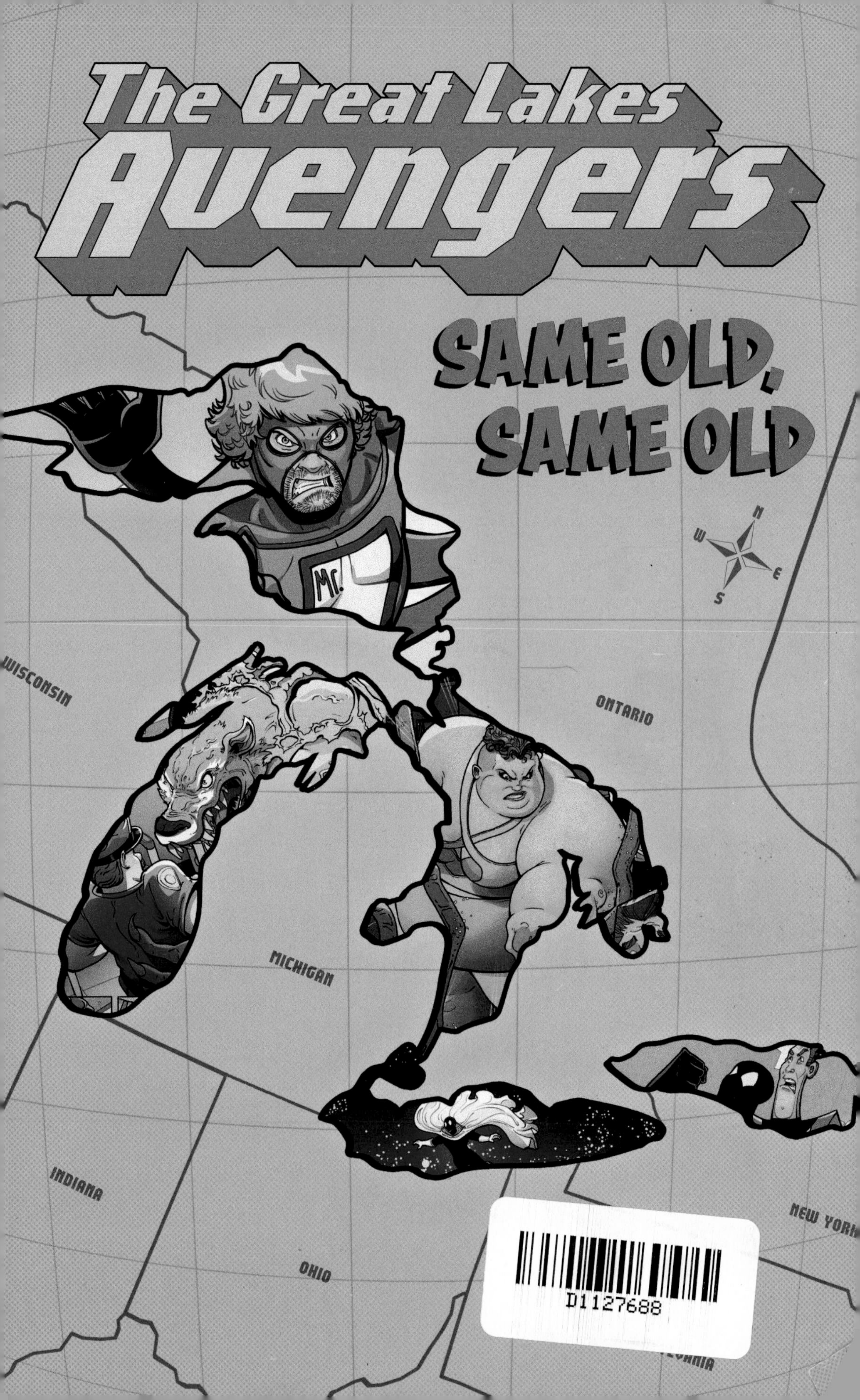
The Great Lakes
Avengers
SAME OLD,
SAME OLD
Mr.
N
W
E
S
WISCONSIN
ONTARIO
MICHIGAN
INDIANA
OHIO
NEW YORK

# The Great Lakes Avengers

## SAME OLD, SAME OLD

ZAC GORMAN
WRITER

WILL ROBSON (#1-3 & #5-7) & JACOB CHABOT (#4)
ARTISTS

SCOTT HANNA
ADDITIONAL INKS, #7

TAMRA BONVILLAIN WITH MARISSA LOUISE (#4)
COLOR ARTISTS

VC's JOE CARAMAGNA
LETTERER

WILL ROBSON WITH IAN HERRING (#1) & TAMRA BONVILLAIN (#2-7)
COVER ARTISTS

ALANNA SMITH
ASSISTANT TOR

TOM BREVOORT
EDITOR

AVENGERS CREATED BY STAN LEE & JACK KIRBY

COLLECTION EDITOR: JENNIFER GRÜNWALD
ASSISTANT EDITOR: CAITLIN O'CONNELL
ASSOCIATE MANAGING EDITOR: KATERI WOODY
EDITOR, SPECIAL PROJECTS: MARK D. BEAZLEY

VP PRODUCTION & SPECIAL PROJECTS: JEFF YOUNGQUIST
SVP PRINT, SALES & MARKETING: DAVID GABRIEL
BOOK DESIGNER: ADAM DEL RE

EDITOR IN CHIEF: AXEL ALONSO
CHIEF CREATIVE OFFICER: JOE QUESADA
PRESIDENT: DAN BUCKLEY
EXECUTIVE PRODUCER: ALAN FINE

**GREAT LAKES AVENGERS: SAME OLD, SAME OLD.** Contains material originally published in magazine form as GREAT LAKES AVENGERS #1-7. First printing 2017. ISBN# 978-1-302-90621-4. Published by MARVEL WORLDWIDE, INC., a subsidiary of MARVEL ENTERTAINMENT, LLC. OFFICE OF PUBLICATION: 135 West 50th Street, New York, NY 10020.  **Printed in the U.S.A.** DAN BUCKLEY, President, Marvel Entertainment; JOE QUESADA, Chief Creative Officer; TOM BREVOORT, SVP of Publishing; DAVID BOGART, SVP of Business Affairs & Operations, Publishing & Partnership; C.B. CEBULSKI, VP of Brand Management & Development, Asia; DAVID GABRIEL, SVP of Sales & Marketing, Publishing; JEFF YOUNGQUIST, VP of Production & Special Projects; DAN CARR, Executive Director of Publishing Technology; ALEX MORALES, Director of Publishing Operations; SUSAN CRESPI, Production Manager; STAN LEE, Chairman Emeritus. For information regarding advertising in Marvel Comics or on Marvel.com, please contact Vit DeBellis, Integrated Sales Manager, at vdebellis@marvel.com. For Marvel subscription inquiries, please call 888-511-5480. **Manufactured between 5/5/2017 and 6/5/2017 by QUAD/GRAPHICS WASECA, WASECA, MN, USA.**

10 9 8 7 6 5 4 3 2 1

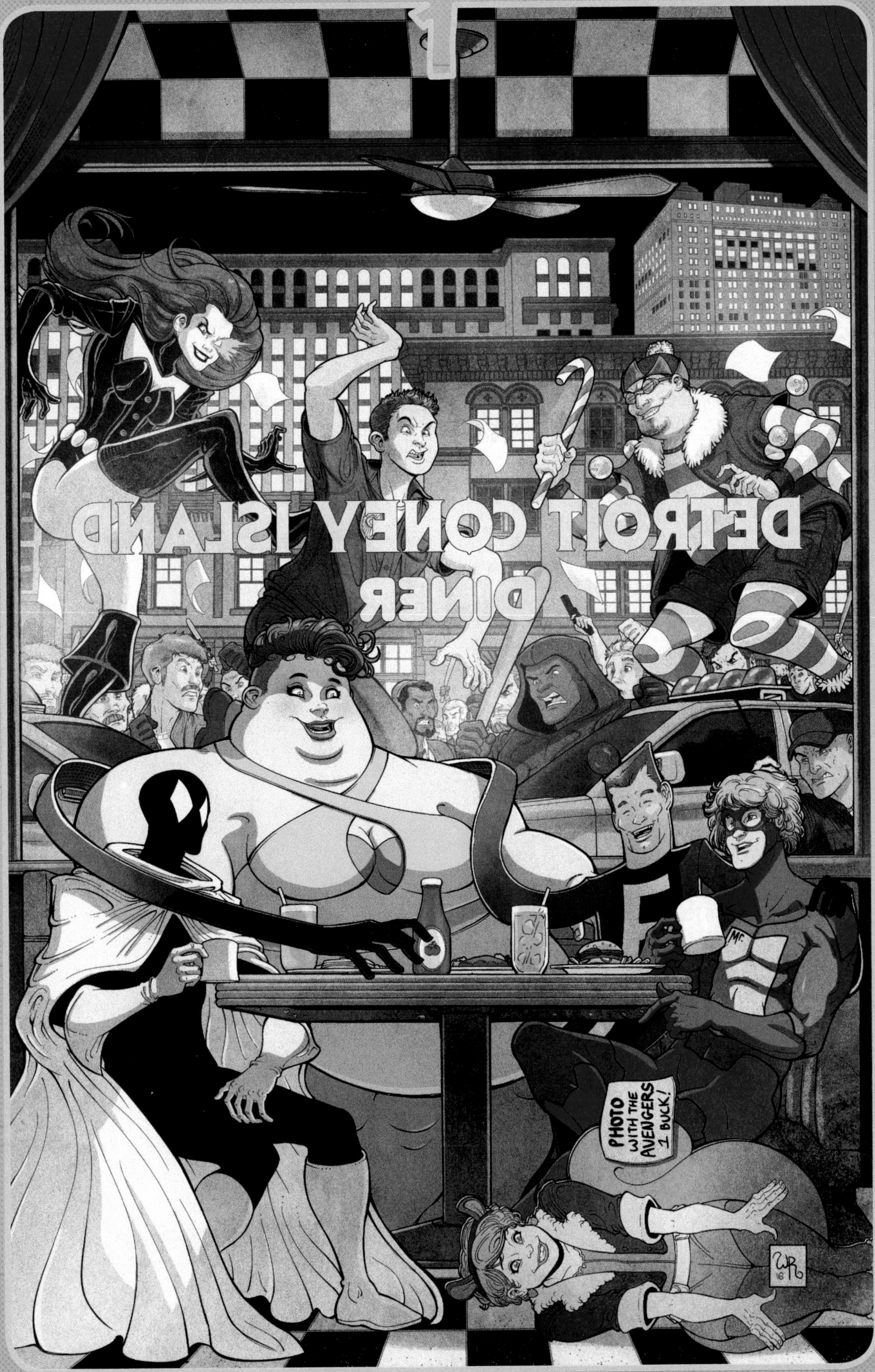
DETROIT CONEY ISLAND
DINER
PHOTO WITH THE AVENGERS 1 BUCK!

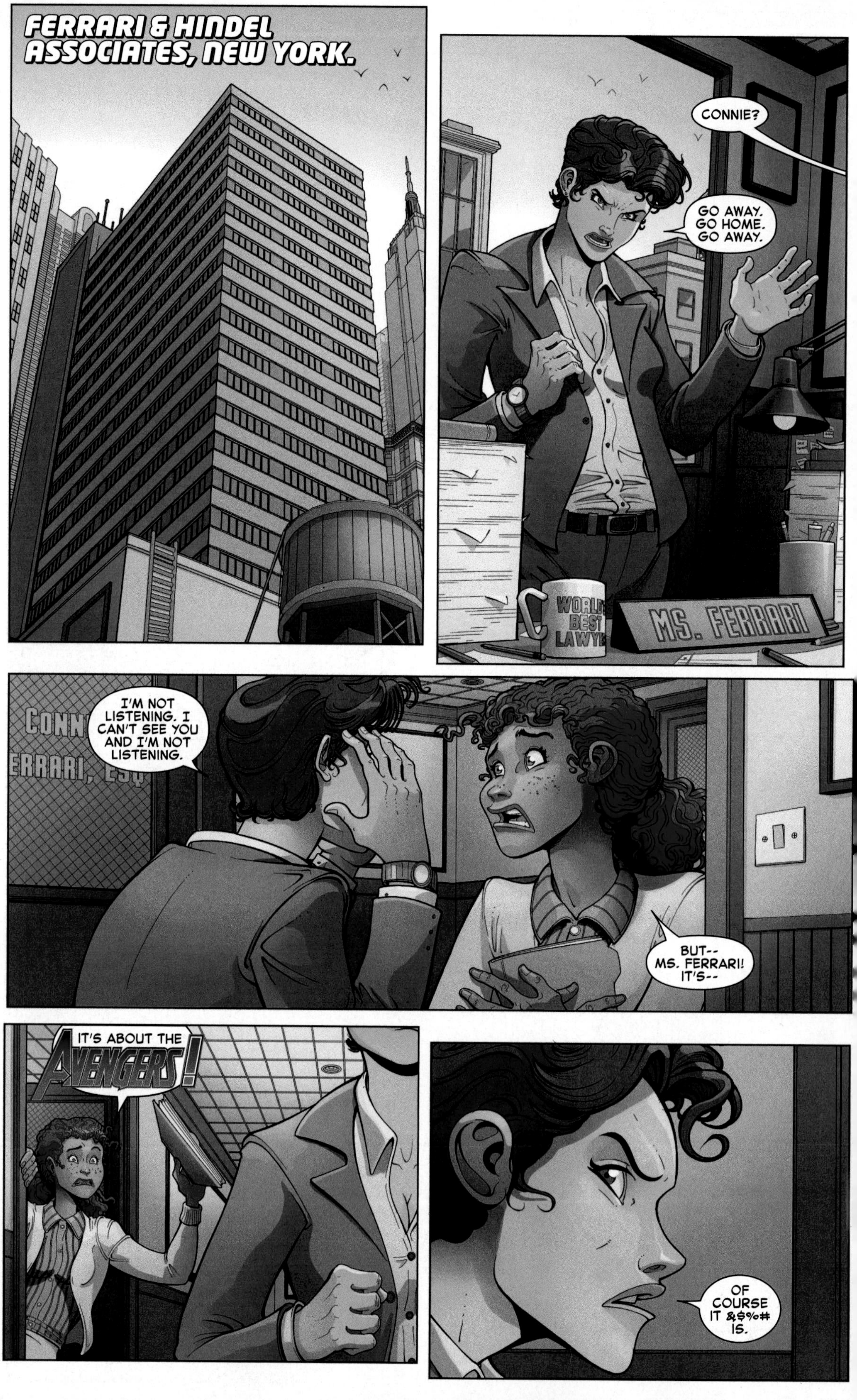
FERRARI & HINDEL ASSOCIATES, NEW YORK.
CONNIE?
GO AWAY. GO HOME. GO AWAY.
WORLD'S BEST LAWYER
MS. FERRARI
I'M NOT LISTENING. I CAN'T SEE YOU AND I'M NOT LISTENING.
BUT-- MS. FERRARI! IT'S--
IT'S ABOUT THE AVENGERS!
OF COURSE IT &$%# IS.

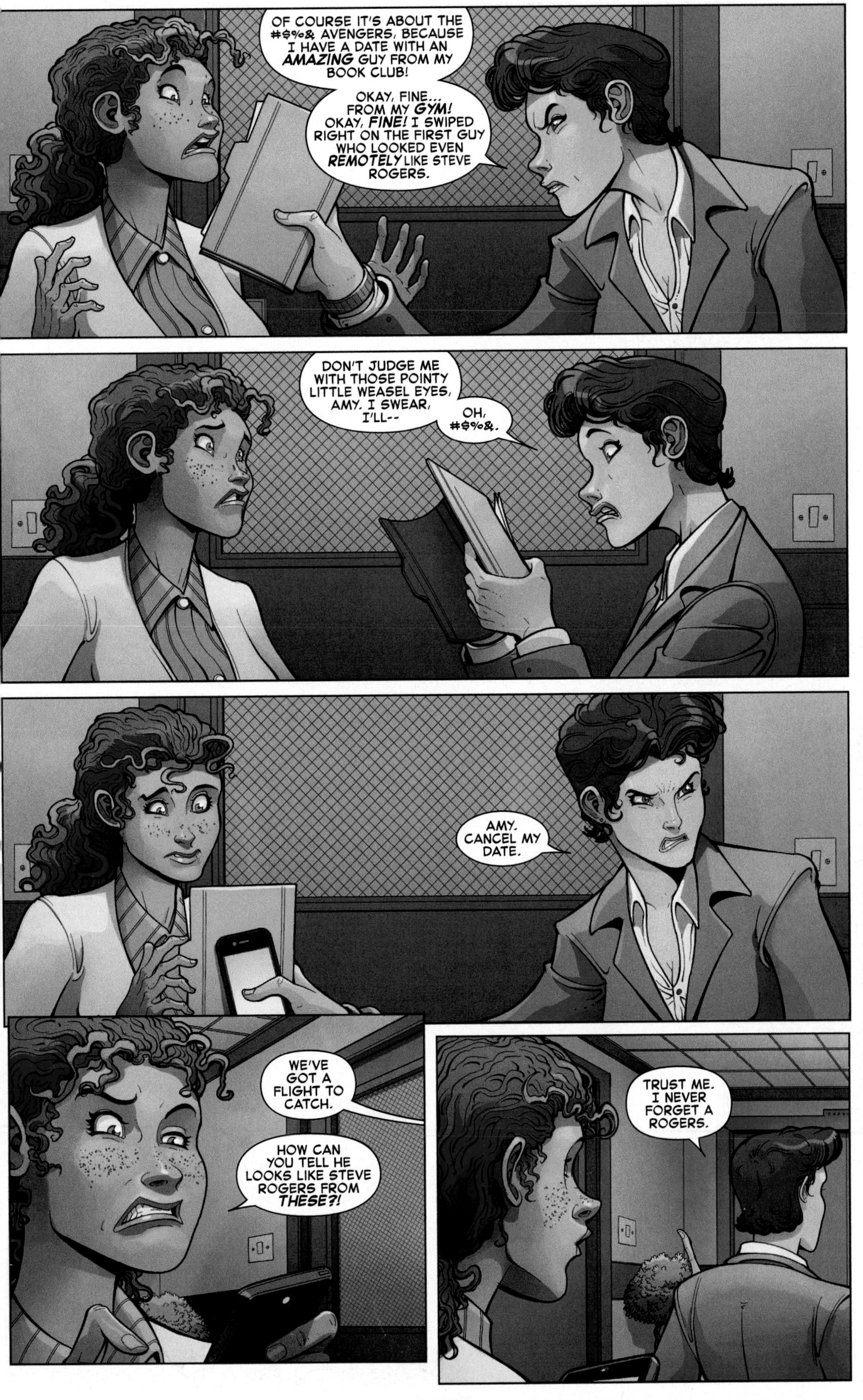
OF COURSE IT'S ABOUT THE #$%& AVENGERS, BECAUSE I HAVE A DATE WITH AN AMAZING GUY FROM MY BOOK CLUB!
OKAY, FINE... FROM MY GYM! OKAY, FINE! I SWIPED RIGHT ON THE FIRST GUY WHO LOOKED EVEN REMOTELY LIKE STEVE ROGERS.
DON'T JUDGE ME WITH THOSE POINTY LITTLE WEASEL EYES, AMY. I SWEAR, I'LL--
OH, #$%&.
AMY. CANCEL MY DATE.
WE'VE GOT A FLIGHT TO CATCH.
HOW CAN YOU TELL HE LOOKS LIKE STEVE ROGERS FROM THESE?!
TRUST ME. I NEVER FORGET A ROGERS.

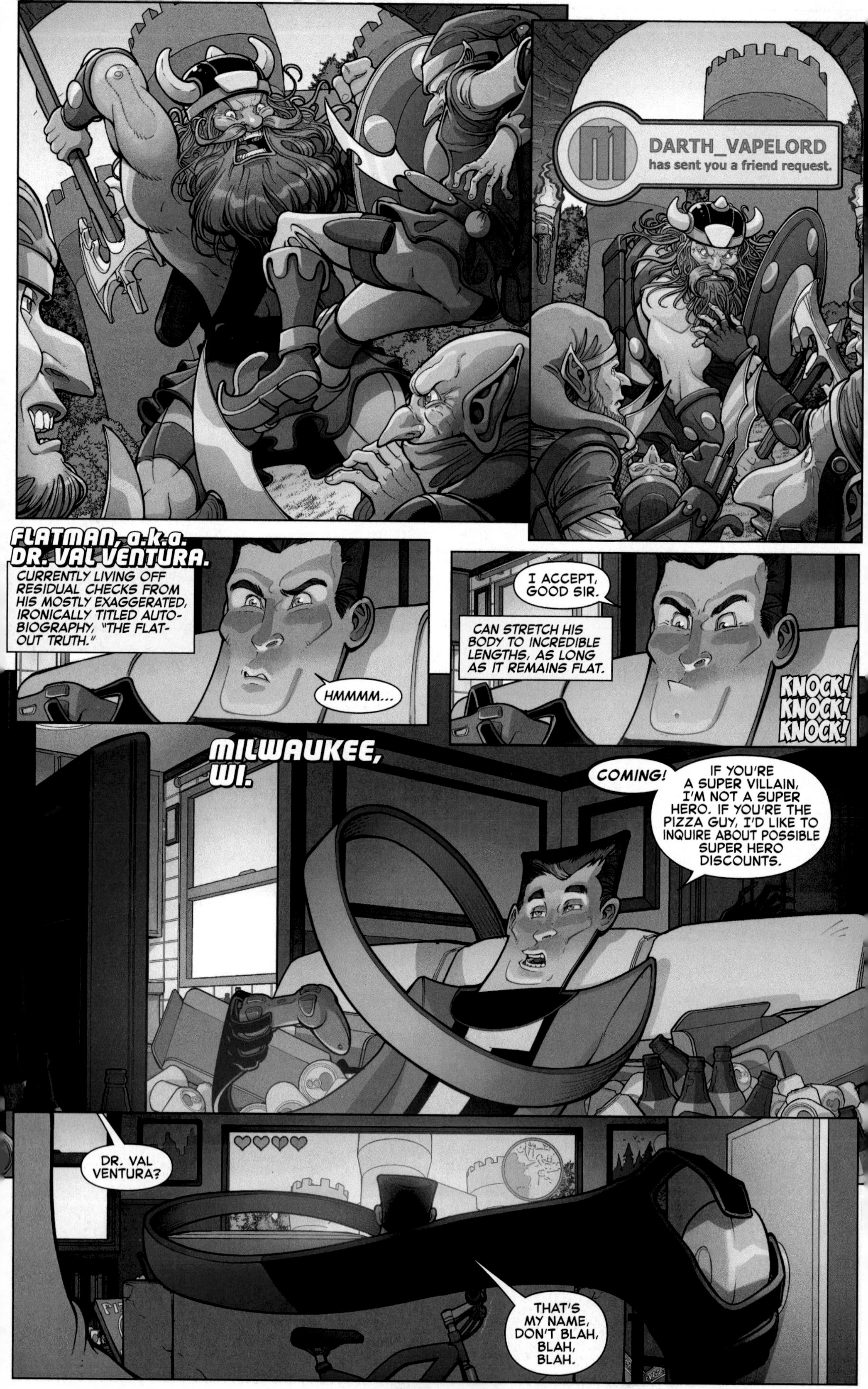
DARTH_VAPELORD
has sent you a friend request.
FLATMAN, a.k.a. DR. VAL VENTURA.
CURRENTLY LIVING OFF RESIDUAL CHECKS FROM HIS MOSTLY EXAGGERATED, IRONICALLY TITLED AUTO-BIOGRAPHY, "THE FLAT-OUT TRUTH."
HMMMM...
I ACCEPT, GOOD SIR.
CAN STRETCH HIS BODY TO INCREDIBLE LENGTHS, AS LONG AS IT REMAINS FLAT.
KNOCK! KNOCK! KNOCK!
MILWAUKEE, WI.
COMING!
IF YOU'RE A SUPER VILLAIN, I'M NOT A SUPER HERO. IF YOU'RE THE PIZZA GUY, I'D LIKE TO INQUIRE ABOUT POSSIBLE SUPER HERO DISCOUNTS.
DR. VAL VENTURA?
THAT'S MY NAME, DON'T BLAH, BLAH, BLAH.

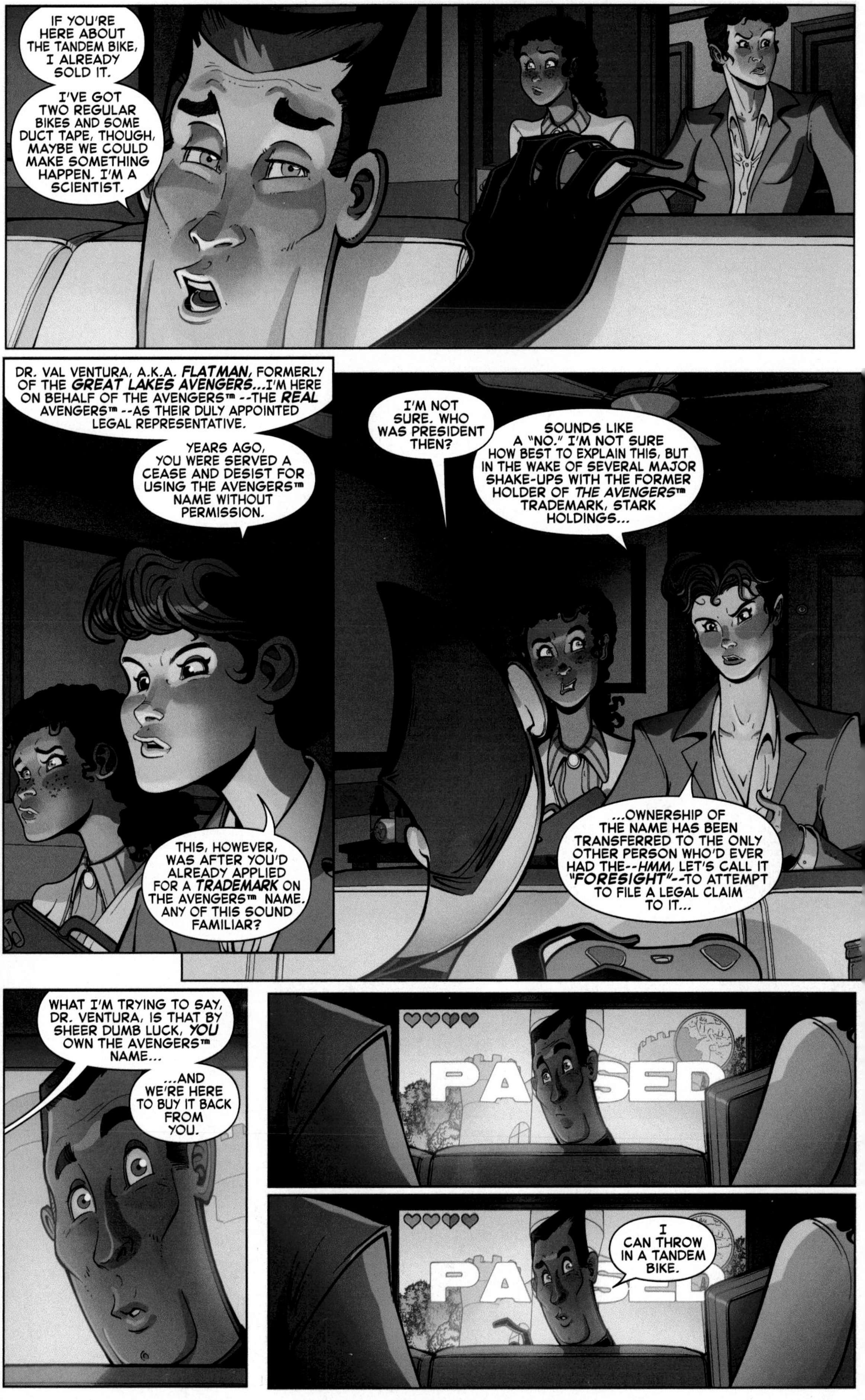
IF YOU'RE HERE ABOUT THE TANDEM BIKE, I ALREADY SOLD IT.
I'VE GOT TWO REGULAR BIKES AND SOME DUCT TAPE, THOUGH. MAYBE WE COULD MAKE SOMETHING HAPPEN. I'M A SCIENTIST.
DR. VAL VENTURA, A.K.A. FLATMAN, FORMERLY OF THE GREAT LAKES AVENGERS...I'M HERE ON BEHALF OF THE AVENGERS™ --THE REAL AVENGERS™ --AS THEIR DULY APPOINTED LEGAL REPRESENTATIVE.
YEARS AGO, YOU WERE SERVED A CEASE AND DESIST FOR USING THE AVENGERS™ NAME WITHOUT PERMISSION.
THIS, HOWEVER, WAS AFTER YOU'D ALREADY APPLIED FOR A TRADEMARK ON THE AVENGERS™ NAME. ANY OF THIS SOUND FAMILIAR?
I'M NOT SURE. WHO WAS PRESIDENT THEN?
SOUNDS LIKE A "NO." I'M NOT SURE HOW BEST TO EXPLAIN THIS, BUT IN THE WAKE OF SEVERAL MAJOR SHAKE-UPS WITH THE FORMER HOLDER OF THE AVENGERS™ TRADEMARK, STARK HOLDINGS...
...OWNERSHIP OF THE NAME HAS BEEN TRANSFERRED TO THE ONLY OTHER PERSON WHO'D EVER HAD THE--HMM, LET'S CALL IT "FORESIGHT"--TO ATTEMPT TO FILE A LEGAL CLAIM TO IT...
WHAT I'M TRYING TO SAY, DR. VENTURA, IS THAT BY SHEER DUMB LUCK, YOU OWN THE AVENGERS™ NAME...
...AND WE'RE HERE TO BUY IT BACK FROM YOU.
PA SED
I CAN THROW IN A TANDEM BIKE.

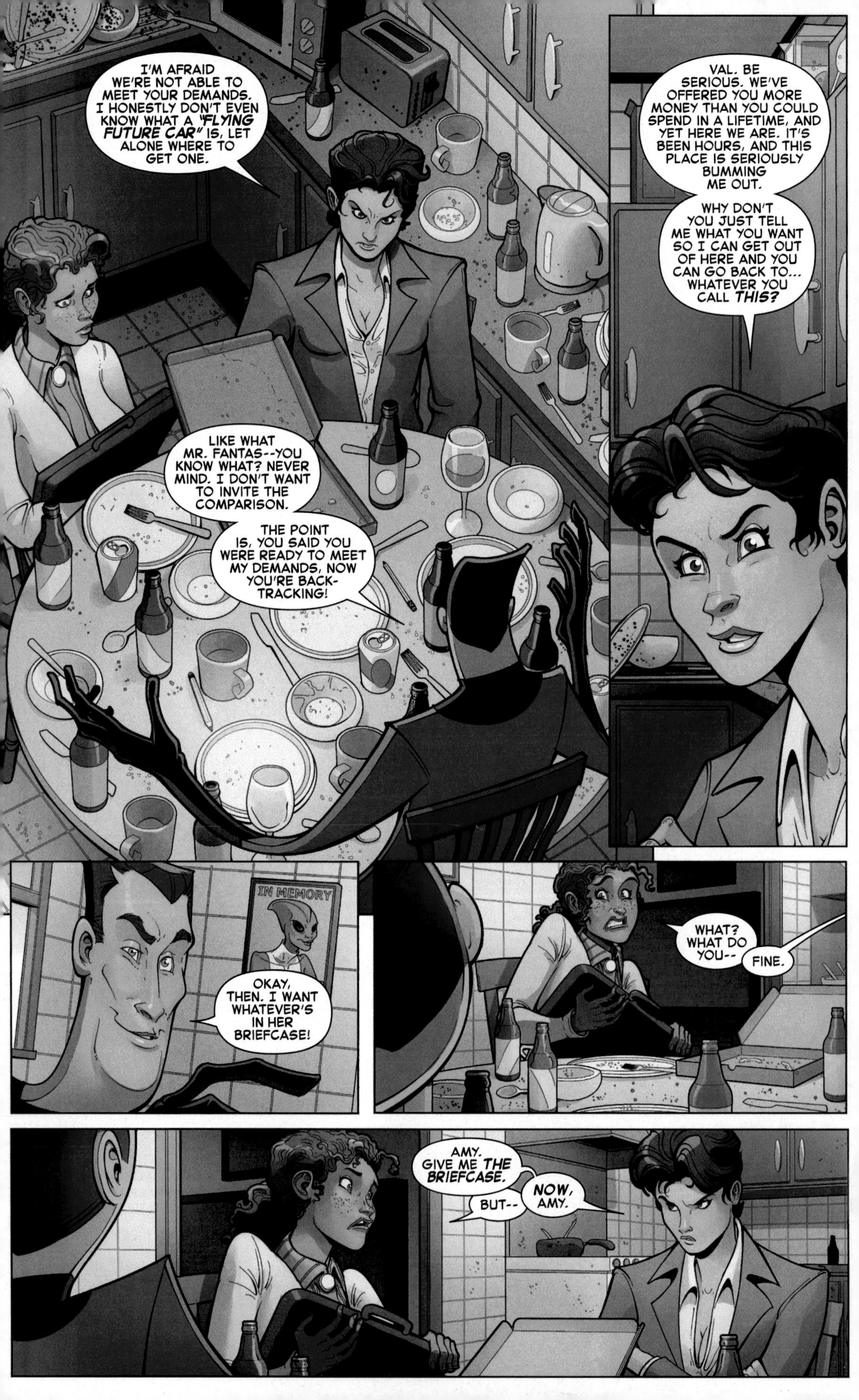
I'M AFRAID WE'RE NOT ABLE TO MEET YOUR DEMANDS. I HONESTLY DON'T EVEN KNOW WHAT A *"FLYING FUTURE CAR"* IS, LET ALONE WHERE TO GET ONE.
LIKE WHAT MR. FANTAS--YOU KNOW WHAT? NEVER MIND. I DON'T WANT TO INVITE THE COMPARISON.
THE POINT IS, YOU SAID YOU WERE READY TO MEET MY DEMANDS, NOW YOU'RE BACK-TRACKING!
VAL. BE SERIOUS. WE'VE OFFERED YOU MORE MONEY THAN YOU COULD SPEND IN A LIFETIME, AND YET HERE WE ARE. IT'S BEEN HOURS, AND THIS PLACE IS SERIOUSLY BUMMING ME OUT.
WHY DON'T YOU JUST TELL ME WHAT YOU WANT SO I CAN GET OUT OF HERE AND YOU CAN GO BACK TO... WHATEVER YOU CALL *THIS?*
IN MEMORY
OKAY, THEN. I WANT WHATEVER'S IN HER BRIEFCASE!
WHAT? WHAT DO YOU--
FINE.
AMY. GIVE ME *THE BRIEFCASE.*
BUT--
*NOW,* AMY.

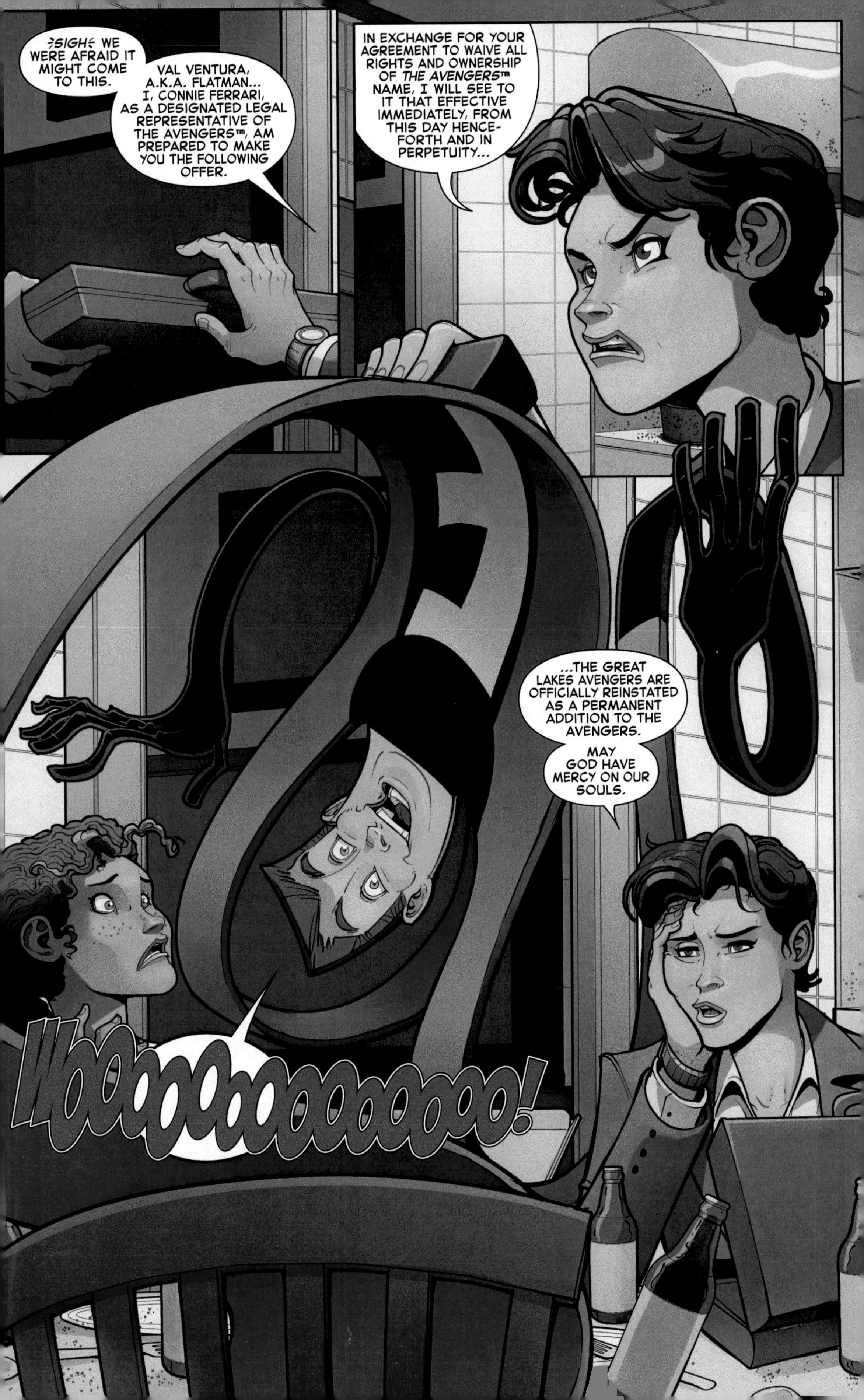

⸗SIGH⸗ WE WERE AFRAID IT MIGHT COME TO THIS.
VAL VENTURA, A.K.A. FLATMAN... I, CONNIE FERRARI, AS A DESIGNATED LEGAL REPRESENTATIVE OF THE AVENGERS™, AM PREPARED TO MAKE YOU THE FOLLOWING OFFER.
IN EXCHANGE FOR YOUR AGREEMENT TO WAIVE ALL RIGHTS AND OWNERSHIP OF *THE AVENGERS™* NAME, I WILL SEE TO IT THAT EFFECTIVE IMMEDIATELY, FROM THIS DAY HENCE-FORTH AND IN PERPETUITY...
...THE GREAT LAKES AVENGERS ARE OFFICIALLY REINSTATED AS A PERMANENT ADDITION TO THE AVENGERS.
MAY GOD HAVE MERCY ON OUR SOULS.
WOOOOOOOOOOOOOOOO!

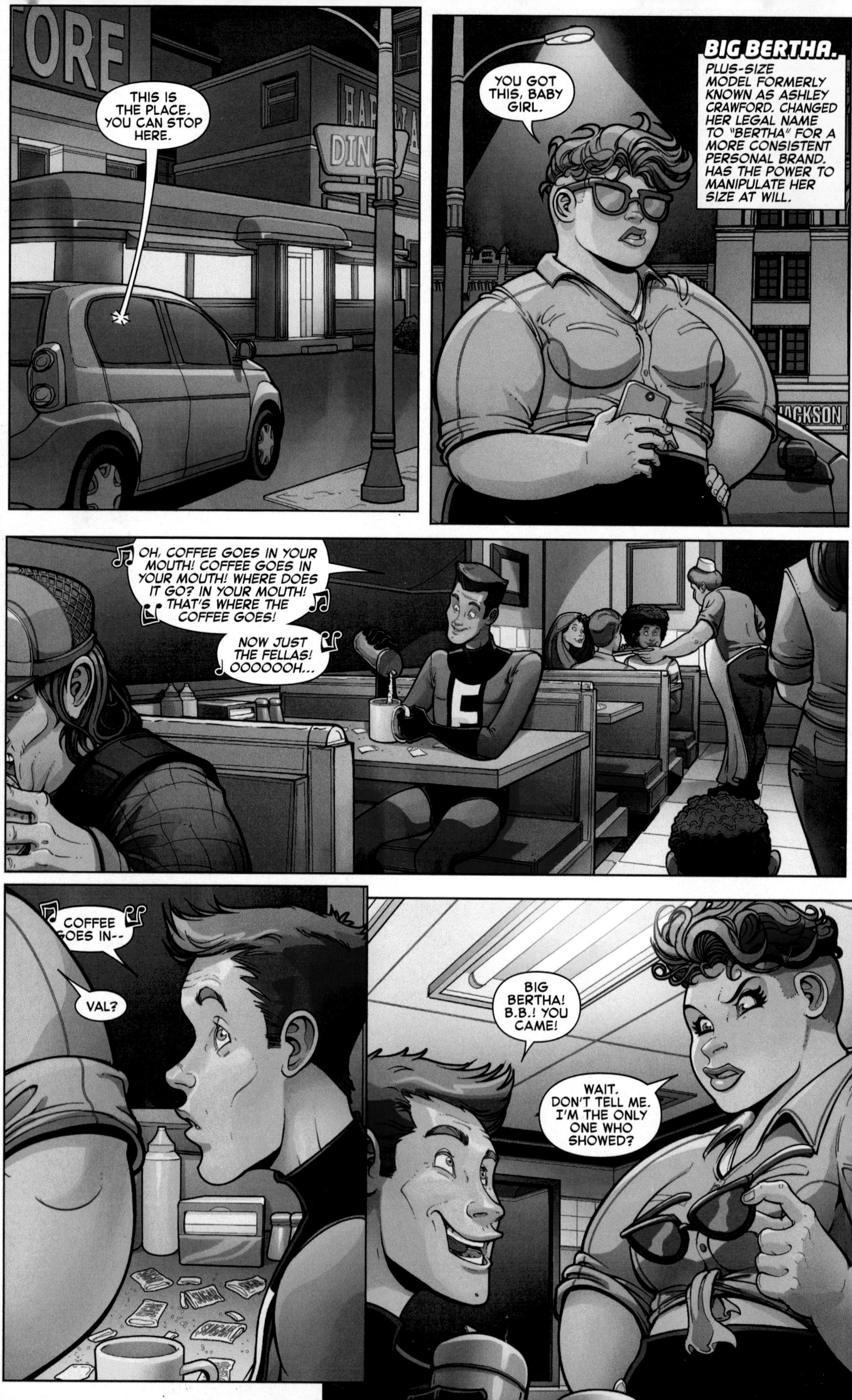
ORE
THIS IS THE PLACE. YOU CAN STOP HERE.
DINE
YOU GOT THIS, BABY GIRL.
BIG BERTHA.
PLUS-SIZE MODEL FORMERLY KNOWN AS ASHLEY CRAWFORD. CHANGED HER LEGAL NAME TO "BERTHA" FOR A MORE CONSISTENT PERSONAL BRAND. HAS THE POWER TO MANIPULATE HER SIZE AT WILL.
JACKSON
OH, COFFEE GOES IN YOUR MOUTH! COFFEE GOES IN YOUR MOUTH! WHERE DOES IT GO? IN YOUR MOUTH! THAT'S WHERE THE COFFEE GOES!
NOW JUST THE FELLAS! OOOOOOH...
COFFEE GOES IN--
VAL?
BIG BERTHA! B.B.! YOU CAME!
WAIT. DON'T TELL ME. I'M THE ONLY ONE WHO SHOWED?

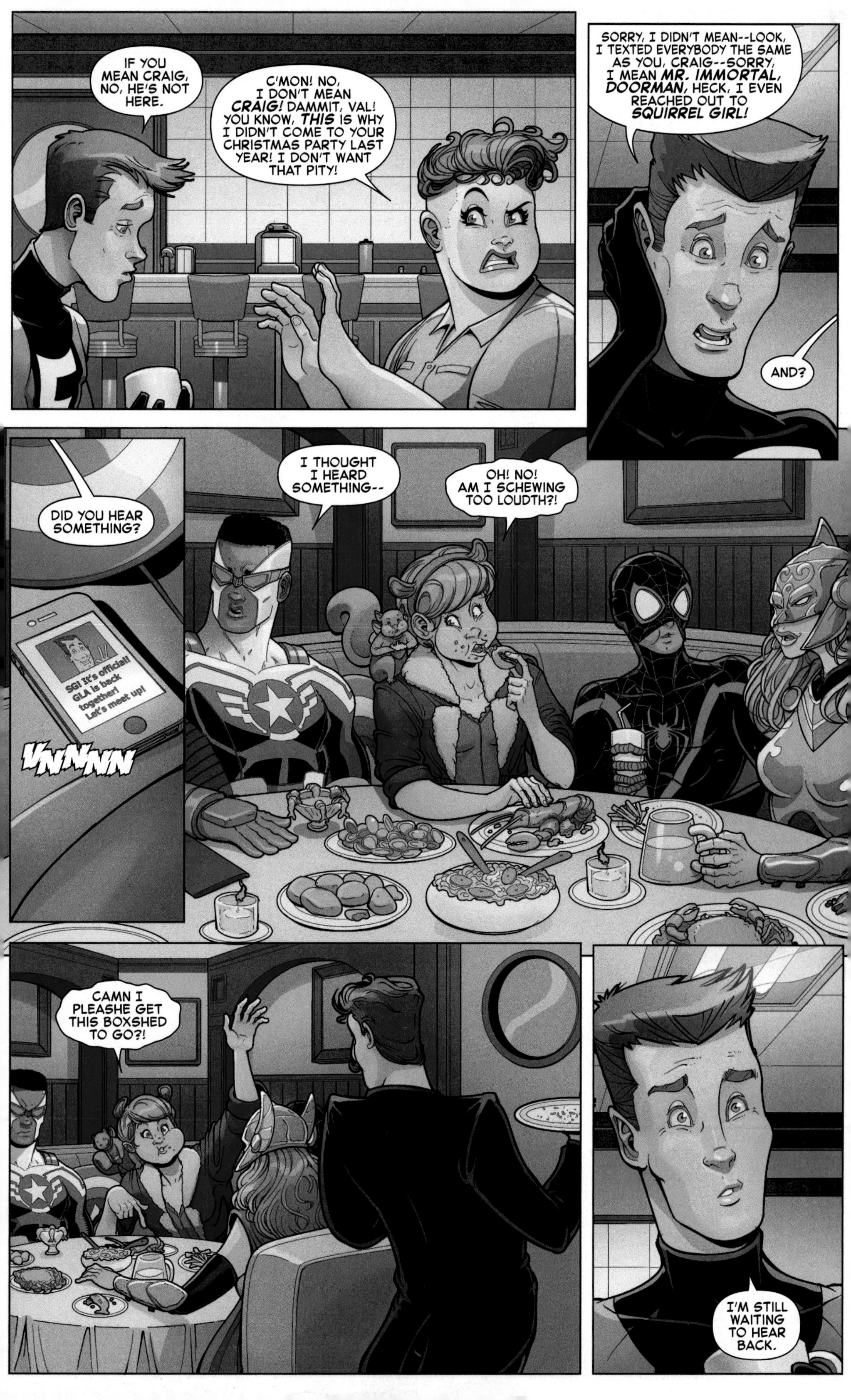
IF YOU MEAN CRAIG, NO, HE'S NOT HERE.
C'MON! NO, I DON'T MEAN CRAIG! DAMMIT, VAL! YOU KNOW, THIS IS WHY I DIDN'T COME TO YOUR CHRISTMAS PARTY LAST YEAR! I DON'T WANT THAT PITY!
SORRY, I DIDN'T MEAN--LOOK, I TEXTED EVERYBODY THE SAME AS YOU, CRAIG--SORRY, I MEAN MR. IMMORTAL, DOORMAN, HECK, I EVEN REACHED OUT TO SQUIRREL GIRL!
AND?
DID YOU HEAR SOMETHING?
SG! It's official! GLA is back together! Let's meet up!
VNNNN
I THOUGHT I HEARD SOMETHING--
OH! NO! AM I SCHEWING TOO LOUDTH?!
CAMN I PLEASHE GET THIS BOXSHED TO GO?!
I'M STILL WAITING TO HEAR BACK.

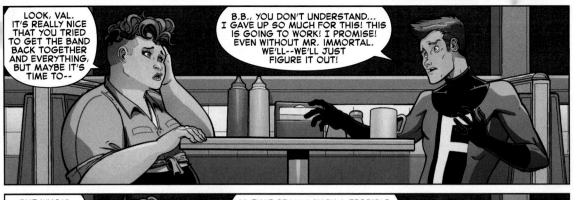

LOOK, VAL. IT'S REALLY NICE THAT YOU TRIED TO GET THE BAND BACK TOGETHER AND EVERYTHING, BUT MAYBE IT'S TIME TO--

B.B., YOU DON'T UNDERSTAND... I GAVE UP SO MUCH FOR THIS! THIS IS GOING TO WORK! I PROMISE! EVEN WITHOUT MR. IMMORTAL, WE'LL--WE'LL JUST FIGURE IT OUT!

BUT WHO'S GOING TO LEAD THE TEAM? YOU?

IS THAT REALLY SUCH A TERRIBLE IDEA? IT'S NOT LIKE MR. IMMORTAL SET A HIGH BAR! ALL I HAVE TO DO IS NOT GET ANYBODY KILLED. HOW HARD IS THAT? I CAN BE LEADER!

SHOULDN'T WE AT LEAST PUT IT TO A VOTE? I MEAN, THIS IS A DEMOCRACY...RIGHT? RIGHT? I'M SERIOUSLY ASKING. I'VE BEEN IN THE DARKFORCE DIMENSION FOR SO LONG, I FORGOT WHAT MY MOTHER LOOKED LIKE.

I THINK HER HAIR WAS BROWN. LIKE WET FALL LEAVES.

DOORMAN!

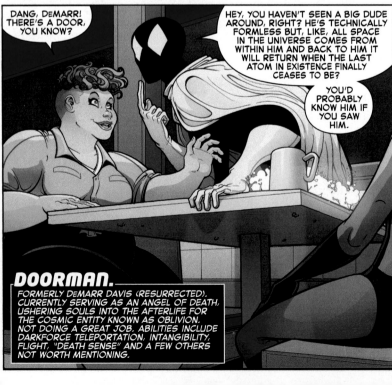

DANG, DEMARR! THERE'S A DOOR, YOU KNOW?

HEY, YOU HAVEN'T SEEN A BIG DUDE AROUND, RIGHT? HE'S TECHNICALLY FORMLESS BUT, LIKE, ALL SPACE IN THE UNIVERSE COMES FROM WITHIN HIM AND BACK TO HIM IT WILL RETURN WHEN THE LAST ATOM IN EXISTENCE FINALLY CEASES TO BE?

YOU'D PROBABLY KNOW HIM IF YOU SAW HIM.

WHOA! HEY! YOU'RE 3-D!

THAT'S NEW!

**DOORMAN.**
FORMERLY DEMARR DAVIS (RESURRECTED). CURRENTLY SERVING AS AN ANGEL OF DEATH, USHERING SOULS INTO THE AFTERLIFE FOR THE COSMIC ENTITY KNOWN AS OBLIVION. NOT DOING A GREAT JOB. ABILITIES INCLUDE DARKFORCE TELEPORTATION, INTANGIBILITY, FLIGHT, "DEATH SENSE" AND A FEW OTHERS NOT WORTH MENTIONING.

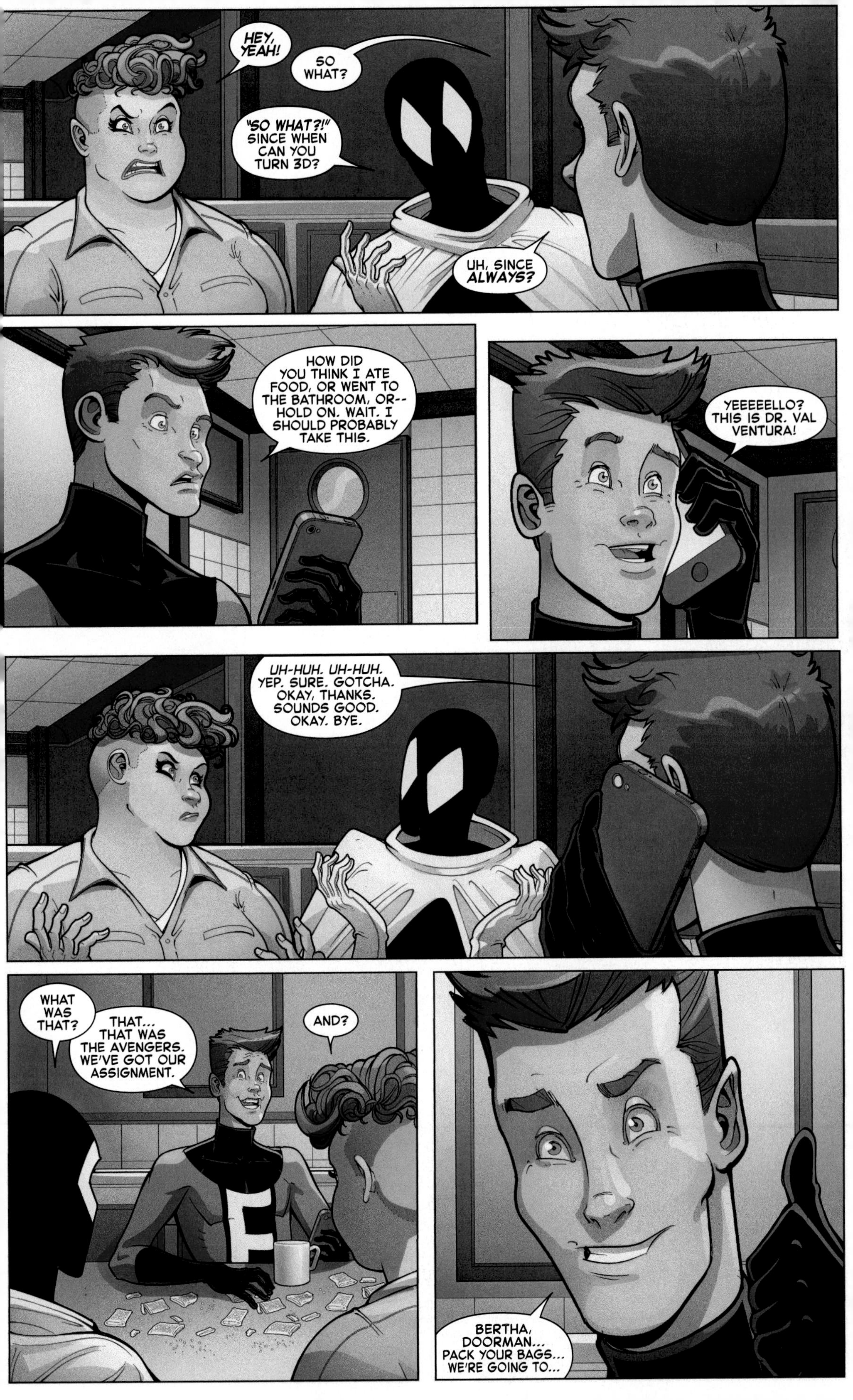

HEY, YEAH!
SO WHAT?
"SO WHAT?!" SINCE WHEN CAN YOU TURN 3D?
UH, SINCE ALWAYS?
HOW DID YOU THINK I ATE FOOD, OR WENT TO THE BATHROOM, OR-- HOLD ON. WAIT. I SHOULD PROBABLY TAKE THIS.
YEEEEELLO? THIS IS DR. VAL VENTURA!
UH-HUH. UH-HUH. YEP. SURE. GOTCHA. OKAY, THANKS. SOUNDS GOOD. OKAY. BYE.
WHAT WAS THAT?
THAT... THAT WAS THE AVENGERS. WE'VE GOT OUR ASSIGNMENT.
AND?
BERTHA, DOORMAN... PACK YOUR BAGS... WE'RE GOING TO...

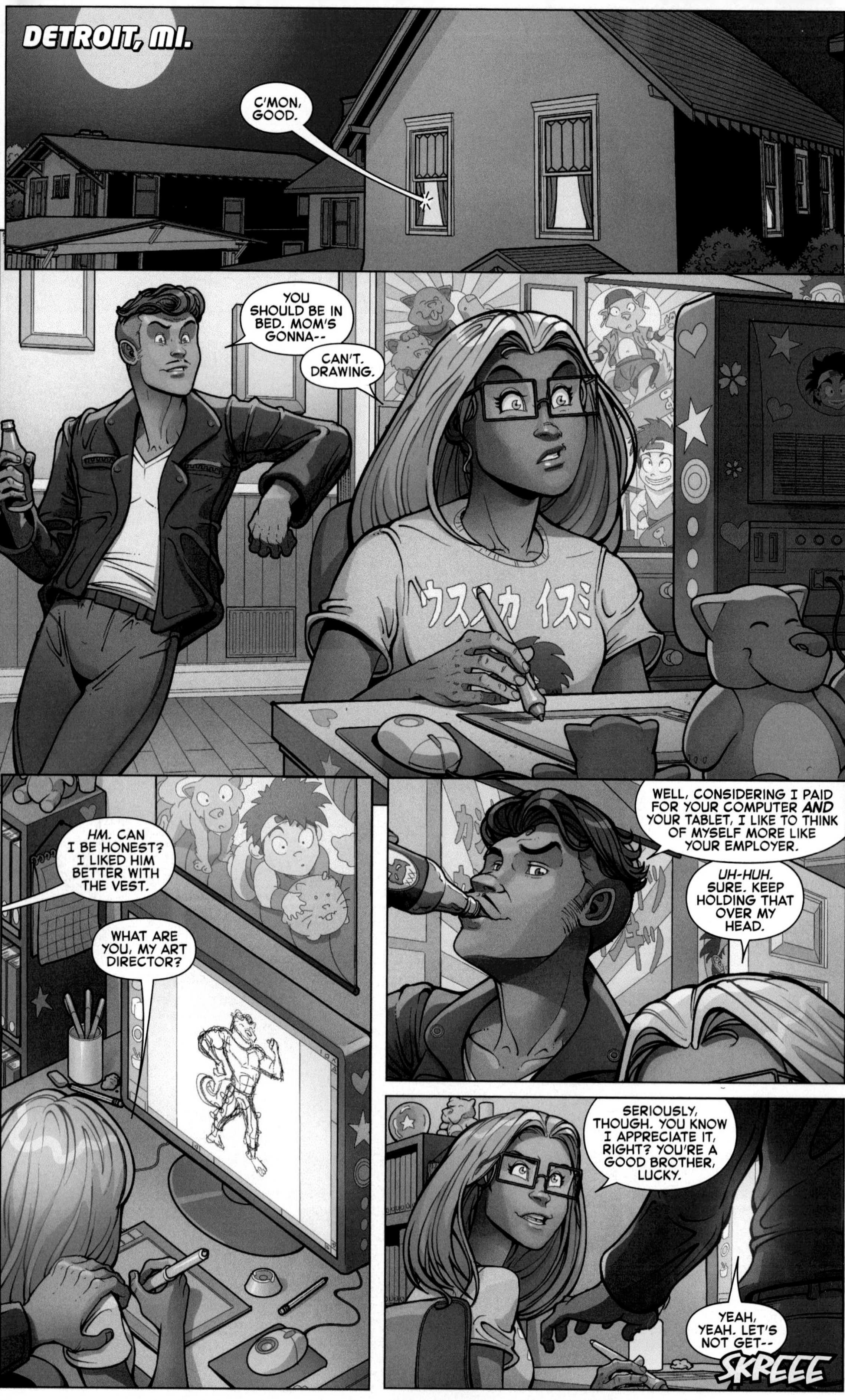
DETROIT, MI.
C'MON, GOOD.
YOU SHOULD BE IN BED. MOM'S GONNA--
CAN'T. DRAWING.
HM. CAN I BE HONEST? I LIKED HIM BETTER WITH THE VEST.
WHAT ARE YOU, MY ART DIRECTOR?
WELL, CONSIDERING I PAID FOR YOUR COMPUTER AND YOUR TABLET, I LIKE TO THINK OF MYSELF MORE LIKE YOUR EMPLOYER.
UH-HUH. SURE. KEEP HOLDING THAT OVER MY HEAD.
SERIOUSLY, THOUGH. YOU KNOW I APPRECIATE IT, RIGHT? YOU'RE A GOOD BROTHER, LUCKY.
YEAH, YEAH. LET'S NOT GET--
SKREEE

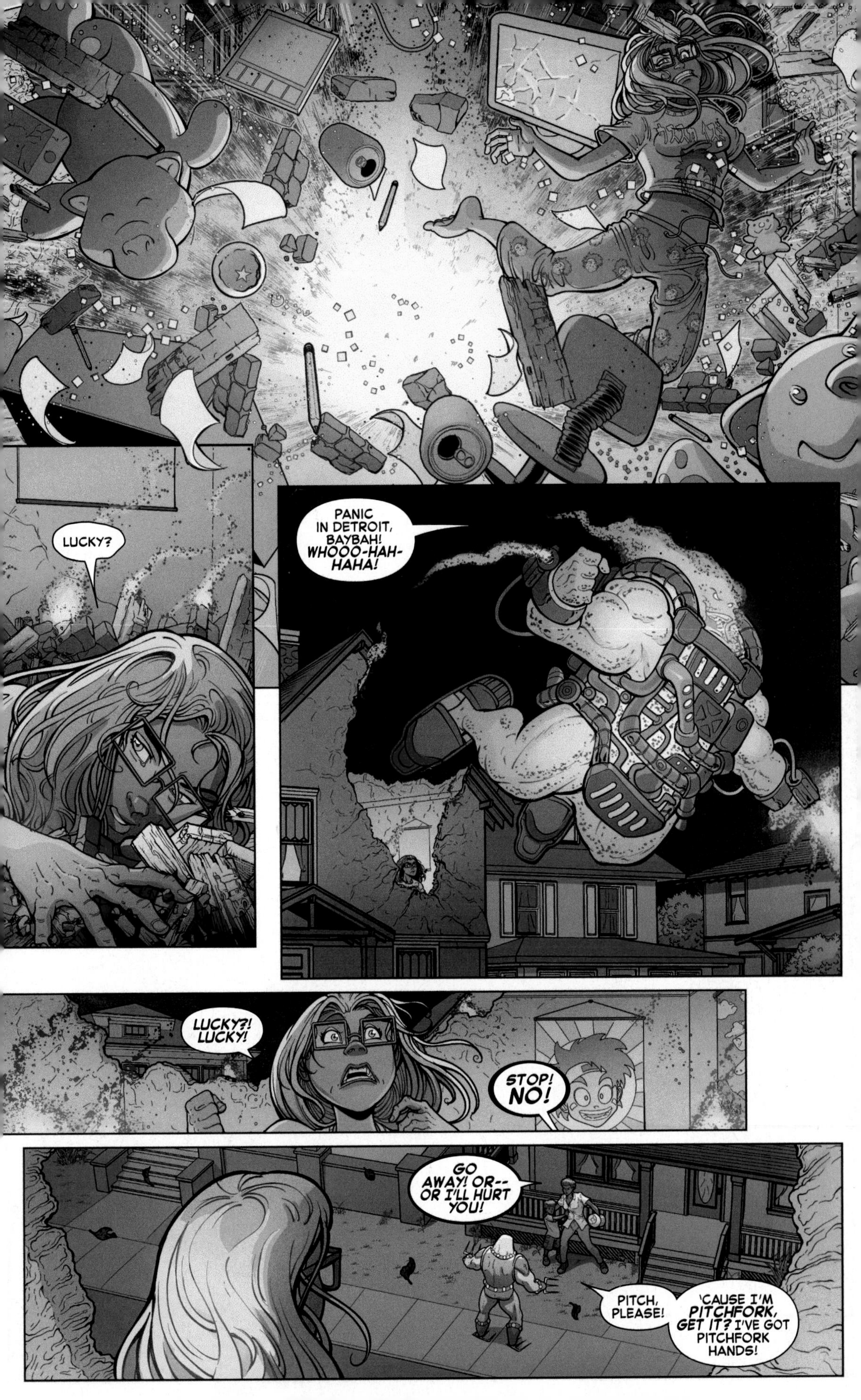
LUCKY?
PANIC IN DETROIT, BAYBAH! WHOOO-HAH-HAHA!
LUCKY?! LUCKY!
STOP! NO!
GO AWAY! OR-- OR I'LL HURT YOU!
PITCH, PLEASE!
'CAUSE I'M PITCHFORK, GET IT? I'VE GOT PITCHFORK HANDS!

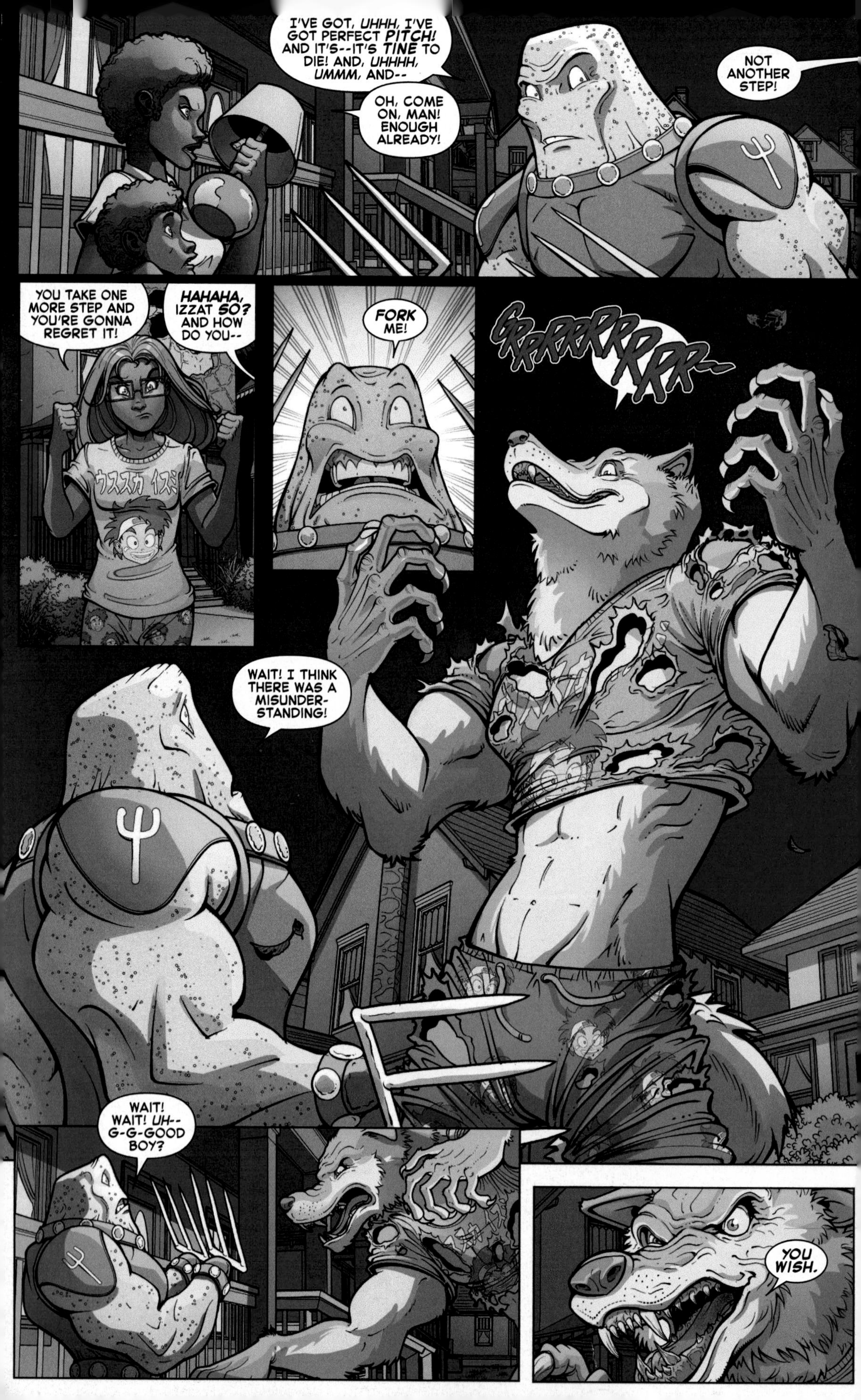
I'VE GOT, UHHH, I'VE GOT PERFECT PITCH! AND IT'S--IT'S TINE TO DIE! AND, UHHHH, UMMM, AND--
OH, COME ON, MAN! ENOUGH ALREADY!
NOT ANOTHER STEP!
YOU TAKE ONE MORE STEP AND YOU'RE GONNA REGRET IT!
HAHAHA, IZZAT SO? AND HOW DO YOU--
FORK ME!
GRRRRRRRRRR--
WAIT! I THINK THERE WAS A MISUNDER-STANDING!
WAIT! WAIT! UH-- G-G-GOOD BOY?
YOU WISH.

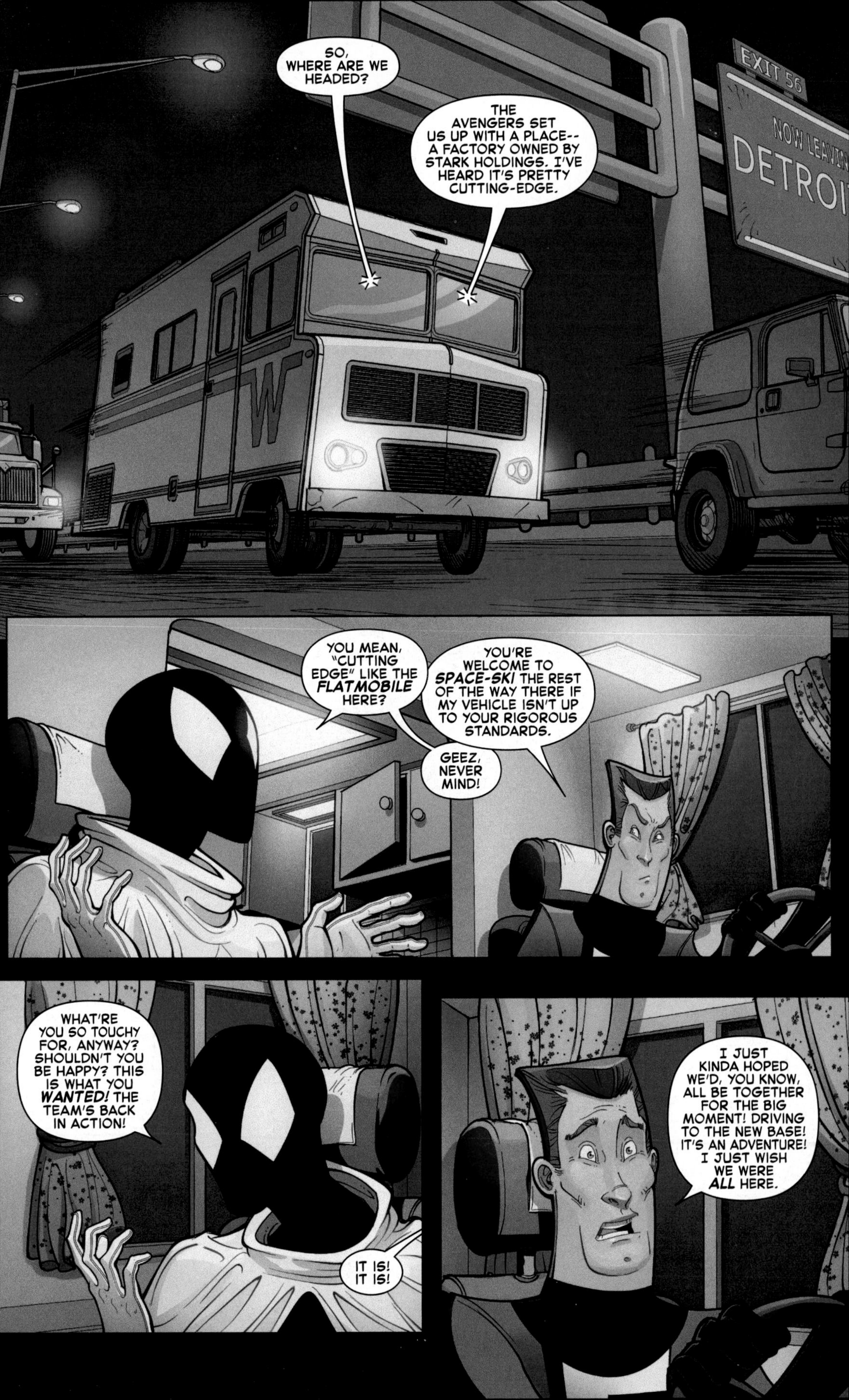
EXIT 56
NOW LEAVING
DETROIT
SO, WHERE ARE WE HEADED?
THE AVENGERS SET US UP WITH A PLACE-- A FACTORY OWNED BY STARK HOLDINGS. I'VE HEARD IT'S PRETTY CUTTING-EDGE.
YOU MEAN, "CUTTING EDGE" LIKE THE *FLATMOBILE* HERE?
YOU'RE WELCOME TO *SPACE-SKI* THE REST OF THE WAY THERE IF MY VEHICLE ISN'T UP TO YOUR RIGOROUS STANDARDS.
GEEZ, NEVER MIND!
WHAT'RE YOU SO TOUCHY FOR, ANYWAY? SHOULDN'T YOU BE HAPPY? THIS IS WHAT YOU *WANTED!* THE TEAM'S BACK IN ACTION!
IT IS! IT IS!
I JUST KINDA HOPED WE'D, YOU KNOW, ALL BE TOGETHER FOR THE BIG MOMENT! DRIVING TO THE NEW BASE! IT'S AN ADVENTURE! I JUST WISH WE WERE *ALL* HERE.

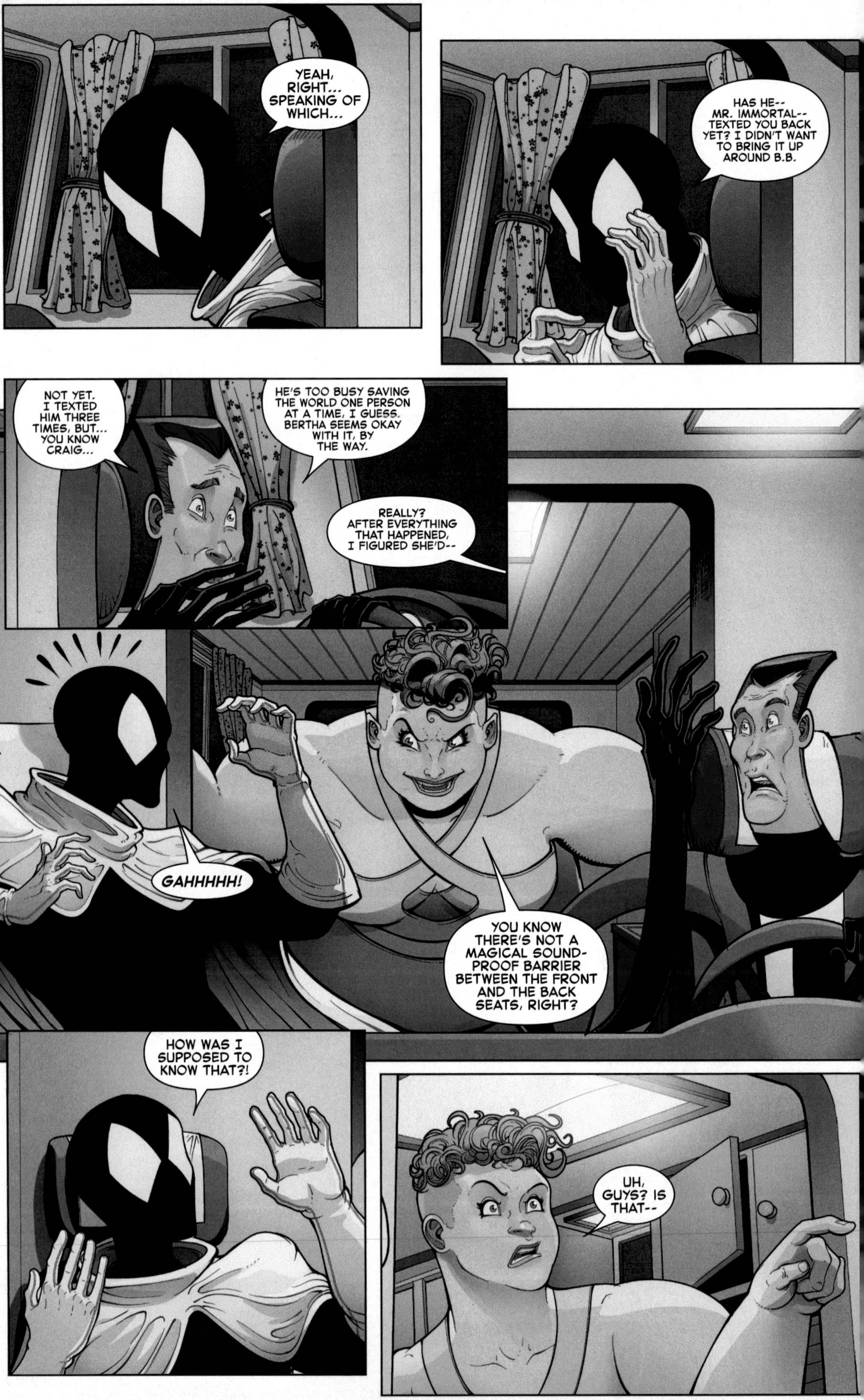
YEAH, RIGHT... SPEAKING OF WHICH...
HAS HE-- MR. IMMORTAL-- TEXTED YOU BACK YET? I DIDN'T WANT TO BRING IT UP AROUND B.B.
NOT YET. I TEXTED HIM THREE TIMES, BUT... YOU KNOW CRAIG...
HE'S TOO BUSY SAVING THE WORLD ONE PERSON AT A TIME, I GUESS. BERTHA SEEMS OKAY WITH IT, BY THE WAY.
REALLY? AFTER EVERYTHING THAT HAPPENED, I FIGURED SHE'D--
GAHHHHH!
YOU KNOW THERE'S NOT A MAGICAL SOUND-PROOF BARRIER BETWEEN THE FRONT AND THE BACK SEATS, RIGHT?
HOW WAS I SUPPOSED TO KNOW THAT?!
UH, GUYS? IS THAT--

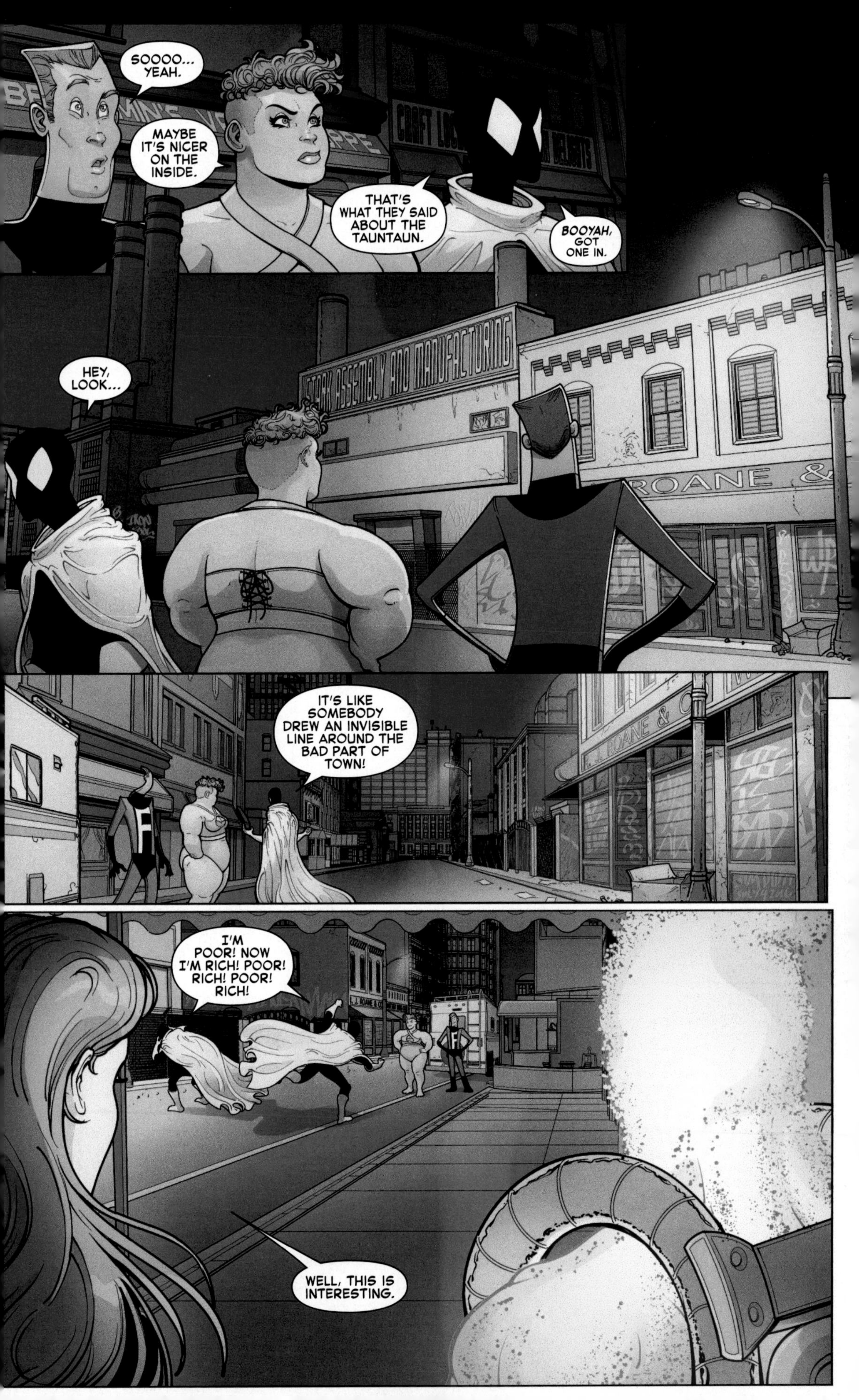
SOOOO... YEAH.
MAYBE IT'S NICER ON THE INSIDE.
THAT'S WHAT THEY SAID ABOUT THE TAUNTAUN.
BOOYAH, GOT ONE IN.
STARK ASSEMBLY AND MANUFACTURING
HEY, LOOK...
ROANE &
IT'S LIKE SOMEBODY DREW AN INVISIBLE LINE AROUND THE BAD PART OF TOWN!
I'M POOR! NOW I'M RICH! POOR! RICH! POOR! RICH!
WELL, THIS IS INTERESTING.

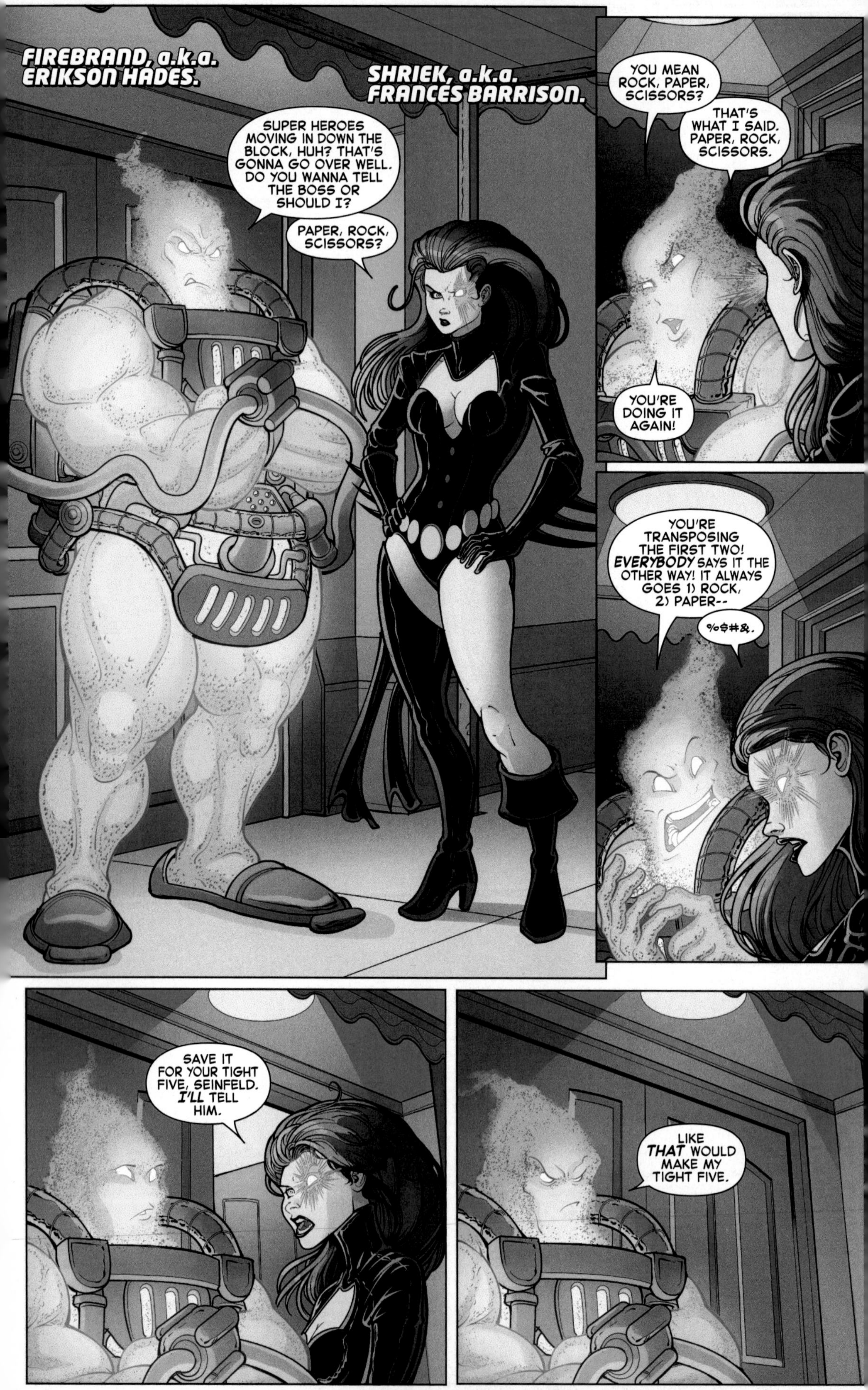
FIREBRAND, a.k.a. ERIKSON HADES.
SHRIEK, a.k.a. FRANCES BARRISON.
SUPER HEROES MOVING IN DOWN THE BLOCK, HUH? THAT'S GONNA GO OVER WELL. DO YOU WANNA TELL THE BOSS OR SHOULD I?
PAPER, ROCK, SCISSORS?
YOU MEAN ROCK, PAPER, SCISSORS?
THAT'S WHAT I SAID. PAPER, ROCK, SCISSORS.
YOU'RE DOING IT AGAIN!
YOU'RE TRANSPOSING THE FIRST TWO! EVERYBODY SAYS IT THE OTHER WAY! IT ALWAYS GOES 1) ROCK, 2) PAPER--
%$#&.
SAVE IT FOR YOUR TIGHT FIVE, SEINFELD. I'LL TELL HIM.
LIKE THAT WOULD MAKE MY TIGHT FIVE.

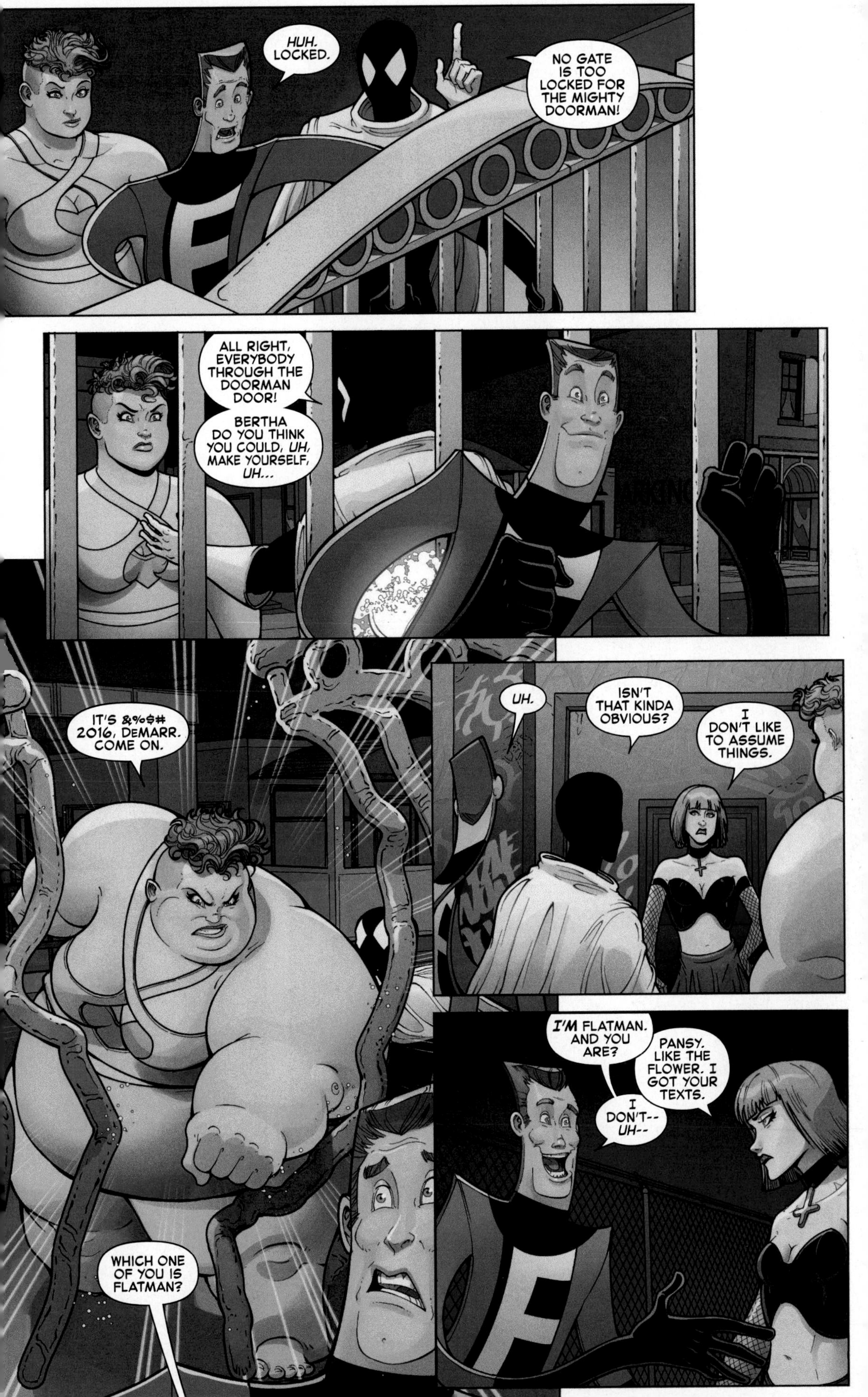
HUH. LOCKED.
NO GATE IS TOO LOCKED FOR THE MIGHTY DOORMAN!
ALL RIGHT, EVERYBODY THROUGH THE DOORMAN DOOR!
BERTHA DO YOU THINK YOU COULD, UH, MAKE YOURSELF, UH...
IT'S &%$# 2016, DEMARR. COME ON.
UH.
ISN'T THAT KINDA OBVIOUS?
I DON'T LIKE TO ASSUME THINGS.
WHICH ONE OF YOU IS FLATMAN?
I'M FLATMAN. AND YOU ARE?
PANSY. LIKE THE FLOWER. I GOT YOUR TEXTS.
I DON'T-- UH--

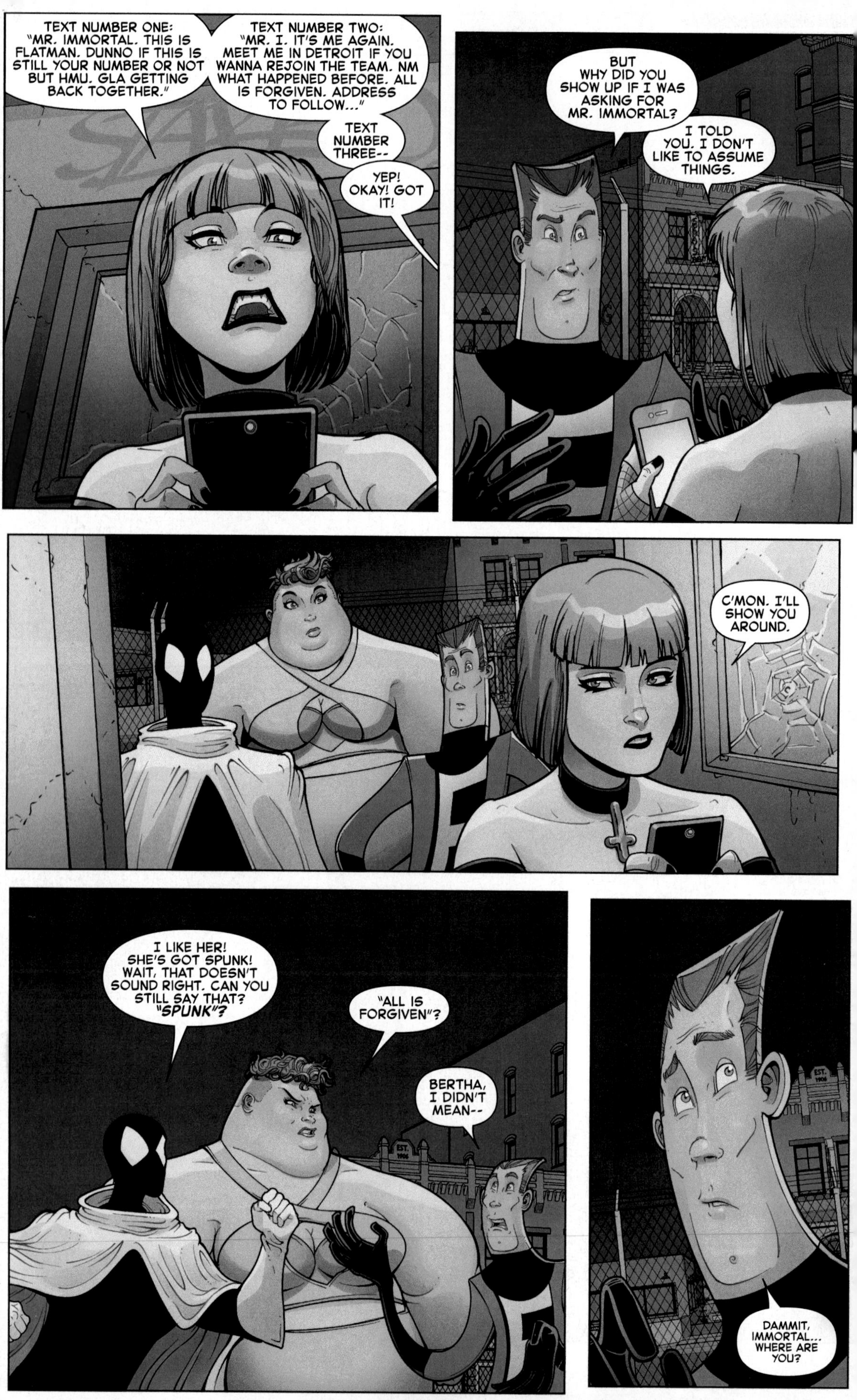
TEXT NUMBER ONE: "MR. IMMORTAL. THIS IS FLATMAN. DUNNO IF THIS IS STILL YOUR NUMBER OR NOT BUT HMU. GLA GETTING BACK TOGETHER."
TEXT NUMBER TWO: "MR. I. IT'S ME AGAIN. MEET ME IN DETROIT IF YOU WANNA REJOIN THE TEAM. NM WHAT HAPPENED BEFORE. ALL IS FORGIVEN. ADDRESS TO FOLLOW..."
TEXT NUMBER THREE--
YEP! OKAY! GOT IT!
BUT WHY DID YOU SHOW UP IF I WAS ASKING FOR MR. IMMORTAL?
I TOLD YOU. I DON'T LIKE TO ASSUME THINGS.
C'MON. I'LL SHOW YOU AROUND.
I LIKE HER! SHE'S GOT SPUNK! WAIT, THAT DOESN'T SOUND RIGHT. CAN YOU STILL SAY THAT? "SPUNK"?
"ALL IS FORGIVEN"?
BERTHA, I DIDN'T MEAN--
DAMMIT, IMMORTAL... WHERE ARE YOU?

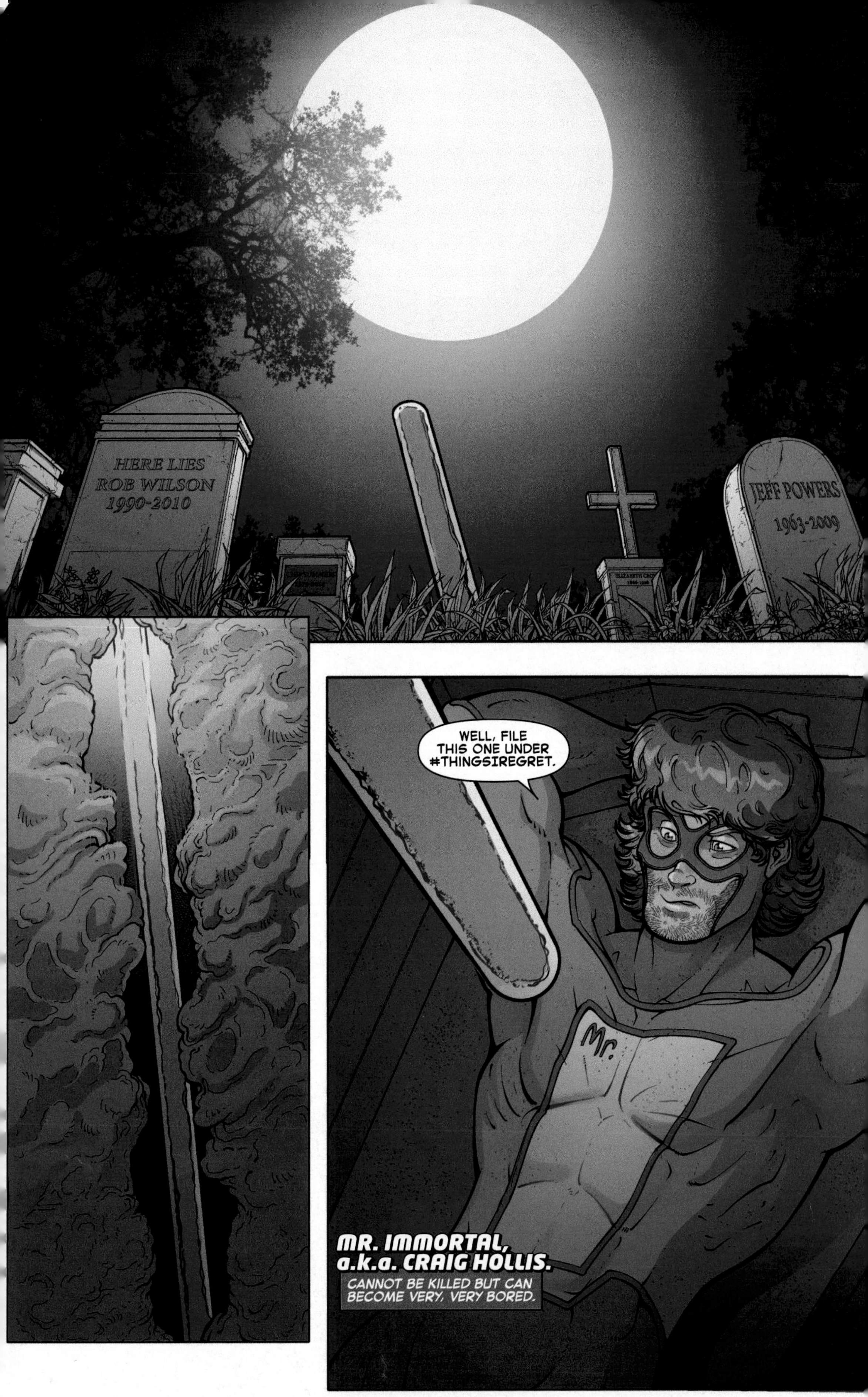
HERE LIES
ROB WILSON
1990-2010
JEFF POWERS
1963-2009
WELL, FILE THIS ONE UNDER #THINGSIREGRET.
Mr.
MR. IMMORTAL, a.k.a. CRAIG HOLLIS.
CANNOT BE KILLED BUT CAN BECOME VERY, VERY BORED.

2

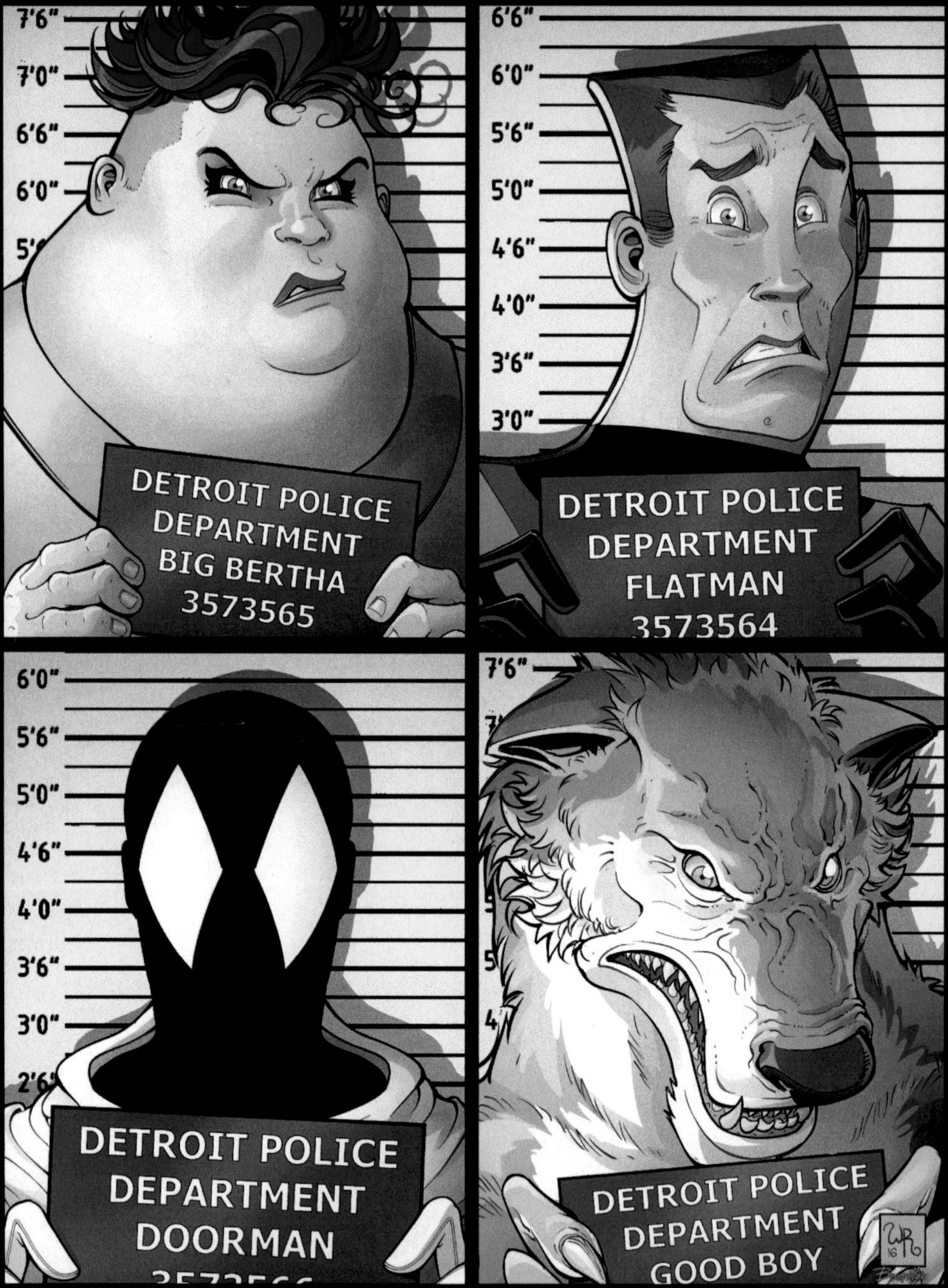

7'6"
7'0"
6'6"
6'0"
DETROIT POLICE
DEPARTMENT
BIG BERTHA
3573565
6'6"
6'0"
5'6"
5'0"
4'6"
4'0"
3'6"
3'0"
DETROIT POLICE
DEPARTMENT
FLATMAN
3573564
6'0"
5'6"
5'0"
4'6"
4'0"
3'6"
3'0"
DETROIT POLICE
DEPARTMENT
DOORMAN
7'6"
DETROIT POLICE
DEPARTMENT
GOOD BOY

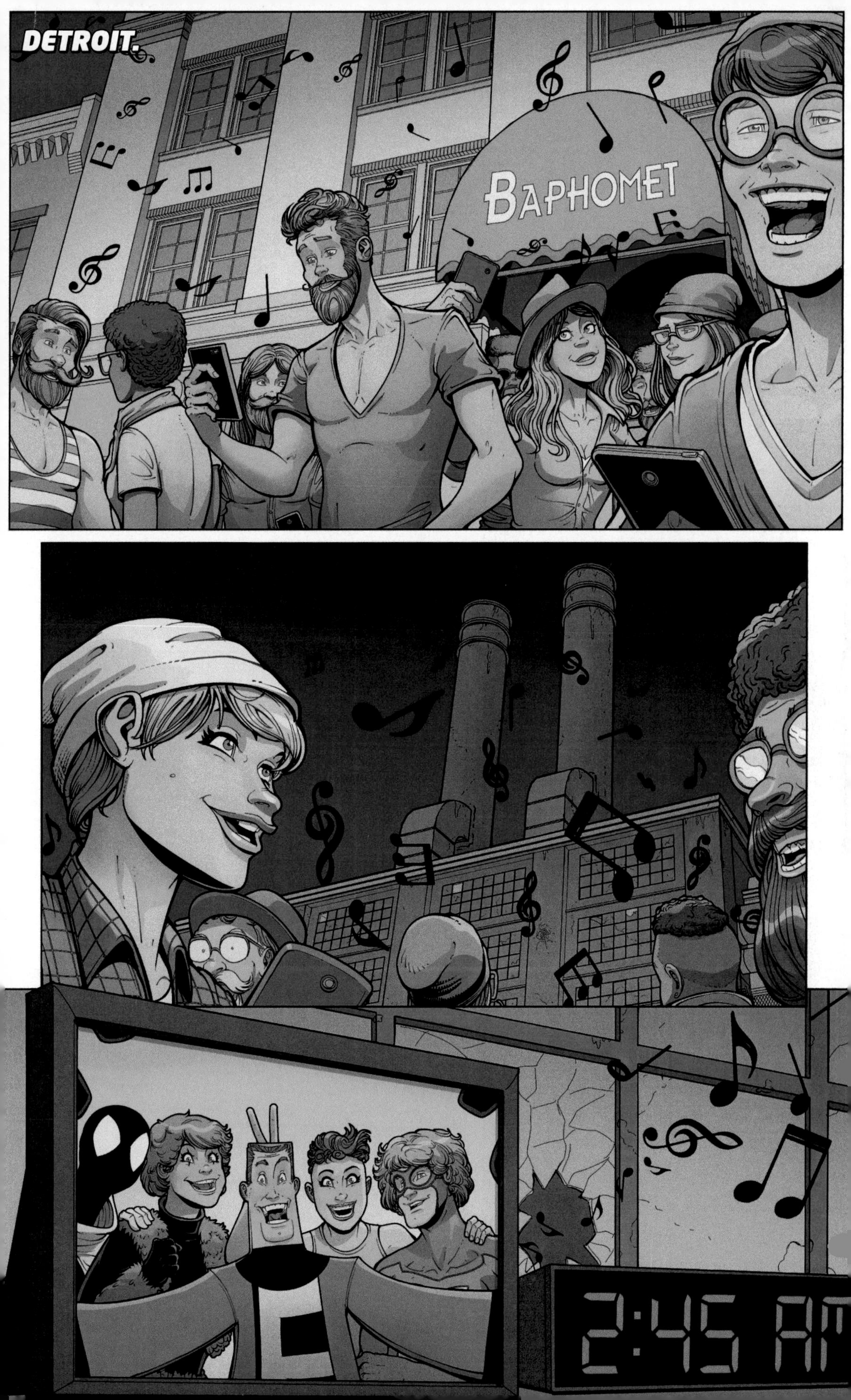
DETROIT.
BAPHOMET
2:45 AM

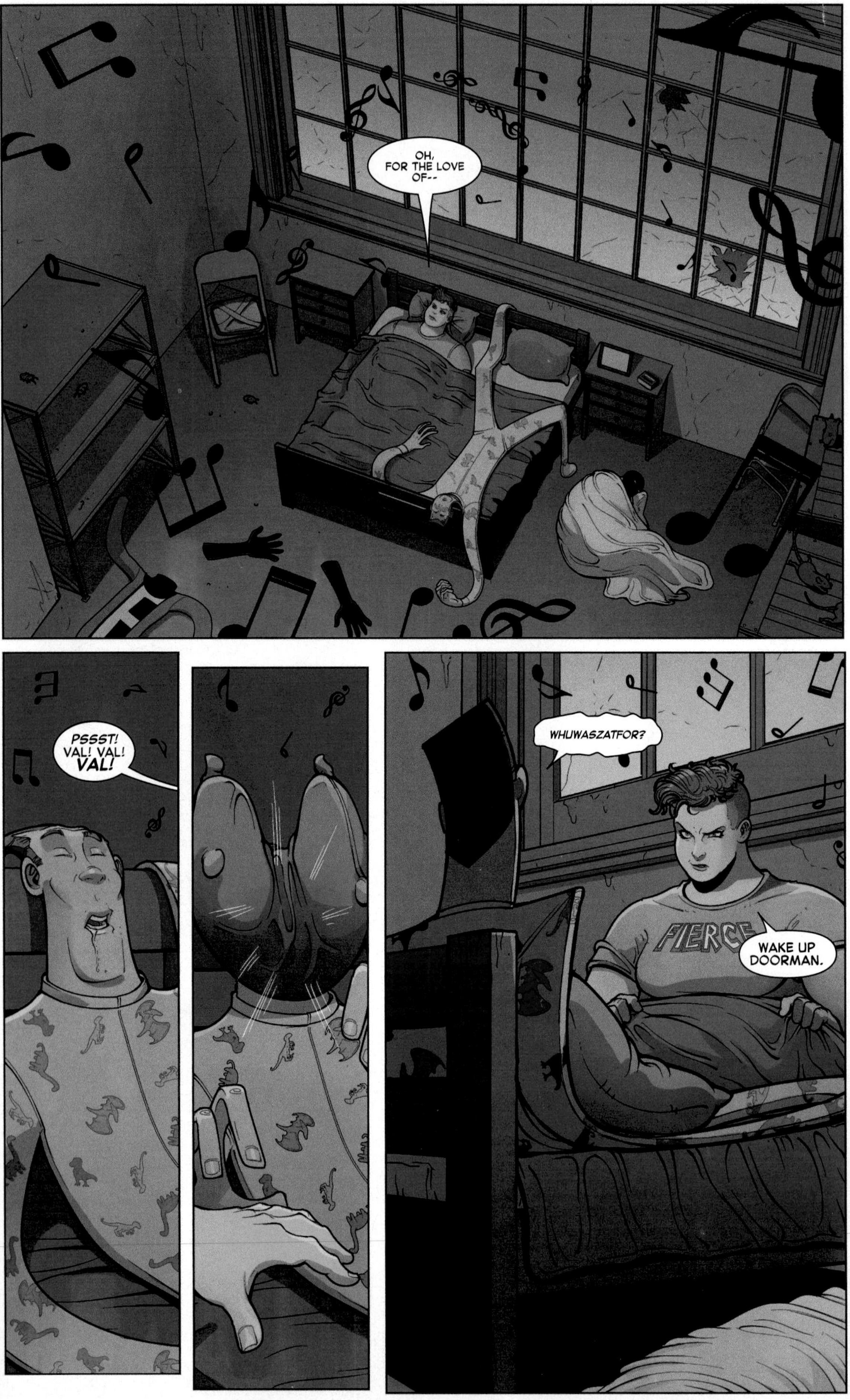
OH, FOR THE LOVE OF--
PSSST! VAL! VAL! VAL!
WHUWASZATFOR?
FIERCE
WAKE UP DOORMAN.

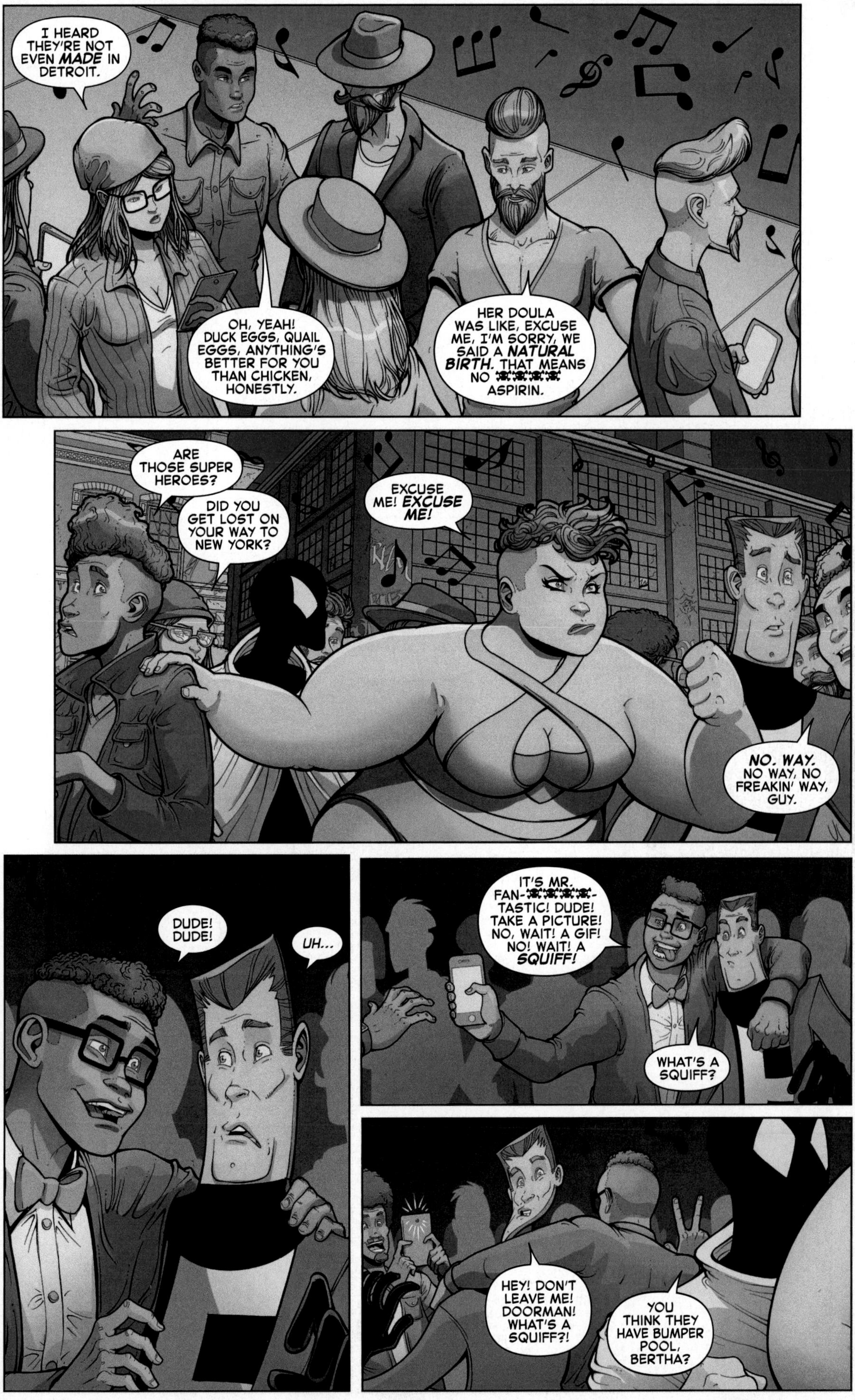
I HEARD THEY'RE NOT EVEN *MADE* IN DETROIT.
OH, YEAH! DUCK EGGS, QUAIL EGGS, ANYTHING'S BETTER FOR YOU THAN CHICKEN, HONESTLY.
HER DOULA WAS LIKE, EXCUSE ME, I'M SORRY, WE SAID A ***NATURAL BIRTH.*** THAT MEANS NO ☠☠☠☠ ASPIRIN.
ARE THOSE SUPER HEROES?
DID YOU GET LOST ON YOUR WAY TO NEW YORK?
EXCUSE ME! ***EXCUSE ME!***
***NO. WAY.*** NO WAY, NO FREAKIN' WAY, GUY.
DUDE! DUDE!
*UH...*
IT'S MR. FAN-☠☠☠☠☠-TASTIC! DUDE! TAKE A PICTURE! NO, WAIT! A GIF! NO! WAIT! A ***SQUIFF!***
WHAT'S A SQUIFF?
HEY! DON'T LEAVE ME! DOORMAN! WHAT'S A SQUIFF?!
YOU THINK THEY HAVE BUMPER POOL, BERTHA?

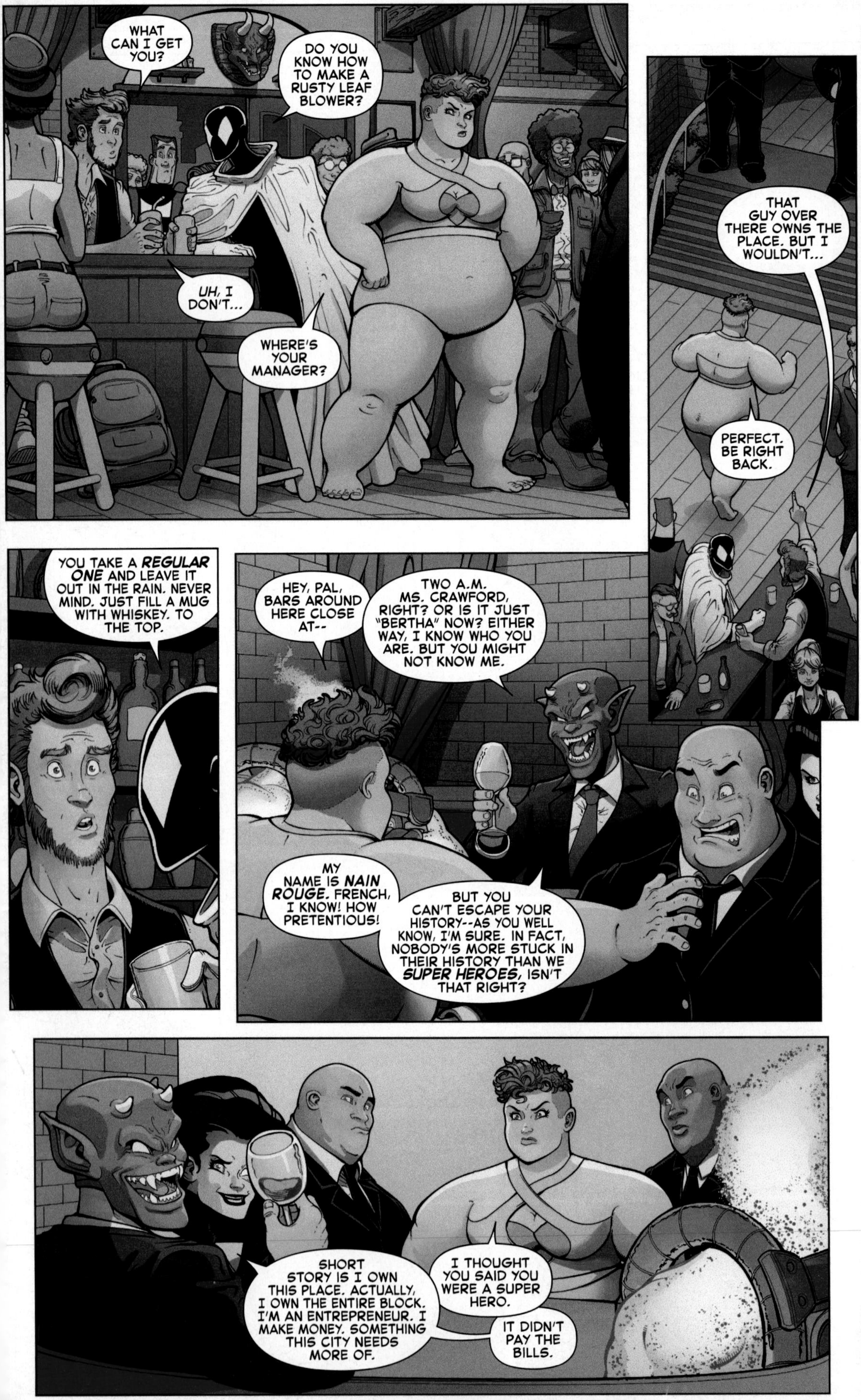
WHAT CAN I GET YOU?
DO YOU KNOW HOW TO MAKE A RUSTY LEAF BLOWER?
UH, I DON'T...
WHERE'S YOUR MANAGER?
THAT GUY OVER THERE OWNS THE PLACE. BUT I WOULDN'T...
PERFECT. BE RIGHT BACK.
YOU TAKE A REGULAR ONE AND LEAVE IT OUT IN THE RAIN. NEVER MIND. JUST FILL A MUG WITH WHISKEY. TO THE TOP.
HEY, PAL, BARS AROUND HERE CLOSE AT--
TWO A.M. MS. CRAWFORD, RIGHT? OR IS IT JUST "BERTHA" NOW? EITHER WAY, I KNOW WHO YOU ARE. BUT YOU MIGHT NOT KNOW ME.
MY NAME IS NAIN ROUGE. FRENCH, I KNOW! HOW PRETENTIOUS!
BUT YOU CAN'T ESCAPE YOUR HISTORY--AS YOU WELL KNOW, I'M SURE. IN FACT, NOBODY'S MORE STUCK IN THEIR HISTORY THAN WE SUPER HEROES, ISN'T THAT RIGHT?
SHORT STORY IS I OWN THIS PLACE. ACTUALLY, I OWN THE ENTIRE BLOCK. I'M AN ENTREPRENEUR. I MAKE MONEY. SOMETHING THIS CITY NEEDS MORE OF.
I THOUGHT YOU SAID YOU WERE A SUPER HERO.
IT DIDN'T PAY THE BILLS.

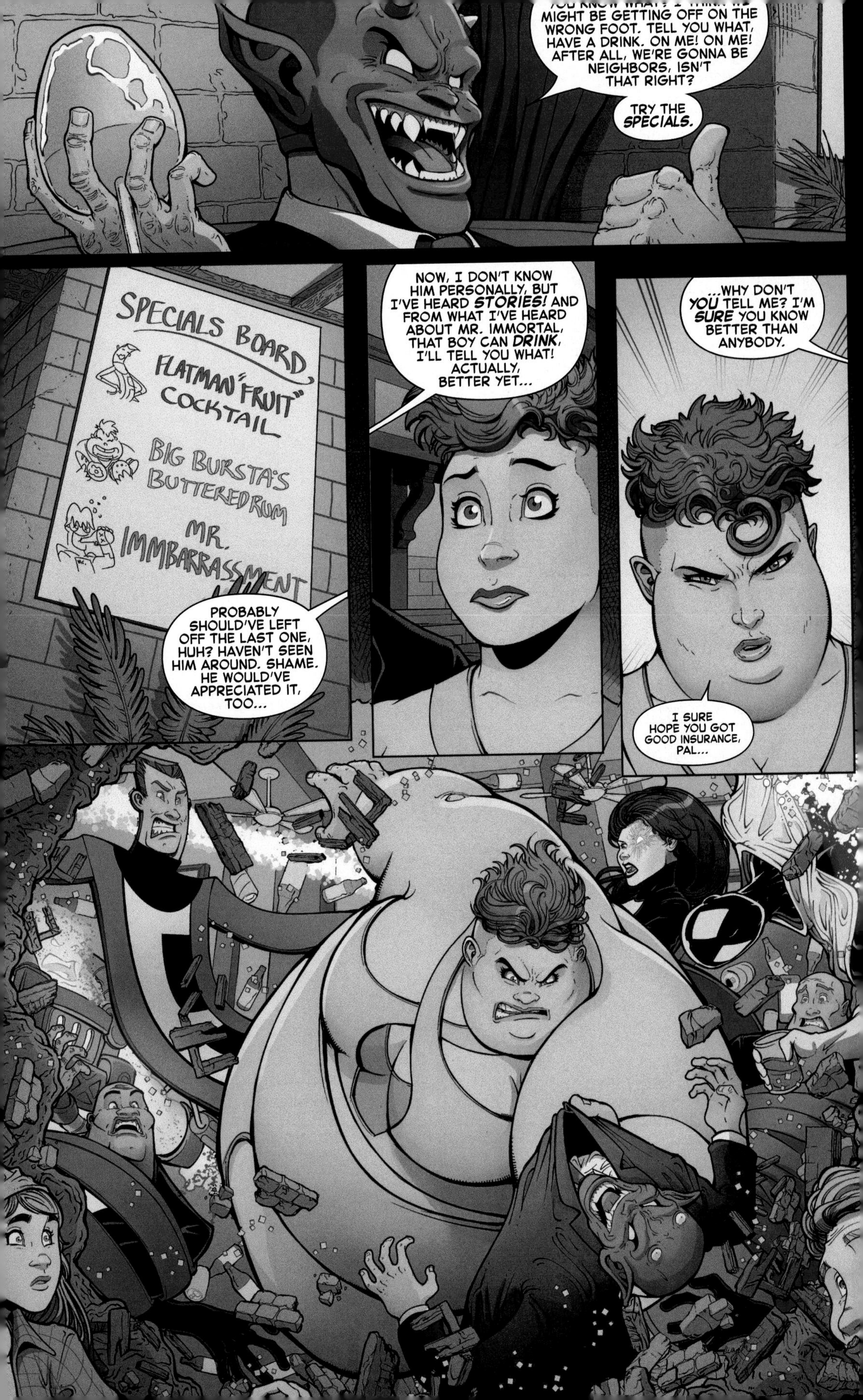

MIGHT BE GETTING OFF ON THE WRONG FOOT. TELL YOU WHAT, HAVE A DRINK. ON ME! ON ME! AFTER ALL, WE'RE GONNA BE NEIGHBORS, ISN'T THAT RIGHT?
TRY THE *SPECIALS.*
SPECIALS BOARD
FLATMAN "FRUIT" COCKTAIL
BIG BURSTA'S BUTTERED RUM
MR. IMMBARRASSMENT
PROBABLY SHOULD'VE LEFT OFF THE LAST ONE, HUH? HAVEN'T SEEN HIM AROUND. SHAME. HE WOULD'VE APPRECIATED IT, TOO...
NOW, I DON'T KNOW HIM PERSONALLY, BUT I'VE HEARD *STORIES!* AND FROM WHAT I'VE HEARD ABOUT MR. IMMORTAL, THAT BOY CAN *DRINK,* I'LL TELL YOU WHAT! ACTUALLY, BETTER YET...
...WHY DON'T *YOU* TELL ME? I'M *SURE* YOU KNOW BETTER THAN ANYBODY.
I SURE HOPE YOU GOT GOOD INSURANCE, PAL...

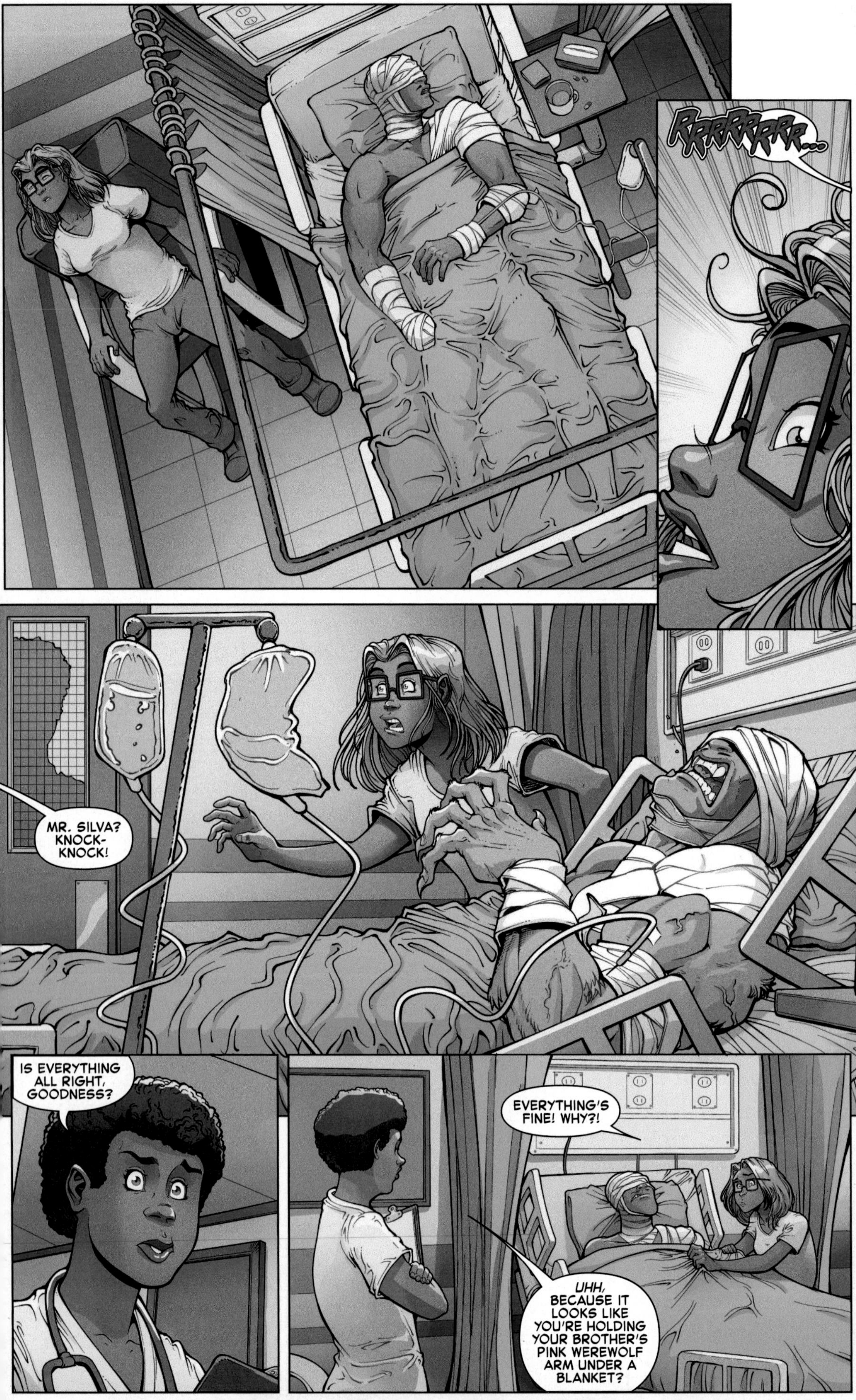
RRRRRRRRR...
MR. SILVA? KNOCK-KNOCK!
IS EVERYTHING ALL RIGHT, GOODNESS?
EVERYTHING'S FINE! WHY?!
UHH, BECAUSE IT LOOKS LIKE YOU'RE HOLDING YOUR BROTHER'S PINK WEREWOLF ARM UNDER A BLANKET?

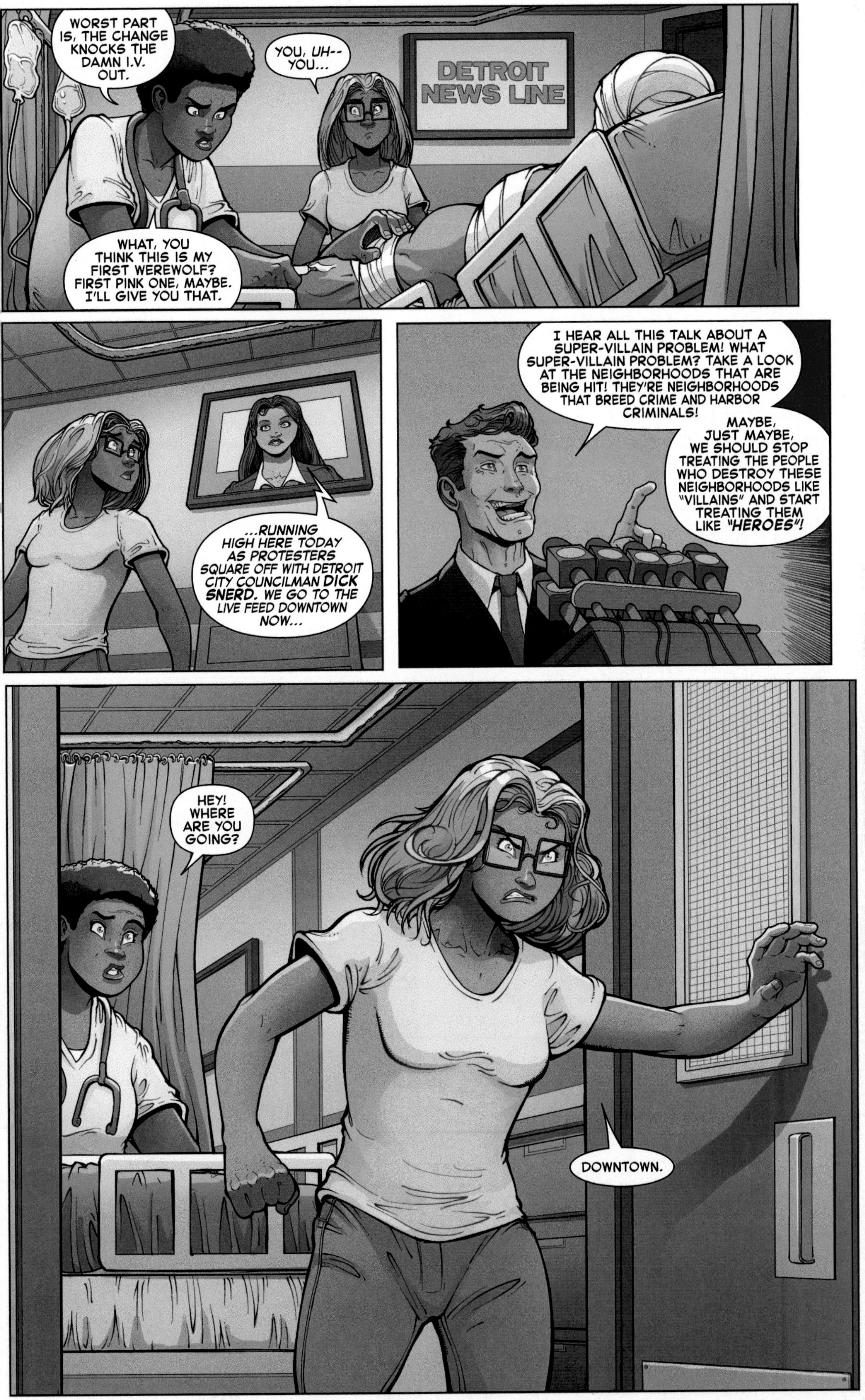
WORST PART IS, THE CHANGE KNOCKS THE DAMN I.V. OUT.
YOU, UH-- YOU...
DETROIT NEWS LINE
WHAT, YOU THINK THIS IS MY FIRST WEREWOLF? FIRST PINK ONE, MAYBE. I'LL GIVE YOU THAT.
...RUNNING HIGH HERE TODAY AS PROTESTERS SQUARE OFF WITH DETROIT CITY COUNCILMAN DICK SNERD. WE GO TO THE LIVE FEED DOWNTOWN NOW...
I HEAR ALL THIS TALK ABOUT A SUPER-VILLAIN PROBLEM! WHAT SUPER-VILLAIN PROBLEM? TAKE A LOOK AT THE NEIGHBORHOODS THAT ARE BEING HIT! THEY'RE NEIGHBORHOODS THAT BREED CRIME AND HARBOR CRIMINALS!
MAYBE, JUST MAYBE, WE SHOULD STOP TREATING THE PEOPLE WHO DESTROY THESE NEIGHBORHOODS LIKE "VILLAINS" AND START TREATING THEM LIKE "HEROES"!
HEY! WHERE ARE YOU GOING?
DOWNTOWN.

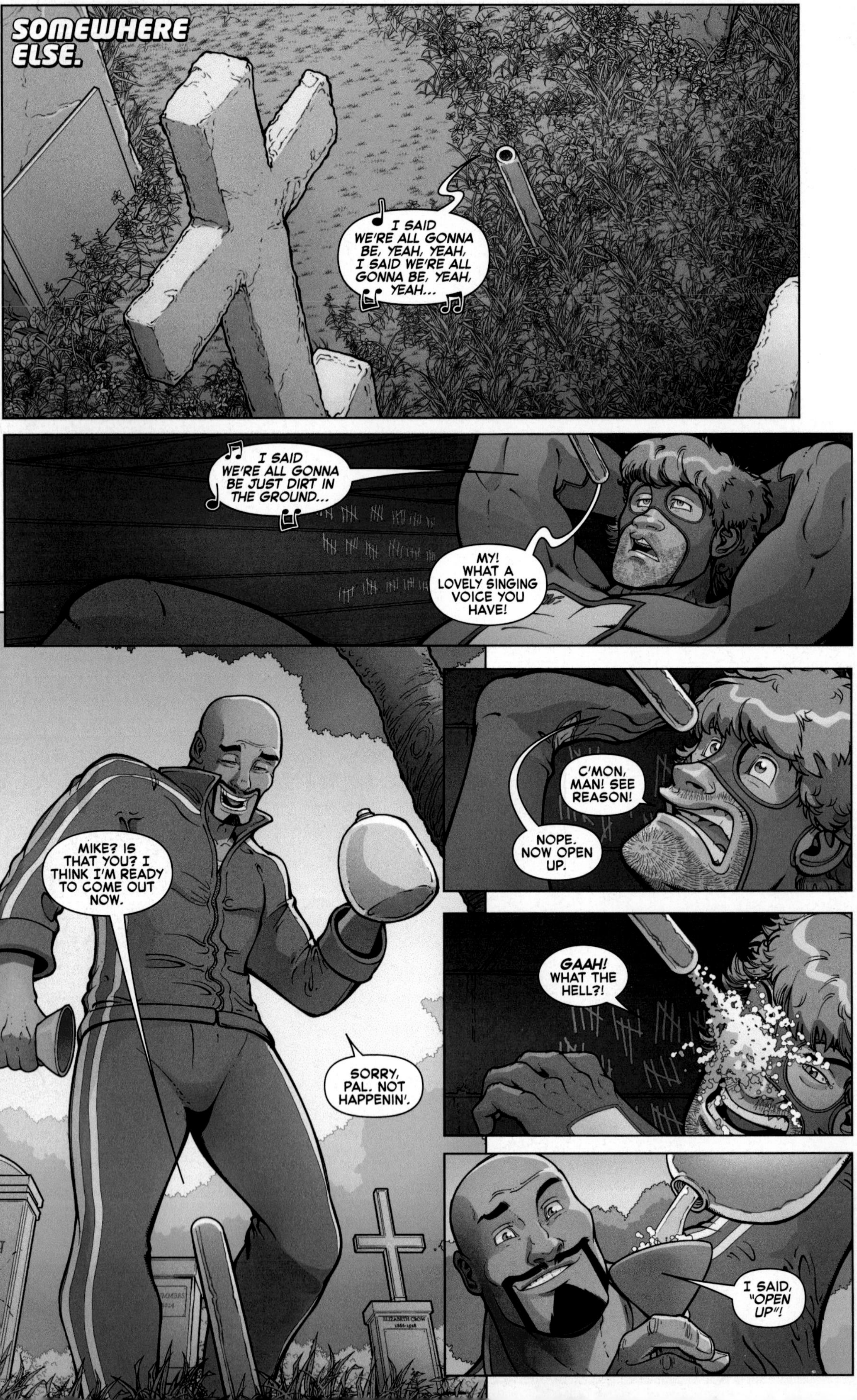
SOMEWHERE ELSE.
I SAID WE'RE ALL GONNA BE, YEAH, YEAH, I SAID WE'RE ALL GONNA BE, YEAH, YEAH...
I SAID WE'RE ALL GONNA BE JUST DIRT IN THE GROUND...
MY! WHAT A LOVELY SINGING VOICE YOU HAVE!
MIKE? IS THAT YOU? I THINK I'M READY TO COME OUT NOW.
SORRY, PAL. NOT HAPPENIN'.
C'MON, MAN! SEE REASON!
NOPE. NOW OPEN UP.
GAAH! WHAT THE HELL?!
I SAID, "OPEN UP"!

DAMMIT! YOU ✕✕✕✕! ARE YOU TRYIN' TO DROWN ME?

ACTUALLY, THAT'S NOT SUCH A BAD IDEA. MIX THINGS UP A LITTLE.

POUR SOME MORE WATER DOWN THE TUBE, I'M GONNA TRY TO GET IT UP MY NOSE! MIKE? *MIKE?*

DAMMIT! MIKE!

✕✕✕✕. WELL, I'M DEFINITELY NOT *STARVING* TO DEATH AGAIN.

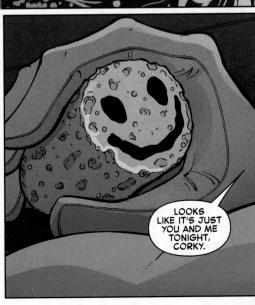

LOOKS LIKE IT'S JUST YOU AND ME TONIGHT, CORKY.

DON'T GIVE ME THAT LOOK, CORKY.

CORKY, YOU CONDESCENDING BASTARD.

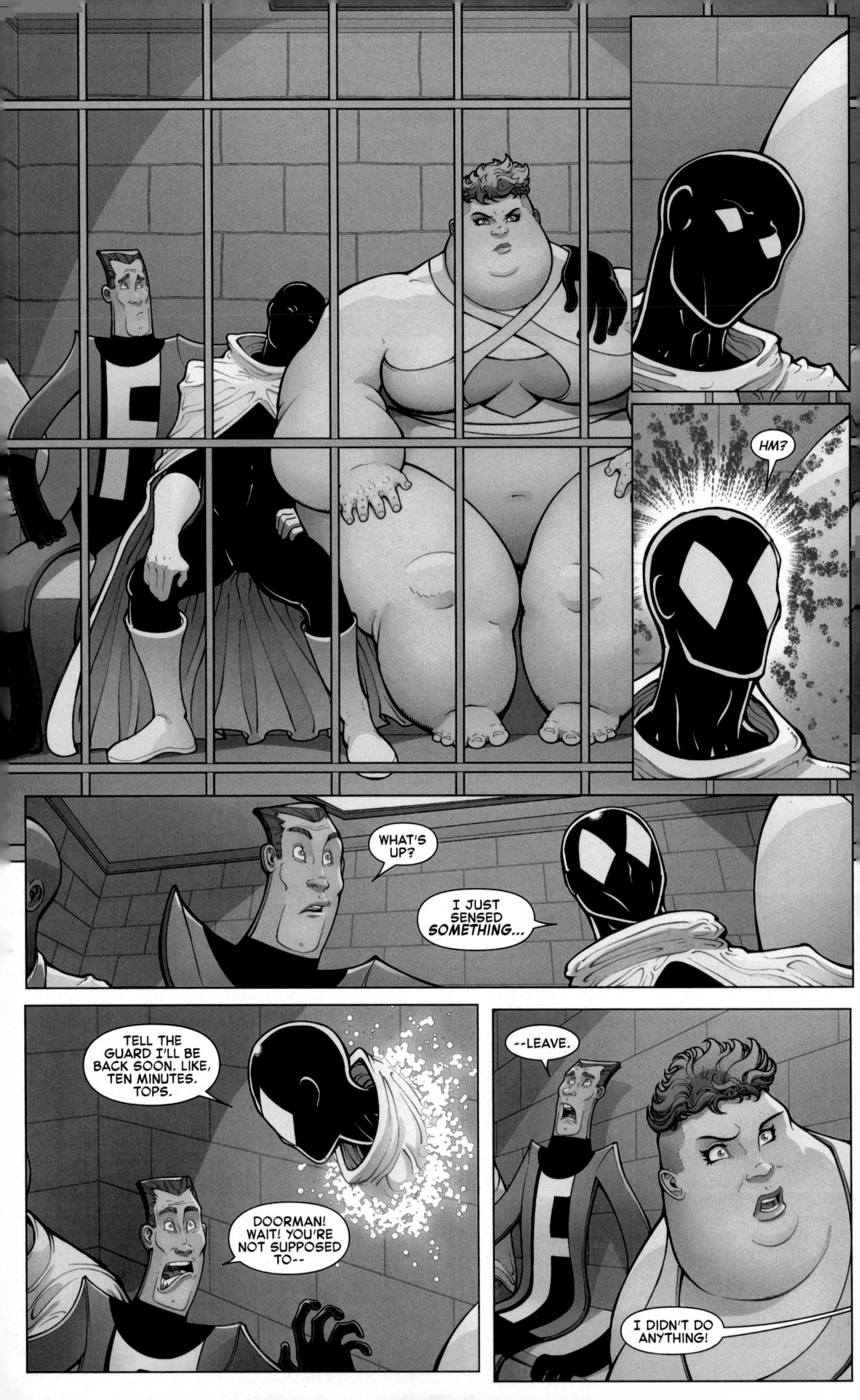
HM?
WHAT'S UP?
I JUST SENSED SOMETHING...
TELL THE GUARD I'LL BE BACK SOON. LIKE, TEN MINUTES. TOPS.
DOORMAN! WAIT! YOU'RE NOT SUPPOSED TO--
--LEAVE.
I DIDN'T DO ANYTHING!

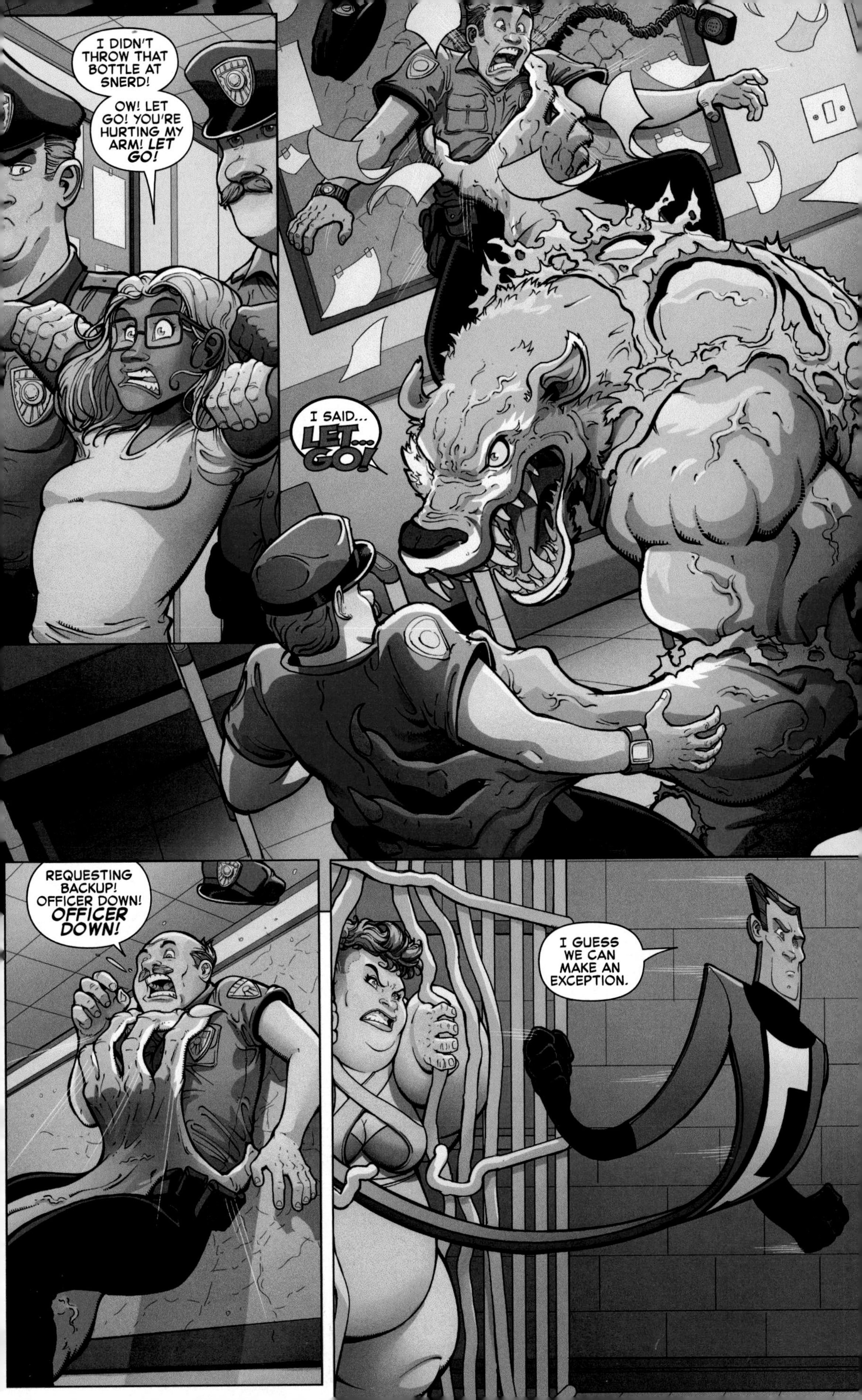
I DIDN'T THROW THAT BOTTLE AT SNERD!
OW! LET GO! YOU'RE HURTING MY ARM! LET GO!
I SAID... LET... GO!
REQUESTING BACKUP! OFFICER DOWN! OFFICER DOWN!
I GUESS WE CAN MAKE AN EXCEPTION.

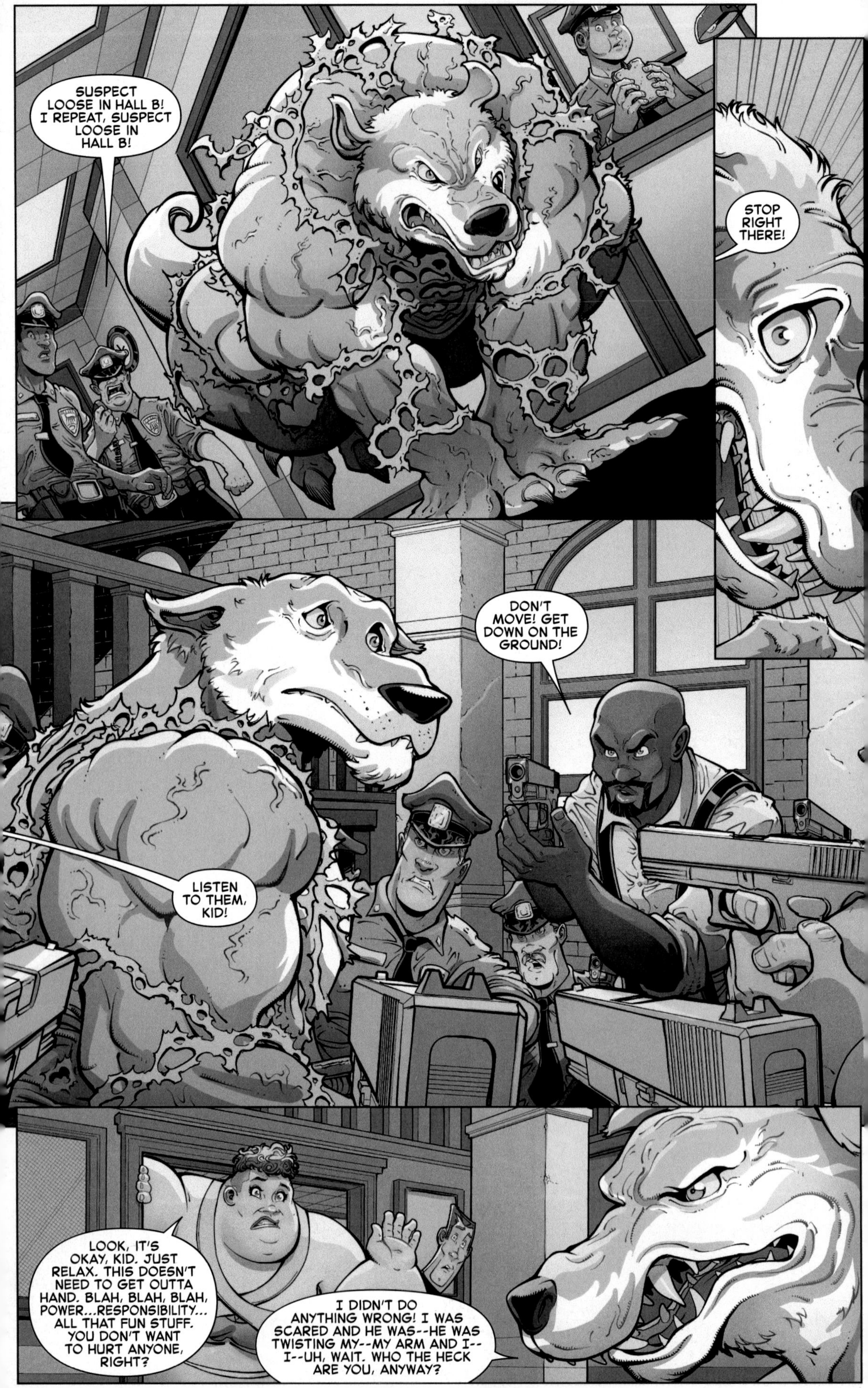
SUSPECT LOOSE IN HALL B! I REPEAT, SUSPECT LOOSE IN HALL B!
STOP RIGHT THERE!
DON'T MOVE! GET DOWN ON THE GROUND!
LISTEN TO THEM, KID!
LOOK, IT'S OKAY, KID. JUST RELAX. THIS DOESN'T NEED TO GET OUTTA HAND. BLAH, BLAH, BLAH, POWER...RESPONSIBILITY... ALL THAT FUN STUFF. YOU DON'T WANT TO HURT ANYONE, RIGHT?
I DIDN'T DO ANYTHING WRONG! I WAS SCARED AND HE WAS--HE WAS TWISTING MY--MY ARM AND I--I--UH, WAIT. WHO THE HECK ARE YOU, ANYWAY?

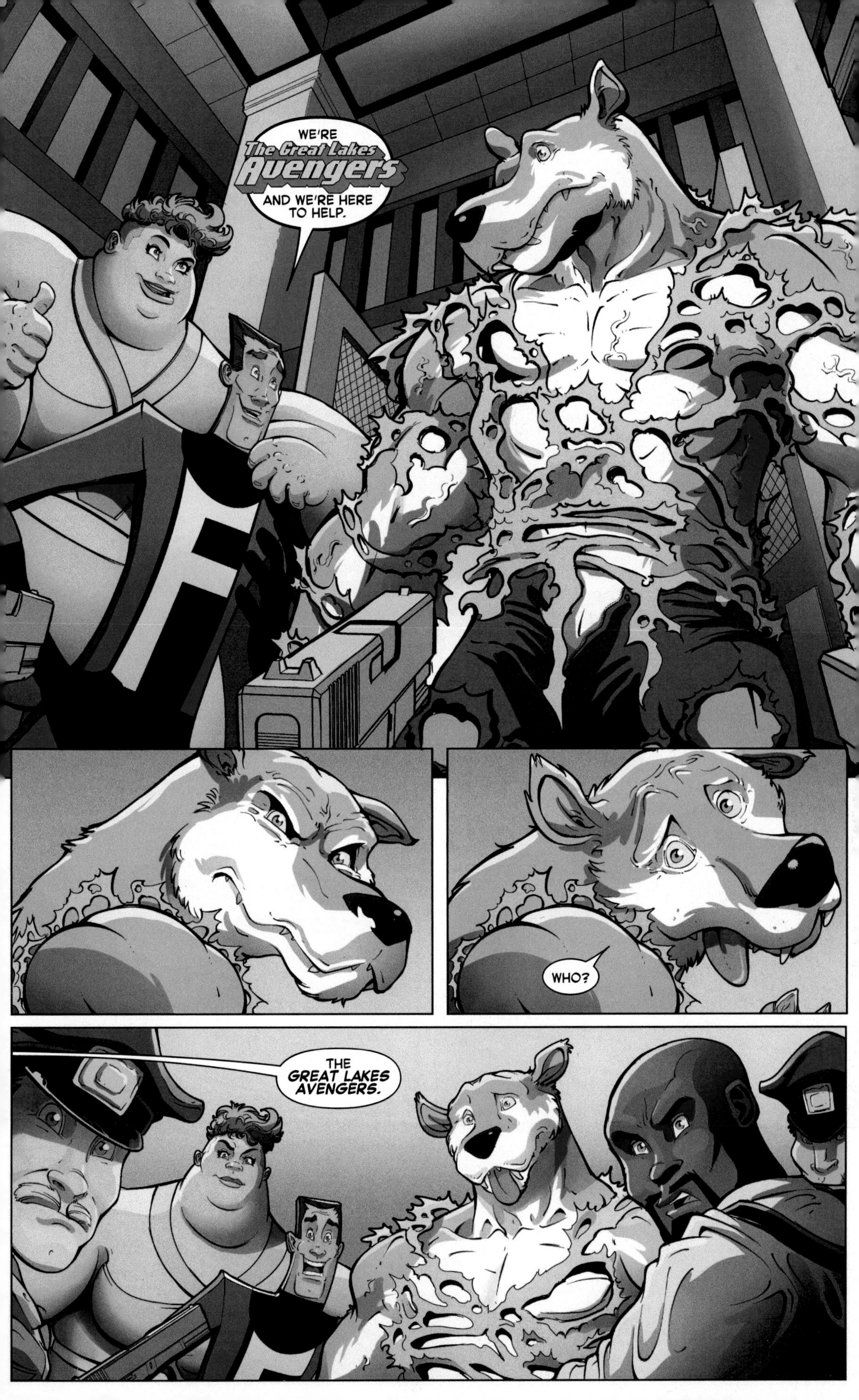
WE'RE
The Great Lakes
Avengers
AND WE'RE HERE TO HELP.
WHO?
THE GREAT LAKES AVENGERS.

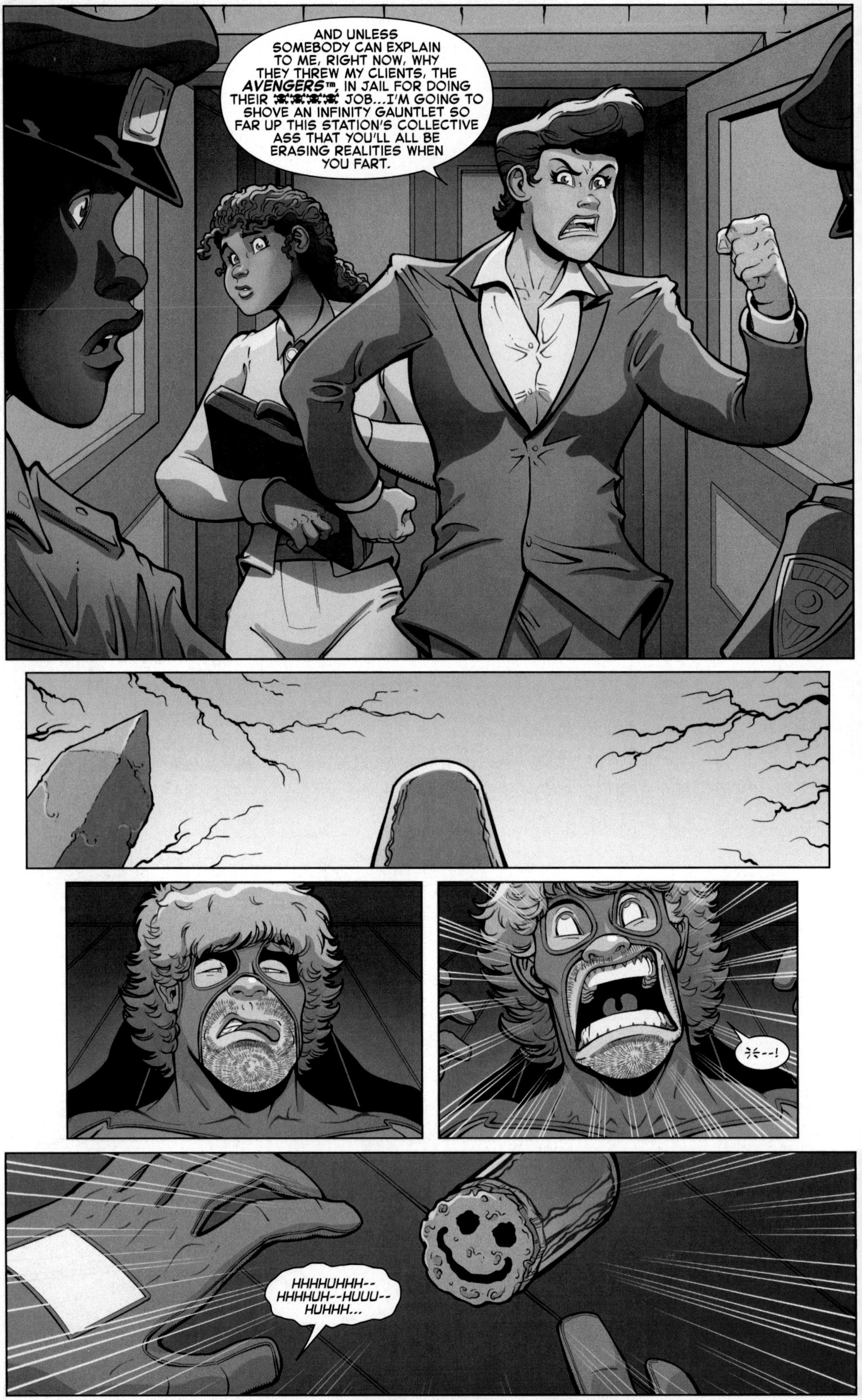
AND UNLESS SOMEBODY CAN EXPLAIN TO ME, RIGHT NOW, WHY THEY THREW MY CLIENTS, THE AVENGERS™, IN JAIL FOR DOING THEIR ☠☠☠☠ JOB...I'M GOING TO SHOVE AN INFINITY GAUNTLET SO FAR UP THIS STATION'S COLLECTIVE ASS THAT YOU'LL ALL BE ERASING REALITIES WHEN YOU FART.
HHHHUHHH-- HHHHUH--HUUU-- HUHHH...

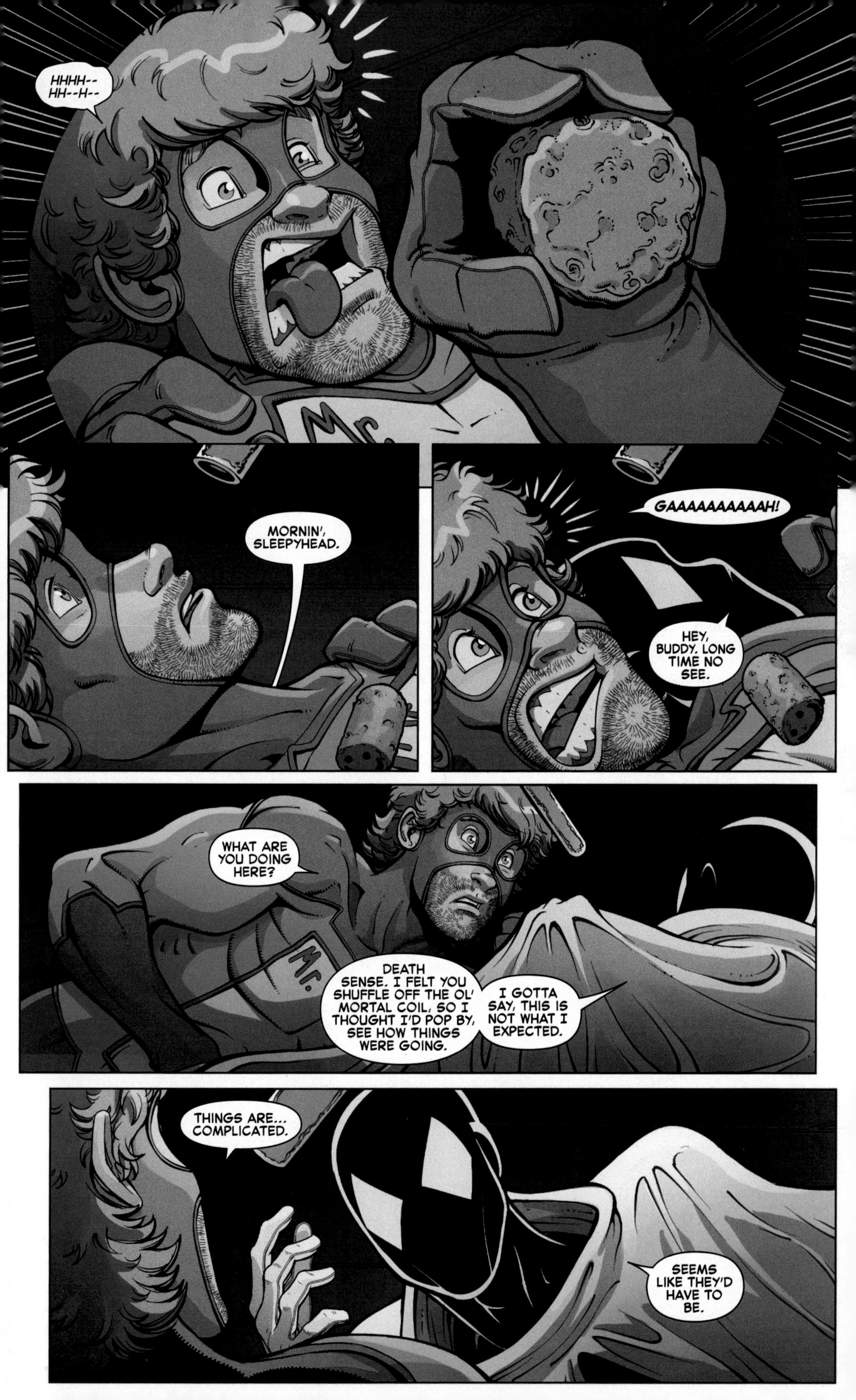
HHHH-- HH--H--
MORNIN', SLEEPYHEAD.
GAAAAAAAAAAH!
HEY, BUDDY. LONG TIME NO SEE.
WHAT ARE YOU DOING HERE?
DEATH SENSE. I FELT YOU SHUFFLE OFF THE OL' MORTAL COIL, SO I THOUGHT I'D POP BY, SEE HOW THINGS WERE GOING.
I GOTTA SAY, THIS IS NOT WHAT I EXPECTED.
THINGS ARE... COMPLICATED.
SEEMS LIKE THEY'D HAVE TO BE.

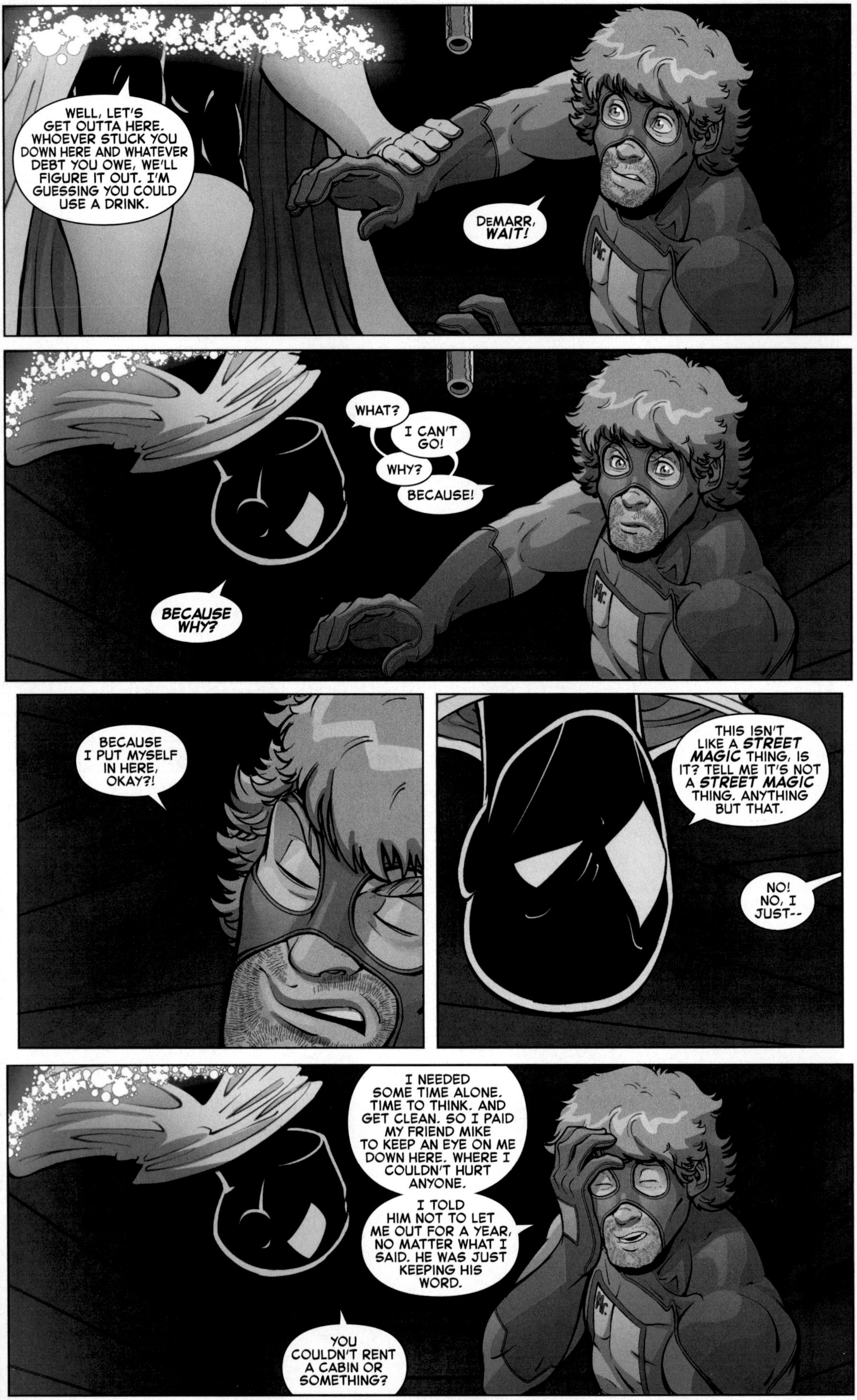

WELL, LET'S GET OUTTA HERE. WHOEVER STUCK YOU DOWN HERE AND WHATEVER DEBT YOU OWE, WE'LL FIGURE IT OUT. I'M GUESSING YOU COULD USE A DRINK.
DEMARR, WAIT!
WHAT?
I CAN'T GO!
WHY?
BECAUSE!
BECAUSE WHY?
BECAUSE I PUT MYSELF IN HERE, OKAY?!
THIS ISN'T LIKE A STREET MAGIC THING, IS IT? TELL ME IT'S NOT A STREET MAGIC THING. ANYTHING BUT THAT.
NO! NO, I JUST--
I NEEDED SOME TIME ALONE. TIME TO THINK. AND GET CLEAN. SO I PAID MY FRIEND MIKE TO KEEP AN EYE ON ME DOWN HERE. WHERE I COULDN'T HURT ANYONE.
I TOLD HIM NOT TO LET ME OUT FOR A YEAR, NO MATTER WHAT I SAID. HE WAS JUST KEEPING HIS WORD.
YOU COULDN'T RENT A CABIN OR SOMETHING?

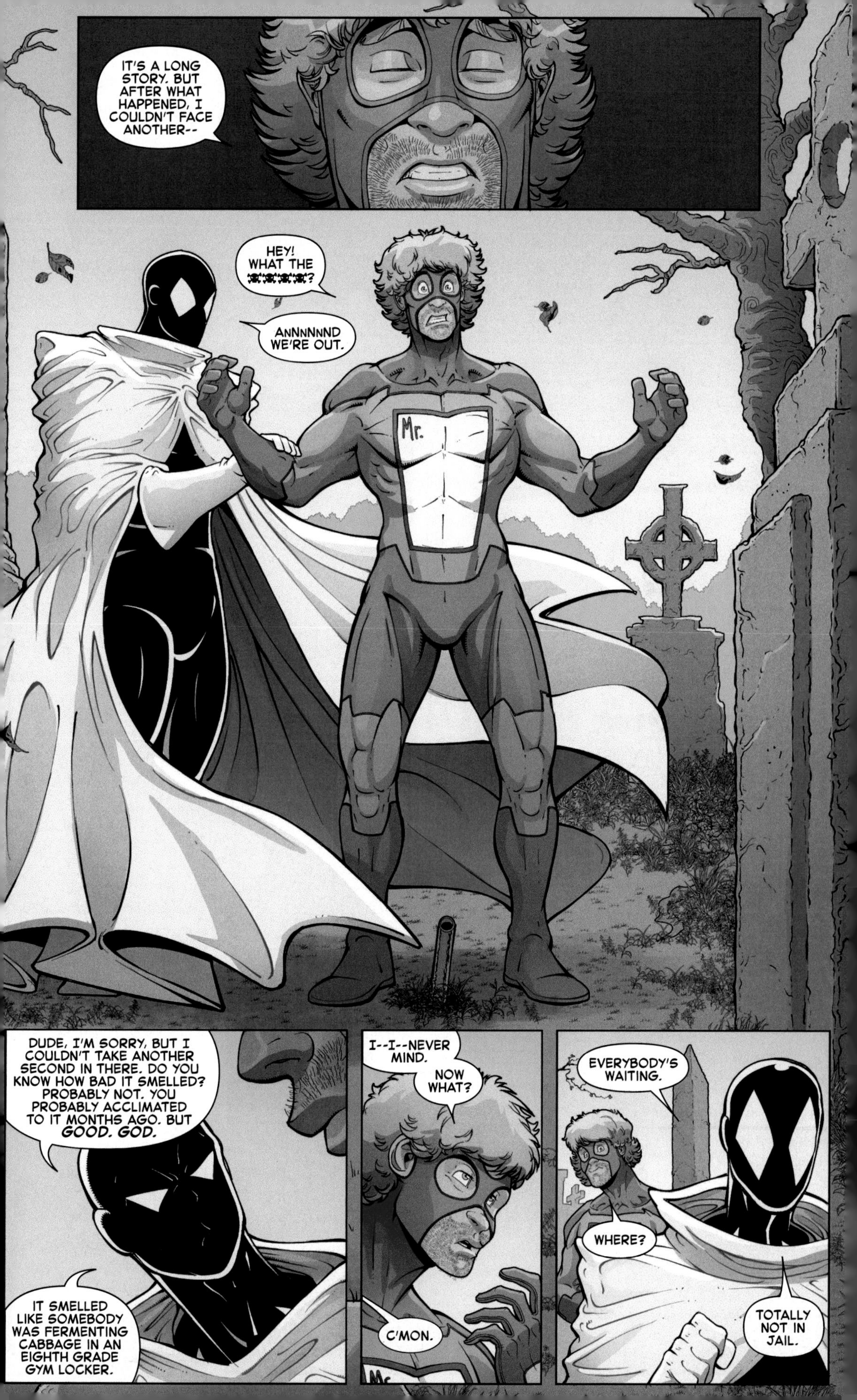
IT'S A LONG STORY. BUT AFTER WHAT HAPPENED, I COULDN'T FACE ANOTHER--
HEY! WHAT THE ☠☠☠☠?
ANNNNNND WE'RE OUT.
DUDE, I'M SORRY, BUT I COULDN'T TAKE ANOTHER SECOND IN THERE. DO YOU KNOW HOW BAD IT SMELLED? PROBABLY NOT. YOU PROBABLY ACCLIMATED TO IT MONTHS AGO. BUT ***GOOD. GOD.***
IT SMELLED LIKE SOMEBODY WAS FERMENTING CABBAGE IN AN EIGHTH GRADE GYM LOCKER.
I--I--NEVER MIND.
NOW WHAT?
C'MON.
EVERYBODY'S WAITING.
WHERE?
TOTALLY NOT IN JAIL.

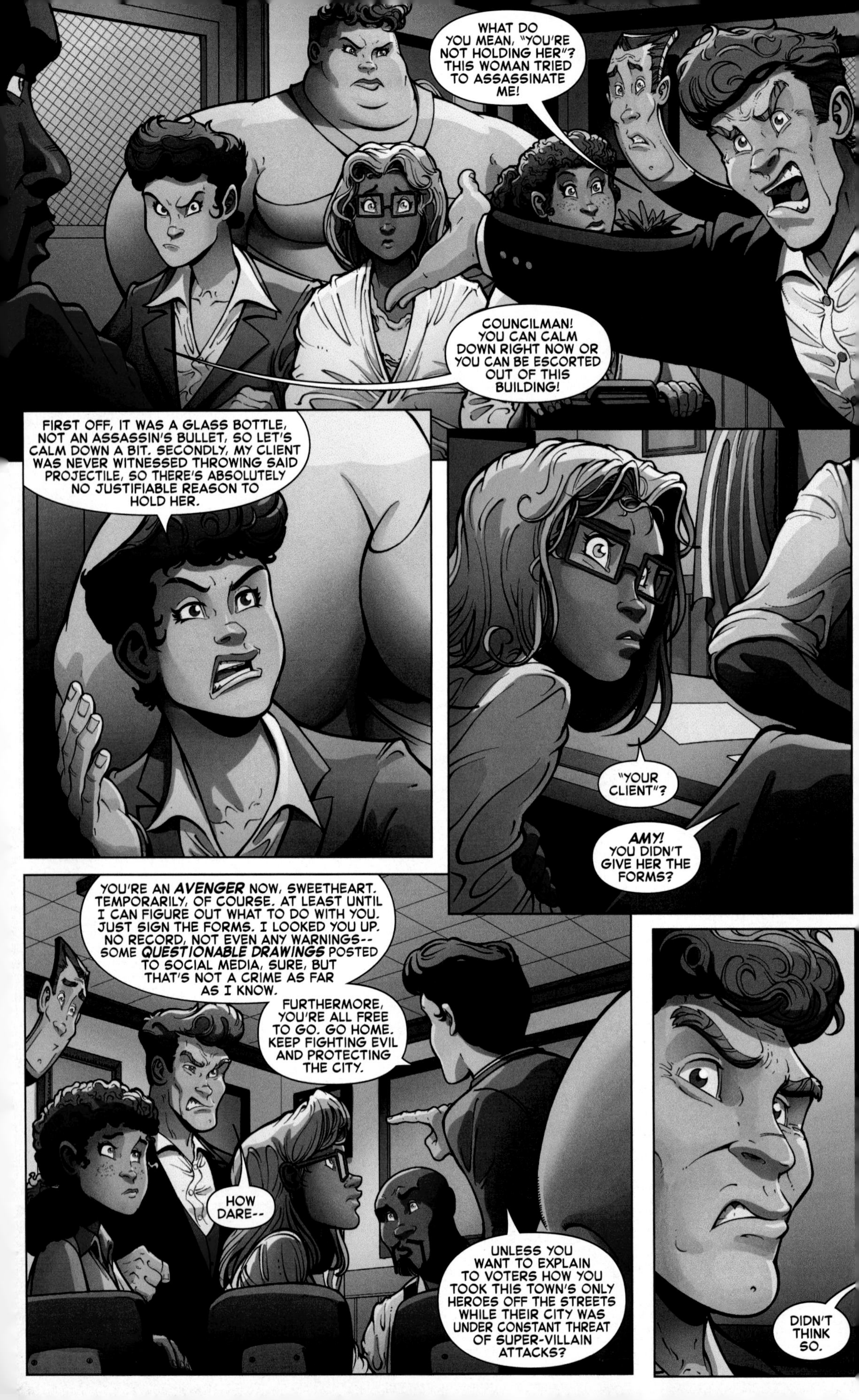
WHAT DO YOU MEAN, "YOU'RE NOT HOLDING HER"? THIS WOMAN TRIED TO ASSASSINATE ME!
COUNCILMAN! YOU CAN CALM DOWN RIGHT NOW OR YOU CAN BE ESCORTED OUT OF THIS BUILDING!
FIRST OFF, IT WAS A GLASS BOTTLE, NOT AN ASSASSIN'S BULLET, SO LET'S CALM DOWN A BIT. SECONDLY, MY CLIENT WAS NEVER WITNESSED THROWING SAID PROJECTILE, SO THERE'S ABSOLUTELY NO JUSTIFIABLE REASON TO HOLD HER.
"YOUR CLIENT"?
AMY! YOU DIDN'T GIVE HER THE FORMS?
YOU'RE AN AVENGER NOW, SWEETHEART. TEMPORARILY, OF COURSE. AT LEAST UNTIL I CAN FIGURE OUT WHAT TO DO WITH YOU. JUST SIGN THE FORMS. I LOOKED YOU UP. NO RECORD, NOT EVEN ANY WARNINGS-- SOME QUESTIONABLE DRAWINGS POSTED TO SOCIAL MEDIA, SURE, BUT THAT'S NOT A CRIME AS FAR AS I KNOW.
FURTHERMORE, YOU'RE ALL FREE TO GO. GO HOME. KEEP FIGHTING EVIL AND PROTECTING THE CITY.
HOW DARE--
UNLESS YOU WANT TO EXPLAIN TO VOTERS HOW YOU TOOK THIS TOWN'S ONLY HEROES OFF THE STREETS WHILE THEIR CITY WAS UNDER CONSTANT THREAT OF SUPER-VILLAIN ATTACKS?
DIDN'T THINK SO.

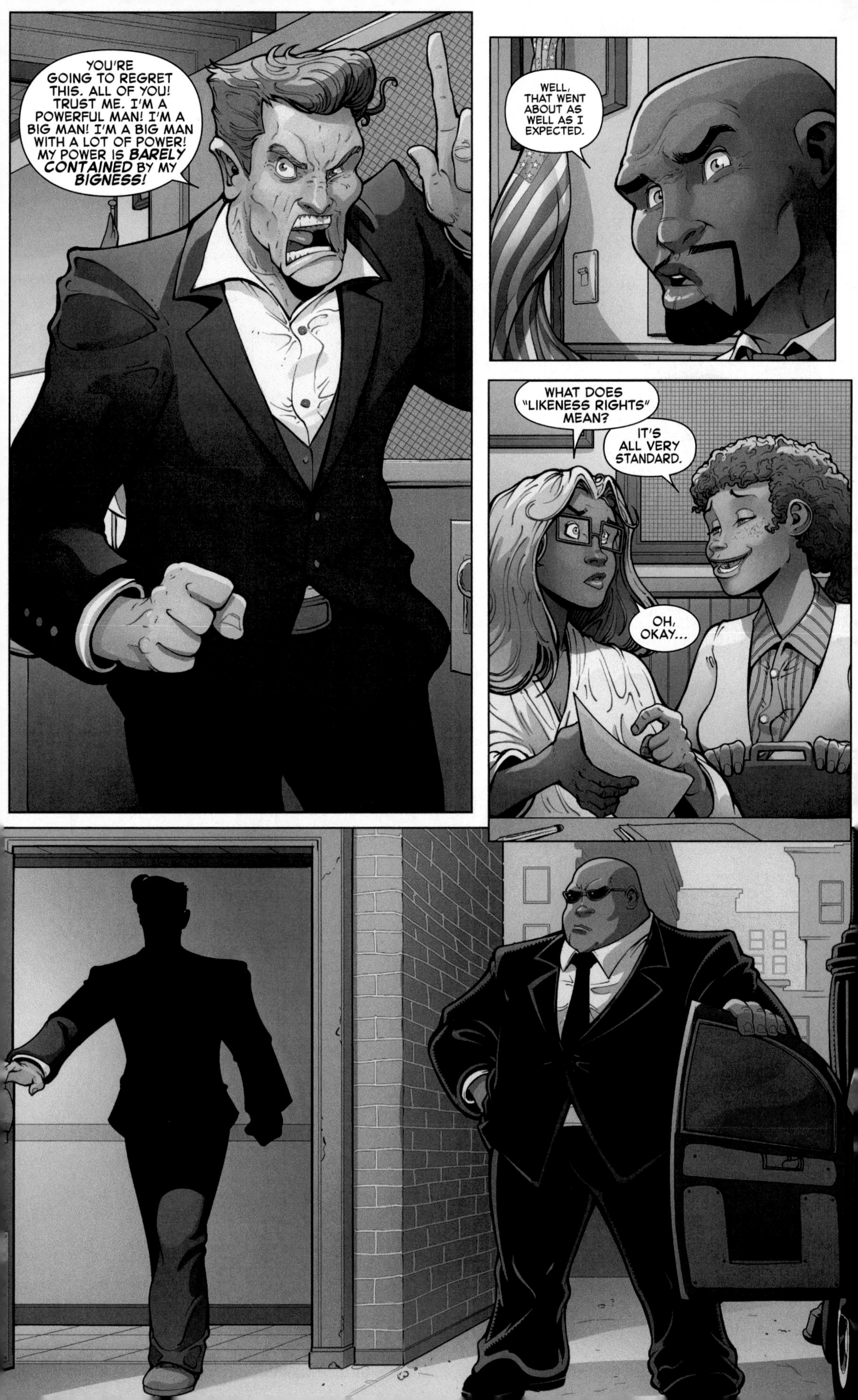

YOU'RE GOING TO REGRET THIS. ALL OF YOU! TRUST ME. I'M A POWERFUL MAN! I'M A BIG MAN! I'M A BIG MAN WITH A LOT OF POWER! MY POWER IS ***BARELY CONTAINED*** BY MY ***BIGNESS!***
WELL, THAT WENT ABOUT AS WELL AS I EXPECTED.
WHAT DOES "LIKENESS RIGHTS" MEAN?
IT'S ALL VERY STANDARD.
OH, OKAY...

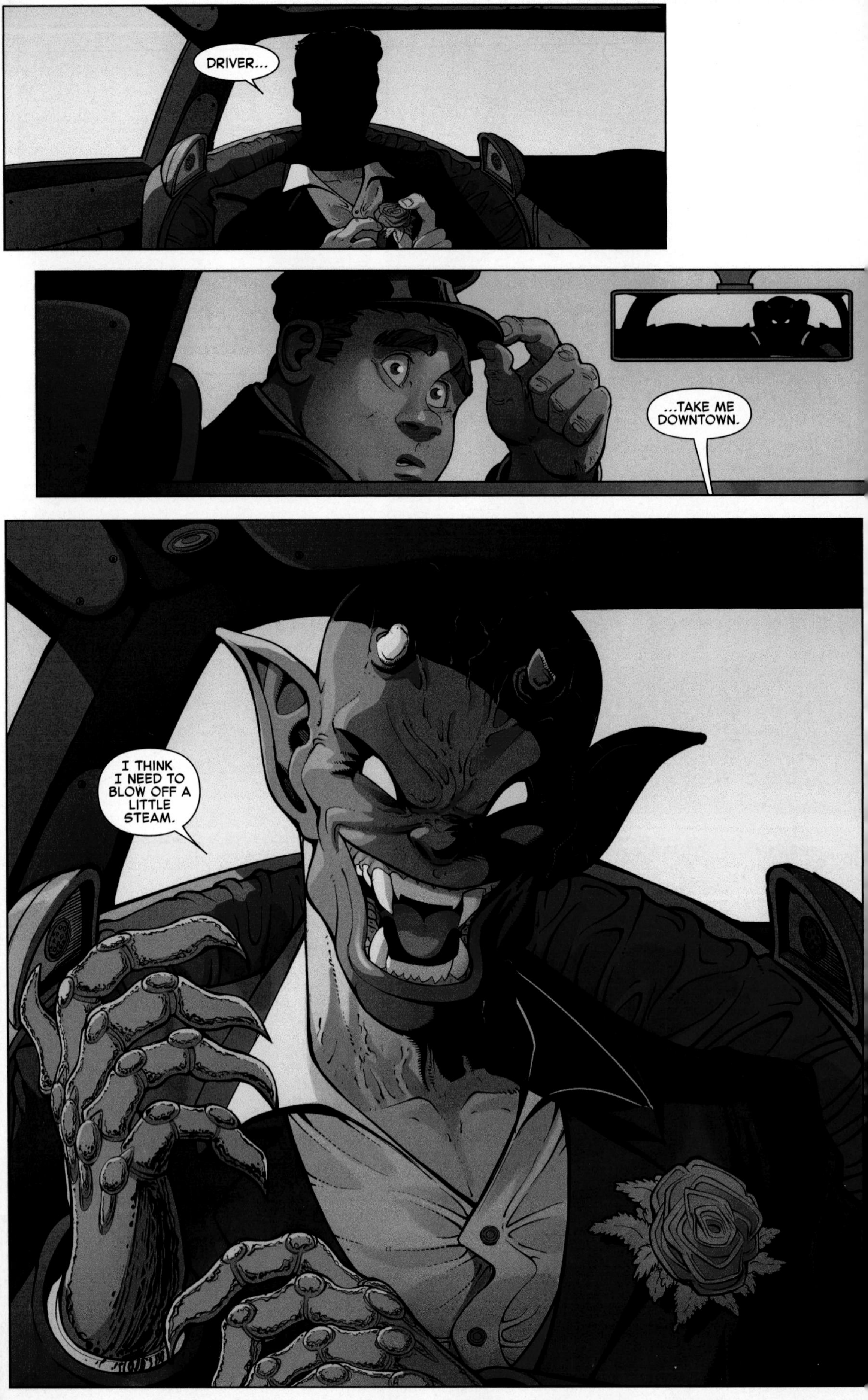
DRIVER...
...TAKE ME DOWNTOWN.
I THINK I NEED TO BLOW OFF A LITTLE STEAM.

# The Great Lakes Avengers

Send letters to MHEROES@MARVEL.COM marked "Okay to Print"!

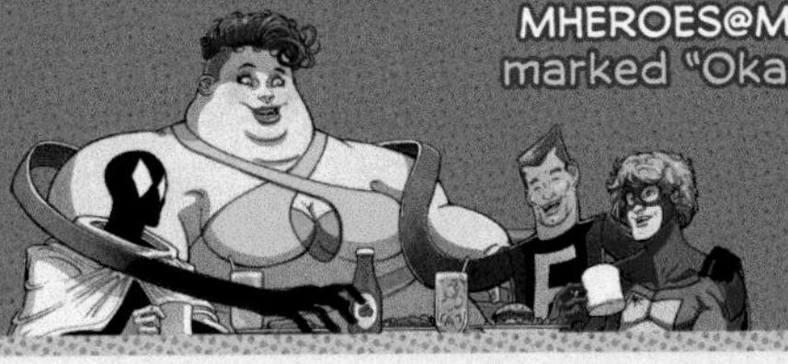

We said the Great Lakes Avengers will take just about anybody, and we meant it! But can our enthusiastically mundane candidates make it past the gauntlet that is writer and GLA hiring director Zac Gorman? Let's find out!

---

I would like to apply for the Great Lakes Avengers. My name is Awesome Shucks Man. I can talk almost anyone into anything with my ability to distract them with my country folksy ways. I would call in and order a pizza and say I have a coupon. When I get there, I talk them up and use my powers. I get the discount but never give them the coupon. I would be great for the GLA in getting us food and stuff. Might be able to distract a bad guy and such. Please consider me.

Thank u,
John "Awwww Shucks Man" Brooks

**Dear Awesome Shucks Man,**

**Your powers are great, there's no doubt about that, but considering your example, are you sure that you aren't better suited to a life of villainy? Coupons, my friend, are the backbone of capitalist commerce! The fair exchange of a little slip of paper for an order of free cheesy bread is the stuff that America was built on! By circumventing this hallowed tradition, I'm afraid that you've outed yourself. Still, we are always looking for new villains, so we'll keep you in mind.**

Dear GLA,

As a Wisconsinite, I was very sad to see the GLA move to Detroit in the first issue. I guess that leaves an opening for a super hero in the Badger State, and who better to step up than the Cheesemonger! Cheddar, pepper jack, muenster, you name a cheese and I'll eat it. The eating of cheese is not my super-power per se, but rather what happens during the digestion process--that's where the real magic happens.

Anyway, just wanted to say thanks for giving one of my favorite teams some long overdue love. That said, please, please, please make my dream come true and somehow, some place, have Big Bertha and the Blob meet. I want them to fall in love, but I'd settle for a "Battle of the Bellies"!

Chad "the Cheesemonger" Holloway

**Dear Cheesemonger,**

**Cheese digestion is indeed magical! Did you know that, according to even most conservative estimates, well over half the world's population loses their lactase enzymes after weaning? Lactose intolerance is a cruel mistress! You are an anomaly, my friend! But with great power comes great responsibility. Please remember to always cheese responsibly and stay away from the canned stuff. It's basically just yellow caulk.**

I wanna join the Great Lakes Avengers...I wanna be called...there are options: Mr. Owes Sallie Mae, with the powers to ignore Sallie Mae phone calls or mail, etc.

Nominal Muslim Guy...I drink beer. I'm Muslim, but did I mention I drink beer?

Fatherhood Education Facilitator Guy. I teach dads the importance of being dads...if villains got it...they'd be better people.

I want in, where's my suit?

The Mega Horbz
WEST TEXAS GOMAB HQ
El Paso, TX

**Dear Mega Horbz,**

**I find it interesting that a person named "The Mega Horbz" decided not to work that into their super hero persona, but perhaps your real super-power is your ability to think outside the box. In that spirit, I say why not combine all three of your suggestions? Maybe you're a Muslim gentleman who drinks beer during the day and a Fatherhood Education Facilitator by night! Why? Because you have bills to pay!**

Hello, my name is Brian Knight, and I am a huge fan of the GREAT LAKES AVENGERS! I am super excited that there is a new series! I am also excited that I have a chance to be an honorary member of the Great Lakes Avengers! EYE have a very special super-power. Just like a mood ring, my eyes change color depending on my mood! It ranges anywhere from blue to greenish and even to gray! I hope this special ability will earn me a spot on the GLA! Thanks!

Brian Knight

**Dear Brian Knight,**

**It seems like you forgot to mention that with each color shift of your eyes, you become capable of blasting different elemental lasers from them. A freeze ray when your eyes are blue with sadness, a heat ray when your eyes are red from anger, a boredom ray when your eyes are gray with indifference! I'm sure that you just ran out of room in your letter to mention the whole laser eyes thing, but next time I might lead with that! Either way, welcome aboard!**

Greetings, fellow heroes, it is I--the Perfect Parker!

It was a dark and stormy lunchtime when I rolled up to a local restaurant for lunch, and there was a spot less than five feet from the door. My friend and work colleague Dave said, "Did you ever notice that Brian always gets the best parking spot? It's, like, it's his super-power!"

My faithful chum was correct. Years earlier I had helped a blind elderly woman cross the street. When we arrived safely at our destination, she asked me what was troubling me. I told her that I had parked several blocks away and was worried I might get a ticket. She placed her hand on my arm and looked deep into my eyes. In that instant, it was like the clouds in her eyes parted, and electricity raced up my arm. "You shall never have trouble parking again," she said.

Since that day I have always found the perfect spot. I am always the designated driver, and I use my power to ferry friends around. I am the Perfect Parker!

Brian Garside

**Dear Perfect Parker,**

**I have good news and I have bad news. The good news is that you have it all: a compelling origin story, a helpful super-power, even your own car! But now the bad news. I spoke with Peter Parker about the name and he said, "No freakin' way. I'm the perfect Parker." I tried my best to explain it to him, but he just wasn't having it. I took this thing all the way up to the top brass at Marvel but it turns out that when you're the most iconic character in your company set to star in their newest line of cinematic blockbusters, you get your way.**

After reading your first issue, I believe that the skill set of my alter ego, Baron Von Papergreat, could benefit the Great Lakes Avengers. He is, to my knowledge, the only ephemera-centric super hero.

Papergreat's powers include the ability to decipher any handwriting, no matter how loopy or chicken-scratchy, on old postcards; the ability to find clues, currency and gum wrappers tucked away inside old books; and the ability to save worthless piles of old papers from certain destruction and hoard them for future evaluation.

I believe this kind of paper-focused perspective could help an Avengers-level group. Or, if you prefer, he's also willing to just answer the phone, sort the mail and do light dusting.

Chris Otto
York, Pennsylvania

**Dear Baron Von Papergreat,**

**You had me hooked with your powers but you reeled me in with "light dusting." You're hired!**

**Zac**

---

**The Great Lakes Avengers still needs more applicants--they're all sure to get killed by Doctor Tannenbaum sooner or later. Send your qualifications to be on the team to MHEROES@MARVEL.COM marked "OKAY TO PRINT." Literally, we'll even take someone who's just really good at cuticle management at this point. Have we mentioned we're desperate?**

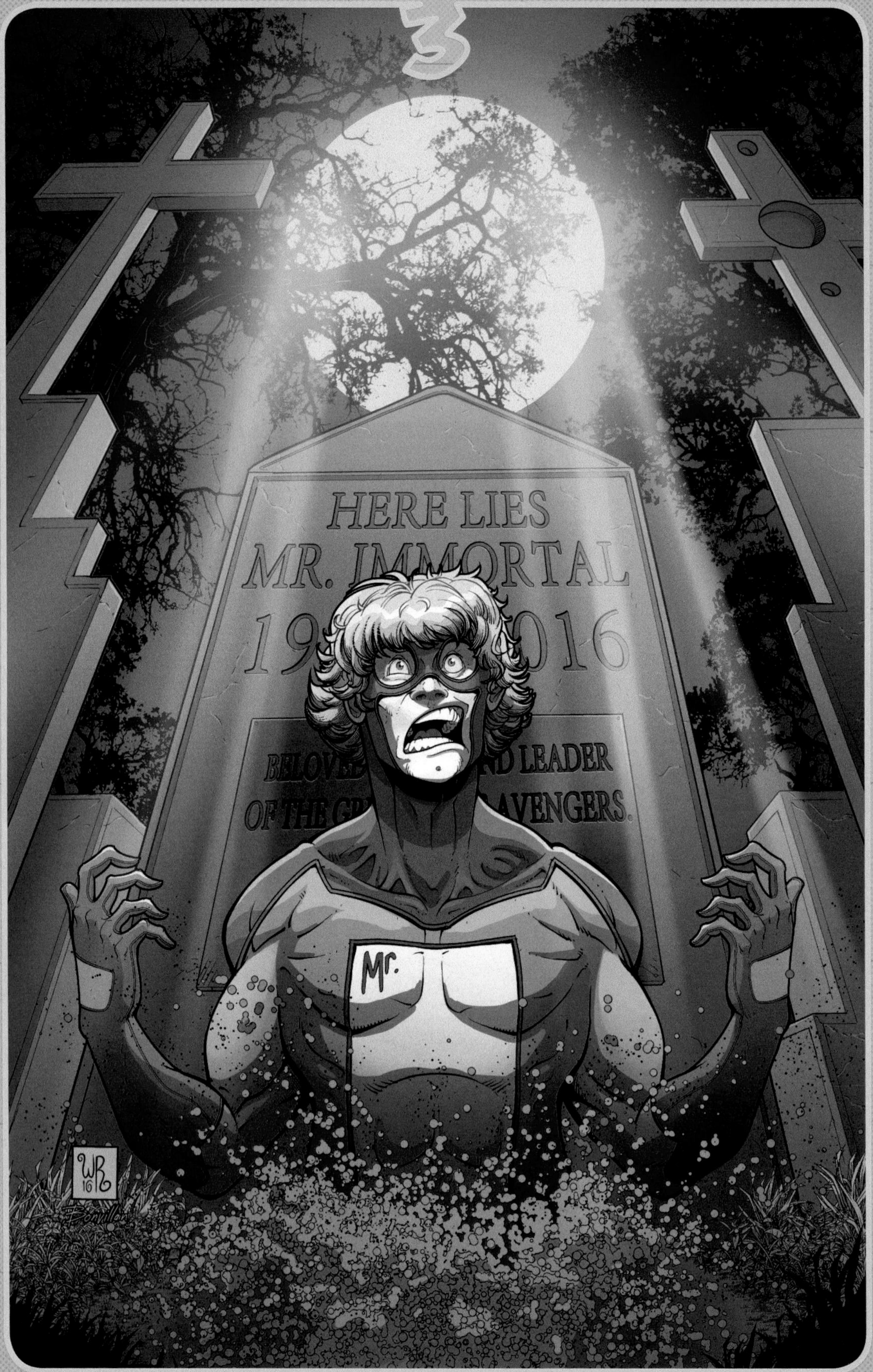
3
HERE LIES
MR. IMMORTAL
Mr.

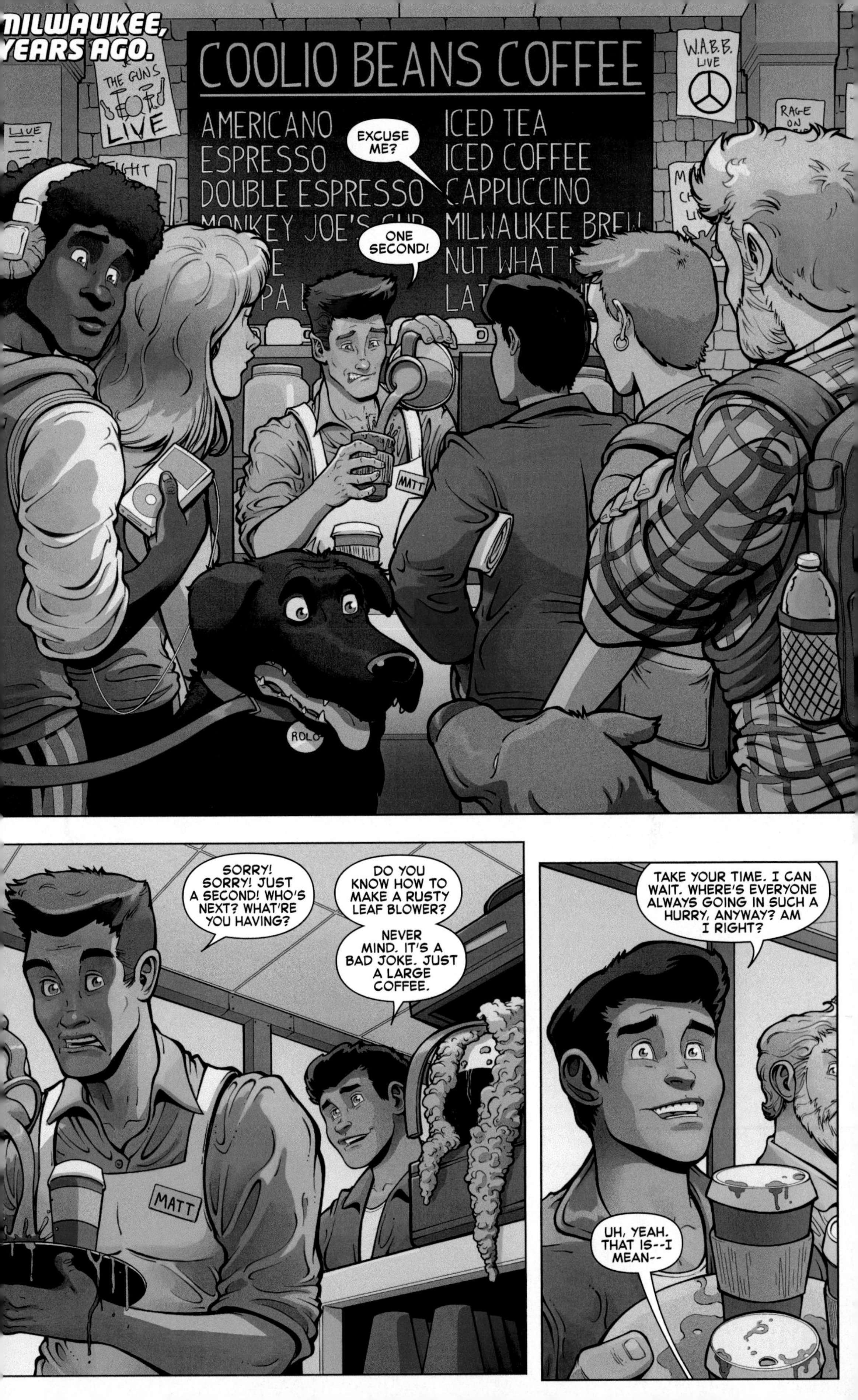
MILWAUKEE, YEARS AGO.
COOLIO BEANS COFFEE
AMERICANO
ESPRESSO
DOUBLE ESPRESSO
ICED TEA
ICED COFFEE
CAPPUCCINO
W.A.B.B. LIVE
THE GUNS LIVE
EXCUSE ME?
ONE SECOND!
MATT
ROLO
SORRY! SORRY! JUST A SECOND! WHO'S NEXT? WHAT'RE YOU HAVING?
DO YOU KNOW HOW TO MAKE A RUSTY LEAF BLOWER?
NEVER MIND. IT'S A BAD JOKE. JUST A LARGE COFFEE.
MATT
TAKE YOUR TIME. I CAN WAIT. WHERE'S EVERYONE ALWAYS GOING IN SUCH A HURRY, ANYWAY? AM I RIGHT?
UH, YEAH. THAT IS--I MEAN--

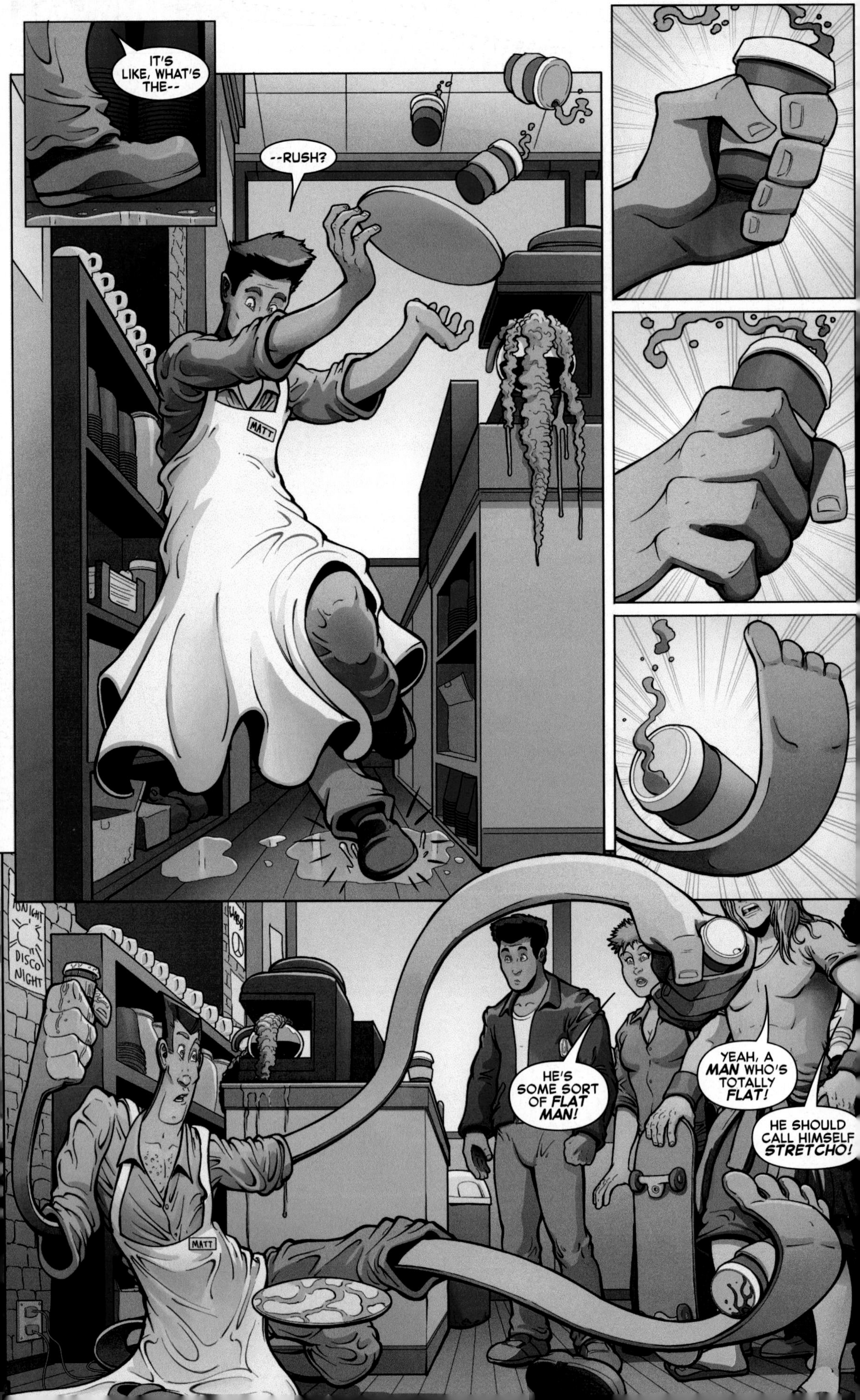
IT'S LIKE, WHAT'S THE--
--RUSH?
TONIGHT DISCO NIGHT
HE'S SOME SORT OF FLAT MAN!
YEAH, A MAN WHO'S TOTALLY FLAT!
HE SHOULD CALL HIMSELF STRETCHO!

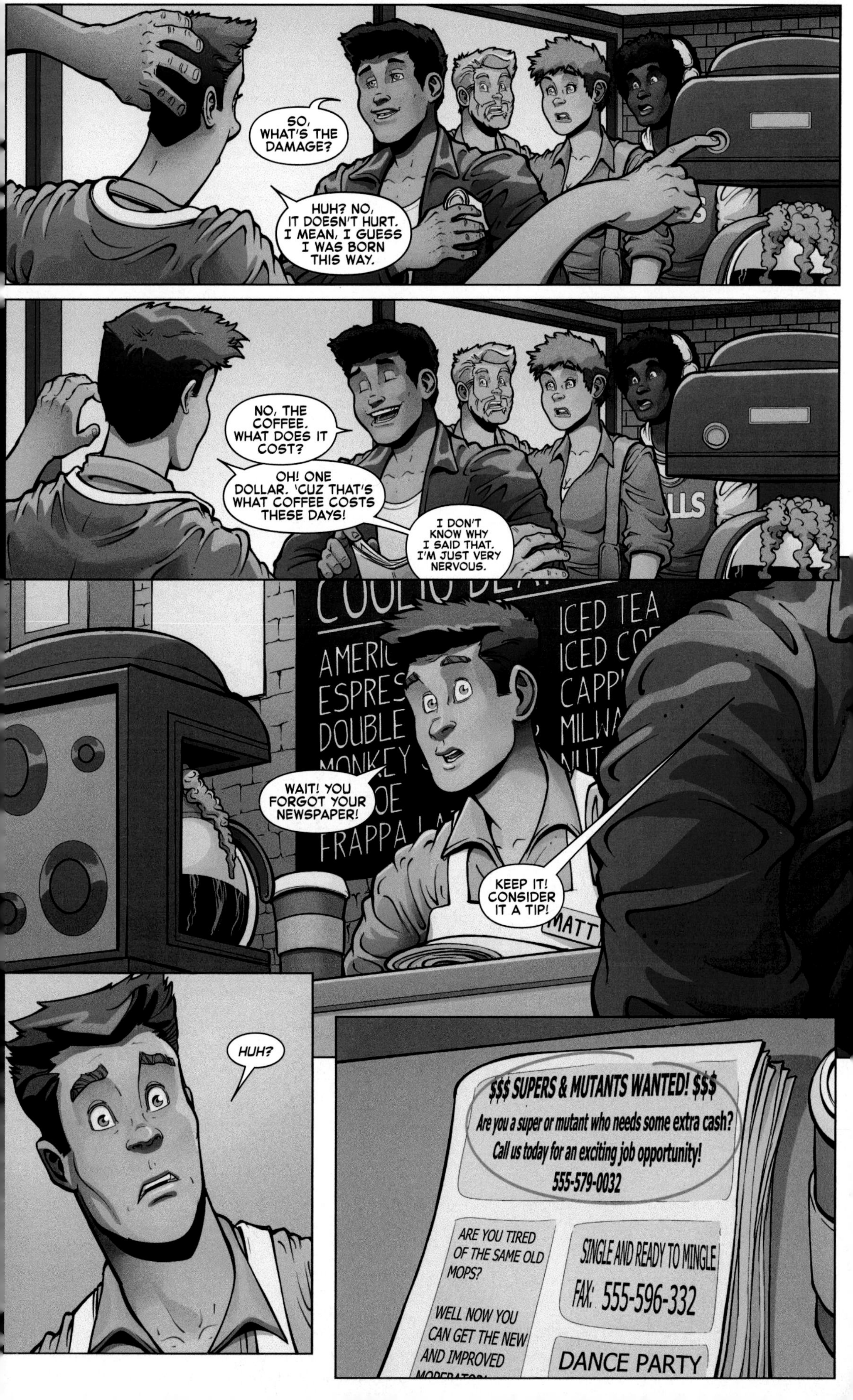
SO, WHAT'S THE DAMAGE?
HUH? NO, IT DOESN'T HURT. I MEAN, I GUESS I WAS BORN THIS WAY.
NO, THE COFFEE. WHAT DOES IT COST?
OH! ONE DOLLAR. 'CUZ THAT'S WHAT COFFEE COSTS THESE DAYS!
I DON'T KNOW WHY I SAID THAT. I'M JUST VERY NERVOUS.
ICED TEA
WAIT! YOU FORGOT YOUR NEWSPAPER!
KEEP IT! CONSIDER IT A TIP!
MATT
HUH?
$$$ SUPERS & MUTANTS WANTED! $$$
Are you a super or mutant who needs some extra cash?
Call us today for an exciting job opportunity!
555-579-0032
ARE YOU TIRED OF THE SAME OLD MOPS?
WELL NOW YOU CAN GET THE NEW AND IMPROVED
SINGLE AND READY TO MINGLE
FAX: 555-596-332
DANCE PARTY

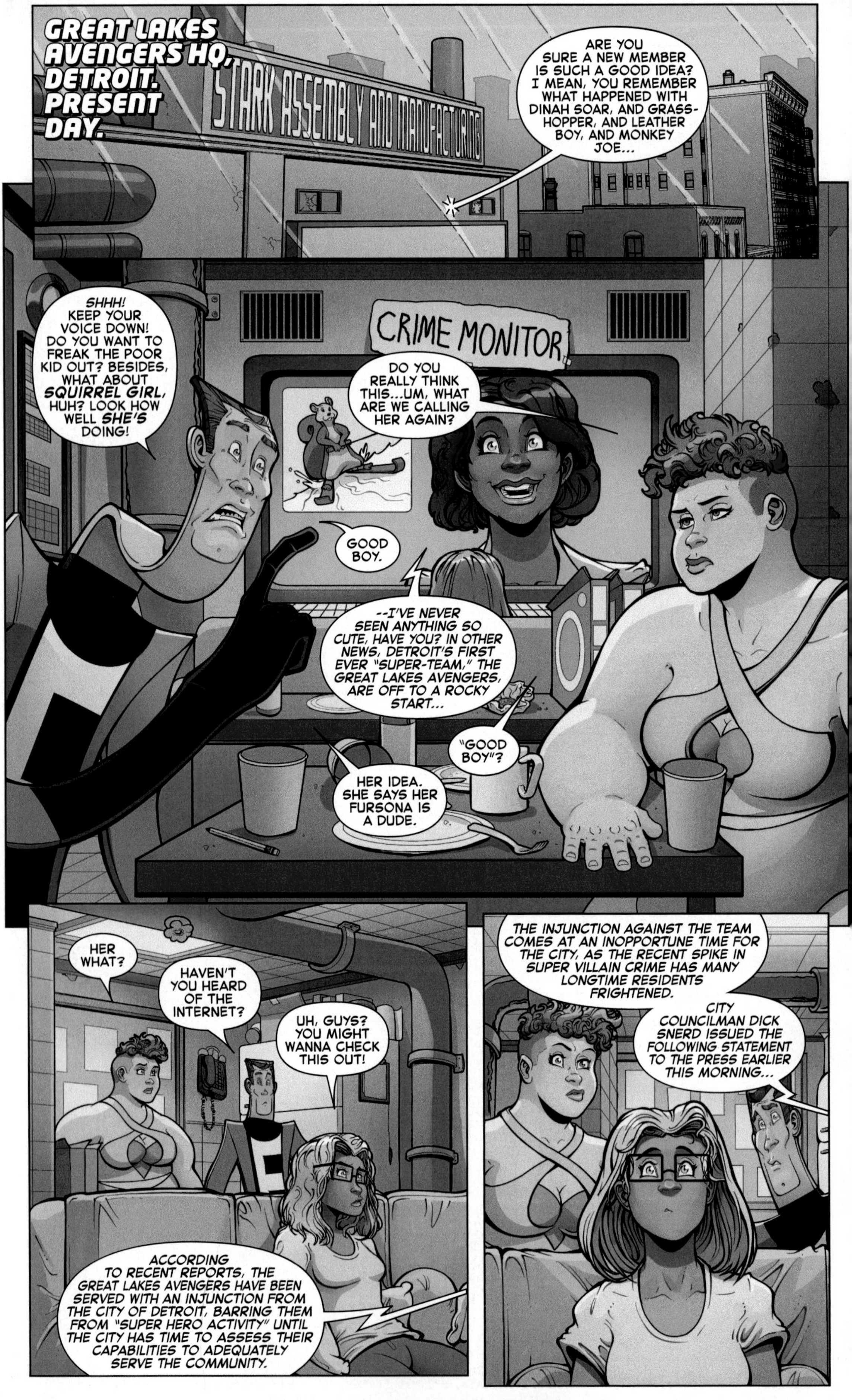
GREAT LAKES AVENGERS HQ, DETROIT. PRESENT DAY.
STARK ASSEMBLY AND MANUFACTURING
ARE YOU SURE A NEW MEMBER IS SUCH A GOOD IDEA? I MEAN, YOU REMEMBER WHAT HAPPENED WITH DINAH SOAR, AND GRASS-HOPPER, AND LEATHER BOY, AND MONKEY JOE...
SHHH! KEEP YOUR VOICE DOWN! DO YOU WANT TO FREAK THE POOR KID OUT? BESIDES, WHAT ABOUT SQUIRREL GIRL, HUH? LOOK HOW WELL SHE'S DOING!
CRIME MONITOR
DO YOU REALLY THINK THIS...UM, WHAT ARE WE CALLING HER AGAIN?
GOOD BOY.
--I'VE NEVER SEEN ANYTHING SO CUTE, HAVE YOU? IN OTHER NEWS, DETROIT'S FIRST EVER "SUPER-TEAM," THE GREAT LAKES AVENGERS, ARE OFF TO A ROCKY START...
"GOOD BOY"?
HER IDEA. SHE SAYS HER FURSONA IS A DUDE.
HER WHAT?
HAVEN'T YOU HEARD OF THE INTERNET?
UH, GUYS? YOU MIGHT WANNA CHECK THIS OUT!
ACCORDING TO RECENT REPORTS, THE GREAT LAKES AVENGERS HAVE BEEN SERVED WITH AN INJUNCTION FROM THE CITY OF DETROIT, BARRING THEM FROM "SUPER HERO ACTIVITY" UNTIL THE CITY HAS TIME TO ASSESS THEIR CAPABILITIES TO ADEQUATELY SERVE THE COMMUNITY.
THE INJUNCTION AGAINST THE TEAM COMES AT AN INOPPORTUNE TIME FOR THE CITY, AS THE RECENT SPIKE IN SUPER VILLAIN CRIME HAS MANY LONGTIME RESIDENTS FRIGHTENED.
CITY COUNCILMAN DICK SNERD ISSUED THE FOLLOWING STATEMENT TO THE PRESS EARLIER THIS MORNING...

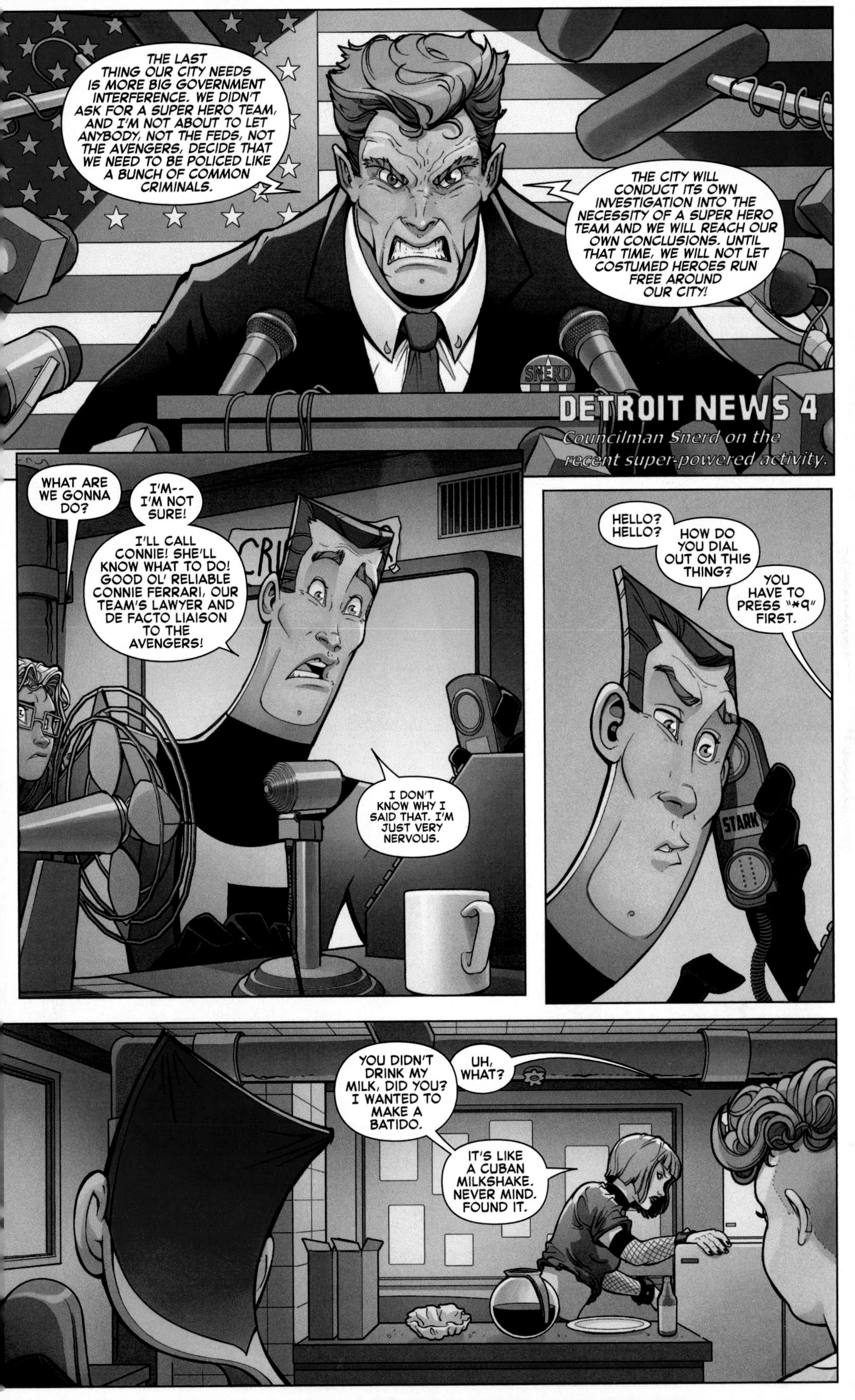
THE LAST THING OUR CITY NEEDS IS MORE BIG GOVERNMENT INTERFERENCE. WE DIDN'T ASK FOR A SUPER HERO TEAM, AND I'M NOT ABOUT TO LET ANYBODY, NOT THE FEDS, NOT THE AVENGERS, DECIDE THAT WE NEED TO BE POLICED LIKE A BUNCH OF COMMON CRIMINALS.
THE CITY WILL CONDUCT ITS OWN INVESTIGATION INTO THE NECESSITY OF A SUPER HERO TEAM AND WE WILL REACH OUR OWN CONCLUSIONS. UNTIL THAT TIME, WE WILL NOT LET COSTUMED HEROES RUN FREE AROUND OUR CITY!
SNERD
DETROIT NEWS 4
Councilman Snerd on the recent super-powered activity.
WHAT ARE WE GONNA DO?
I'M-- I'M NOT SURE!
I'LL CALL CONNIE! SHE'LL KNOW WHAT TO DO! GOOD OL' RELIABLE CONNIE FERRARI, OUR TEAM'S LAWYER AND DE FACTO LIAISON TO THE AVENGERS!
I DON'T KNOW WHY I SAID THAT. I'M JUST VERY NERVOUS.
HELLO? HELLO?
HOW DO YOU DIAL OUT ON THIS THING?
YOU HAVE TO PRESS "*9" FIRST.
STARK
YOU DIDN'T DRINK MY MILK, DID YOU? I WANTED TO MAKE A BATIDO.
UH, WHAT?
IT'S LIKE A CUBAN MILKSHAKE. NEVER MIND. FOUND IT.

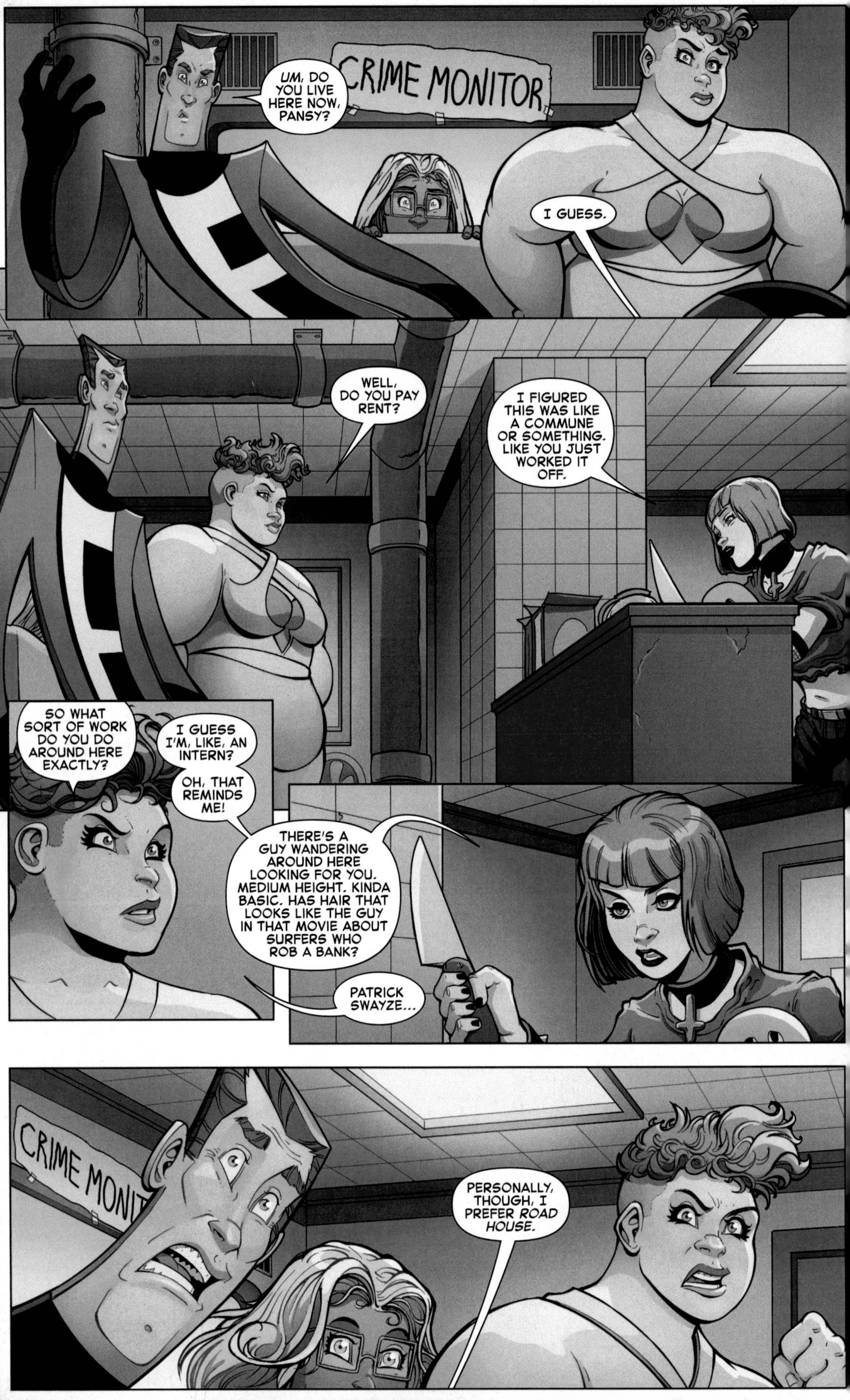
CRIME MONITOR
UM, DO YOU LIVE HERE NOW, PANSY?
I GUESS.
WELL, DO YOU PAY RENT?
I FIGURED THIS WAS LIKE A COMMUNE OR SOMETHING. LIKE YOU JUST WORKED IT OFF.
SO WHAT SORT OF WORK DO YOU DO AROUND HERE EXACTLY?
I GUESS I'M, LIKE, AN INTERN?
OH, THAT REMINDS ME!
THERE'S A GUY WANDERING AROUND HERE LOOKING FOR YOU. MEDIUM HEIGHT. KINDA BASIC. HAS HAIR THAT LOOKS LIKE THE GUY IN THAT MOVIE ABOUT SURFERS WHO ROB A BANK?
PATRICK SWAYZE...
CRIME MONIT
PERSONALLY, THOUGH, I PREFER *ROAD HOUSE.*

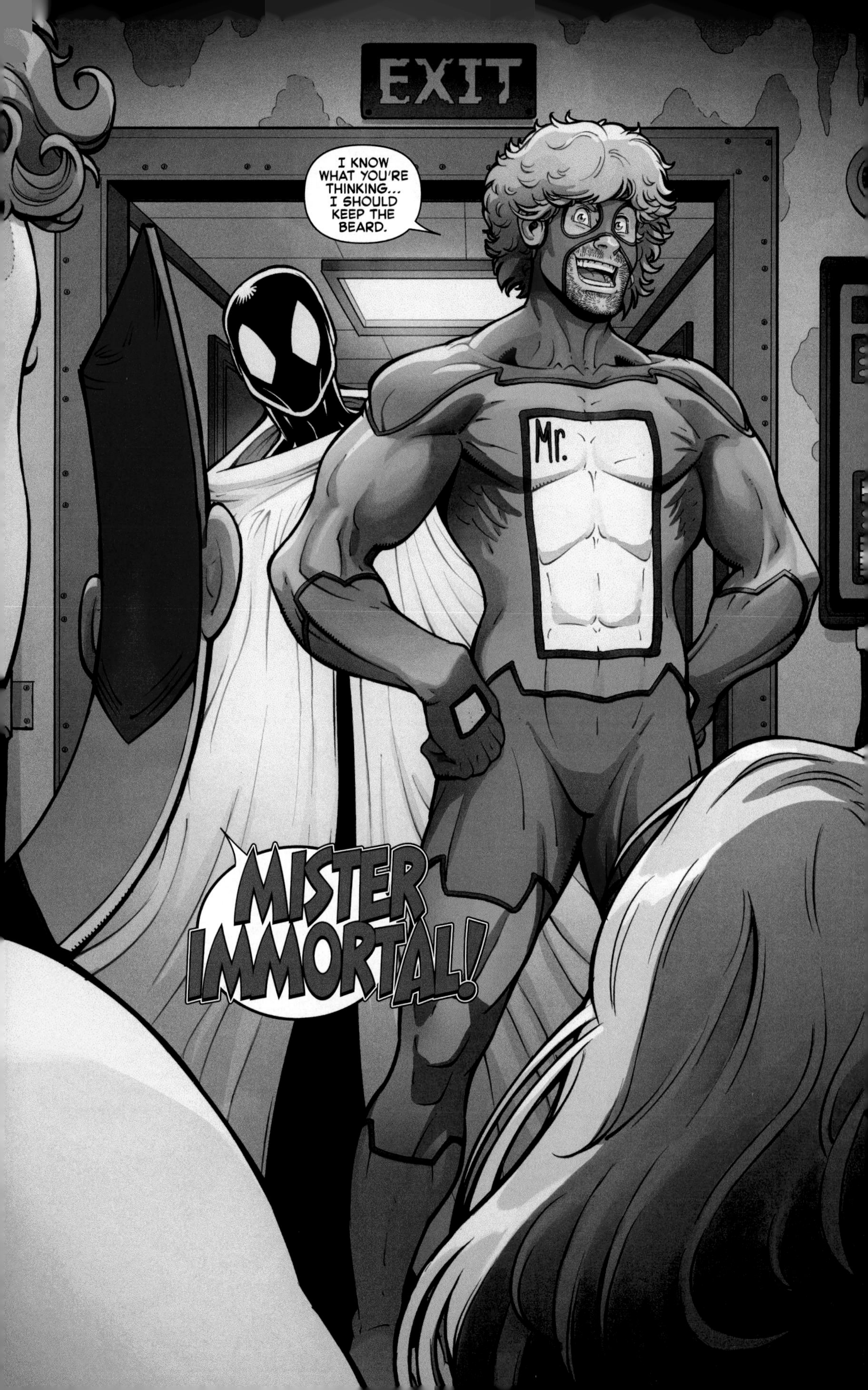
EXIT
I KNOW WHAT YOU'RE THINKING... I SHOULD KEEP THE BEARD.
Mr.
MISTER IMMORTAL!

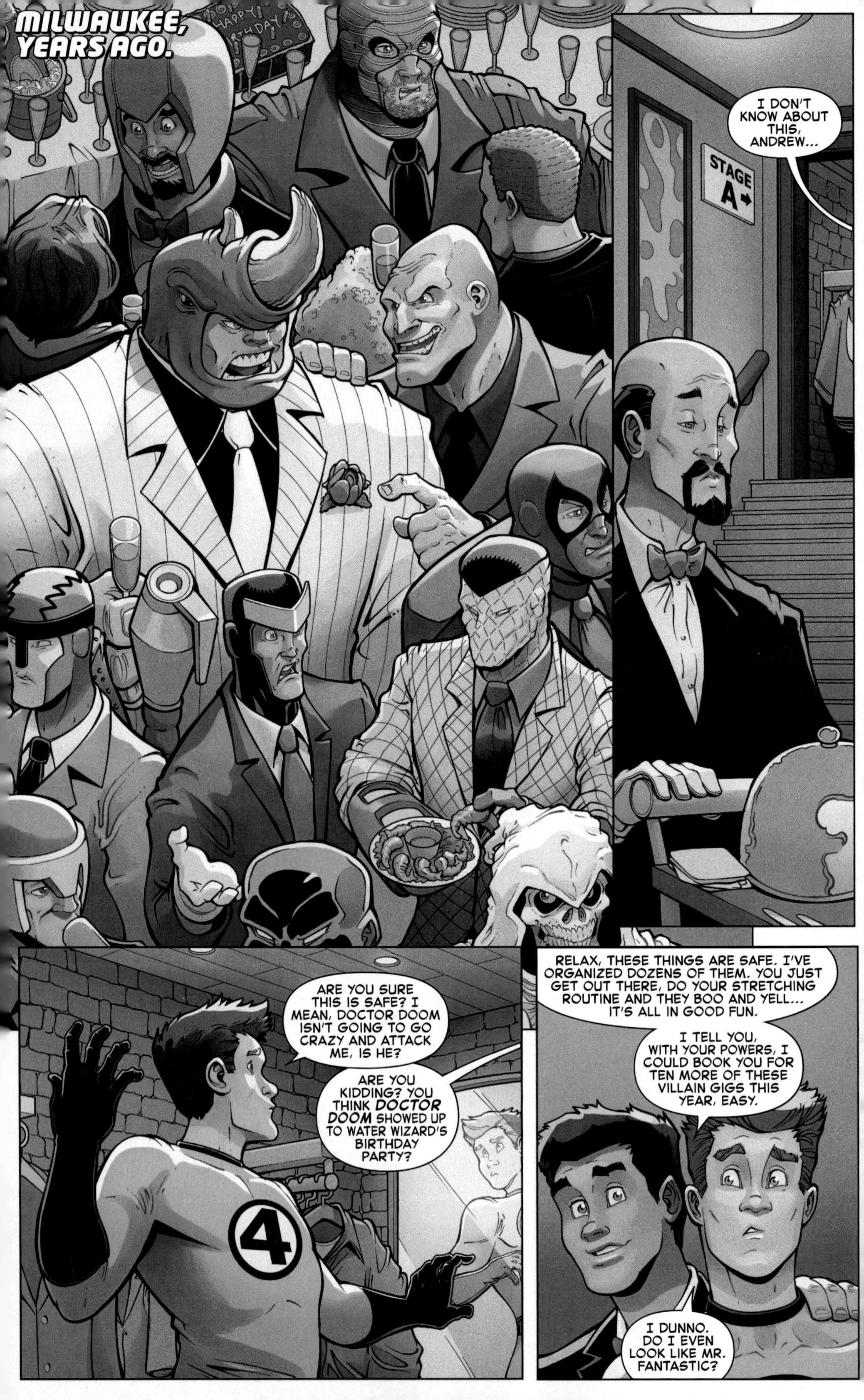
MILWAUKEE, YEARS AGO.
STAGE A
I DON'T KNOW ABOUT THIS, ANDREW...
ARE YOU SURE THIS IS SAFE? I MEAN, DOCTOR DOOM ISN'T GOING TO GO CRAZY AND ATTACK ME, IS HE?
ARE YOU KIDDING? YOU THINK *DOCTOR DOOM* SHOWED UP TO WATER WIZARD'S BIRTHDAY PARTY?
RELAX, THESE THINGS ARE SAFE. I'VE ORGANIZED DOZENS OF THEM. YOU JUST GET OUT THERE, DO YOUR STRETCHING ROUTINE AND THEY BOO AND YELL... IT'S ALL IN GOOD FUN.
I TELL YOU, WITH YOUR POWERS, I COULD BOOK YOU FOR TEN MORE OF THESE VILLAIN GIGS THIS YEAR, EASY.
I DUNNO. DO I EVEN LOOK LIKE MR. FANTASTIC?

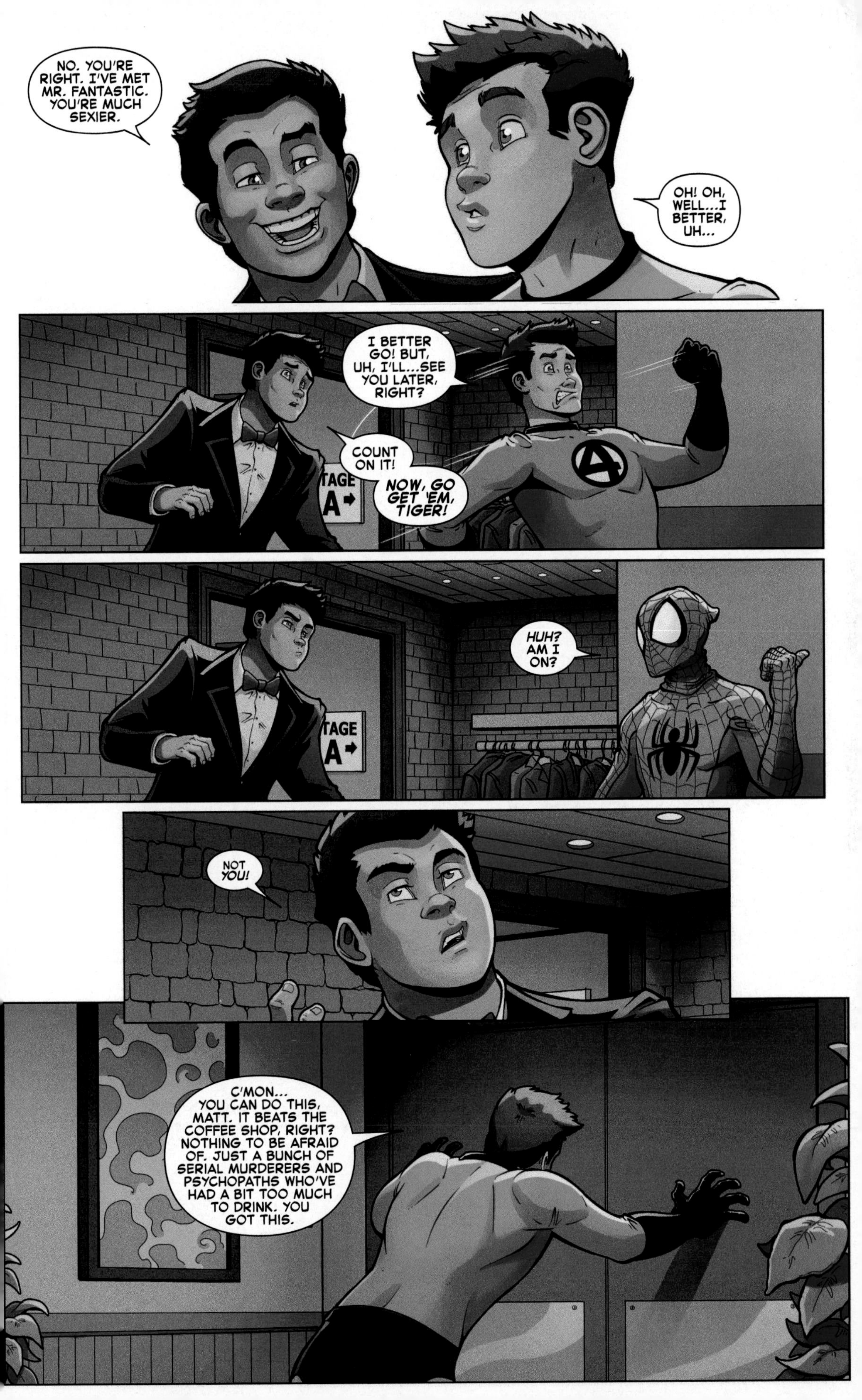
NO. YOU'RE RIGHT. I'VE MET MR. FANTASTIC. YOU'RE MUCH SEXIER.
OH! OH, WELL...I BETTER, UH...
I BETTER GO! BUT, UH, I'LL...SEE YOU LATER, RIGHT?
COUNT ON IT!
NOW, GO GET 'EM, TIGER!
TAGE
A
HUH? AM I ON?
TAGE
A
NOT YOU!
C'MON... YOU CAN DO THIS, MATT. IT BEATS THE COFFEE SHOP, RIGHT? NOTHING TO BE AFRAID OF. JUST A BUNCH OF SERIAL MURDERERS AND PSYCHOPATHS WHO'VE HAD A BIT TOO MUCH TO DRINK. YOU GOT THIS.

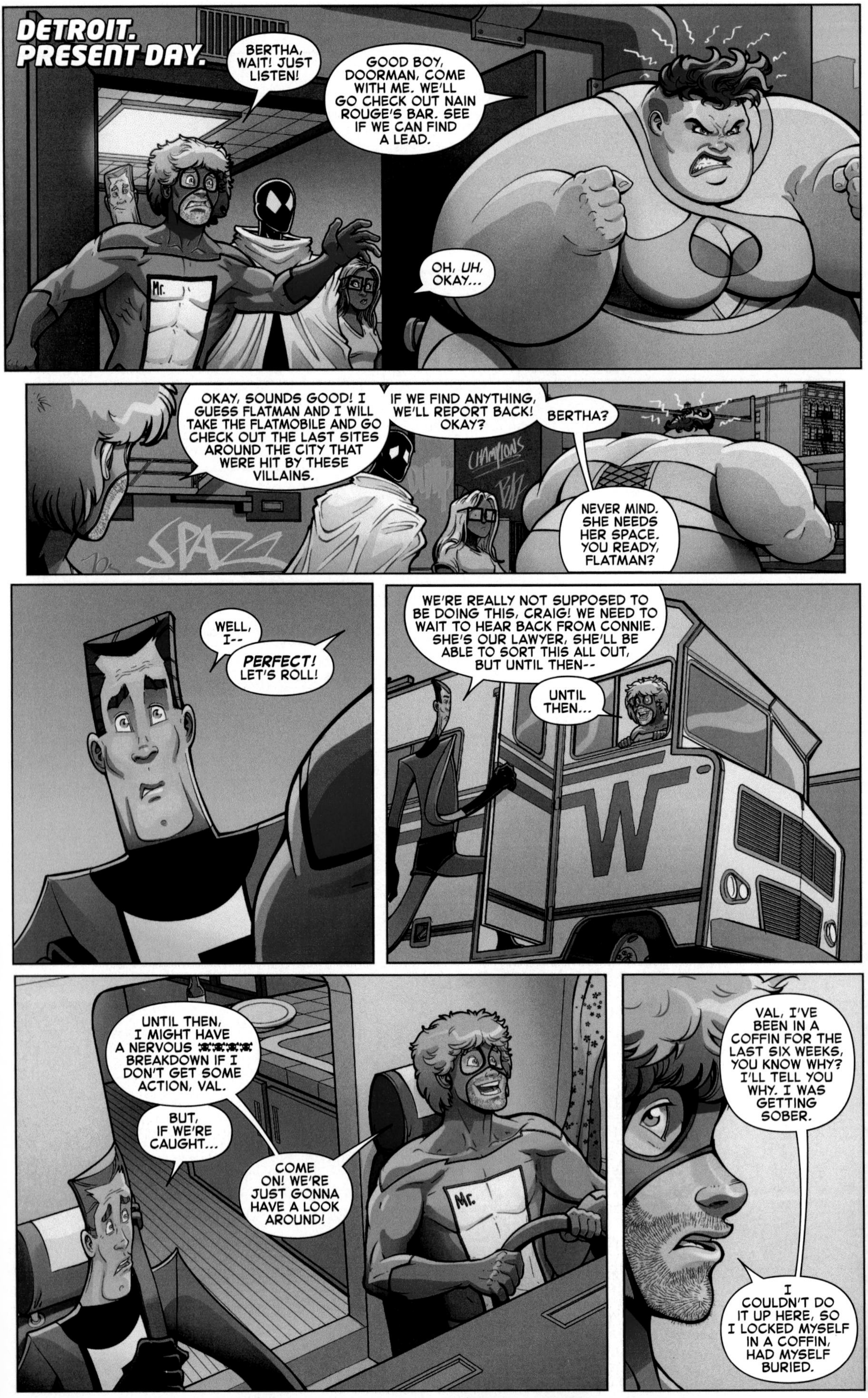
DETROIT. PRESENT DAY.
BERTHA, WAIT! JUST LISTEN!
GOOD BOY, DOORMAN, COME WITH ME. WE'LL GO CHECK OUT NAIN ROUGE'S BAR. SEE IF WE CAN FIND A LEAD.
OH, UH, OKAY...
OKAY, SOUNDS GOOD! I GUESS FLATMAN AND I WILL TAKE THE FLATMOBILE AND GO CHECK OUT THE LAST SITES AROUND THE CITY THAT WERE HIT BY THESE VILLAINS.
IF WE FIND ANYTHING, WE'LL REPORT BACK! OKAY?
BERTHA?
NEVER MIND. SHE NEEDS HER SPACE. YOU READY, FLATMAN?
WELL, I--
PERFECT! LET'S ROLL!
WE'RE REALLY NOT SUPPOSED TO BE DOING THIS, CRAIG! WE NEED TO WAIT TO HEAR BACK FROM CONNIE. SHE'S OUR LAWYER, SHE'LL BE ABLE TO SORT THIS ALL OUT, BUT UNTIL THEN--
UNTIL THEN...
UNTIL THEN, I MIGHT HAVE A NERVOUS ☠✱☠✱☠ BREAKDOWN IF I DON'T GET SOME ACTION, VAL.
BUT, IF WE'RE CAUGHT...
COME ON! WE'RE JUST GONNA HAVE A LOOK AROUND!
VAL, I'VE BEEN IN A COFFIN FOR THE LAST SIX WEEKS, YOU KNOW WHY? I'LL TELL YOU WHY. I WAS GETTING SOBER.
I COULDN'T DO IT UP HERE, SO I LOCKED MYSELF IN A COFFIN, HAD MYSELF BURIED.

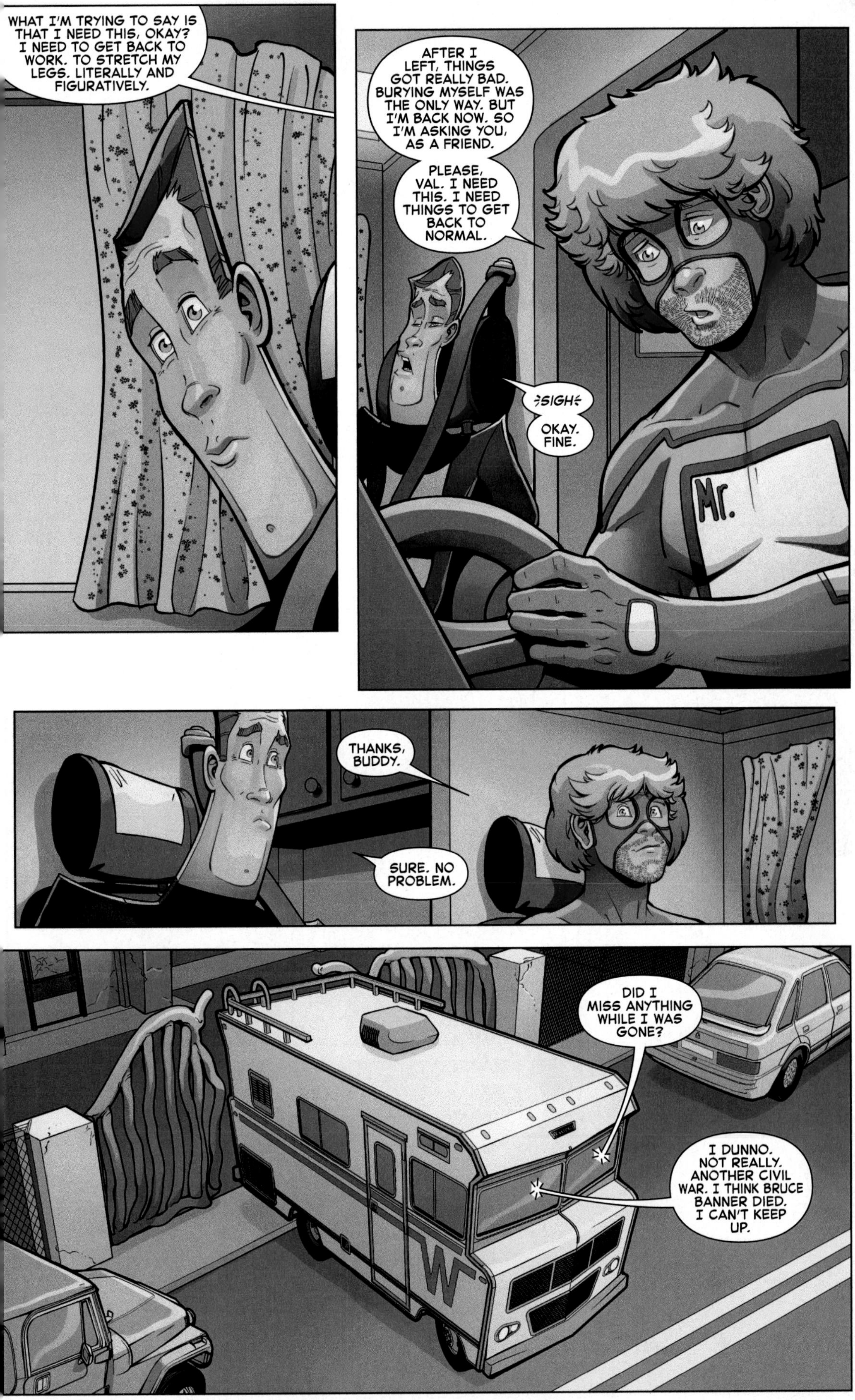
WHAT I'M TRYING TO SAY IS THAT I NEED THIS, OKAY? I NEED TO GET BACK TO WORK. TO STRETCH MY LEGS. LITERALLY AND FIGURATIVELY.
AFTER I LEFT, THINGS GOT REALLY BAD. BURYING MYSELF WAS THE ONLY WAY. BUT I'M BACK NOW. SO I'M ASKING YOU, AS A FRIEND.
PLEASE, VAL. I NEED THIS. I NEED THINGS TO GET BACK TO NORMAL.
SIGH
OKAY. FINE.
Mr.
THANKS, BUDDY.
SURE. NO PROBLEM.
DID I MISS ANYTHING WHILE I WAS GONE?
I DUNNO. NOT REALLY. ANOTHER CIVIL WAR. I THINK BRUCE BANNER DIED. I CAN'T KEEP UP.

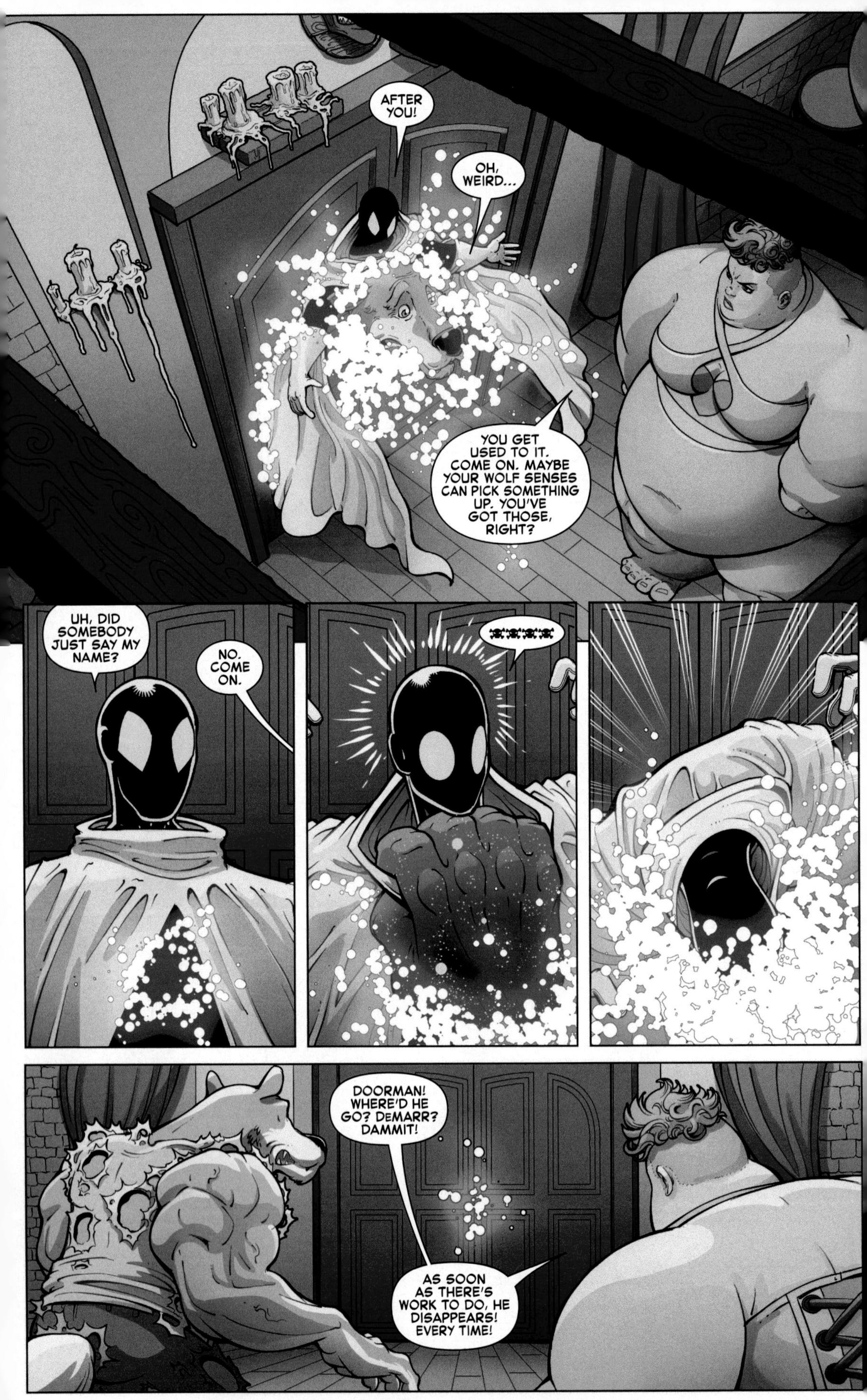
AFTER YOU!
OH, WEIRD...
YOU GET USED TO IT. COME ON. MAYBE YOUR WOLF SENSES CAN PICK SOMETHING UP. YOU'VE GOT THOSE, RIGHT?
UH, DID SOMEBODY JUST SAY MY NAME?
NO. COME ON.
DOORMAN! WHERE'D HE GO? DeMARR? DAMMIT!
AS SOON AS THERE'S WORK TO DO, HE DISAPPEARS! EVERY TIME!

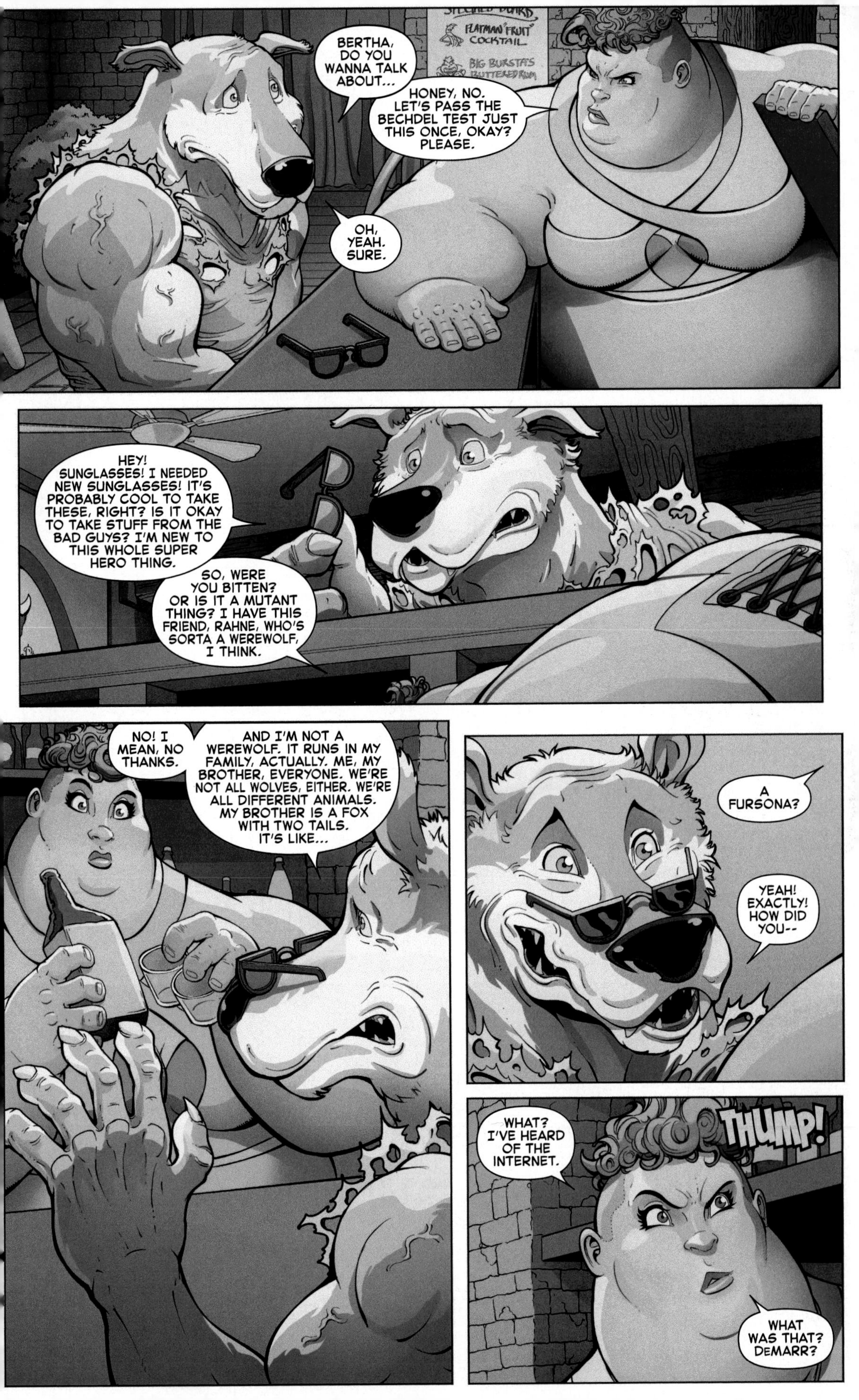
FLATMAN "FRUIT" COCKTAIL
BIG BURSTA'S BUTTERED RUM
BERTHA, DO YOU WANNA TALK ABOUT...
HONEY, NO. LET'S PASS THE BECHDEL TEST JUST THIS ONCE, OKAY? PLEASE.
OH, YEAH. SURE.
HEY! SUNGLASSES! I NEEDED NEW SUNGLASSES! IT'S PROBABLY COOL TO TAKE THESE, RIGHT? IS IT OKAY TO TAKE STUFF FROM THE BAD GUYS? I'M NEW TO THIS WHOLE SUPER HERO THING.
SO, WERE YOU BITTEN? OR IS IT A MUTANT THING? I HAVE THIS FRIEND, RAHNE, WHO'S SORTA A WEREWOLF, I THINK.
NO! I MEAN, NO THANKS.
AND I'M NOT A WEREWOLF. IT RUNS IN MY FAMILY, ACTUALLY. ME, MY BROTHER, EVERYONE. WE'RE NOT ALL WOLVES, EITHER. WE'RE ALL DIFFERENT ANIMALS. MY BROTHER IS A FOX WITH TWO TAILS. IT'S LIKE...
A FURSONA?
YEAH! EXACTLY! HOW DID YOU--
WHAT? I'VE HEARD OF THE INTERNET.
THUMP!
WHAT WAS THAT? DeMARR?

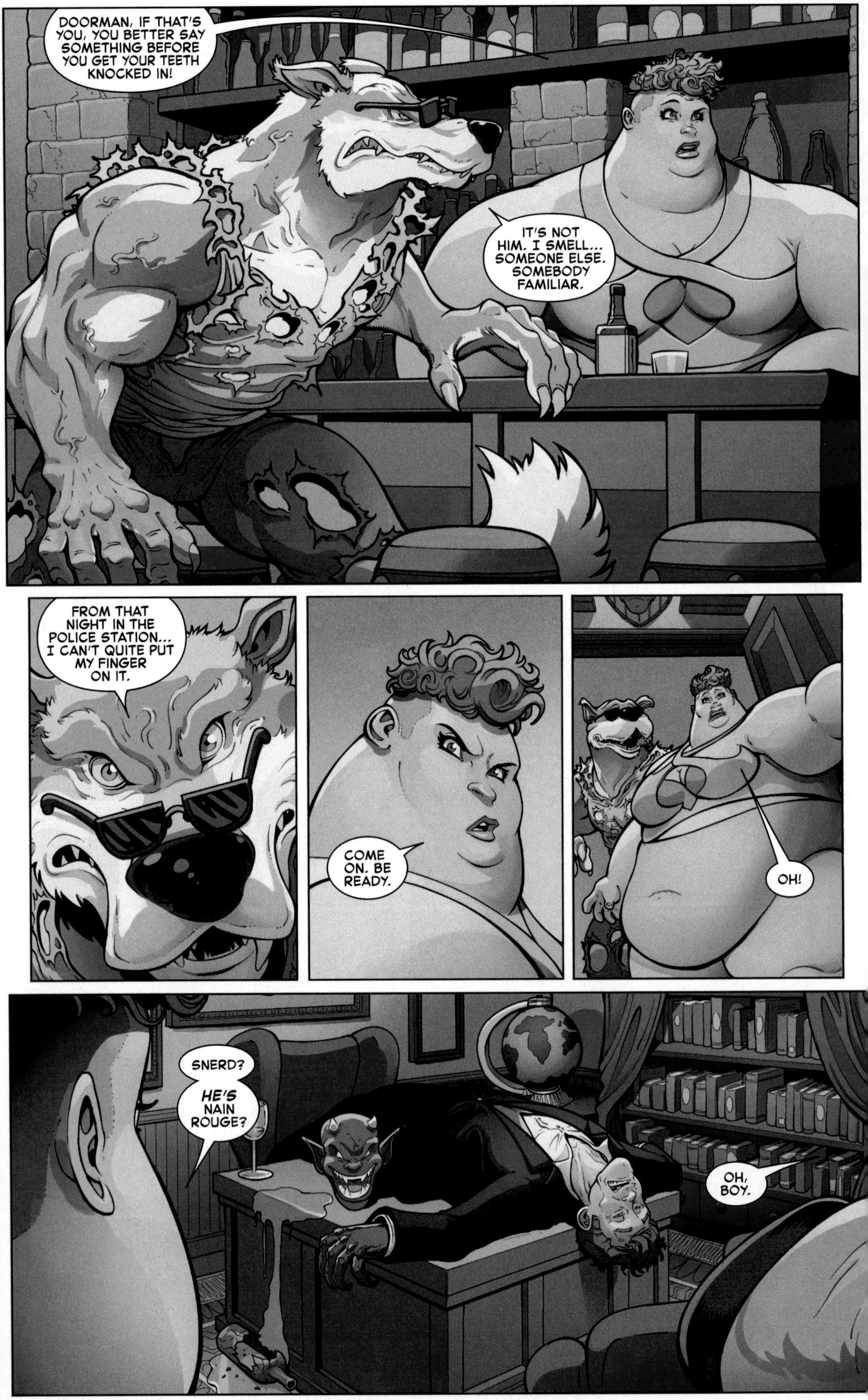
DOORMAN, IF THAT'S YOU, YOU BETTER SAY SOMETHING BEFORE YOU GET YOUR TEETH KNOCKED IN!
IT'S NOT HIM. I SMELL... SOMEONE ELSE. SOMEBODY FAMILIAR.
FROM THAT NIGHT IN THE POLICE STATION... I CAN'T QUITE PUT MY FINGER ON IT.
COME ON. BE READY.
OH!
SNERD? HE'S NAIN ROUGE?
OH, BOY.

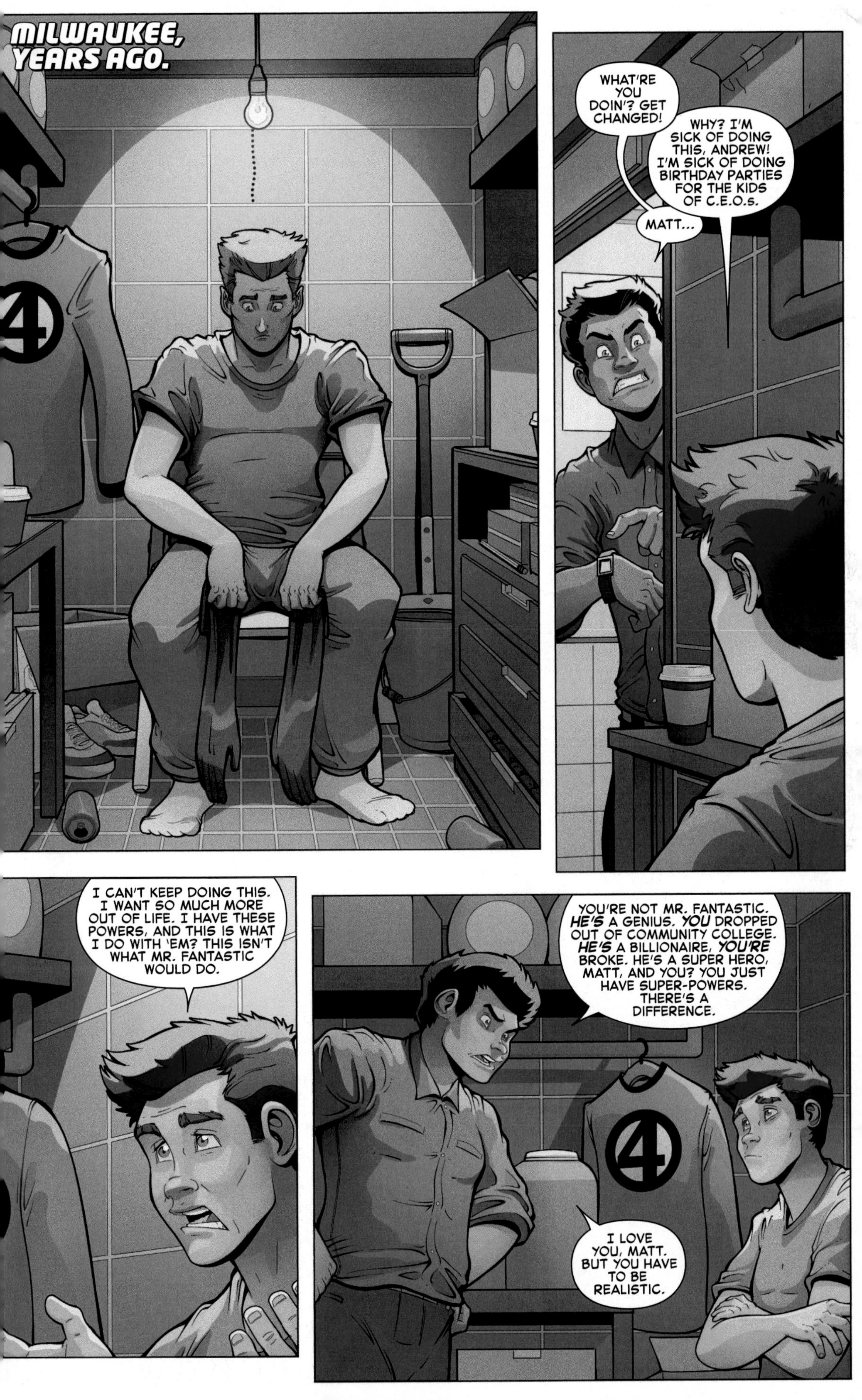
MILWAUKEE, YEARS AGO.
WHAT'RE YOU DOIN'? GET CHANGED!
MATT...
WHY? I'M SICK OF DOING THIS, ANDREW! I'M SICK OF DOING BIRTHDAY PARTIES FOR THE KIDS OF C.E.O.s.
I CAN'T KEEP DOING THIS. I WANT SO MUCH MORE OUT OF LIFE. I HAVE THESE POWERS, AND THIS IS WHAT I DO WITH 'EM? THIS ISN'T WHAT MR. FANTASTIC WOULD DO.
YOU'RE NOT MR. FANTASTIC. HE'S A GENIUS. YOU DROPPED OUT OF COMMUNITY COLLEGE. HE'S A BILLIONAIRE, YOU'RE BROKE. HE'S A SUPER HERO, MATT, AND YOU? YOU JUST HAVE SUPER-POWERS. THERE'S A DIFFERENCE.
I LOVE YOU, MATT. BUT YOU HAVE TO BE REALISTIC.

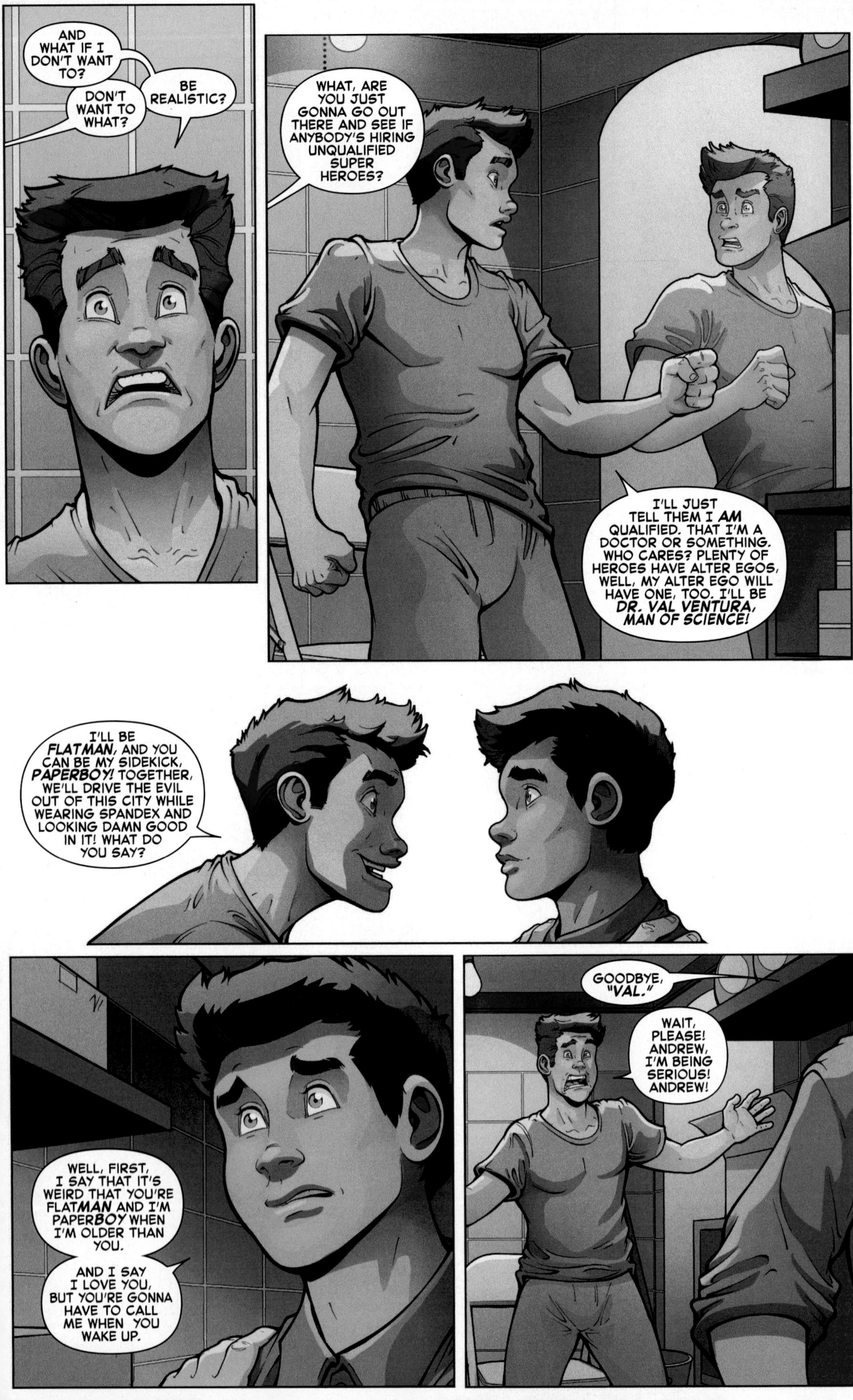

AND WHAT IF I DON'T WANT TO?
DON'T WANT TO WHAT?
BE REALISTIC?
WHAT, ARE YOU JUST GONNA GO OUT THERE AND SEE IF ANYBODY'S HIRING UNQUALIFIED SUPER HEROES?
I'LL JUST TELL THEM I AM QUALIFIED. THAT I'M A DOCTOR OR SOMETHING. WHO CARES? PLENTY OF HEROES HAVE ALTER EGOS, WELL, MY ALTER EGO WILL HAVE ONE, TOO. I'LL BE DR. VAL VENTURA, MAN OF SCIENCE!
I'LL BE FLATMAN, AND YOU CAN BE MY SIDEKICK, PAPERBOY! TOGETHER, WE'LL DRIVE THE EVIL OUT OF THIS CITY WHILE WEARING SPANDEX AND LOOKING DAMN GOOD IN IT! WHAT DO YOU SAY?
WELL, FIRST, I SAY THAT IT'S WEIRD THAT YOU'RE FLATMAN AND I'M PAPERBOY WHEN I'M OLDER THAN YOU.
AND I SAY I LOVE YOU, BUT YOU'RE GONNA HAVE TO CALL ME WHEN YOU WAKE UP.
GOODBYE, "VAL."
WAIT, PLEASE! ANDREW, I'M BEING SERIOUS! ANDREW!

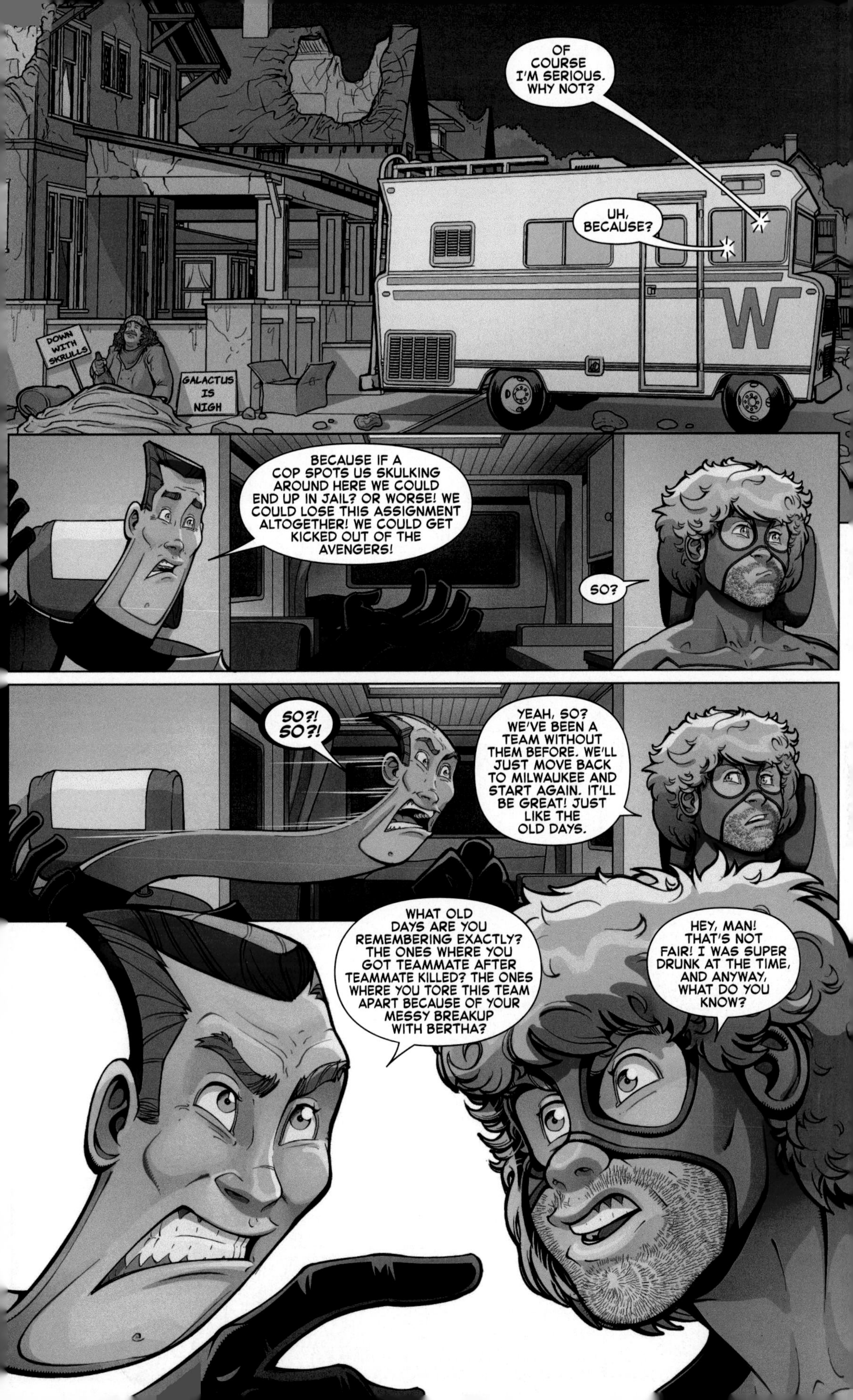
OF COURSE I'M SERIOUS. WHY NOT?
UH, BECAUSE?
DOWN WITH SKRULLS
GALACTUS IS NIGH
W
BECAUSE IF A COP SPOTS US SKULKING AROUND HERE WE COULD END UP IN JAIL? OR WORSE! WE COULD LOSE THIS ASSIGNMENT ALTOGETHER! WE COULD GET KICKED OUT OF THE AVENGERS!
SO?
SO?! SO?!
YEAH, SO? WE'VE BEEN A TEAM WITHOUT THEM BEFORE. WE'LL JUST MOVE BACK TO MILWAUKEE AND START AGAIN. IT'LL BE GREAT! JUST LIKE THE OLD DAYS.
WHAT OLD DAYS ARE YOU REMEMBERING EXACTLY? THE ONES WHERE YOU GOT TEAMMATE AFTER TEAMMATE KILLED? THE ONES WHERE YOU TORE THIS TEAM APART BECAUSE OF YOUR MESSY BREAKUP WITH BERTHA?
HEY, MAN! THAT'S NOT FAIR! I WAS SUPER DRUNK AT THE TIME, AND ANYWAY, WHAT DO YOU KNOW?

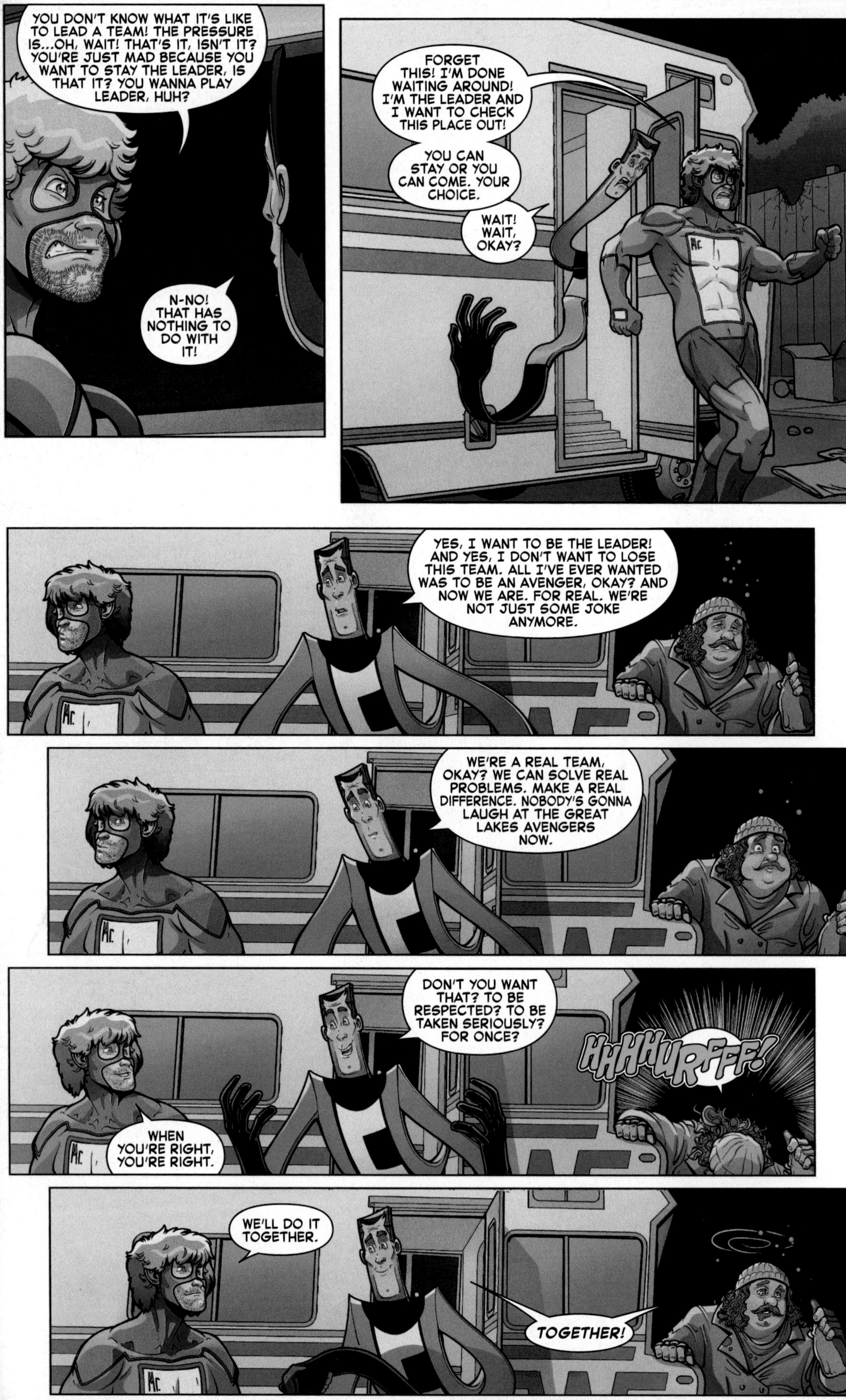
YOU DON'T KNOW WHAT IT'S LIKE TO LEAD A TEAM! THE PRESSURE IS...OH, WAIT! THAT'S IT, ISN'T IT? YOU'RE JUST MAD BECAUSE YOU WANT TO STAY THE LEADER, IS THAT IT? YOU WANNA PLAY LEADER, HUH?
N-NO! THAT HAS NOTHING TO DO WITH IT!
FORGET THIS! I'M DONE WAITING AROUND! I'M THE LEADER AND I WANT TO CHECK THIS PLACE OUT!
YOU CAN STAY OR YOU CAN COME. YOUR CHOICE.
WAIT! WAIT, OKAY?
YES, I WANT TO BE THE LEADER! AND YES, I DON'T WANT TO LOSE THIS TEAM. ALL I'VE EVER WANTED WAS TO BE AN AVENGER, OKAY? AND NOW WE ARE. FOR REAL. WE'RE NOT JUST SOME JOKE ANYMORE.
WE'RE A REAL TEAM, OKAY? WE CAN SOLVE REAL PROBLEMS. MAKE A REAL DIFFERENCE. NOBODY'S GONNA LAUGH AT THE GREAT LAKES AVENGERS NOW.
DON'T YOU WANT THAT? TO BE RESPECTED? TO BE TAKEN SERIOUSLY? FOR ONCE?
HHHHURFFF!
WHEN YOU'RE RIGHT, YOU'RE RIGHT.
WE'LL DO IT TOGETHER.
TOGETHER!

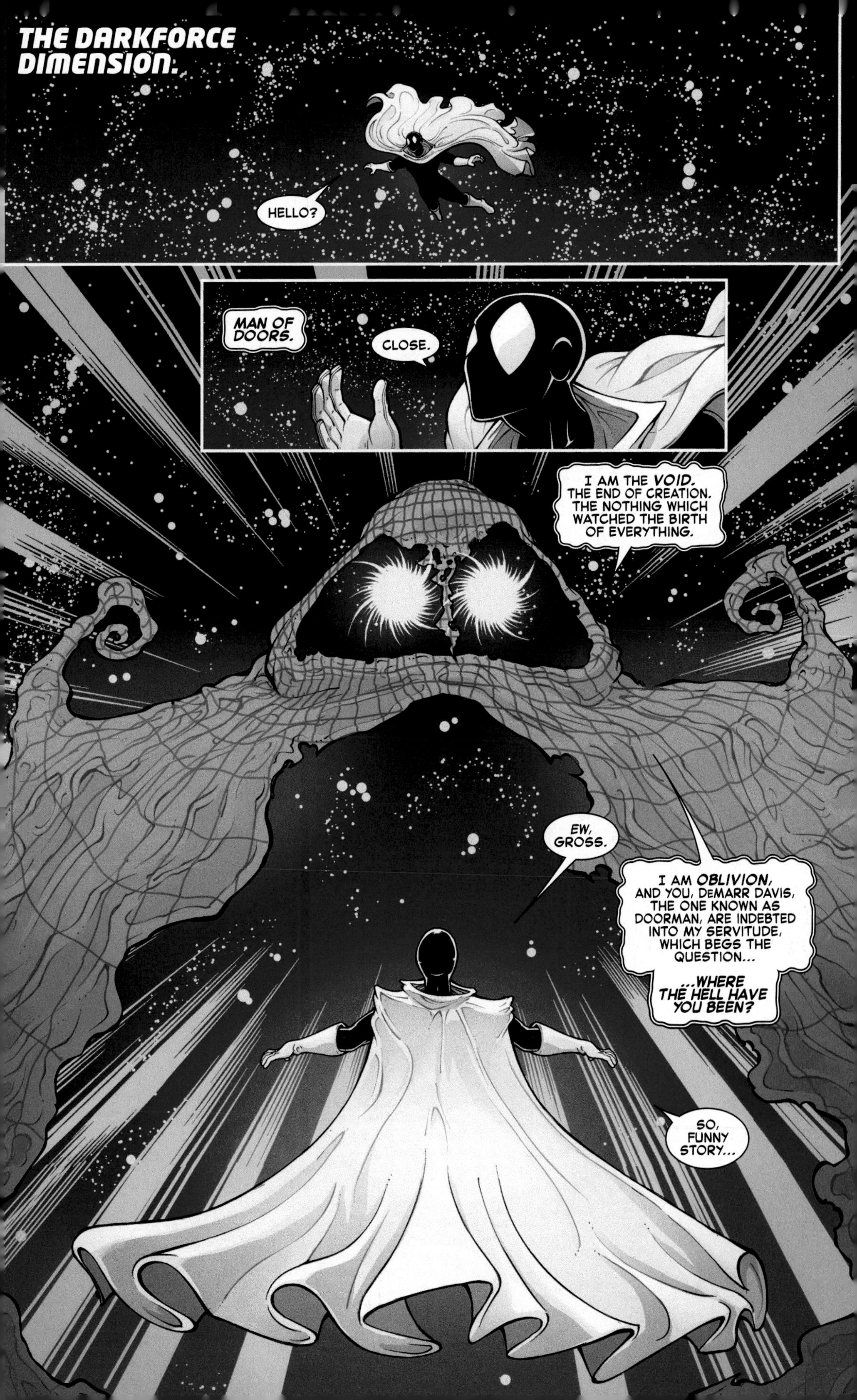
THE DARKFORCE DIMENSION.
HELLO?
MAN OF DOORS.
CLOSE.
I AM THE VOID. THE END OF CREATION. THE NOTHING WHICH WATCHED THE BIRTH OF EVERYTHING.
EW, GROSS.
I AM OBLIVION, AND YOU, DEMARR DAVIS, THE ONE KNOWN AS DOORMAN, ARE INDEBTED INTO MY SERVITUDE, WHICH BEGS THE QUESTION...
...WHERE THE HELL HAVE YOU BEEN?
SO, FUNNY STORY...

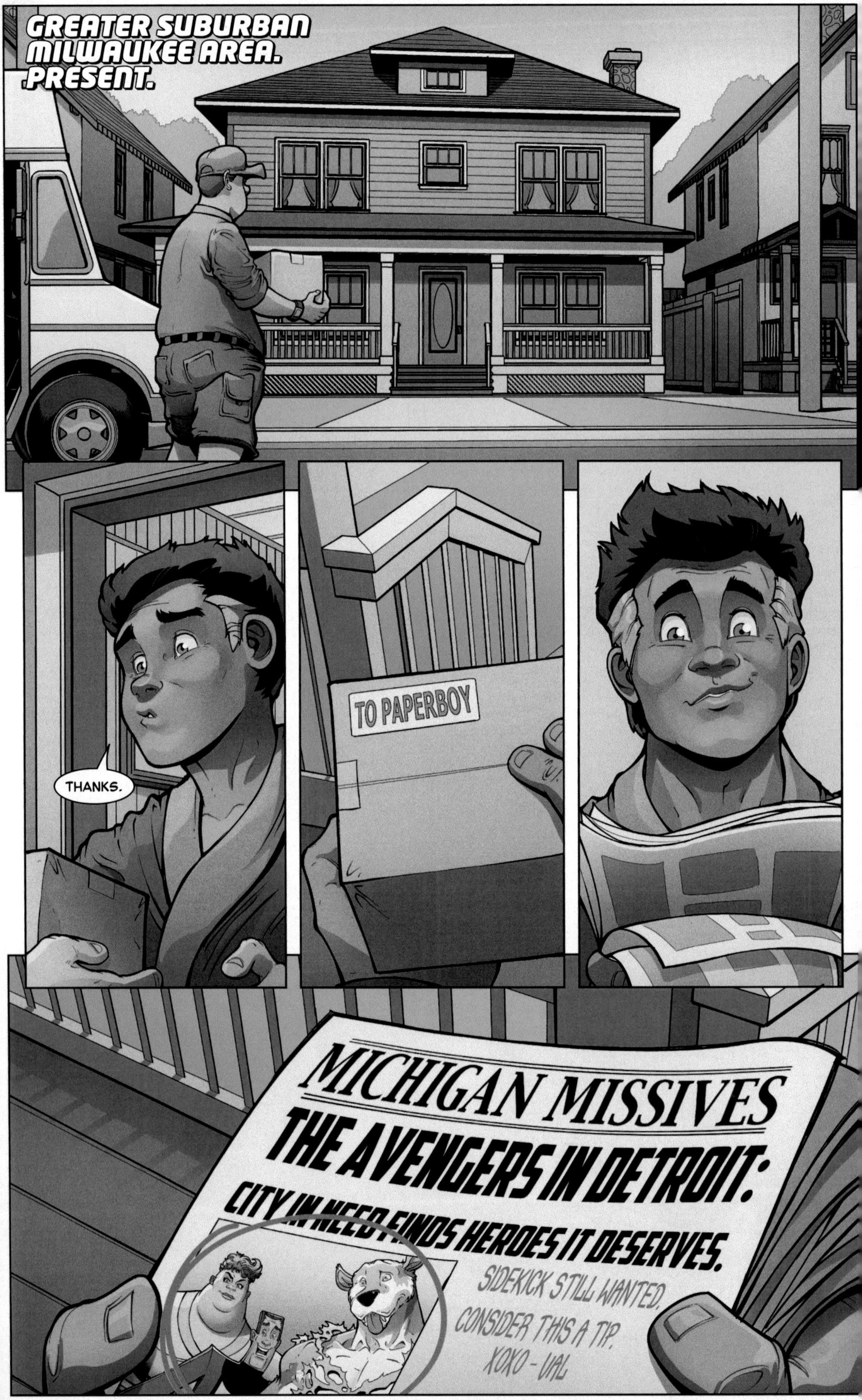
GREATER SUBURBAN MILWAUKEE AREA. PRESENT.
THANKS.
TO PAPERBOY
MICHIGAN MISSIVES
THE AVENGERS IN DETROIT:
CITY IN NEED FINDS HEROES IT DESERVES.
SIDEKICK STILL WANTED,
CONSIDER THIS A TIP.
XOXO - VAL

# The Great Lakes Avengers

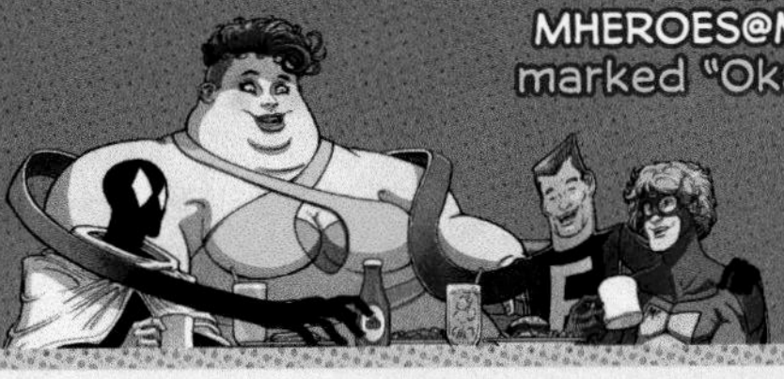

Send letters to MHEROES@MARVEL.COM marked "Okay to Print"!

We said the Great Lakes Avengers will hire just about anybody to be an expendable human shield, and our readers have answered the call! But can our overwhelmingly ordinary applicants impress writer and GLA hiring director Zac Gorman? Let's find out!

---

Super-powers and achievements include (but are not limited to):

1. I don't know who Mr. Fantastic is, and don't care either.
2. Conveniently located in Berlin, WI, where you should NEVER go.
3. I once pretended to be Jeff Loeb... it didn't work. (Editor's note: See AMAZING ADVENTURES #9.)
4. I always A.I.M. to please.
5. I will never leave the team to become a herald of Galactus, no matter how much he begs.
6. I once interned with Doctor Tannenbaum, and am prepared for any Snowman-related mission that might arise.

I have already given my two weeks' notice, and await your acceptance letter.

Tim Mentuis
Berlin, WI

Dear Tim, you showed the right amount of initiative and forward-thinking in quitting your job before sending your letter. There's no substitute for ambition. Unfortunately, your A.I.M. reference has us all a little worried that you might actually be M.O.D.O.K. in disguise. So, I'm sorry, but we must respectfully decline your offer.

Dear Great Lakes Avengers,

My name is Aeromajor and for 30 years I've been fighting crime in the Toledo, Ohio area. I have the mutant ability of naviometry, meaning no matter where I go, people ask me for directions, no matter if that's in the Great Lakes or on the other side of the planet. The side effect is that I cannot get lost. I can help the GLA find their way to wherever they are needed.

Aeromajor

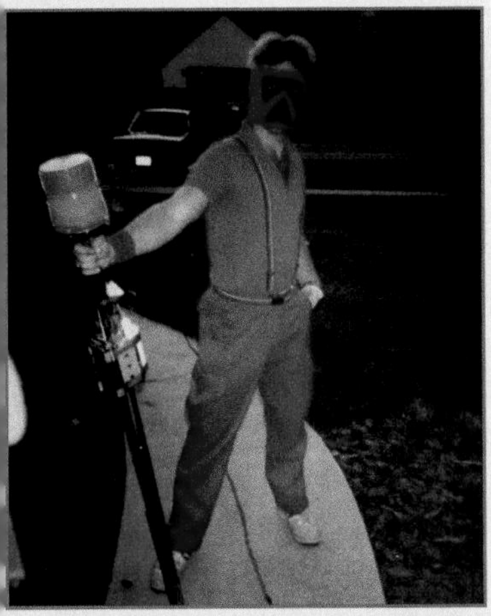

Whoa! You already have your own costume? And an awesome staff? I have to be honest here, I think you might be able to do better than the Great Lakes Avengers. I say why not aim higher? The Guardians of the Galaxy get lost all the time! Dream big, my friend! Dream big!

My super-power isn't a normal one, that is for sure. I was born with an insatiable urge to eat pumpkins: not whole pumpkins but foods with pumpkin in them. I'd even make hamburgers with slices of pumpkin. Weird, I know. But the whole reason I'm writing this isn't because I obsessively eat pumpkins. It is because on my 23rd birthday, I gained the ability to communicate with pumpkins and slowly learned about each one: who and what they were and what faces they wanted to have. That's it, my power. I'm not made of pumpkin, no super-defensive skin or anything cool. Literally not helpful to anyone, but the pumpkins were always more friendly than people. So, I made friends with the pumpkins. The pumpkin patch told me of the reforming of the Great Lakes Avengers, and they're kinda pushing me to join...

Any room for a pumpkin dude?

King Pumpkin
(The pumpkins named me this.)

Peter, Peter, Pumpkin-eater! That's what the pumpkins should've called you! I have to question the rationale of anything which would elect the foremost devourer of its people as their king.

Hi, Great Lake Avengers! First I want to congratulate all of you for receiving official Avengers Membership, way to go! Also, what I can do with my secret super-power is sell official GLA Merchandise, lots and lots of merchandise, exponentially bettering all of your lives and the lives of your neighbors near your new headquarters. I envision a community --no, a GLA Community--where boys and girls are playing with Great Lake Avengers action figures while their parents and grandparents are wearing full Great Lake Avengers cosplay regalia. Team, if you would have me, could you please help me pick a code-name and help me with a costume design? I would greatly appreciate it. Your new grassroots community will become a beacon of hope and a model safe place where everyone is friends and laughs are always with and never at. Make Mine Marvel!

John Bonnett
Coronado, CA

I want everybody to look at this letter. Take a good long look. Read it. Then read it again. Revel in its candor and enthusiasm. Roll around naked on the bear skin rug of its visionary nature. This is exactly what we're looking for when it comes to picking new members of the Great Lakes Avengers! You would do well to remember this man's name. Remember John Bonnett, because one day we'll all be working for him!

Dear Great Lakes Avengers,

I hear you are looking for new members. I would like to take this opportunity to nominate myself. I am Australian, which is quite a good super-power, and better than a lot out there, and should qualify me to be a super hero in the same way that being British makes you automatically eligible to be a super villain.

Please let me know.

Damien White
Adelaide, Australia

I find this letter of particular interest because the artist on our series, Will, is himself British. Before reading this, I thought the only thing that being British made you eligible for was knighthood but apparently I was mistaken. At least that explains his penchant for mustache twirling and his sinister laughter whenever I mention the crown jewels.

Zac

---

The Great Lakes Avengers still need more applicants--the turnover/brutal-murder-in-the-line-of-duty rate is pretty high. Send your qualifications to MHEROES@MARVEL.COM marked "OKAY TO PRINT," even if all you can do is staple papers real good or remember to feed your cat regularly. Have we mentioned how low the bar is here?

---

## NEXT:

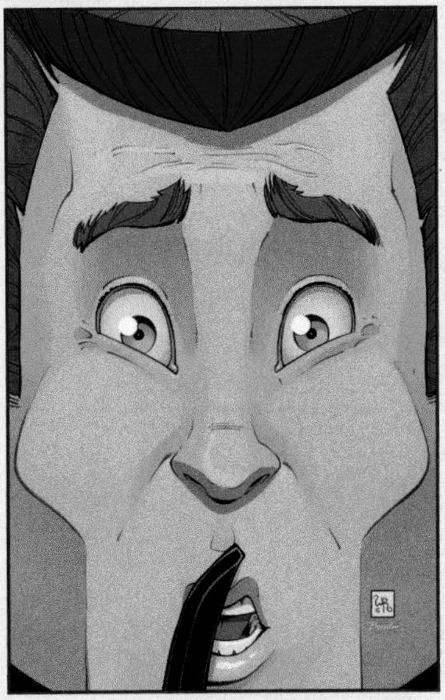

Is this Flatman or a comic? Who can say?

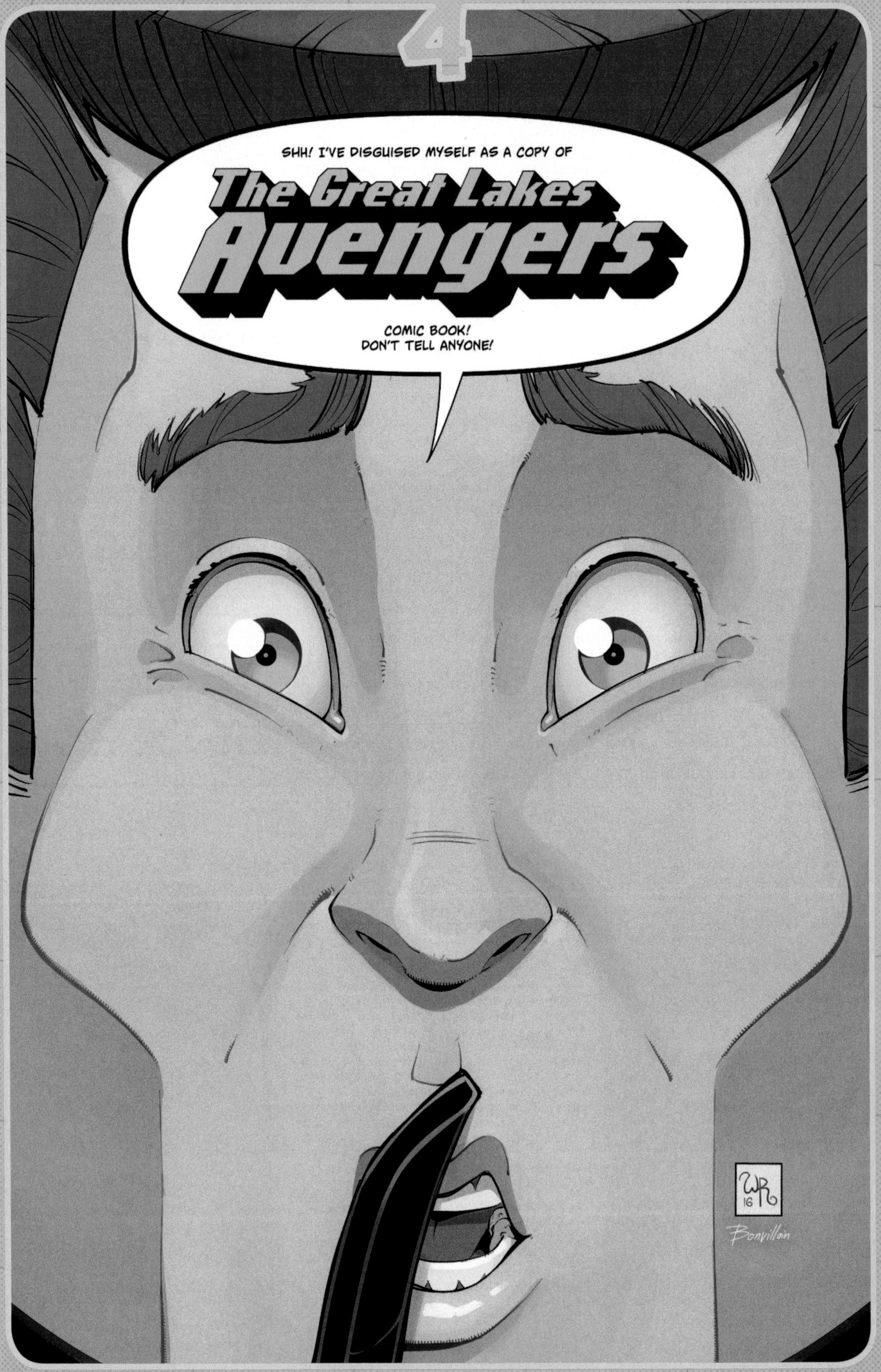
4
SHH! I'VE DISGUISED MYSELF AS A COPY OF
The Great Lakes Avengers
COMIC BOOK!
DON'T TELL ANYONE!
WR 16
Bonvillain

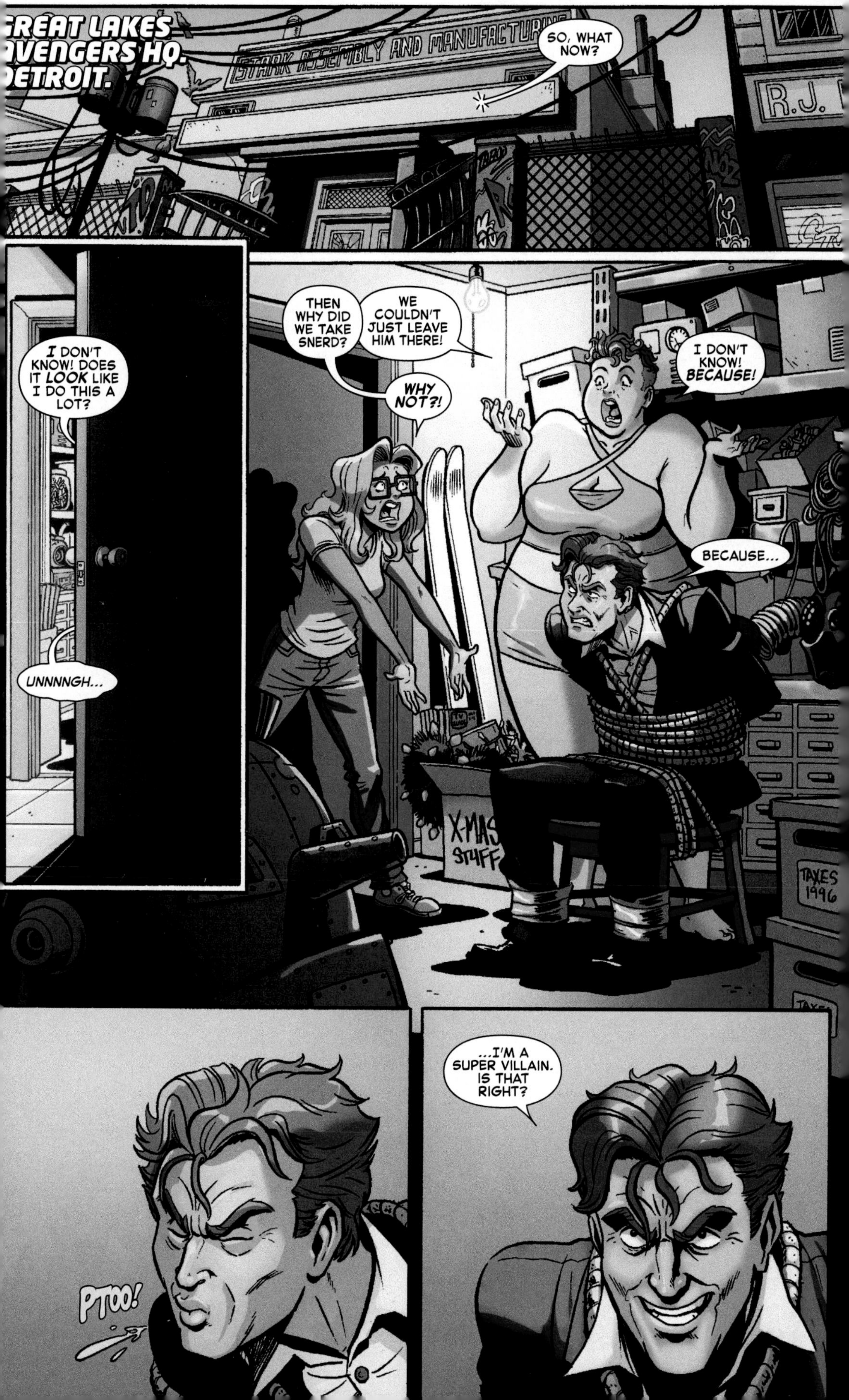

GREAT LAKES AVENGERS HQ. DETROIT.
STARK ASSEMBLY AND MANUFACTURING
R.J.
SO, WHAT NOW?
I DON'T KNOW! DOES IT LOOK LIKE I DO THIS A LOT?
THEN WHY DID WE TAKE SNERD?
WE COULDN'T JUST LEAVE HIM THERE!
WHY NOT?!
I DON'T KNOW! BECAUSE!
BECAUSE...
UNNNNGH...
X-MAS STUFF
TAXES 1996
...I'M A SUPER VILLAIN. IS THAT RIGHT?
PTOO!

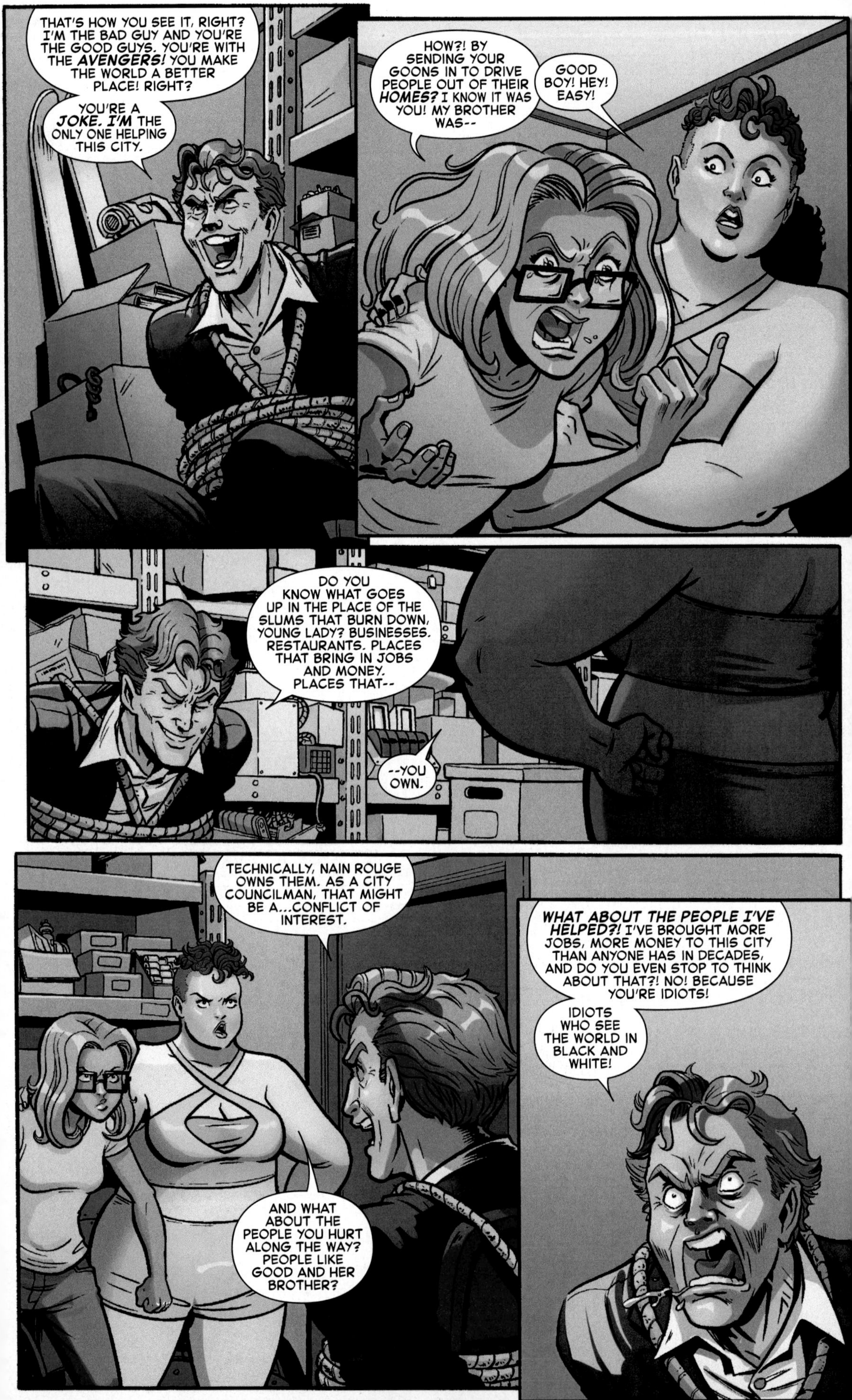
THAT'S HOW YOU SEE IT, RIGHT? I'M THE BAD GUY AND YOU'RE THE GOOD GUYS. YOU'RE WITH THE AVENGERS! YOU MAKE THE WORLD A BETTER PLACE! RIGHT?
YOU'RE A JOKE. I'M THE ONLY ONE HELPING THIS CITY.
HOW?! BY SENDING YOUR GOONS IN TO DRIVE PEOPLE OUT OF THEIR HOMES? I KNOW IT WAS YOU! MY BROTHER WAS--
GOOD BOY! HEY! EASY!
DO YOU KNOW WHAT GOES UP IN THE PLACE OF THE SLUMS THAT BURN DOWN, YOUNG LADY? BUSINESSES. RESTAURANTS. PLACES THAT BRING IN JOBS AND MONEY. PLACES THAT--
--YOU OWN.
TECHNICALLY, NAIN ROUGE OWNS THEM. AS A CITY COUNCILMAN, THAT MIGHT BE A...CONFLICT OF INTEREST.
AND WHAT ABOUT THE PEOPLE YOU HURT ALONG THE WAY? PEOPLE LIKE GOOD AND HER BROTHER?
WHAT ABOUT THE PEOPLE I'VE HELPED?! I'VE BROUGHT MORE JOBS, MORE MONEY TO THIS CITY THAN ANYONE HAS IN DECADES, AND DO YOU EVEN STOP TO THINK ABOUT THAT?! NO! BECAUSE YOU'RE IDIOTS!
IDIOTS WHO SEE THE WORLD IN BLACK AND WHITE!

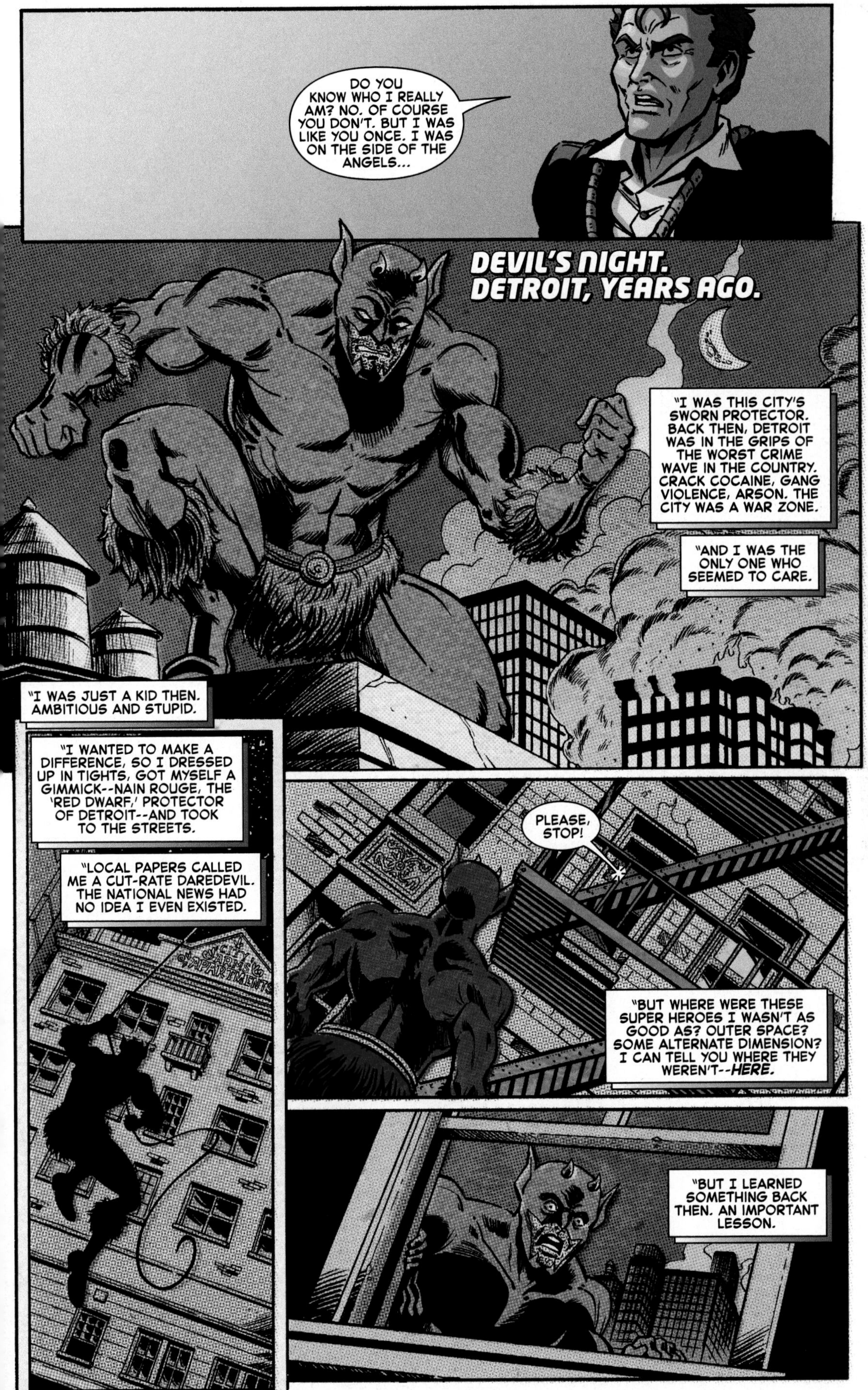
DO YOU KNOW WHO I REALLY AM? NO. OF COURSE YOU DON'T. BUT I WAS LIKE YOU ONCE. I WAS ON THE SIDE OF THE ANGELS...
DEVIL'S NIGHT. DETROIT, YEARS AGO.
"I WAS THIS CITY'S SWORN PROTECTOR. BACK THEN, DETROIT WAS IN THE GRIPS OF THE WORST CRIME WAVE IN THE COUNTRY. CRACK COCAINE, GANG VIOLENCE, ARSON. THE CITY WAS A WAR ZONE.
"AND I WAS THE ONLY ONE WHO SEEMED TO CARE.
"I WAS JUST A KID THEN. AMBITIOUS AND STUPID.
"I WANTED TO MAKE A DIFFERENCE, SO I DRESSED UP IN TIGHTS, GOT MYSELF A GIMMICK--NAIN ROUGE, THE 'RED DWARF,' PROTECTOR OF DETROIT--AND TOOK TO THE STREETS.
"LOCAL PAPERS CALLED ME A CUT-RATE DAREDEVIL. THE NATIONAL NEWS HAD NO IDEA I EVEN EXISTED.
CITY ARMS APARTMENTS
PLEASE, STOP!
"BUT WHERE WERE THESE SUPER HEROES I WASN'T AS GOOD AS? OUTER SPACE? SOME ALTERNATE DIMENSION? I CAN TELL YOU WHERE THEY WEREN'T--HERE.
"BUT I LEARNED SOMETHING BACK THEN. AN IMPORTANT LESSON.

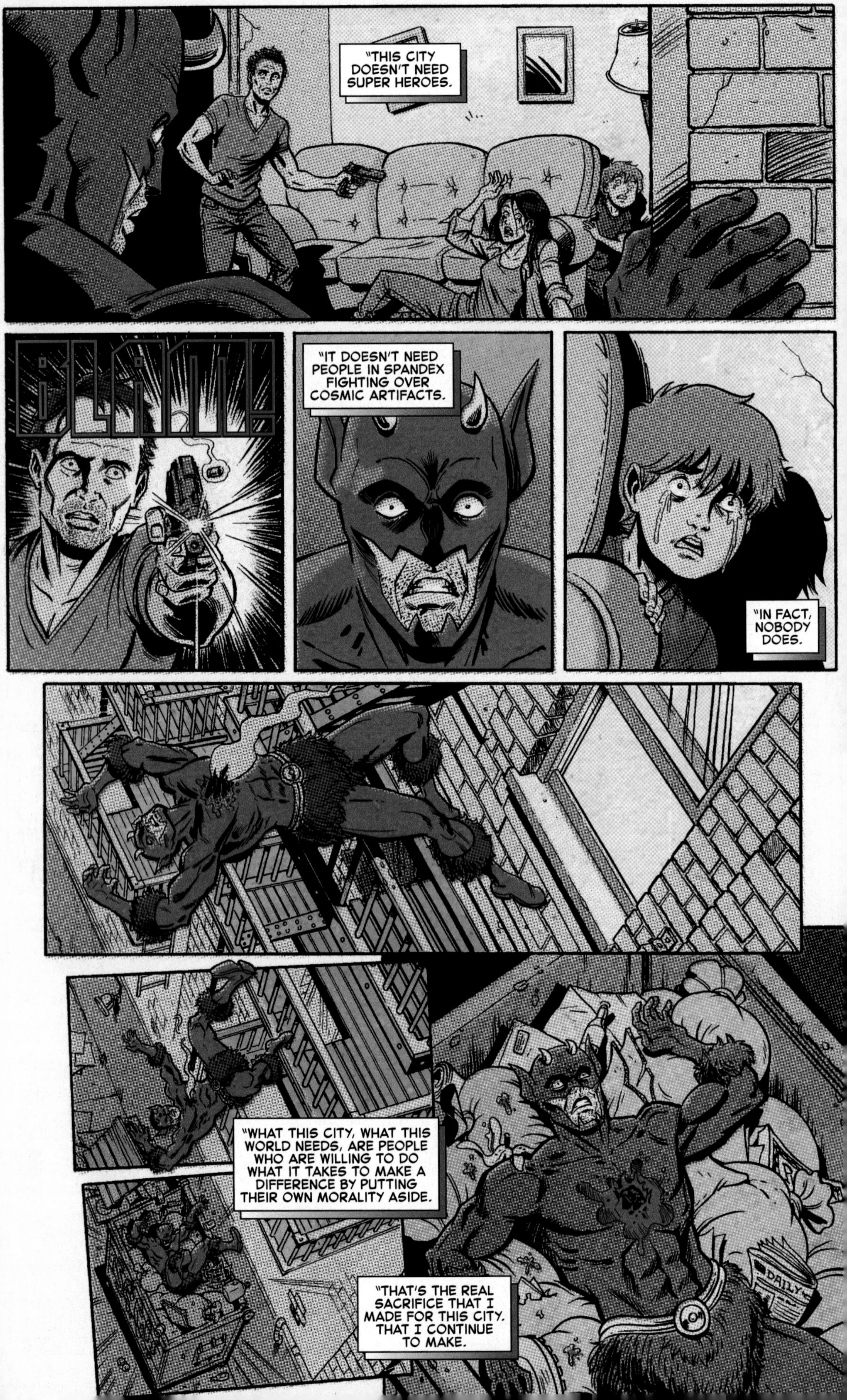
"THIS CITY DOESN'T NEED SUPER HEROES.
BLAM!
"IT DOESN'T NEED PEOPLE IN SPANDEX FIGHTING OVER COSMIC ARTIFACTS.
"IN FACT, NOBODY DOES.
"WHAT THIS CITY, WHAT THIS WORLD NEEDS, ARE PEOPLE WHO ARE WILLING TO DO WHAT IT TAKES TO MAKE A DIFFERENCE BY PUTTING THEIR OWN MORALITY ASIDE.
"THAT'S THE REAL SACRIFICE THAT I MADE FOR THIS CITY. THAT I CONTINUE TO MAKE.
DAILY

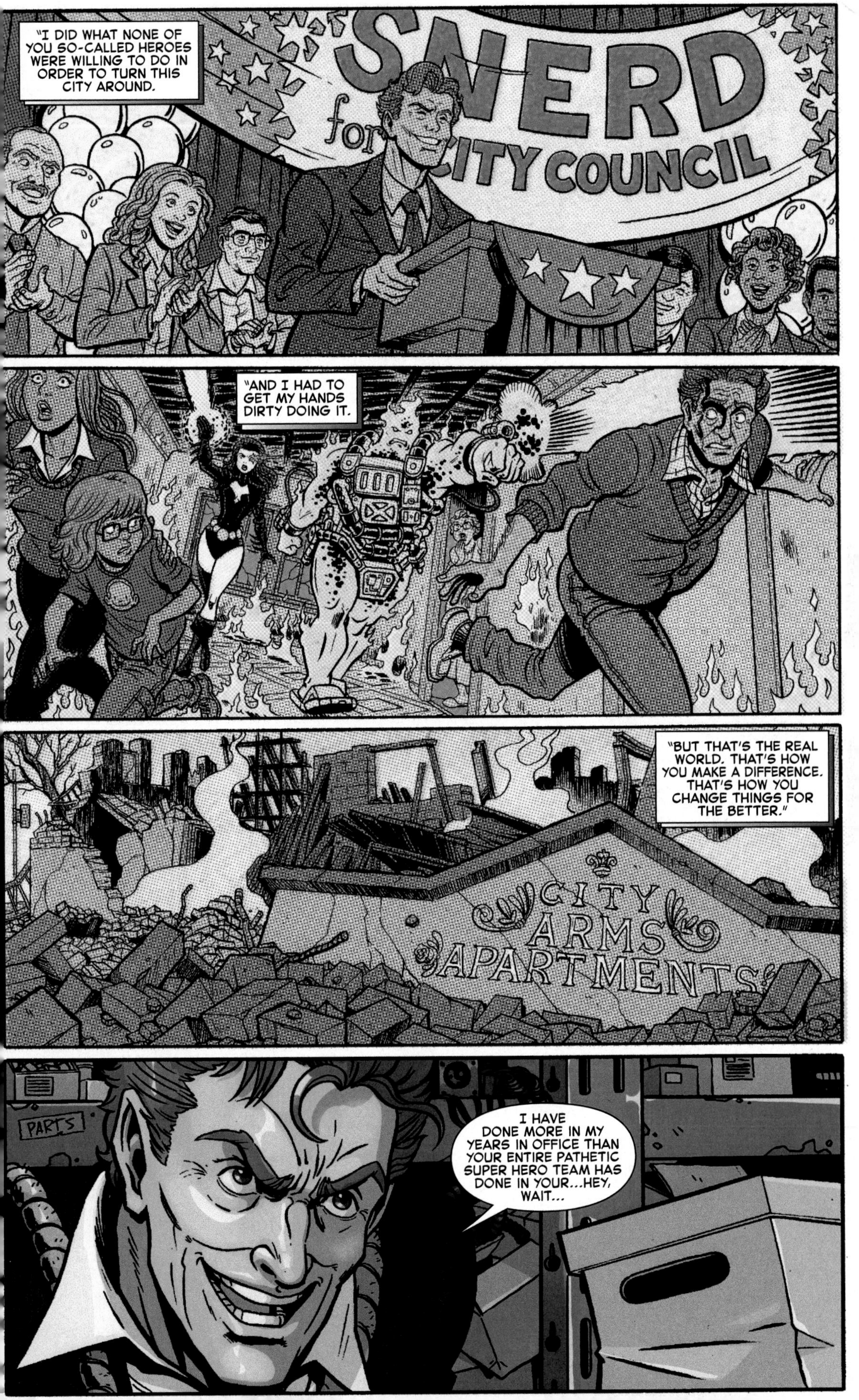
"I DID WHAT NONE OF YOU SO-CALLED HEROES WERE WILLING TO DO IN ORDER TO TURN THIS CITY AROUND.
SNERD for CITY COUNCIL
"AND I HAD TO GET MY HANDS DIRTY DOING IT.
"BUT THAT'S THE REAL WORLD. THAT'S HOW YOU MAKE A DIFFERENCE. THAT'S HOW YOU CHANGE THINGS FOR THE BETTER."
CITY ARMS APARTMENTS
PARTS
I HAVE DONE MORE IN MY YEARS IN OFFICE THAN YOUR ENTIRE PATHETIC SUPER HERO TEAM HAS DONE IN YOUR...HEY, WAIT...

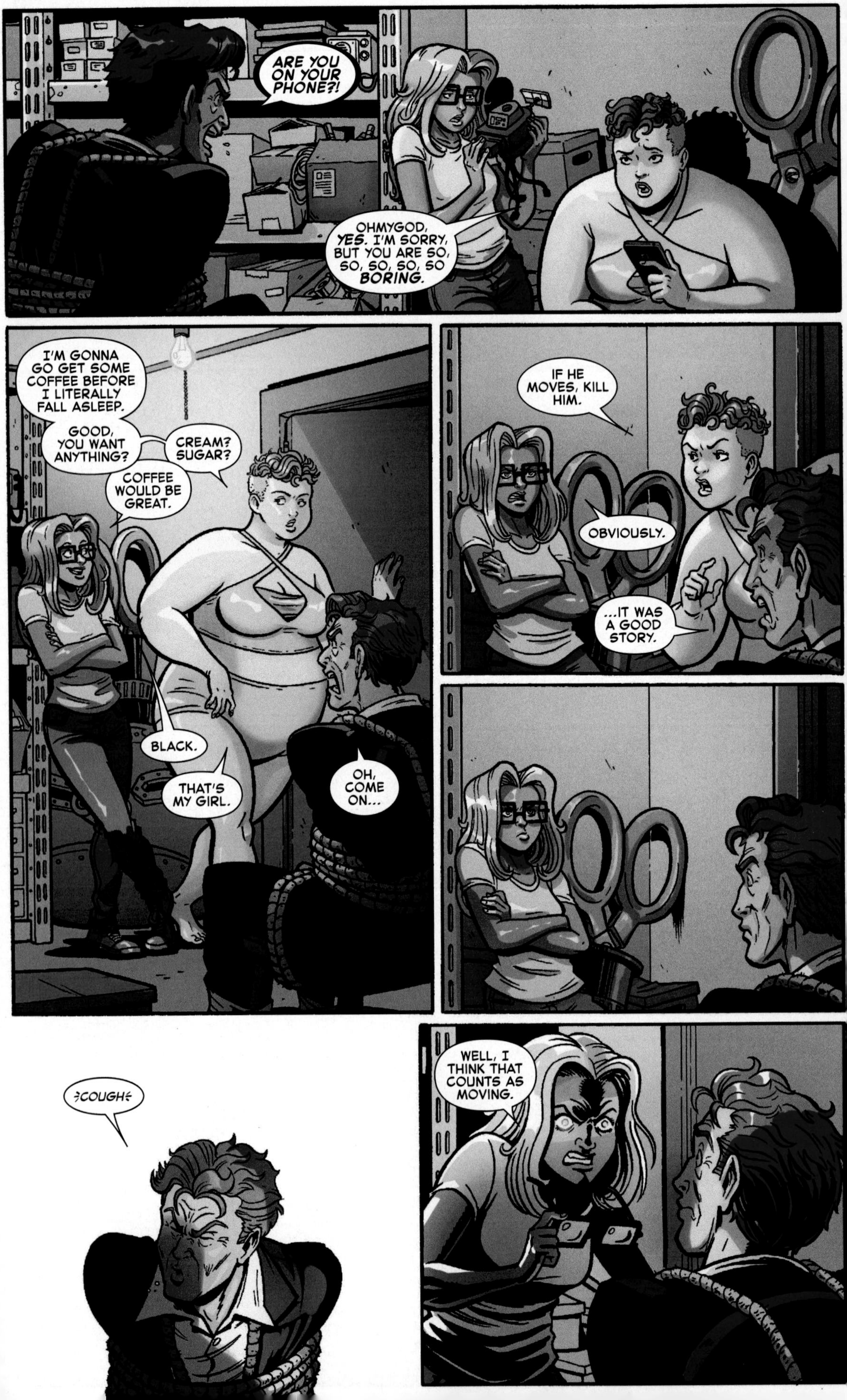
ARE YOU ON YOUR PHONE?!
OHMYGOD, YES. I'M SORRY, BUT YOU ARE SO, SO, SO, SO, SO BORING.
I'M GONNA GO GET SOME COFFEE BEFORE I LITERALLY FALL ASLEEP.
GOOD, YOU WANT ANYTHING?
CREAM? SUGAR?
COFFEE WOULD BE GREAT.
BLACK.
THAT'S MY GIRL.
OH, COME ON...
IF HE MOVES, KILL HIM.
OBVIOUSLY.
...IT WAS A GOOD STORY.
*COUGH*
WELL, I THINK THAT COUNTS AS MOVING.

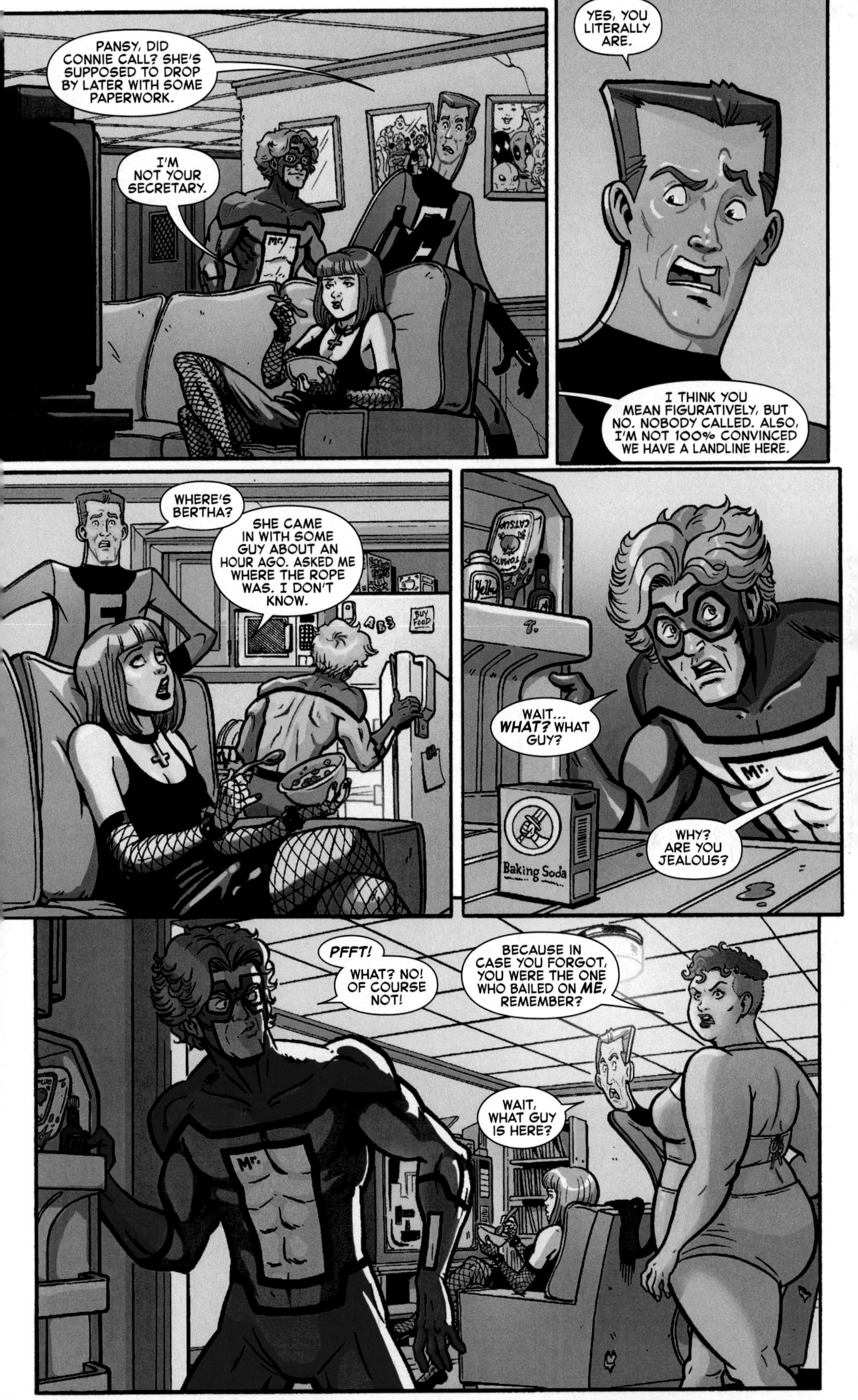
PANSY, DID CONNIE CALL? SHE'S SUPPOSED TO DROP BY LATER WITH SOME PAPERWORK.
I'M NOT YOUR SECRETARY.
YES, YOU LITERALLY ARE.
I THINK YOU MEAN FIGURATIVELY, BUT NO. NOBODY CALLED. ALSO, I'M NOT 100% CONVINCED WE HAVE A LANDLINE HERE.
WHERE'S BERTHA?
SHE CAME IN WITH SOME GUY ABOUT AN HOUR AGO. ASKED ME WHERE THE ROPE WAS. I DON'T KNOW.
BUY FOOD
CATSUP
TOMATO
WAIT... WHAT? WHAT GUY?
Mr.
Baking Soda
WHY? ARE YOU JEALOUS?
PFFT!
WHAT? NO! OF COURSE NOT!
BECAUSE IN CASE YOU FORGOT, YOU WERE THE ONE WHO BAILED ON ME, REMEMBER?
WAIT, WHAT GUY IS HERE?

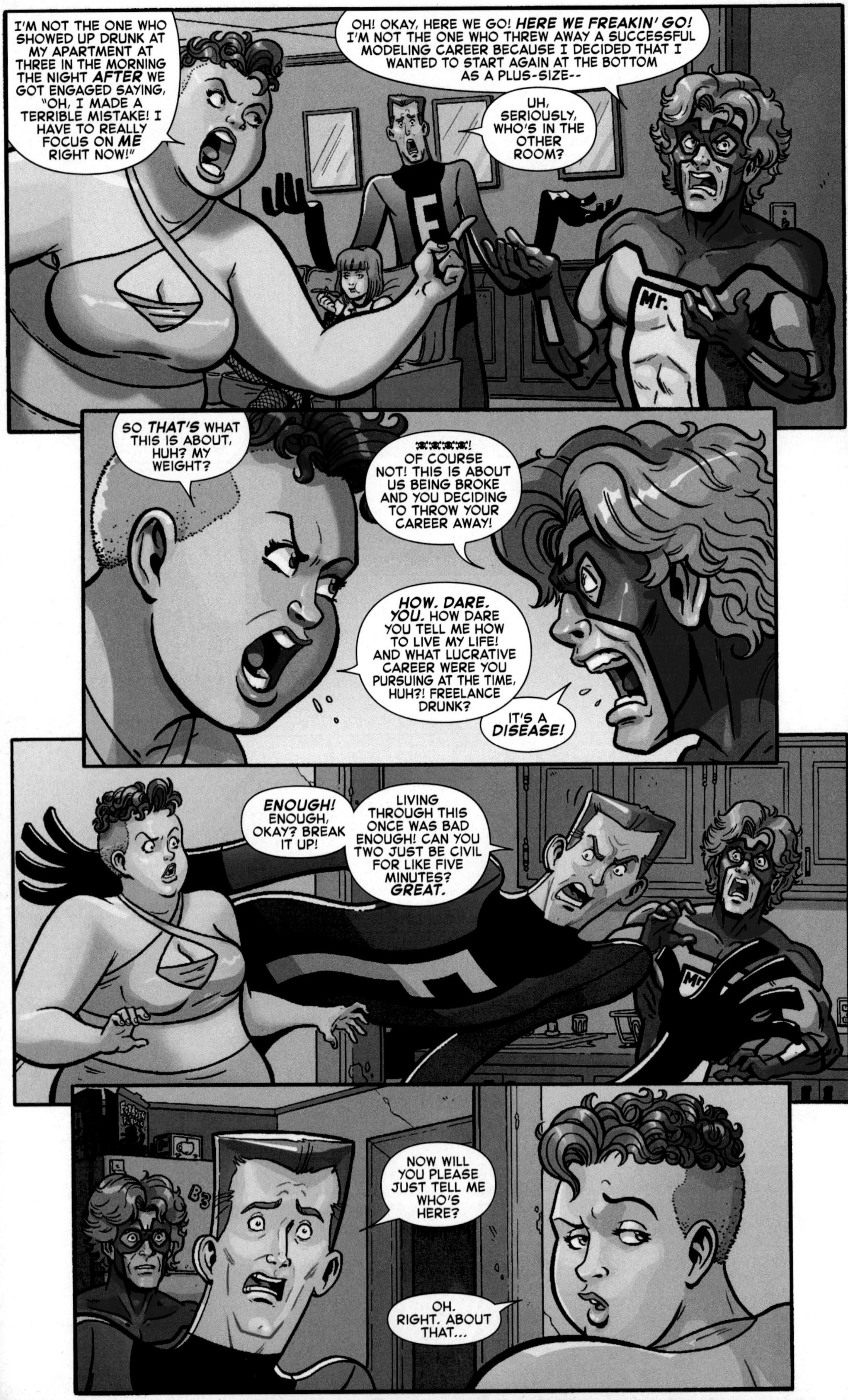
I'M NOT THE ONE WHO SHOWED UP DRUNK AT MY APARTMENT AT THREE IN THE MORNING THE NIGHT *AFTER* WE GOT ENGAGED SAYING, "OH, I MADE A TERRIBLE MISTAKE! I HAVE TO REALLY FOCUS ON *ME* RIGHT NOW!"
OH! OKAY, HERE WE GO! *HERE WE FREAKIN' GO!* I'M NOT THE ONE WHO THREW AWAY A SUCCESSFUL MODELING CAREER BECAUSE I DECIDED THAT I WANTED TO START AGAIN AT THE BOTTOM AS A PLUS-SIZE--
UH, SERIOUSLY, WHO'S IN THE OTHER ROOM?
SO *THAT'S* WHAT THIS IS ABOUT, HUH? MY WEIGHT?
OF COURSE NOT! THIS IS ABOUT US BEING BROKE AND YOU DECIDING TO THROW YOUR CAREER AWAY!
*HOW. DARE. YOU.* HOW DARE YOU TELL ME HOW TO LIVE MY LIFE! AND WHAT LUCRATIVE CAREER WERE YOU PURSUING AT THE TIME, HUH?! FREELANCE DRUNK?
IT'S A *DISEASE!*
*ENOUGH!* ENOUGH, OKAY? BREAK IT UP!
LIVING THROUGH THIS ONCE WAS BAD ENOUGH! CAN YOU TWO JUST BE CIVIL FOR LIKE FIVE MINUTES? *GREAT.*
NOW WILL YOU PLEASE JUST TELL ME WHO'S HERE?
OH. RIGHT. ABOUT THAT...

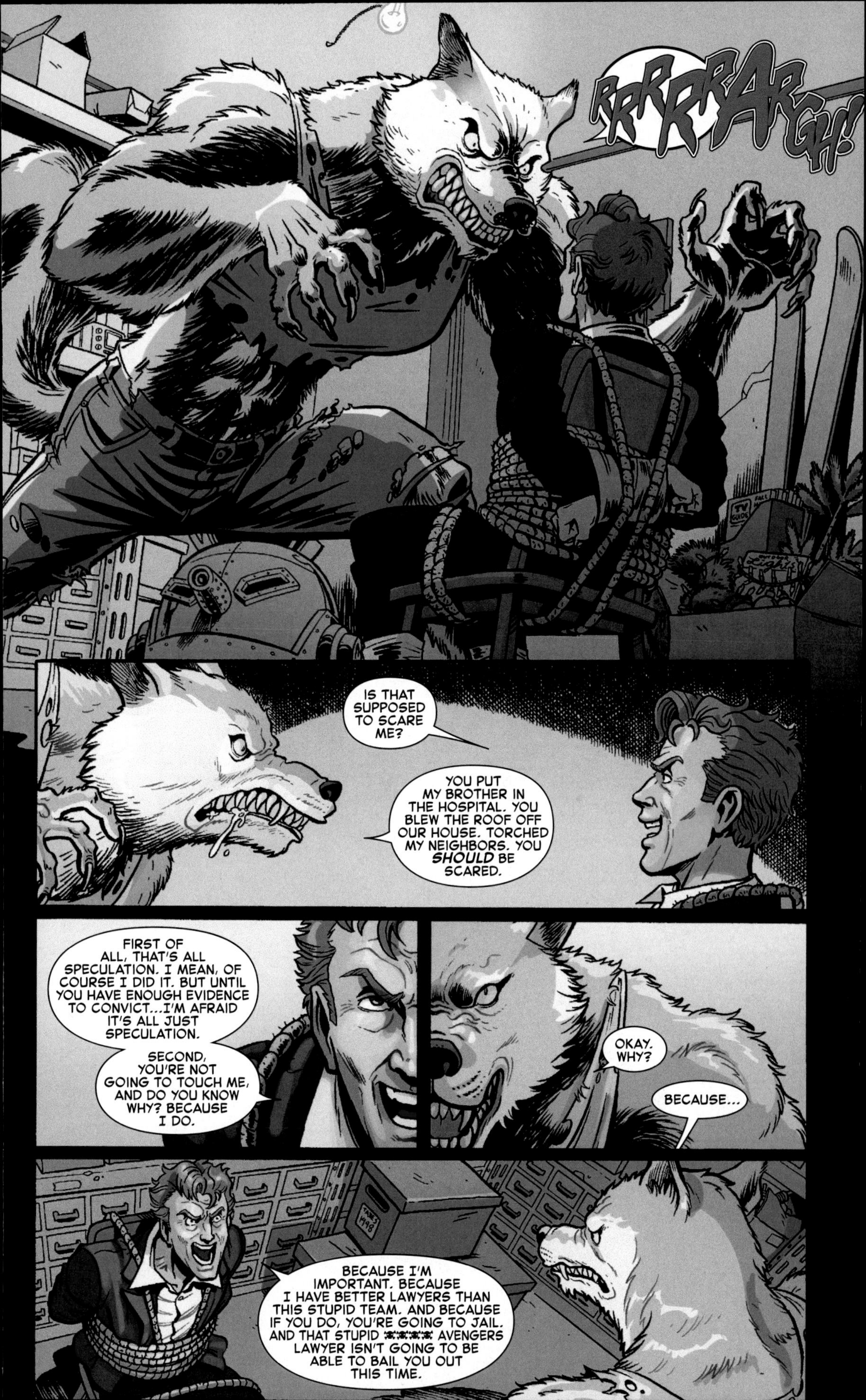

RRRRRARGH!
IS THAT SUPPOSED TO SCARE ME?
YOU PUT MY BROTHER IN THE HOSPITAL. YOU BLEW THE ROOF OFF OUR HOUSE. TORCHED MY NEIGHBORS. YOU *SHOULD* BE SCARED.
FIRST OF ALL, THAT'S ALL SPECULATION. I MEAN, OF COURSE I DID IT. BUT UNTIL YOU HAVE ENOUGH EVIDENCE TO CONVICT...I'M AFRAID IT'S ALL JUST SPECULATION.
SECOND, YOU'RE NOT GOING TO TOUCH ME, AND DO YOU KNOW WHY? BECAUSE I DO.
OKAY. WHY?
BECAUSE...
BECAUSE I'M IMPORTANT. BECAUSE I HAVE BETTER LAWYERS THAN THIS STUPID TEAM. AND BECAUSE IF YOU DO, YOU'RE GOING TO JAIL. AND THAT STUPID ✱✱✱✱ AVENGERS LAWYER ISN'T GOING TO BE ABLE TO BAIL YOU OUT THIS TIME.

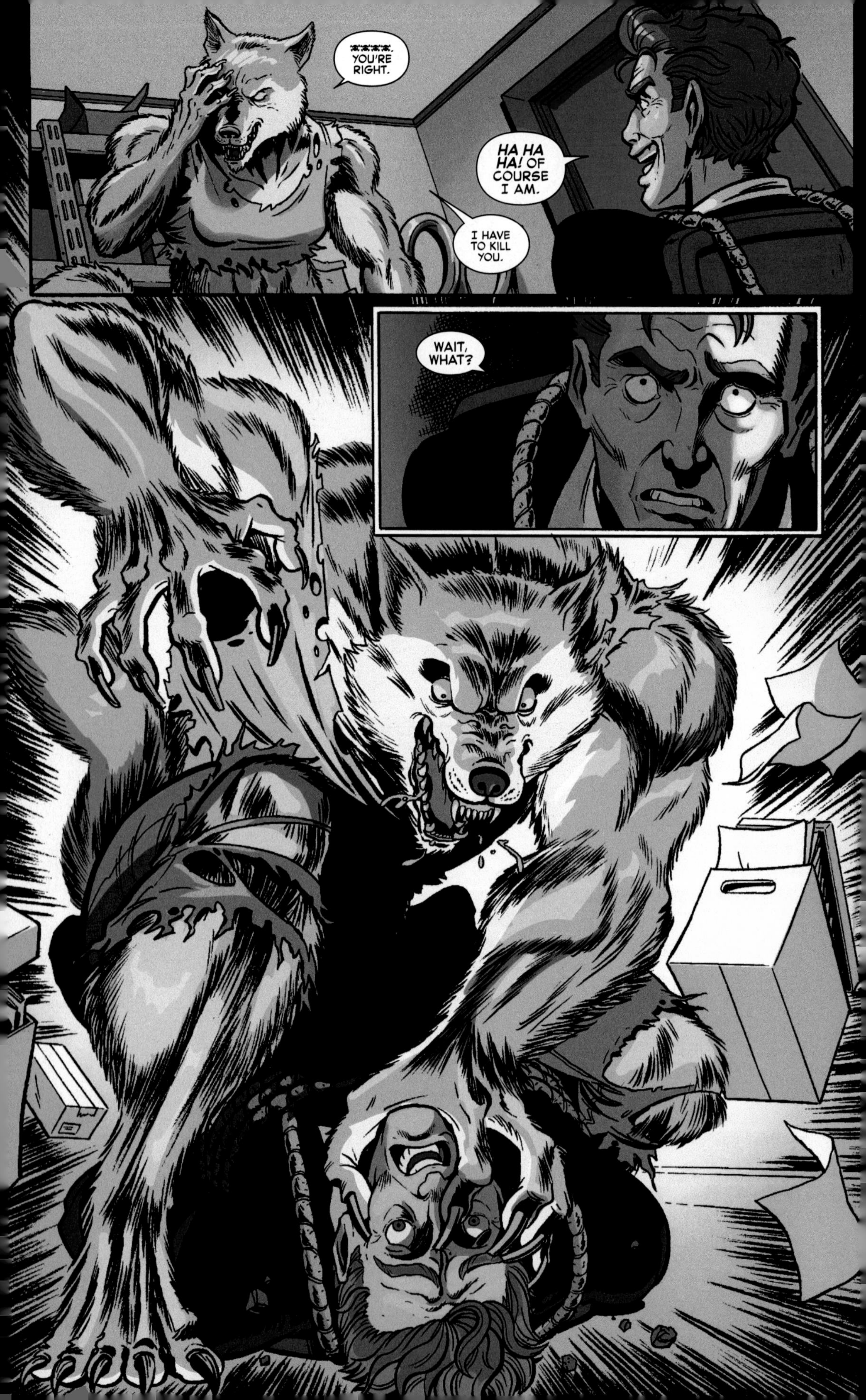

YOU'RE RIGHT.
HA HA HA! OF COURSE I AM.
I HAVE TO KILL YOU.
WAIT, WHAT?

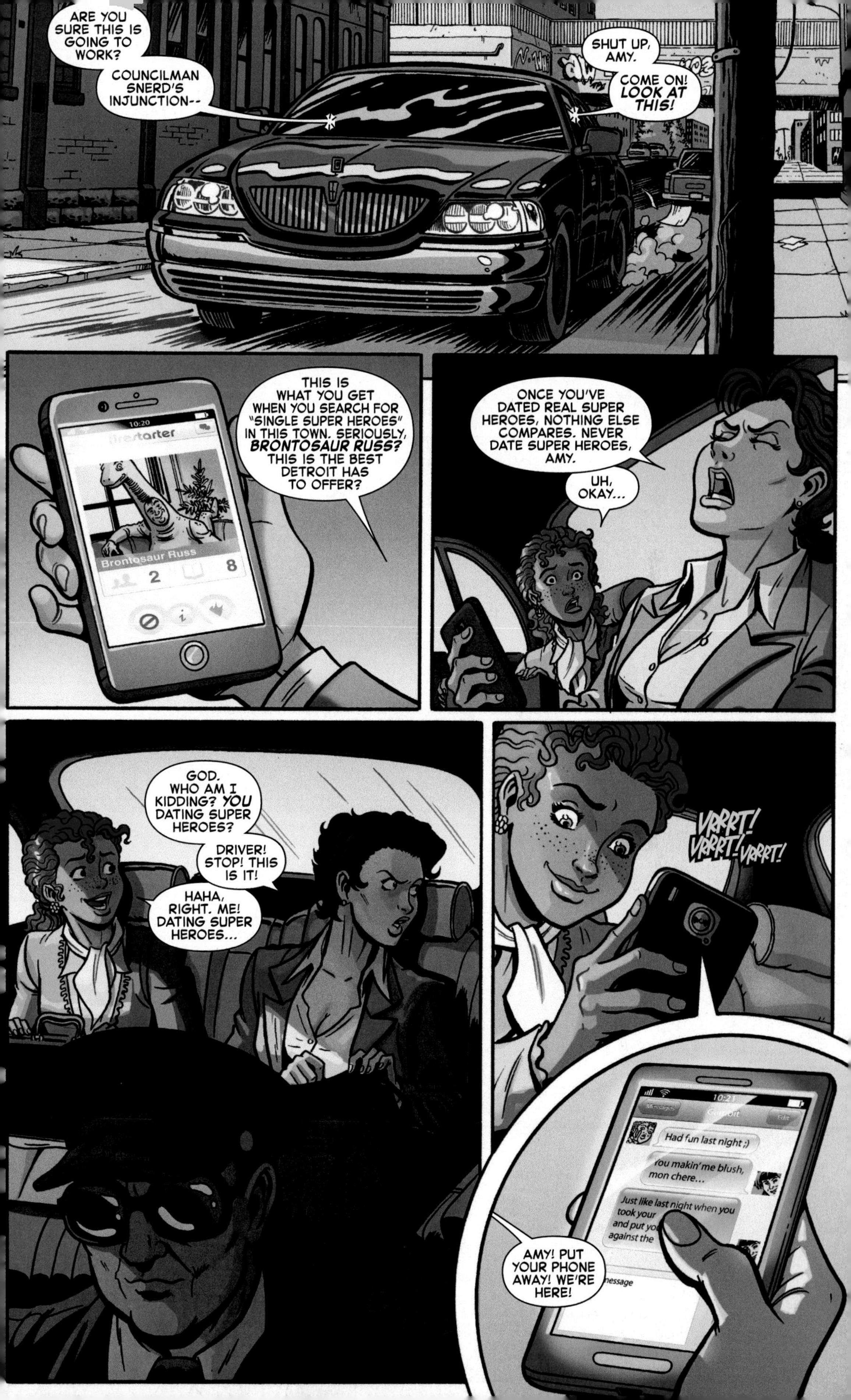
ARE YOU SURE THIS IS GOING TO WORK?
COUNCILMAN SNERD'S INJUNCTION--
SHUT UP, AMY.
COME ON! LOOK AT THIS!
10:20
firestarter
Brontosaur Russ
2
8
THIS IS WHAT YOU GET WHEN YOU SEARCH FOR "SINGLE SUPER HEROES" IN THIS TOWN. SERIOUSLY, BRONTOSAUR RUSS? THIS IS THE BEST DETROIT HAS TO OFFER?
ONCE YOU'VE DATED REAL SUPER HEROES, NOTHING ELSE COMPARES. NEVER DATE SUPER HEROES, AMY.
UH, OKAY...
GOD. WHO AM I KIDDING? YOU DATING SUPER HEROES?
DRIVER! STOP! THIS IS IT!
HAHA, RIGHT. ME! DATING SUPER HEROES...
VRRRT! VRRRT! VRRRT!
10:21
Had fun last night ;)
You makin' me blush, mon chere...
Just like last night when you took your and put yo against the
AMY! PUT YOUR PHONE AWAY! WE'RE HERE!

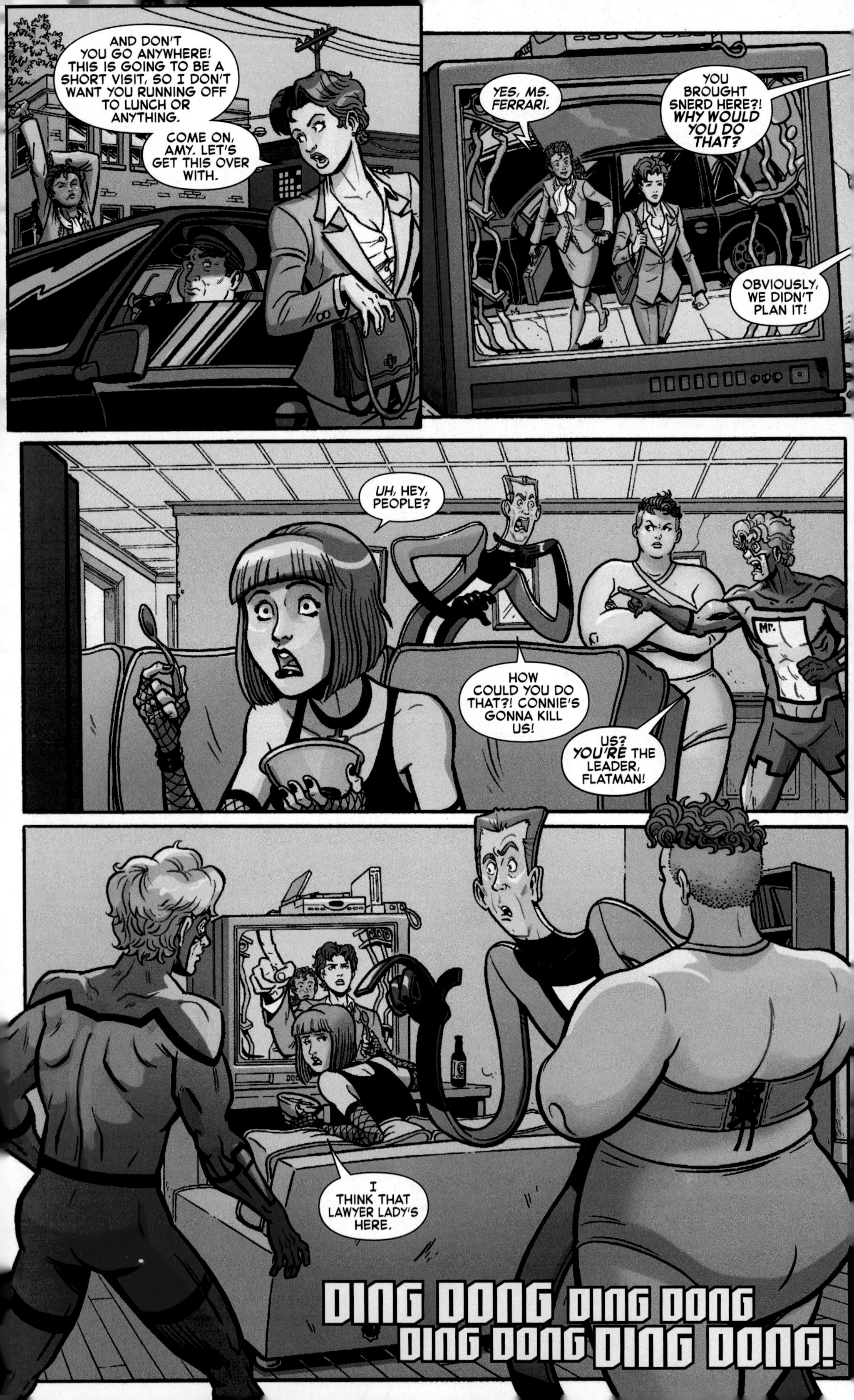
AND DON'T YOU GO ANYWHERE! THIS IS GOING TO BE A SHORT VISIT, SO I DON'T WANT YOU RUNNING OFF TO LUNCH OR ANYTHING.
COME ON, AMY. LET'S GET THIS OVER WITH.
YES, MS. FERRARI.
YOU BROUGHT SNERD HERE?! WHY WOULD YOU DO THAT?
OBVIOUSLY, WE DIDN'T PLAN IT!
UH, HEY, PEOPLE?
HOW COULD YOU DO THAT?! CONNIE'S GONNA KILL US!
US? YOU'RE THE LEADER, FLATMAN!
I THINK THAT LAWYER LADY'S HERE.
DING DONG DING DONG DING DONG DING DONG!

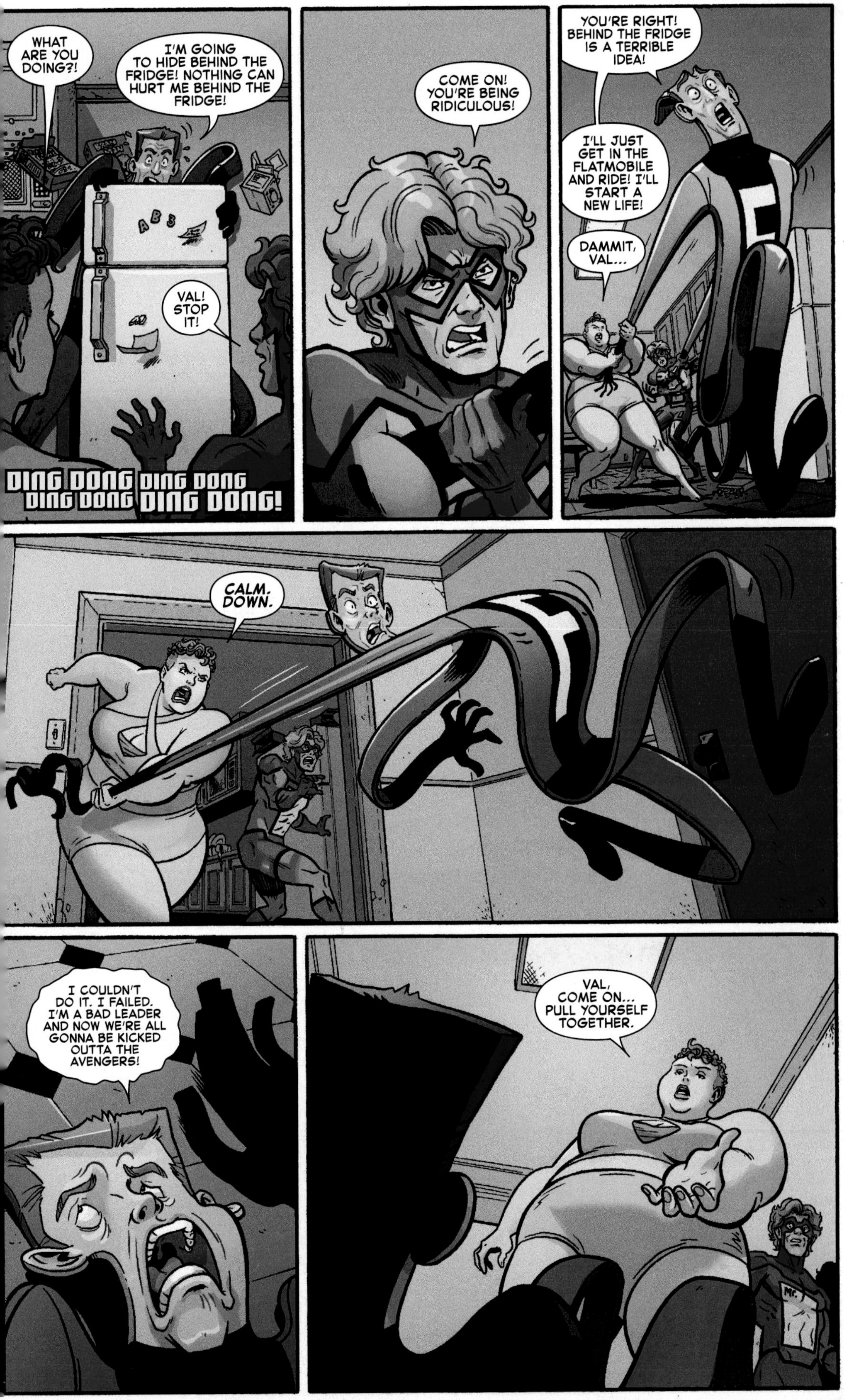
WHAT ARE YOU DOING?!
I'M GOING TO HIDE BEHIND THE FRIDGE! NOTHING CAN HURT ME BEHIND THE FRIDGE!
A B 3
VAL! STOP IT!
DING DONG DING DONG DING DONG DING DONG!
COME ON! YOU'RE BEING RIDICULOUS!
YOU'RE RIGHT! BEHIND THE FRIDGE IS A TERRIBLE IDEA!
I'LL JUST GET IN THE FLATMOBILE AND RIDE! I'LL START A NEW LIFE!
DAMMIT, VAL...
CALM. DOWN.
I COULDN'T DO IT. I FAILED. I'M A BAD LEADER AND NOW WE'RE ALL GONNA BE KICKED OUTTA THE AVENGERS!
VAL, COME ON... PULL YOURSELF TOGETHER.
MR.

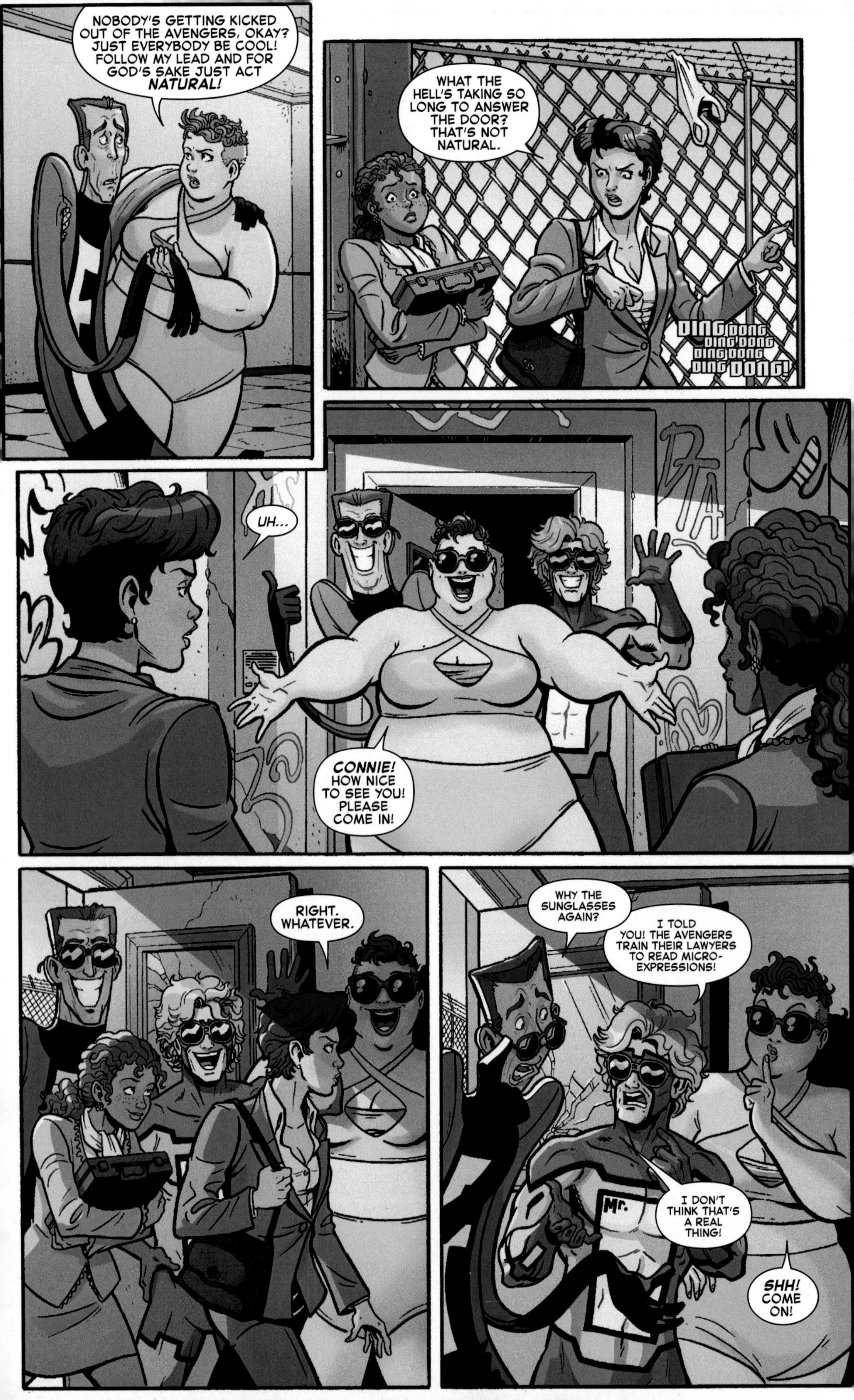
NOBODY'S GETTING KICKED OUT OF THE AVENGERS, OKAY? JUST EVERYBODY BE COOL! FOLLOW MY LEAD AND FOR GOD'S SAKE JUST ACT *NATURAL!*
WHAT THE HELL'S TAKING SO LONG TO ANSWER THE DOOR? THAT'S NOT NATURAL.
DING DONG DING DONG DING DONG DING DONG!
UH...
*CONNIE!* HOW NICE TO SEE YOU! PLEASE COME IN!
RIGHT. WHATEVER.
WHY THE SUNGLASSES AGAIN?
I TOLD YOU! THE AVENGERS TRAIN THEIR LAWYERS TO READ MICRO-EXPRESSIONS!
Mr.
I DON'T THINK THAT'S A REAL THING!
*SHH!* COME ON!

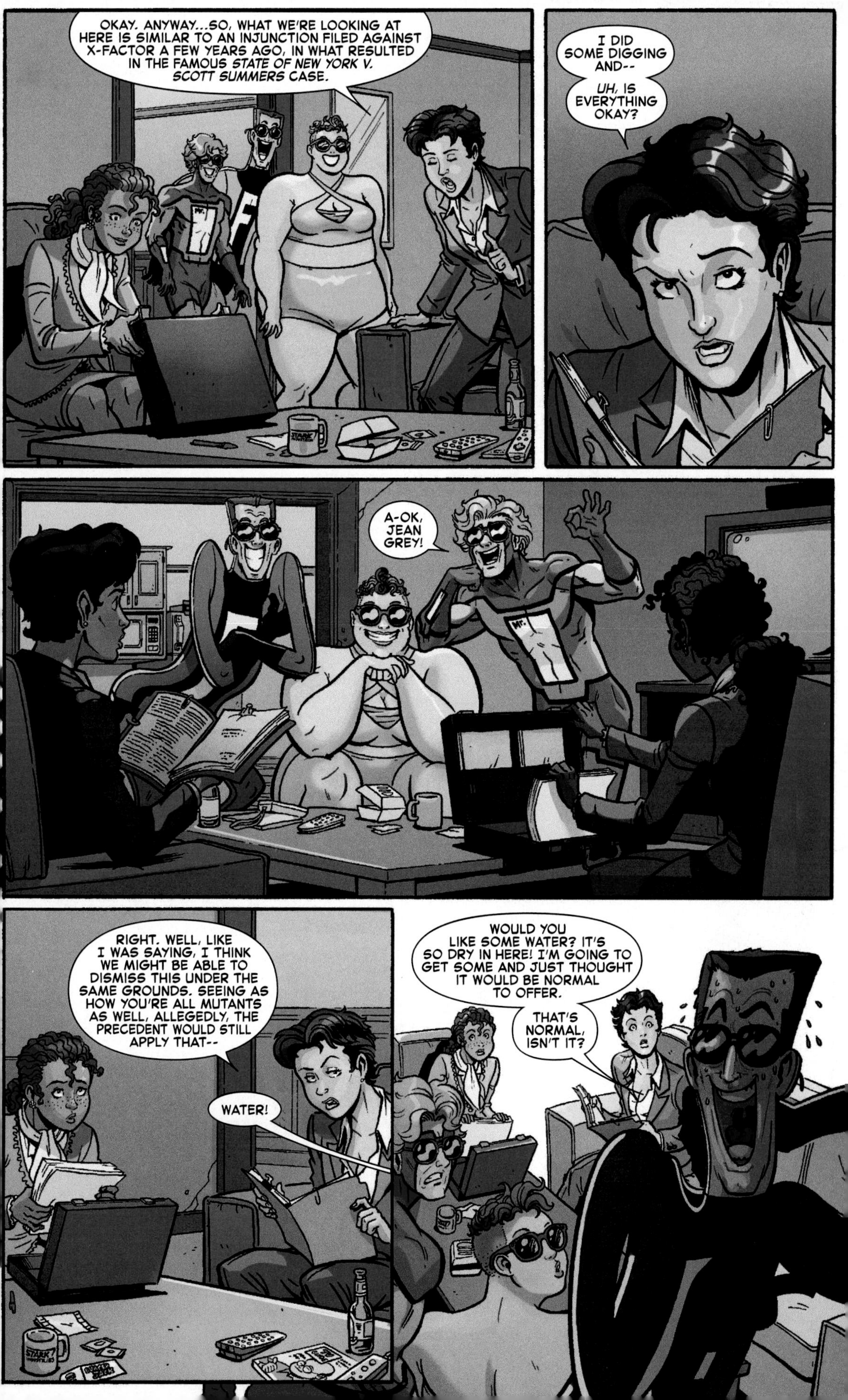
OKAY. ANYWAY...SO, WHAT WE'RE LOOKING AT HERE IS SIMILAR TO AN INJUNCTION FILED AGAINST X-FACTOR A FEW YEARS AGO, IN WHAT RESULTED IN THE FAMOUS *STATE OF NEW YORK V. SCOTT SUMMERS* CASE.
I DID SOME DIGGING AND--
*UH,* IS EVERYTHING OKAY?
A-OK, JEAN GREY!
RIGHT. WELL, LIKE I WAS SAYING, I THINK WE MIGHT BE ABLE TO DISMISS THIS UNDER THE SAME GROUNDS. SEEING AS HOW YOU'RE ALL MUTANTS AS WELL, ALLEGEDLY, THE PRECEDENT WOULD STILL APPLY THAT--
WATER!
WOULD YOU LIKE SOME WATER? IT'S SO DRY IN HERE! I'M GOING TO GET SOME AND JUST THOUGHT IT WOULD BE NORMAL TO OFFER.
THAT'S NORMAL, ISN'T IT?

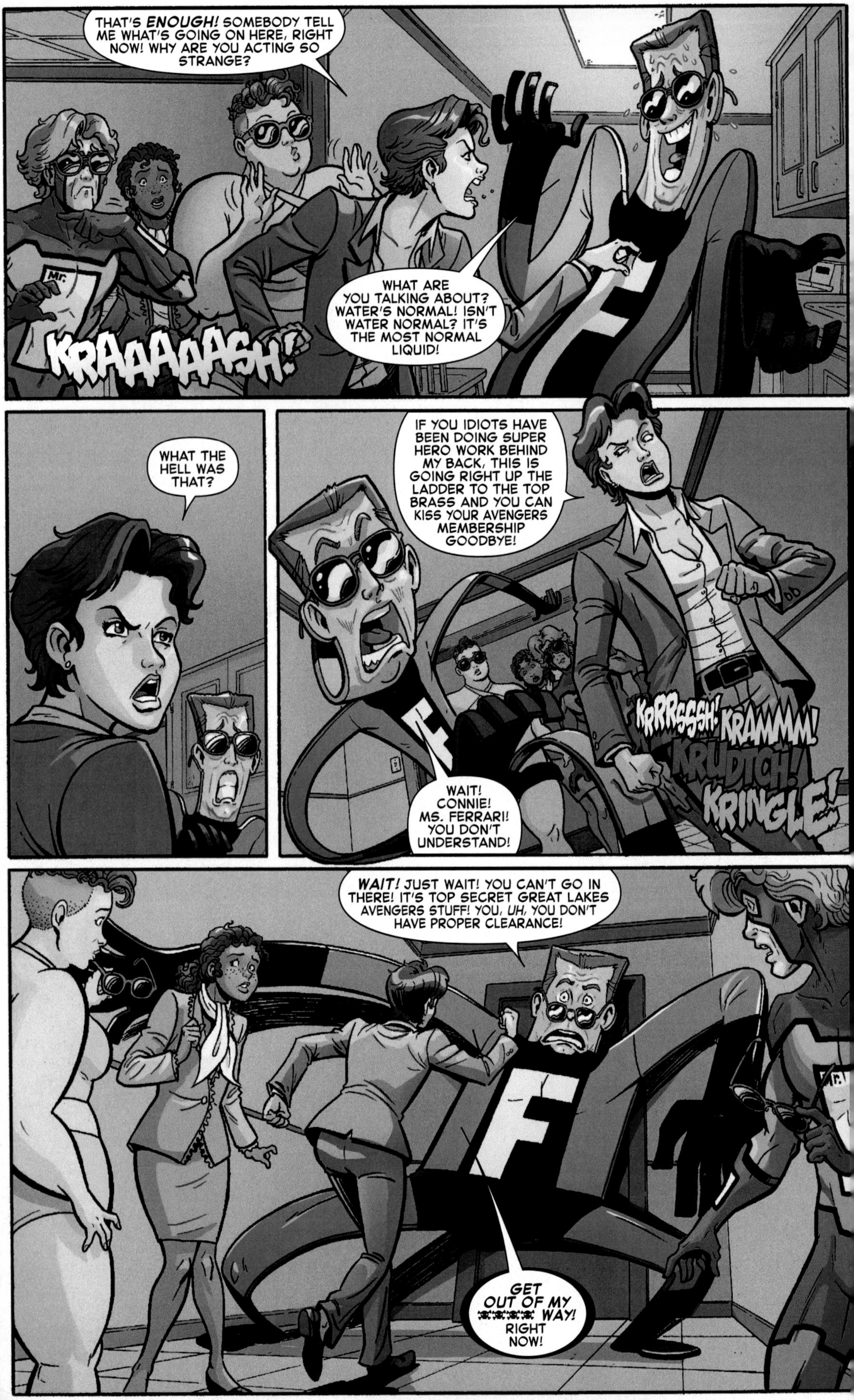
THAT'S ENOUGH! SOMEBODY TELL ME WHAT'S GOING ON HERE, RIGHT NOW! WHY ARE YOU ACTING SO STRANGE?
WHAT ARE YOU TALKING ABOUT? WATER'S NORMAL! ISN'T WATER NORMAL? IT'S THE MOST NORMAL LIQUID!
KRAAAAASH!
Mr.
WHAT THE HELL WAS THAT?
IF YOU IDIOTS HAVE BEEN DOING SUPER HERO WORK BEHIND MY BACK, THIS IS GOING RIGHT UP THE LADDER TO THE TOP BRASS AND YOU CAN KISS YOUR AVENGERS MEMBERSHIP GOODBYE!
WAIT! CONNIE! MS. FERRARI! YOU DON'T UNDERSTAND!
KRRRSSSH! KRAMMM! KRUDTCH! KRINGLE!
WAIT! JUST WAIT! YOU CAN'T GO IN THERE! IT'S TOP SECRET GREAT LAKES AVENGERS STUFF! YOU, UH, YOU DON'T HAVE PROPER CLEARANCE!
GET OUT OF MY WAY! RIGHT NOW!

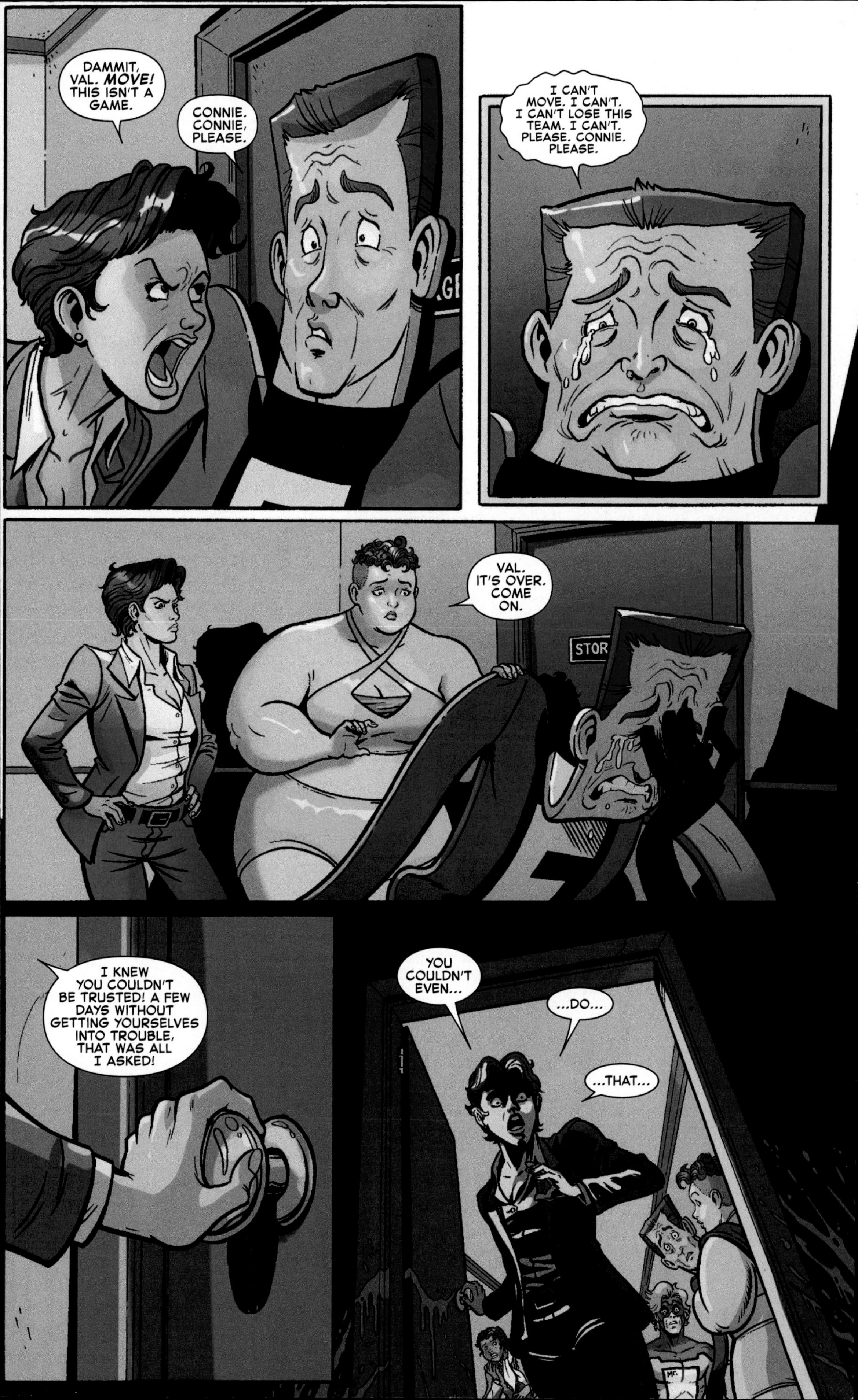
DAMMIT, VAL. MOVE! THIS ISN'T A GAME.
CONNIE. CONNIE, PLEASE.
I CAN'T MOVE. I CAN'T. I CAN'T LOSE THIS TEAM. I CAN'T. PLEASE. CONNIE. PLEASE.
VAL. IT'S OVER. COME ON.
I KNEW YOU COULDN'T BE TRUSTED! A FEW DAYS WITHOUT GETTING YOURSELVES INTO TROUBLE, THAT WAS ALL I ASKED!
YOU COULDN'T EVEN...
...DO...
...THAT...

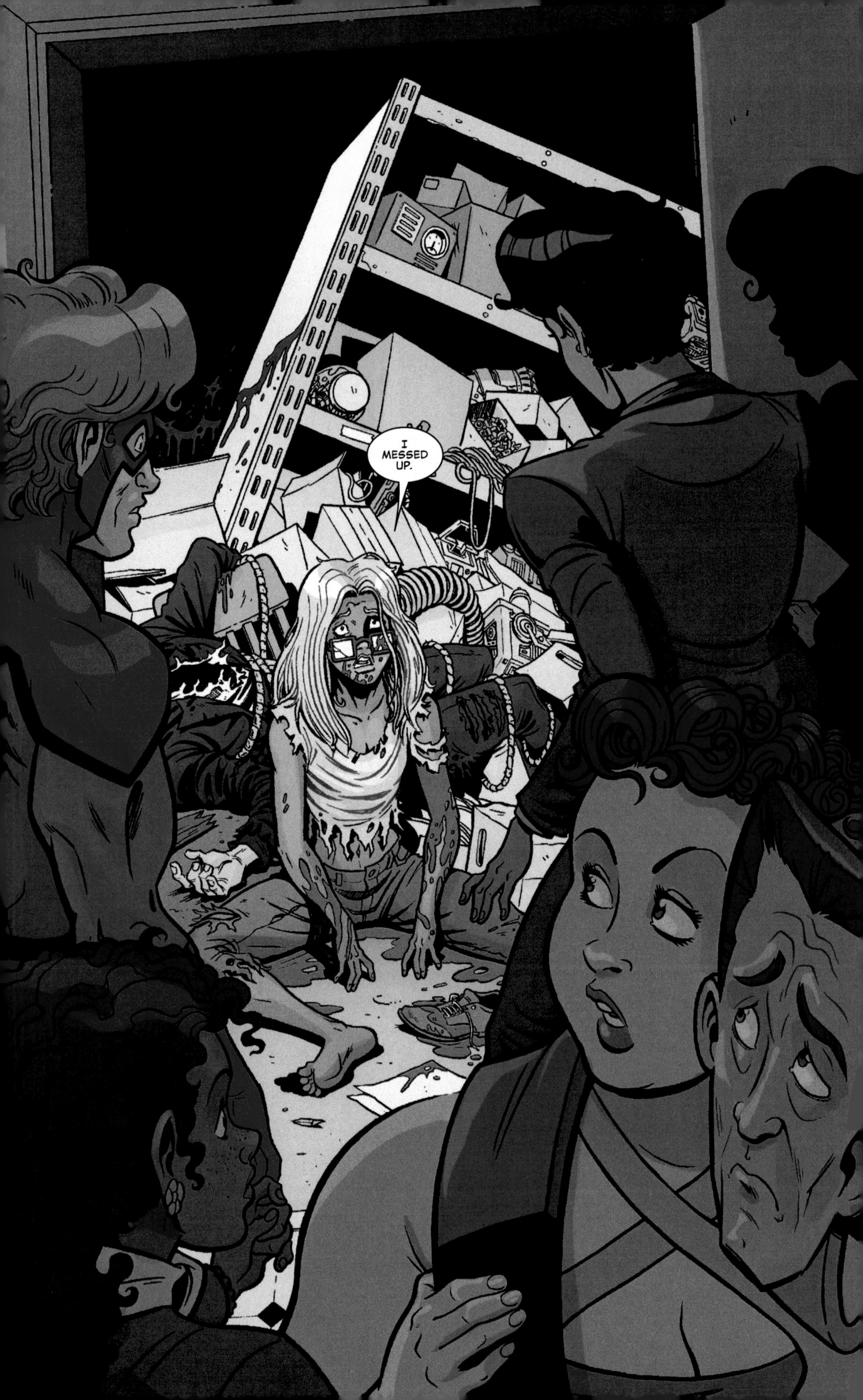
I MESSED UP.

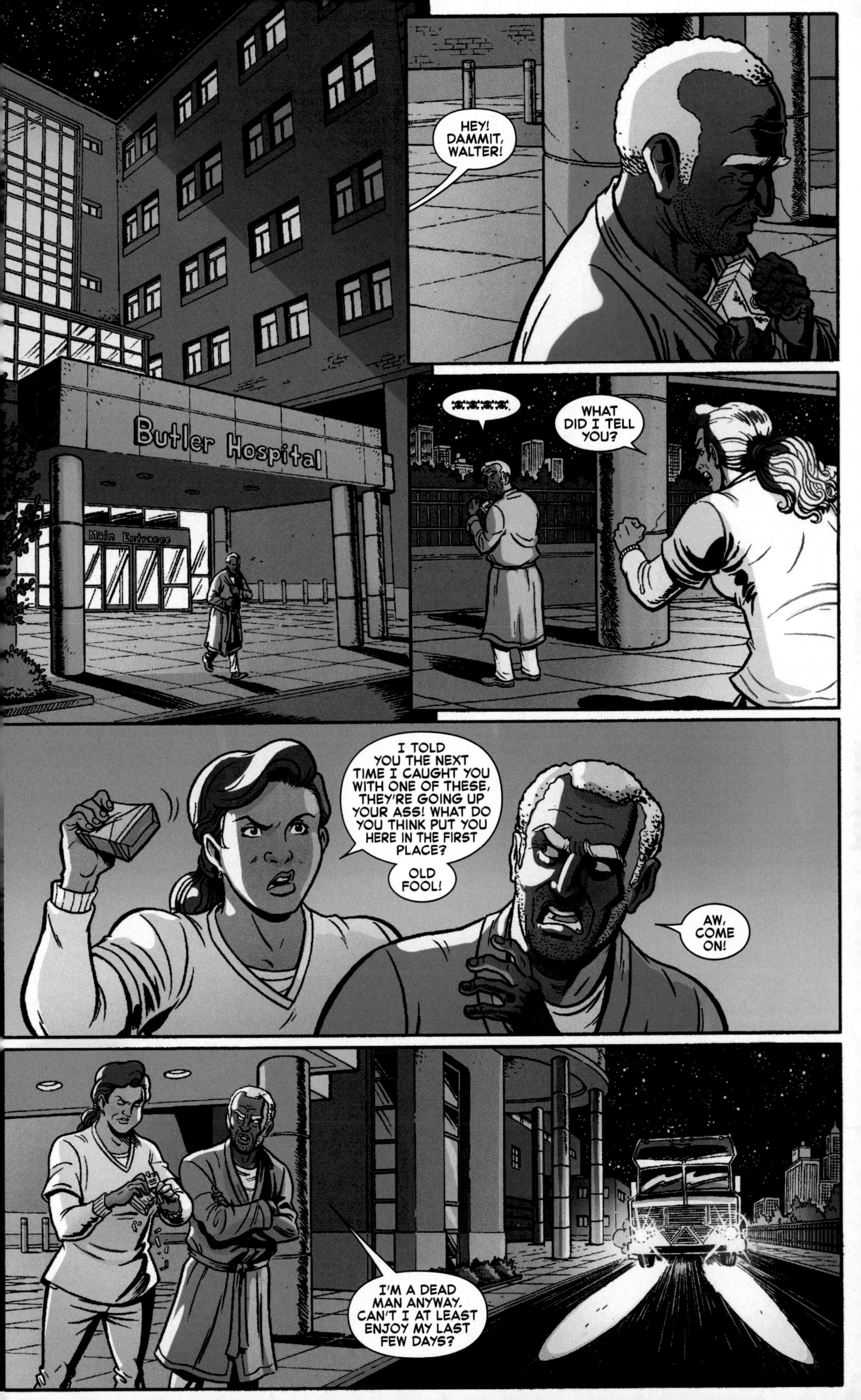
Butler Hospital
Main Entrance
HEY! DAMMIT, WALTER!
WHAT DID I TELL YOU?
I TOLD YOU THE NEXT TIME I CAUGHT YOU WITH ONE OF THESE, THEY'RE GOING UP YOUR ASS! WHAT DO YOU THINK PUT YOU HERE IN THE FIRST PLACE?
OLD FOOL!
AW, COME ON!
I'M A DEAD MAN ANYWAY. CAN'T I AT LEAST ENJOY MY LAST FEW DAYS?

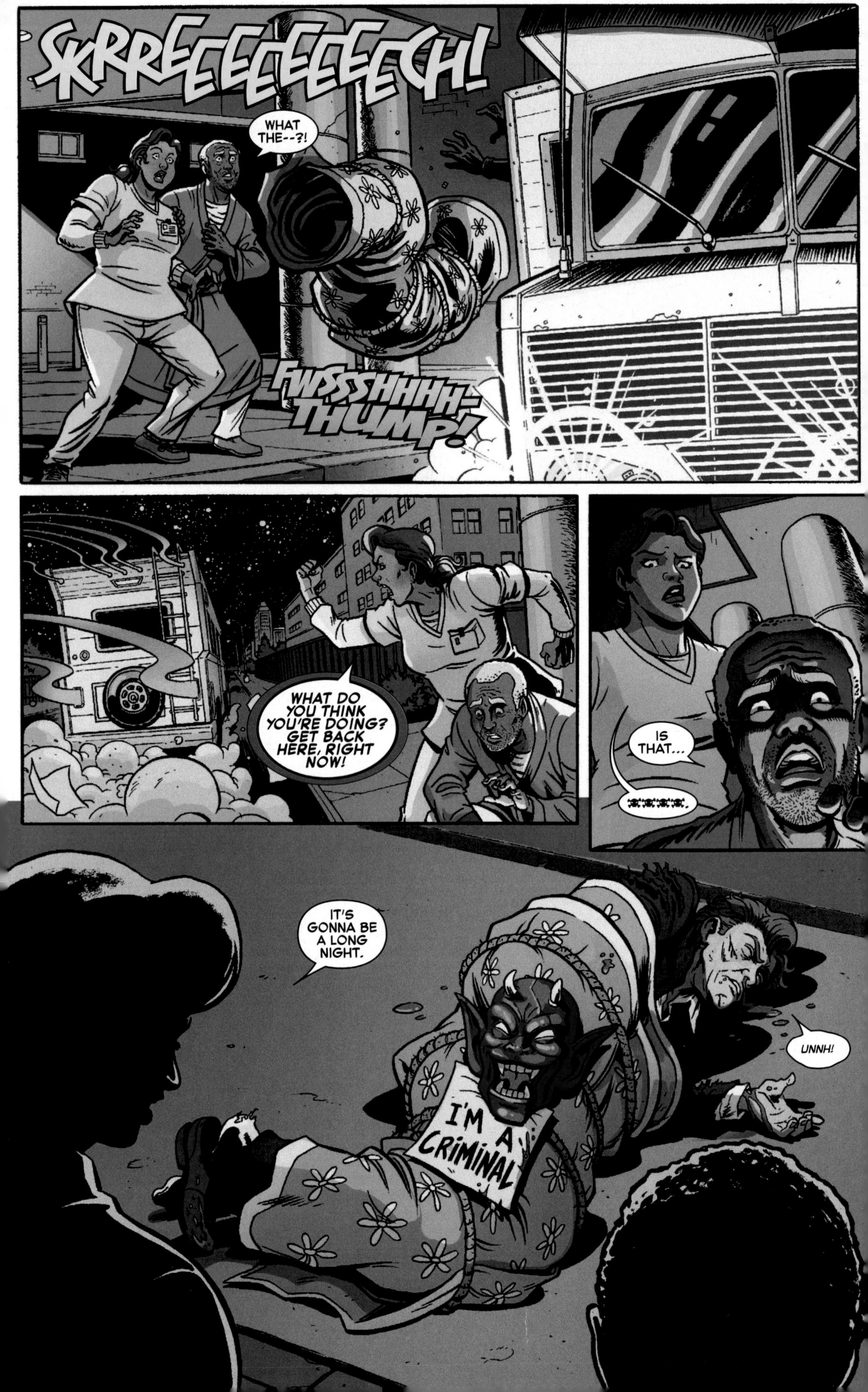
SKRREEEEEEEEEECH!
WHAT THE--?!
FWSSSHHHH-THUMP!
WHAT DO YOU THINK YOU'RE DOING? GET BACK HERE, RIGHT NOW!
IS THAT...
IT'S GONNA BE A LONG NIGHT.
UNNH!
I'M A CRIMINAL

# The Great Lakes Avengers

Send letters to
MHEROES@MARVEL.COM
marked "Okay to Print"!

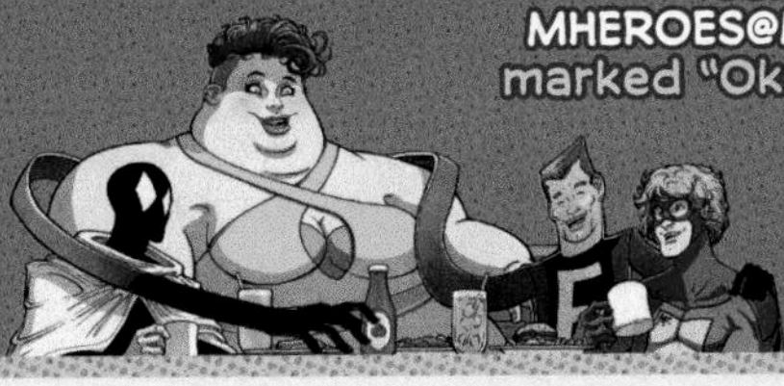

**We said the Great Lakes Avengers will hire just about anybody to join the team that CIVIL WAR II forgot, and our readers have answered the call! But can our astoundingly average applicants impress writer and GLA hiring director Zac Gorman? Let's find out!**

---

The revival of the GREAT LAKES AVENGERS is upon us! Is the Marvel Universe ready for it? Big Bertha, Flat Man, Doorman, and the eternal Mr. Immortal have stayed in the background long enough. Ever since their debut back in WEST COAST AVENGERS #46, I felt like some of those characters should have been featured in the regular Avengers titles a little more through the years. Mr. Immortal has a ton of potential, not to mention the potential of tons of Big Bertha, also a favorite. So here's to a franchise of epic proportions. I just hope it's not all parody and jokes. When they first got together, Hawkeye said, "Your powers are kinda funky...and your codenames stink...but with the proper management...my management...this could be a heckuva team!" And as far as the cool stuff that I can do, how does the ability to keep buying comics and  nding space for them in my studio apartment sound? After all, there's only 500 square feet available and I have been buying comics for years!

Long live the GLA!
Dan Tandarich

**We appreciate the apartment space, Dan! But I guess that means that you won't be purchasing the special edition trade coming next year, which actually measures just a hair over 600 square feet. I tried to warn my editors this might happen. I said, hey, do you think that 600 square feet is too big for a comic? They said no. I wanted it to be the size of a normal comic, Tom wanted it to be 1,200 square feet, so we compromised. It just goes to show!**

I wasn't expecting such a fun comic! It went into my local comic store, and after a quick browse for my usual, I didn't find anything I liked. One of the workers pointed out that I might like the GREAT LAKE AVENGERS, since I like quirky fun comics. I was told that it was "the failed team of Avengers that gets called in when everyone dies."

Big Bertha has to be my favorite so far (plus I love her hair)! I am absolutely enthralled with the art style! Looking forward to the next issue!

Aria Ching

**Thank you for your kind words and cool name, Aria. I can only hope that you enjoy reading the comic as much as I enjoyed reading your name just now.**

Hello to the Marvel Makers,

You have heard the voice of the fans and the GREAT LAKES AVENGERS are finally getting the monthly series they deserve, YES! I have been a fan of the GLA since I first heard of them and have been wanting to see them more than once a year on only one page; now they can be seen every three weeks in over 20 pages. This is a series I have been waiting for, and I hope it goes for the next 3-5 years, and that the writer keeps it good, because I plan to keep on reading to in  nity and beyond.

Henry Spruill from Byron, GA.

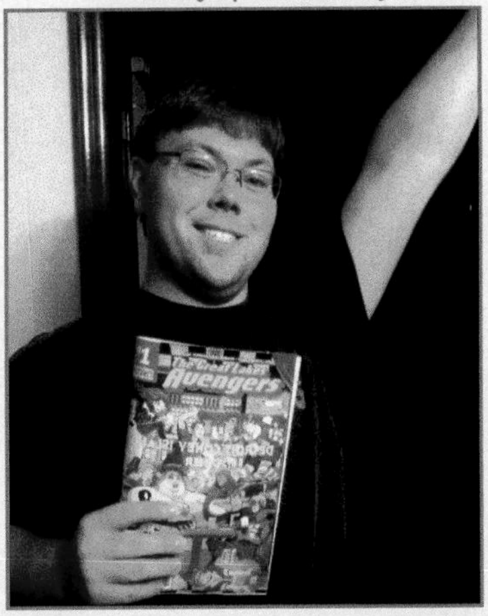

**Thank you for your enthusiasm, Henry! But I have a favor to ask. I was wondering if maybe while you were hoping, you wouldn't mind also hoping for a GREAT LAKES AVENGERS film franchise, preferably one where the creative team would all be asked to stand in as bystanders during a really cool action scene. Thanks again!**

Dear Marvel,

Yo!

So the second I first heard about the new GREAT LAKES AVENGERS ongoing, I rushed to tell literally everyone I knew about it because it's amazing! I bought the whole limited series last year and I ate it up, and I'm super excited that it's taking place in Detroit! Will there be any cool places you're going to be referencing? (Vault of Midnight just opened up there, and it's a super cool comic store. It would be the most meta thing ever!) I can't wait to start reading and collecting this series!

Elisha Deogracias

**I'm excited also! And I don't know if they'll let me print this, Elisha, but Vault of Midnight is my favorite comic store on the planet and everyone should go there! In fact, if you come to the Ann Arbor location on any given Wednesday, there's a good chance I'm walking amongst the racks with my arms full of comics! Thanks for spreading the word!**

**[Spoiler alert: We let him print it.]**

Greetings, Zac Gorman and Will Robson! I really liked GREAT LAKES AVENGERS #1 and I hope you continue the good work. Since this is a team that always cared for minorities, I was wondering: Is there any possibility Starbrand & Nightmask could make an appearance?

Pedro Nogueira

**Thanks for reading, Pedro! We do have a diverse little family of characters here with the Great Lakes Avengers, and I'll never rule out any crossovers, but there are no plans at the moment! Still, our team is a great place to bring back forgotten but beloved characters...**

My name is Mark Duck and I write to join the GLA. I am totally qualified to join, for I have not one, but two "magni  co" powers! My first power is "saiko desu"! I switch English adjectives with their counter parts in "alte" languages. My second power is the ability to write "pobjeda" resumes. They "immer" get accepted! Let's make the world "asfalis" for everyone.

Thank you for your time and consideration!

Andrew Outeiral

**Dear Andrew Outeiral,**

**Are you sure your powers aren't to confuse people who write letters columns?!**

**Zac**

---

**The Great Lakes Avengers still wants YOU (to be their extraordinarily mundane cannon fodder/teammates)! Send your qualifications--like arriving exactly ten minutes late anywhere you go and always finding quarters left behind in vending machines--to MHEROES@MARVEL.COM marked "OKAY TO PRINT" to be considered (our lawyers said we have to tell you there is no pay and that we couldn't put that fact in really really tiny print in the margins anymore).**

---

## NEXT:

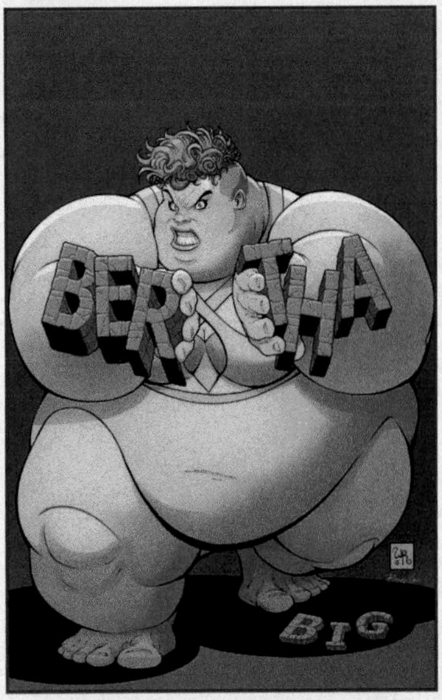
BERTHA
BIG

**BIG BERTHA TAKES DETROIT**

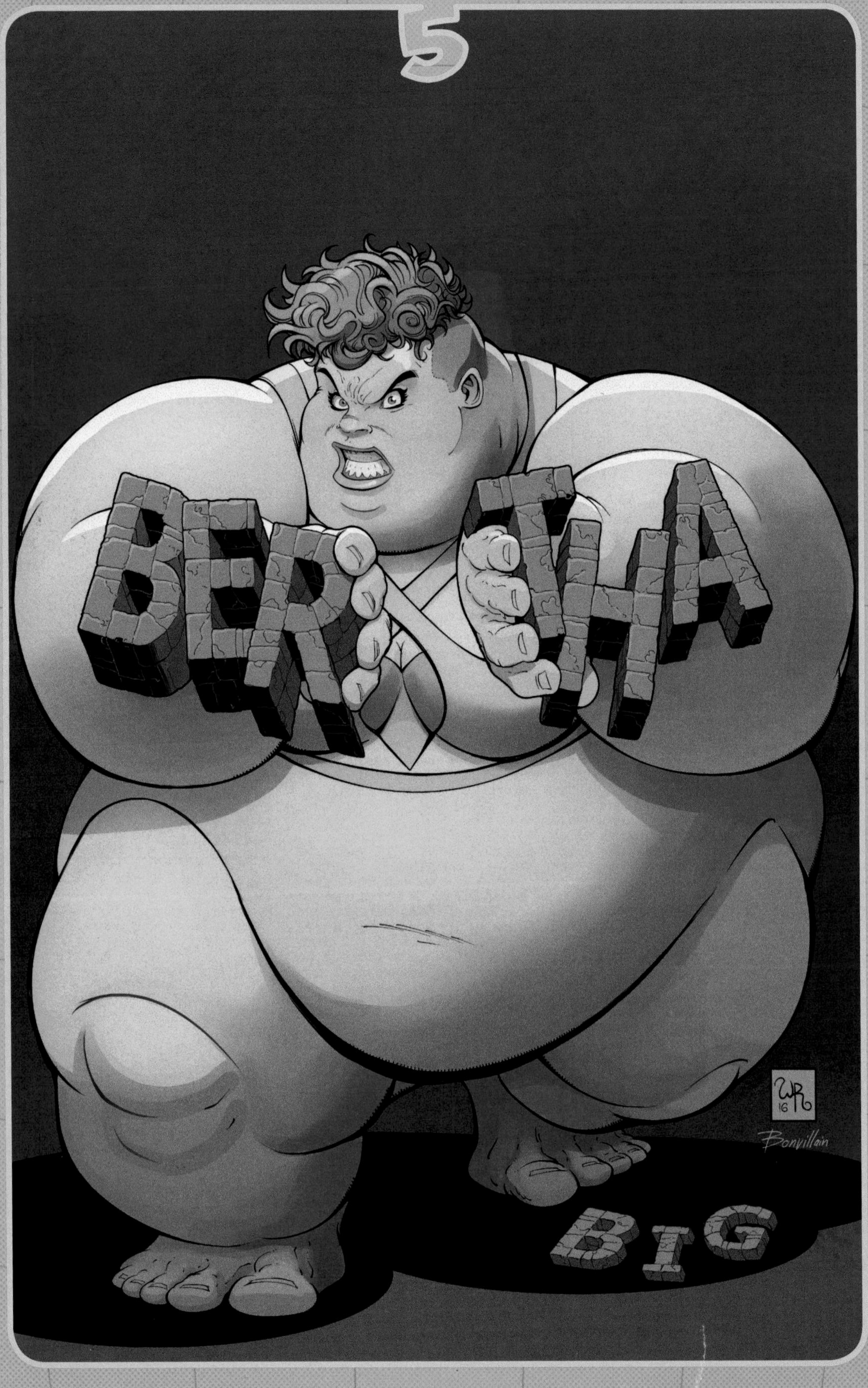
5
BERTHA
BIG
Bonvillain

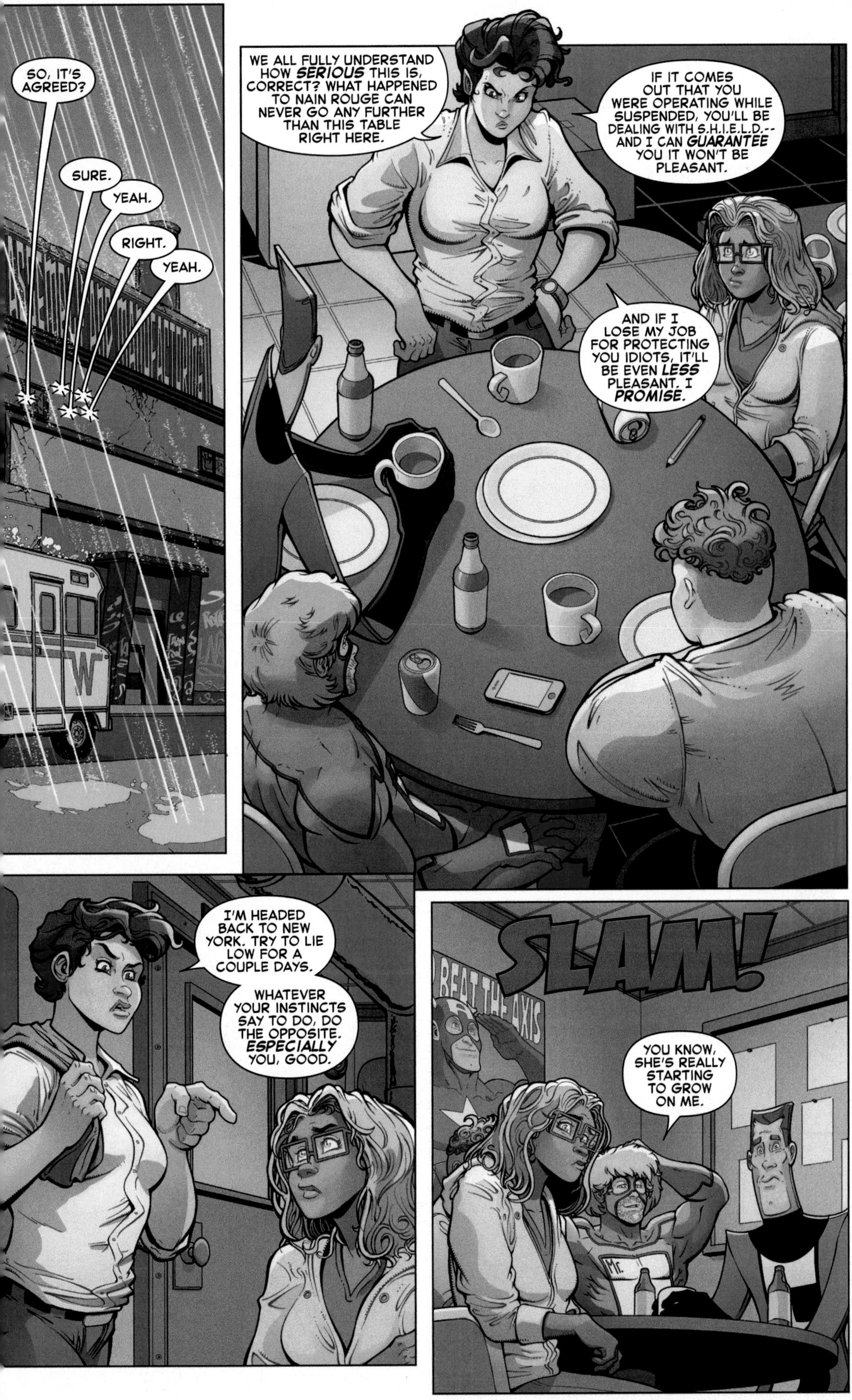
SO, IT'S AGREED?
SURE.
YEAH.
RIGHT.
YEAH.
WE ALL FULLY UNDERSTAND HOW SERIOUS THIS IS, CORRECT? WHAT HAPPENED TO NAIN ROUGE CAN NEVER GO ANY FURTHER THAN THIS TABLE RIGHT HERE.
IF IT COMES OUT THAT YOU WERE OPERATING WHILE SUSPENDED, YOU'LL BE DEALING WITH S.H.I.E.L.D.-- AND I CAN GUARANTEE YOU IT WON'T BE PLEASANT.
AND IF I LOSE MY JOB FOR PROTECTING YOU IDIOTS, IT'LL BE EVEN LESS PLEASANT. I PROMISE.
I'M HEADED BACK TO NEW YORK. TRY TO LIE LOW FOR A COUPLE DAYS.
WHATEVER YOUR INSTINCTS SAY TO DO, DO THE OPPOSITE. ESPECIALLY YOU, GOOD.
SLAM!
BEAT THE AXIS
YOU KNOW, SHE'S REALLY STARTING TO GROW ON ME.

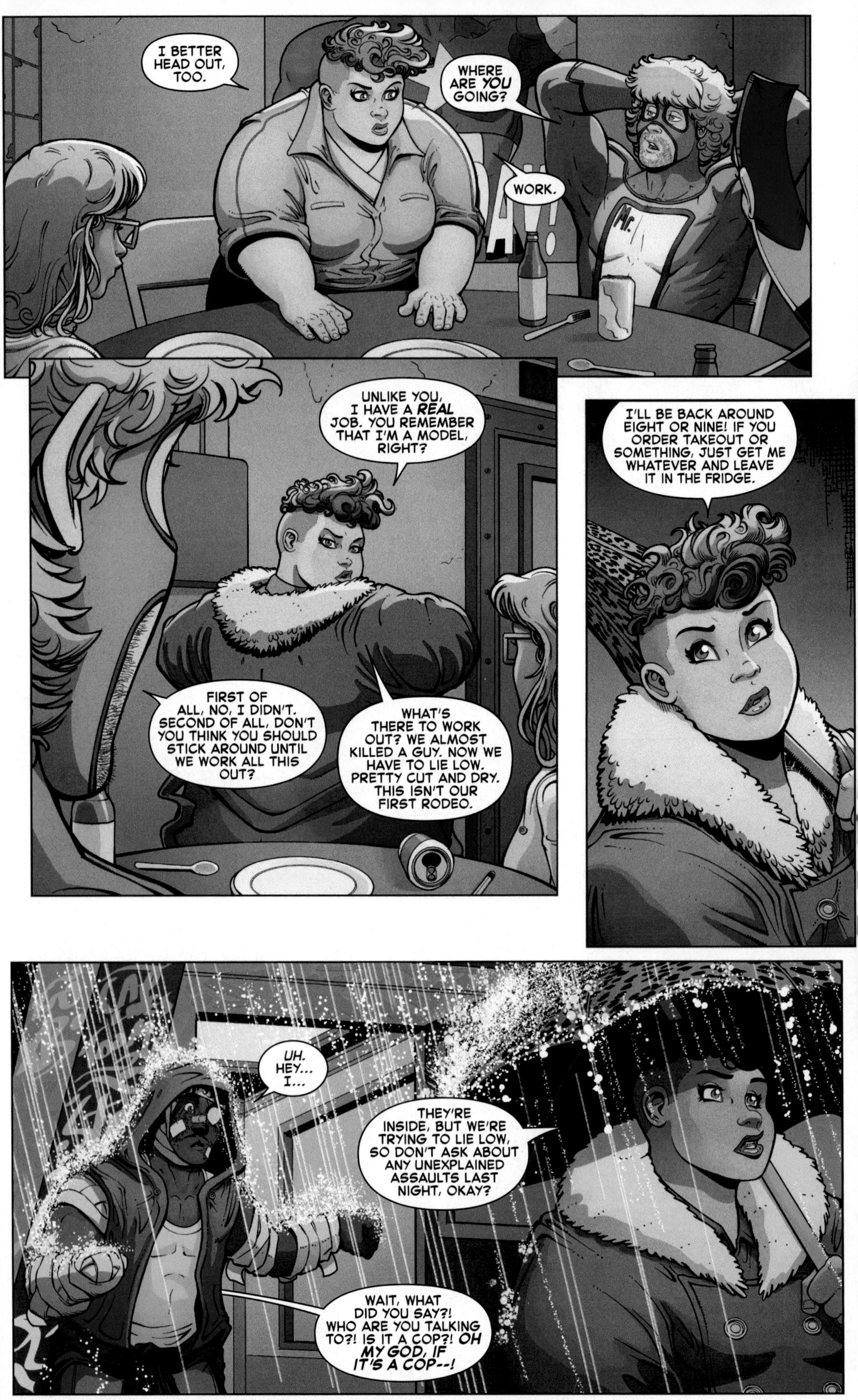
I BETTER HEAD OUT, TOO.
WHERE ARE *YOU* GOING?
WORK.
UNLIKE YOU, I HAVE A *REAL* JOB. YOU REMEMBER THAT I'M A MODEL, RIGHT?
FIRST OF ALL, NO, I DIDN'T. SECOND OF ALL, DON'T YOU THINK YOU SHOULD STICK AROUND UNTIL WE WORK ALL THIS OUT?
WHAT'S THERE TO WORK OUT? WE ALMOST KILLED A GUY. NOW WE HAVE TO LIE LOW. PRETTY CUT AND DRY. THIS ISN'T OUR FIRST RODEO.
I'LL BE BACK AROUND EIGHT OR NINE! IF YOU ORDER TAKEOUT OR SOMETHING, JUST GET ME WHATEVER AND LEAVE IT IN THE FRIDGE.
*UH. HEY... I...*
THEY'RE INSIDE, BUT WE'RE TRYING TO LIE LOW, SO DON'T ASK ABOUT ANY UNEXPLAINED ASSAULTS LAST NIGHT, OKAY?
WAIT, WHAT DID YOU SAY?! WHO ARE YOU TALKING TO?! IS IT A COP?! *OH MY GOD, IF IT'S A COP--!*

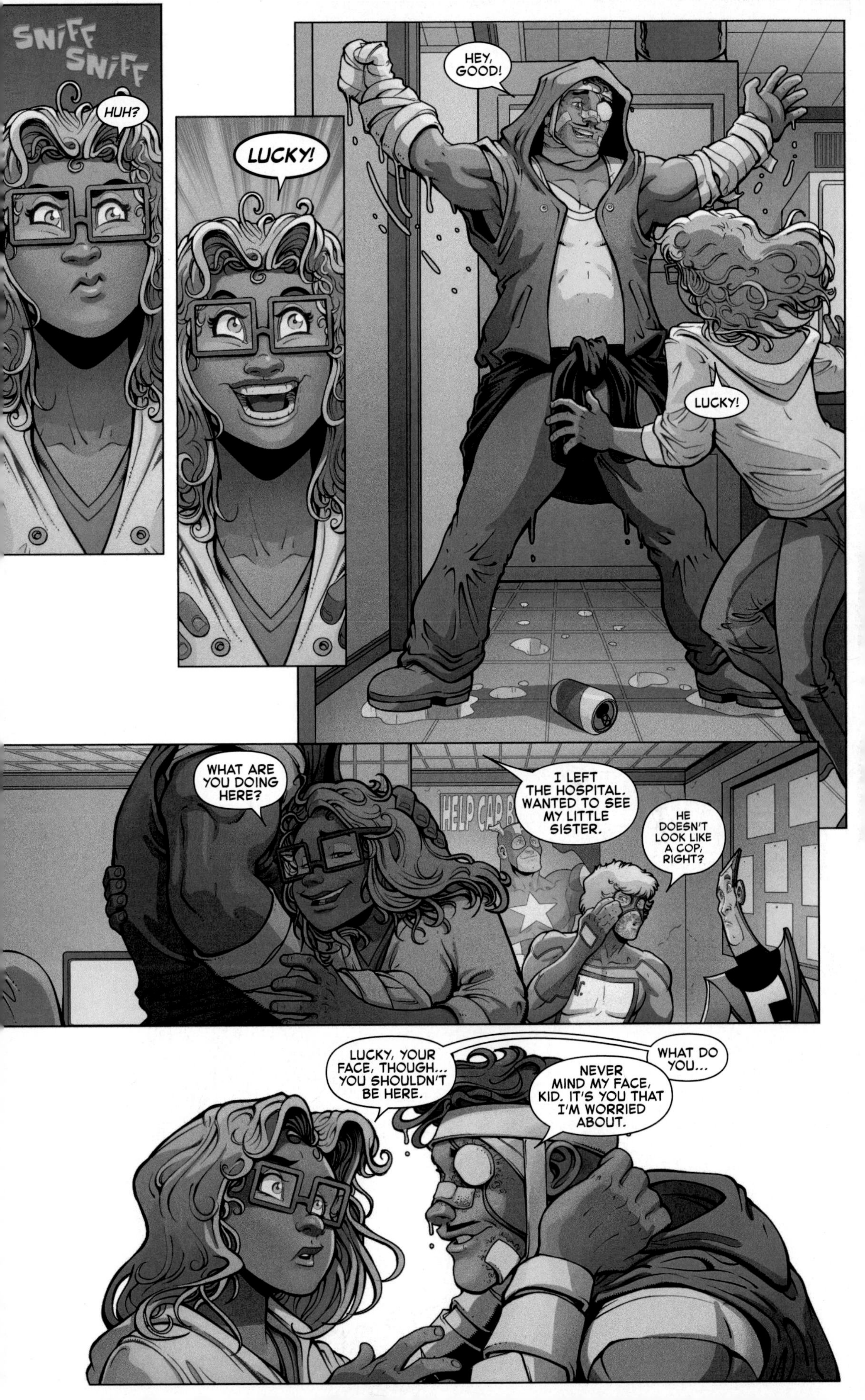
SNIFF SNIFF
HUH?
LUCKY!
HEY, GOOD!
LUCKY!
WHAT ARE YOU DOING HERE?
I LEFT THE HOSPITAL. WANTED TO SEE MY LITTLE SISTER.
HE DOESN'T LOOK LIKE A COP, RIGHT?
LUCKY, YOUR FACE, THOUGH... YOU SHOULDN'T BE HERE.
WHAT DO YOU...
NEVER MIND MY FACE, KID. IT'S YOU THAT I'M WORRIED ABOUT.

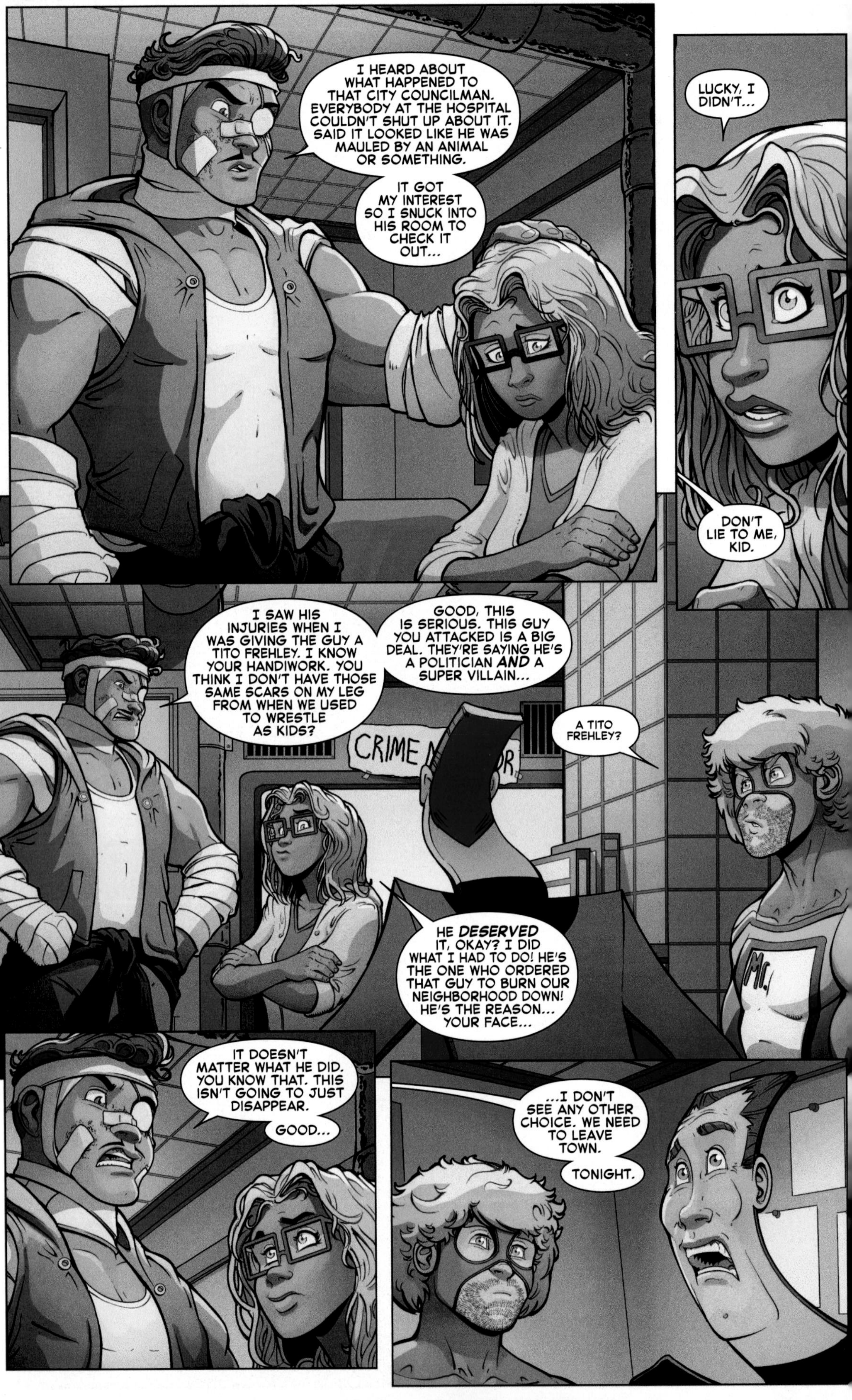
I HEARD ABOUT WHAT HAPPENED TO THAT CITY COUNCILMAN. EVERYBODY AT THE HOSPITAL COULDN'T SHUT UP ABOUT IT. SAID IT LOOKED LIKE HE WAS MAULED BY AN ANIMAL OR SOMETHING.
IT GOT MY INTEREST SO I SNUCK INTO HIS ROOM TO CHECK IT OUT...
LUCKY, I DIDN'T...
DON'T LIE TO ME, KID.
I SAW HIS INJURIES WHEN I WAS GIVING THE GUY A TITO FREHLEY. I KNOW YOUR HANDIWORK. YOU THINK I DON'T HAVE THOSE SAME SCARS ON MY LEG FROM WHEN WE USED TO WRESTLE AS KIDS?
GOOD, THIS IS SERIOUS. THIS GUY YOU ATTACKED IS A BIG DEAL. THEY'RE SAYING HE'S A POLITICIAN *AND* A SUPER VILLAIN...
A TITO FREHLEY?
HE *DESERVED* IT, OKAY? I DID WHAT I HAD TO DO! HE'S THE ONE WHO ORDERED THAT GUY TO BURN OUR NEIGHBORHOOD DOWN! HE'S THE REASON... YOUR FACE...
IT DOESN'T MATTER WHAT HE DID. YOU KNOW THAT. THIS ISN'T GOING TO JUST DISAPPEAR.
GOOD...
...I DON'T SEE ANY OTHER CHOICE. WE NEED TO LEAVE TOWN.
TONIGHT.

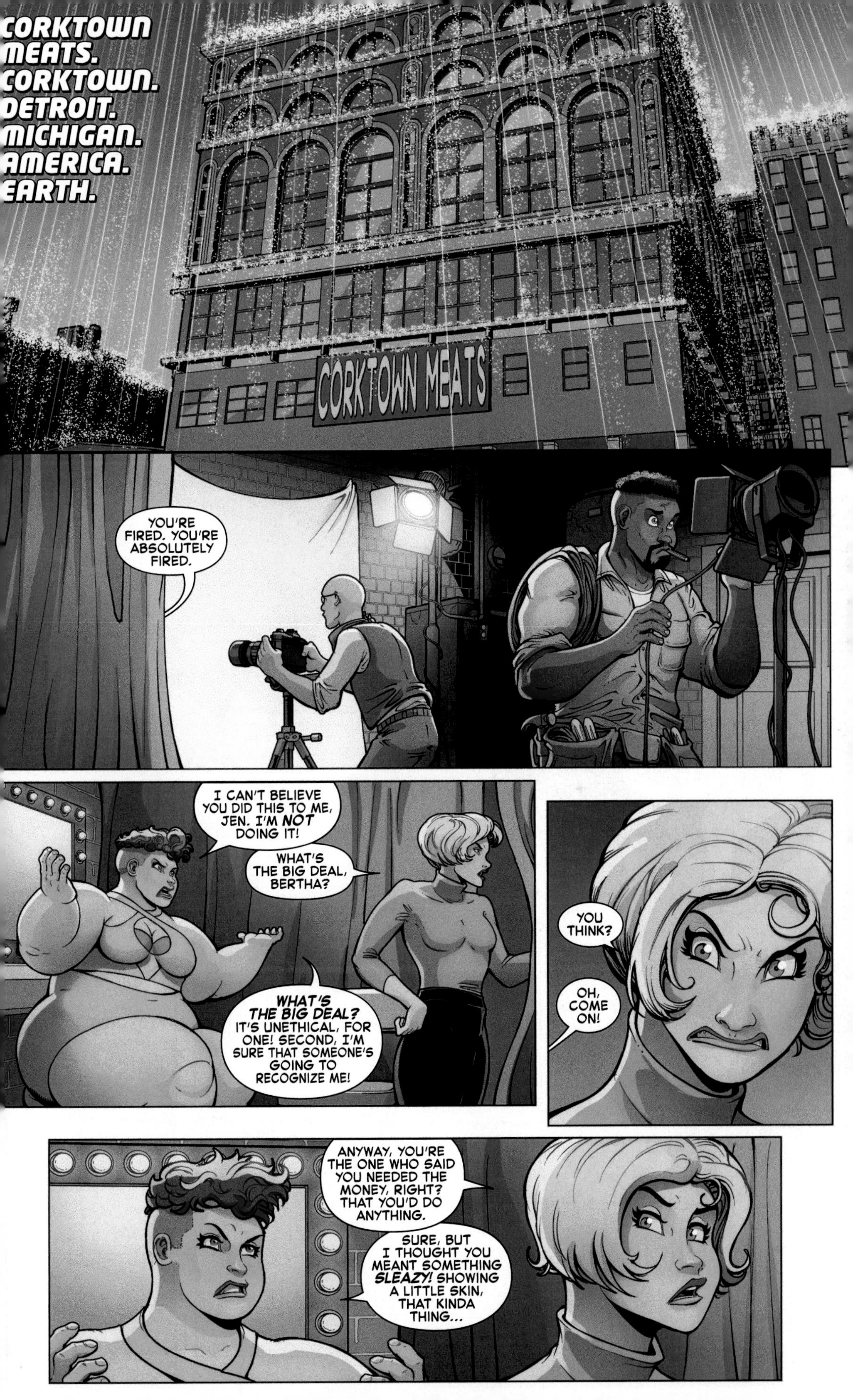
CORKTOWN MEATS. CORKTOWN. DETROIT. MICHIGAN. AMERICA. EARTH.
CORKTOWN MEATS
YOU'RE FIRED. YOU'RE ABSOLUTELY FIRED.
I CAN'T BELIEVE YOU DID THIS TO ME, JEN. I'M NOT DOING IT!
WHAT'S THE BIG DEAL, BERTHA?
WHAT'S THE BIG DEAL? IT'S UNETHICAL, FOR ONE! SECOND, I'M SURE THAT SOMEONE'S GOING TO RECOGNIZE ME!
YOU THINK?
OH, COME ON!
ANYWAY, YOU'RE THE ONE WHO SAID YOU NEEDED THE MONEY, RIGHT? THAT YOU'D DO ANYTHING.
SURE, BUT I THOUGHT YOU MEANT SOMETHING SLEAZY! SHOWING A LITTLE SKIN, THAT KINDA THING...

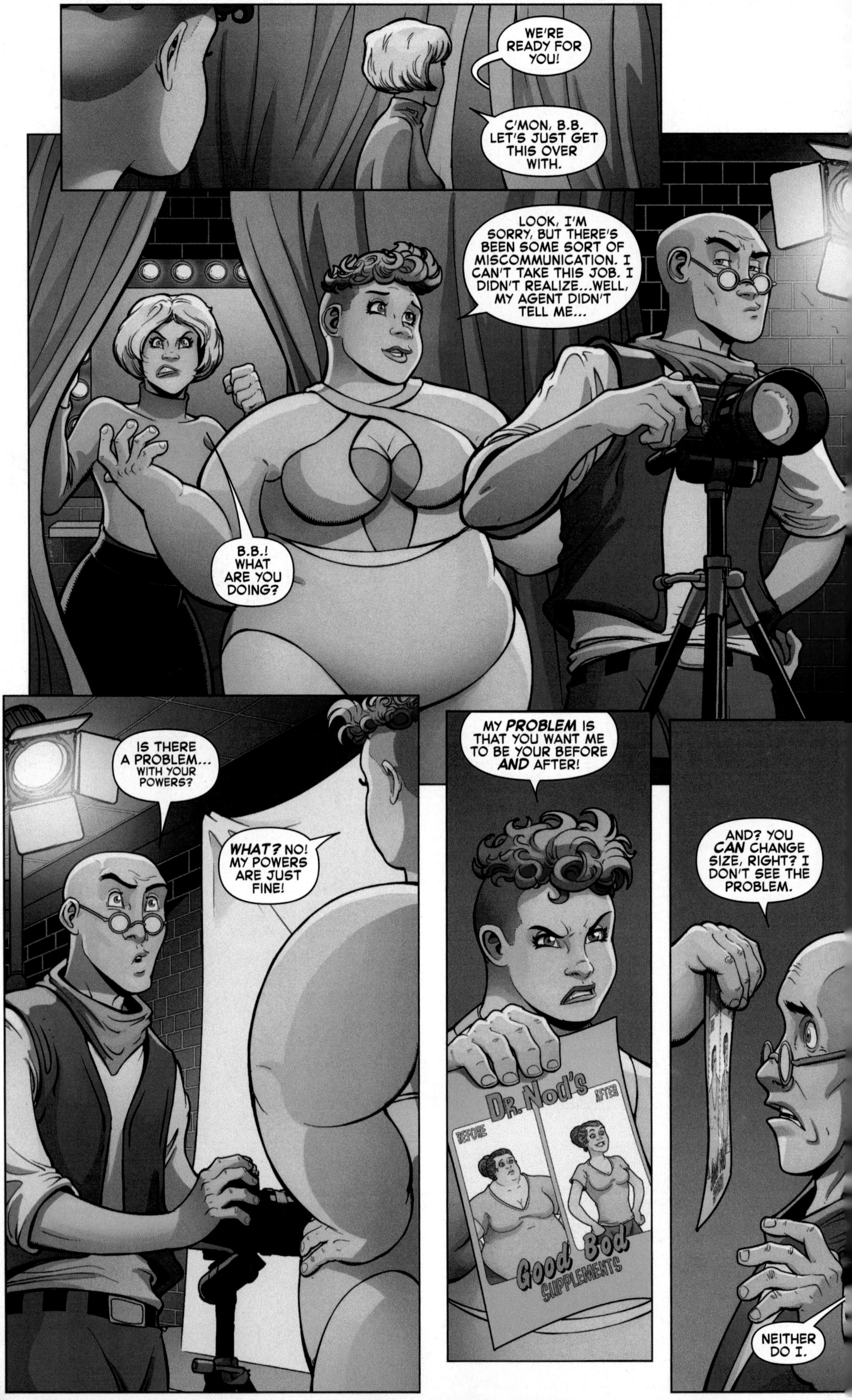

WE'RE READY FOR YOU!
C'MON, B.B. LET'S JUST GET THIS OVER WITH.
LOOK, I'M SORRY, BUT THERE'S BEEN SOME SORT OF MISCOMMUNICATION. I CAN'T TAKE THIS JOB. I DIDN'T REALIZE...WELL, MY AGENT DIDN'T TELL ME...
B.B.! WHAT ARE YOU DOING?
IS THERE A PROBLEM... WITH YOUR POWERS?
WHAT? NO! MY POWERS ARE JUST FINE!
MY PROBLEM IS THAT YOU WANT ME TO BE YOUR BEFORE AND AFTER!
DR. NOD'S
BEFORE
AFTER
GOOD BOD
SUPPLEMENTS
AND? YOU CAN CHANGE SIZE, RIGHT? I DON'T SEE THE PROBLEM.
NEITHER DO I.

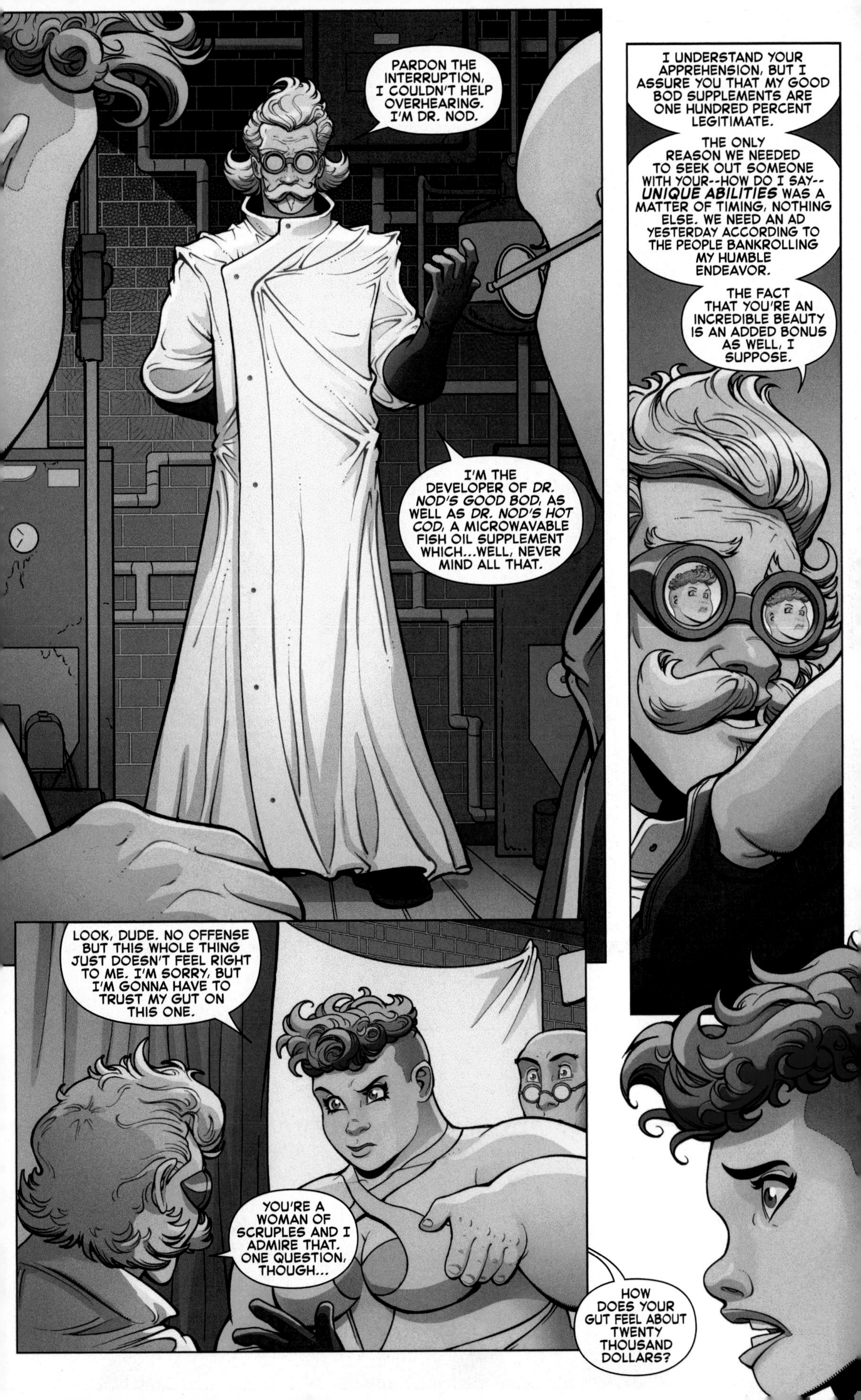
PARDON THE INTERRUPTION, I COULDN'T HELP OVERHEARING. I'M DR. NOD.
I'M THE DEVELOPER OF DR. NOD'S GOOD BOD, AS WELL AS DR. NOD'S HOT COD, A MICROWAVABLE FISH OIL SUPPLEMENT WHICH...WELL, NEVER MIND ALL THAT.
I UNDERSTAND YOUR APPREHENSION, BUT I ASSURE YOU THAT MY GOOD BOD SUPPLEMENTS ARE ONE HUNDRED PERCENT LEGITIMATE.
THE ONLY REASON WE NEEDED TO SEEK OUT SOMEONE WITH YOUR--HOW DO I SAY--UNIQUE ABILITIES WAS A MATTER OF TIMING, NOTHING ELSE. WE NEED AN AD YESTERDAY ACCORDING TO THE PEOPLE BANKROLLING MY HUMBLE ENDEAVOR.
THE FACT THAT YOU'RE AN INCREDIBLE BEAUTY IS AN ADDED BONUS AS WELL, I SUPPOSE.
LOOK, DUDE. NO OFFENSE BUT THIS WHOLE THING JUST DOESN'T FEEL RIGHT TO ME. I'M SORRY, BUT I'M GONNA HAVE TO TRUST MY GUT ON THIS ONE.
YOU'RE A WOMAN OF SCRUPLES AND I ADMIRE THAT. ONE QUESTION, THOUGH...
HOW DOES YOUR GUT FEEL ABOUT TWENTY THOUSAND DOLLARS?

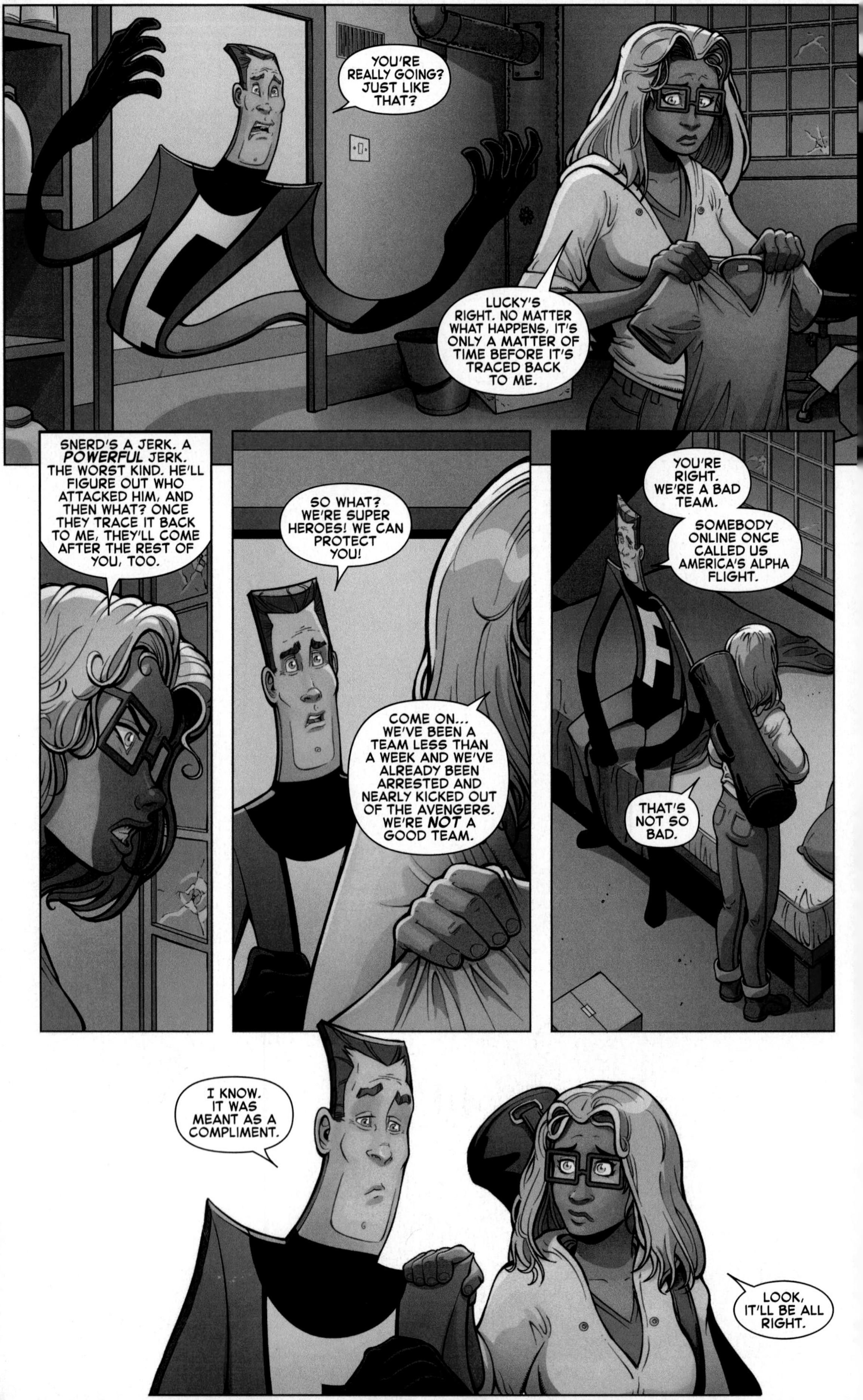
YOU'RE REALLY GOING? JUST LIKE THAT?
LUCKY'S RIGHT. NO MATTER WHAT HAPPENS, IT'S ONLY A MATTER OF TIME BEFORE IT'S TRACED BACK TO ME.
SNERD'S A JERK. A *POWERFUL* JERK. THE WORST KIND. HE'LL FIGURE OUT WHO ATTACKED HIM, AND THEN WHAT? ONCE THEY TRACE IT BACK TO ME, THEY'LL COME AFTER THE REST OF YOU, TOO.
SO WHAT? WE'RE SUPER HEROES! WE CAN PROTECT YOU!
COME ON... WE'VE BEEN A TEAM LESS THAN A WEEK AND WE'VE ALREADY BEEN ARRESTED AND NEARLY KICKED OUT OF THE AVENGERS. WE'RE *NOT* A GOOD TEAM.
YOU'RE RIGHT. WE'RE A BAD TEAM.
SOMEBODY ONLINE ONCE CALLED US AMERICA'S ALPHA FLIGHT.
THAT'S NOT SO BAD.
I KNOW. IT WAS MEANT AS A COMPLIMENT.
LOOK, IT'LL BE ALL RIGHT.

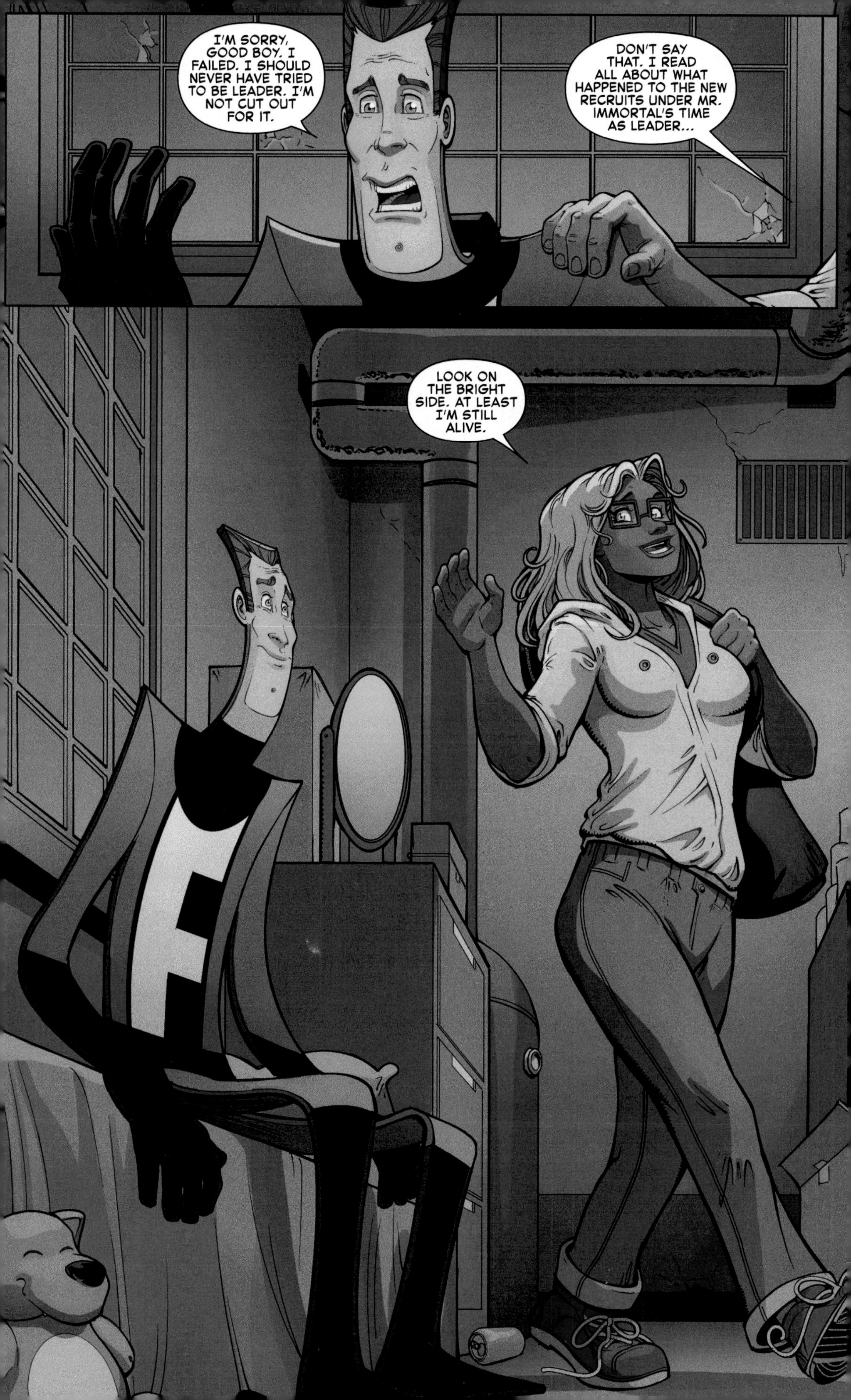
I'M SORRY, GOOD BOY. I FAILED. I SHOULD NEVER HAVE TRIED TO BE LEADER. I'M NOT CUT OUT FOR IT.
DON'T SAY THAT. I READ ALL ABOUT WHAT HAPPENED TO THE NEW RECRUITS UNDER MR. IMMORTAL'S TIME AS LEADER...
LOOK ON THE BRIGHT SIDE. AT LEAST I'M STILL ALIVE.

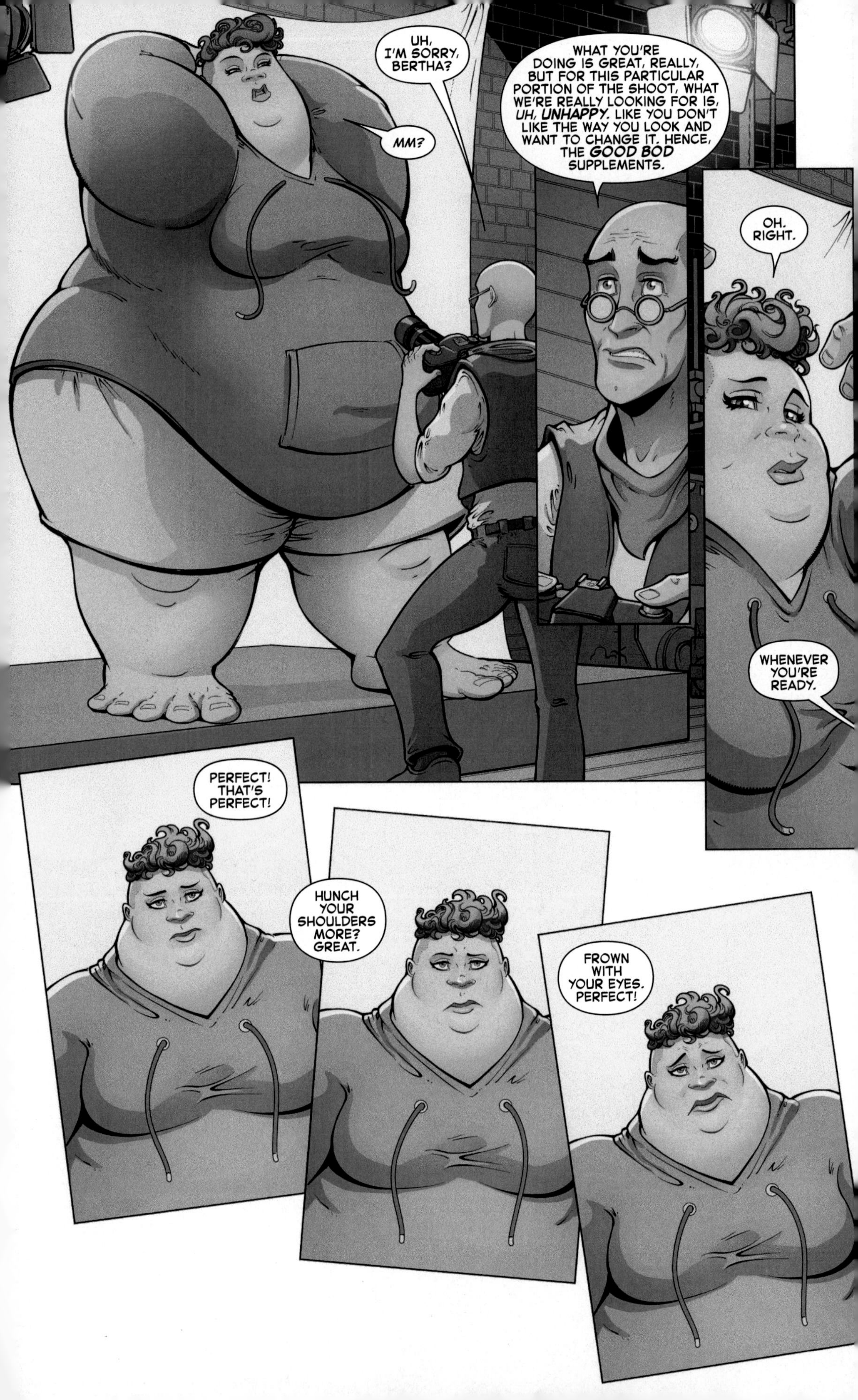
UH, I'M SORRY, BERTHA?
MM?
WHAT YOU'RE DOING IS GREAT, REALLY, BUT FOR THIS PARTICULAR PORTION OF THE SHOOT, WHAT WE'RE REALLY LOOKING FOR IS, *UH,* ***UNHAPPY.*** LIKE YOU DON'T LIKE THE WAY YOU LOOK AND WANT TO CHANGE IT. HENCE, THE ***GOOD BOD*** SUPPLEMENTS.
OH. RIGHT.
WHENEVER YOU'RE READY.
PERFECT! THAT'S PERFECT!
HUNCH YOUR SHOULDERS MORE? GREAT.
FROWN WITH YOUR EYES. PERFECT!

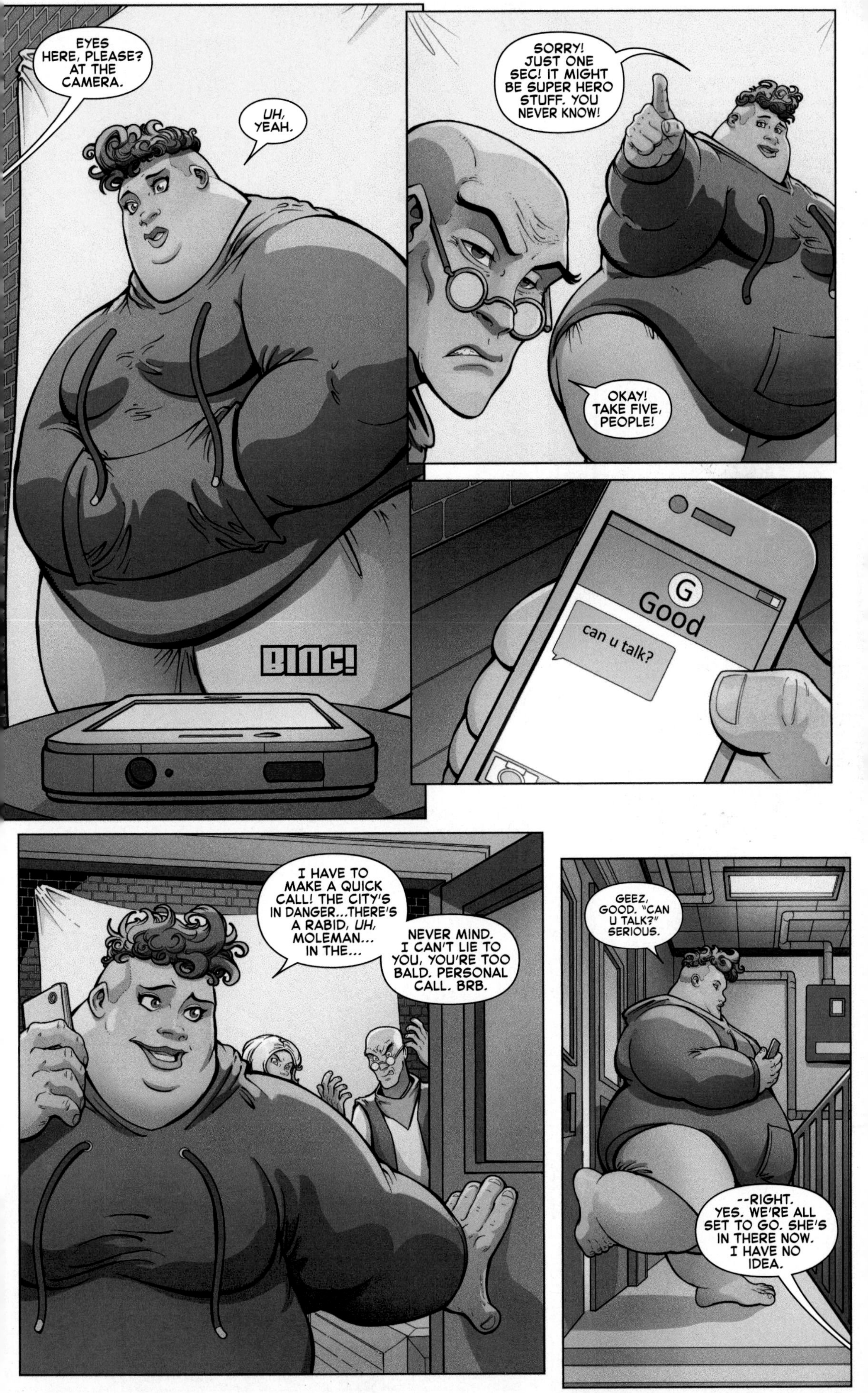
EYES HERE, PLEASE? AT THE CAMERA.
UH, YEAH.
SORRY! JUST ONE SEC! IT MIGHT BE SUPER HERO STUFF. YOU NEVER KNOW!
OKAY! TAKE FIVE, PEOPLE!
BING!
G
Good
can u talk?
I HAVE TO MAKE A QUICK CALL! THE CITY'S IN DANGER...THERE'S A RABID, UH, MOLEMAN... IN THE...
NEVER MIND. I CAN'T LIE TO YOU, YOU'RE TOO BALD. PERSONAL CALL. BRB.
GEEZ, GOOD. "CAN U TALK?" SERIOUS.
--RIGHT. YES. WE'RE ALL SET TO GO. SHE'S IN THERE NOW. I HAVE NO IDEA.

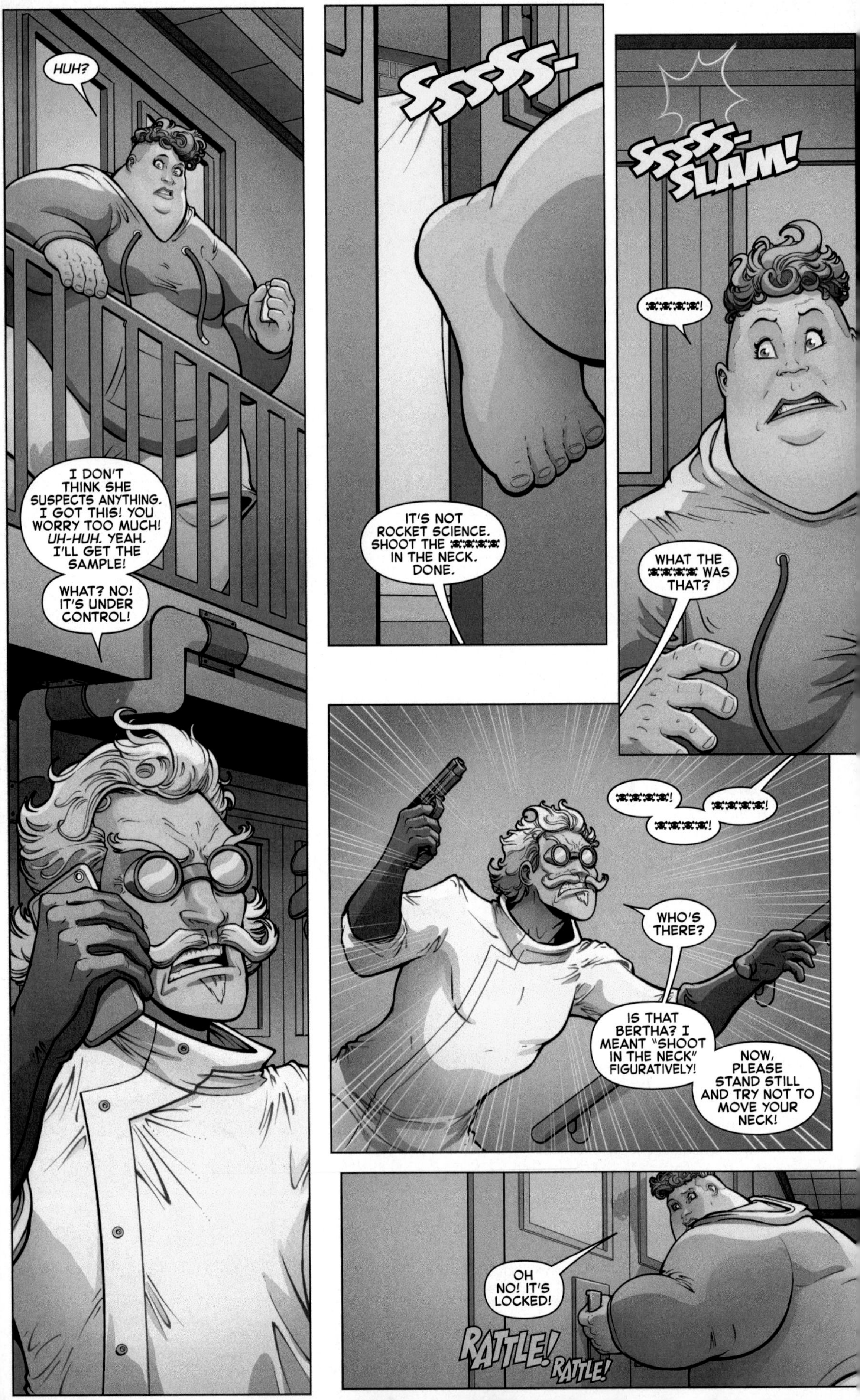
HUH?
I DON'T THINK SHE SUSPECTS ANYTHING. I GOT THIS! YOU WORRY TOO MUCH! *UH-HUH.* YEAH. I'LL GET THE SAMPLE!
WHAT? NO! IT'S UNDER CONTROL!
SSSSS-
IT'S NOT ROCKET SCIENCE. SHOOT THE IN THE NECK. DONE.
SSSSS-SLAM!
WHAT THE WAS THAT?
WHO'S THERE?
IS THAT BERTHA? I MEANT "SHOOT IN THE NECK" FIGURATIVELY!
NOW, PLEASE STAND STILL AND TRY NOT TO MOVE YOUR NECK!
OH NO! IT'S LOCKED!
RATTLE! RATTLE!

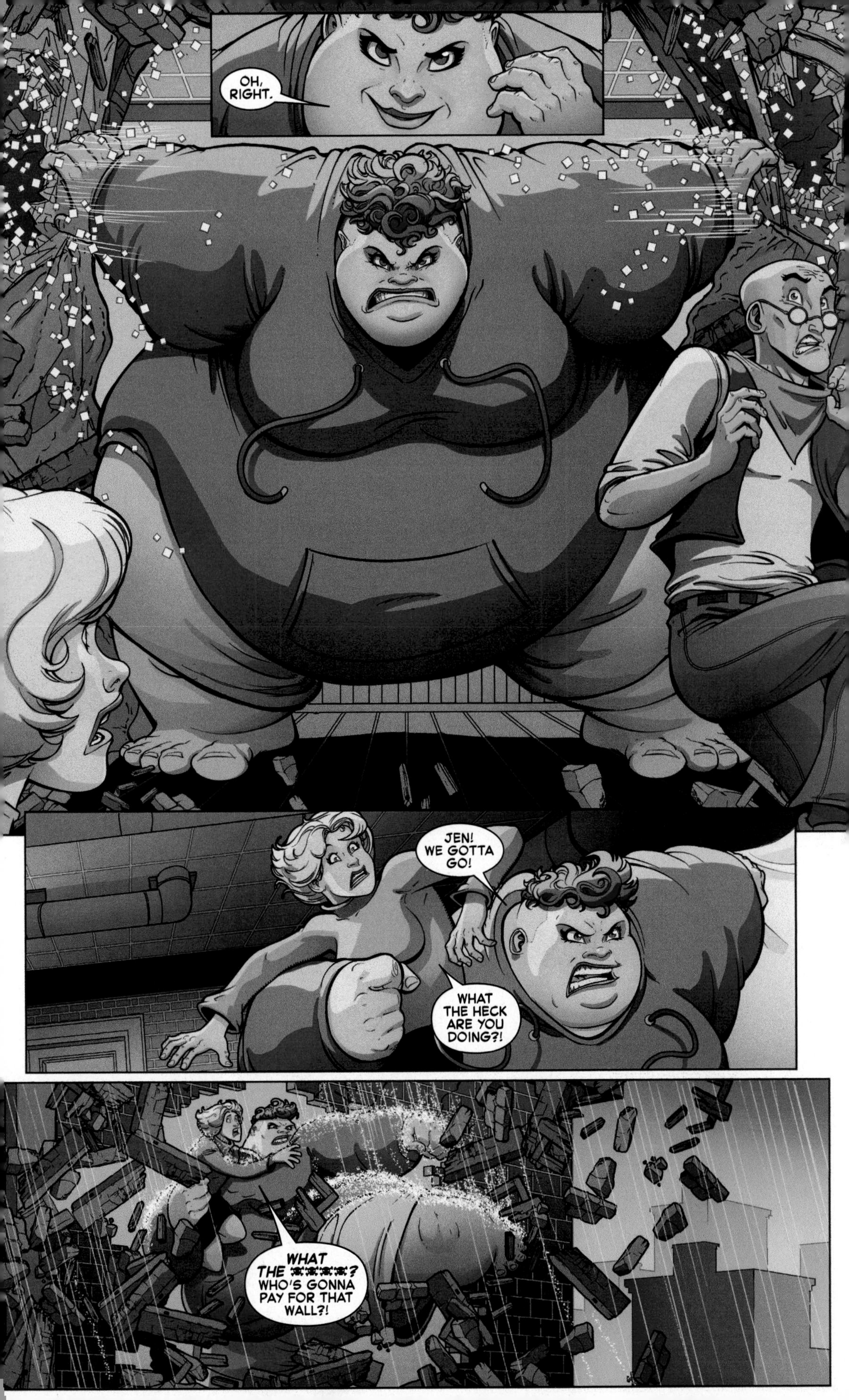
OH, RIGHT.
JEN! WE GOTTA GO!
WHAT THE HECK ARE YOU DOING?!
WHAT THE ✹✹✹✹? WHO'S GONNA PAY FOR THAT WALL?!

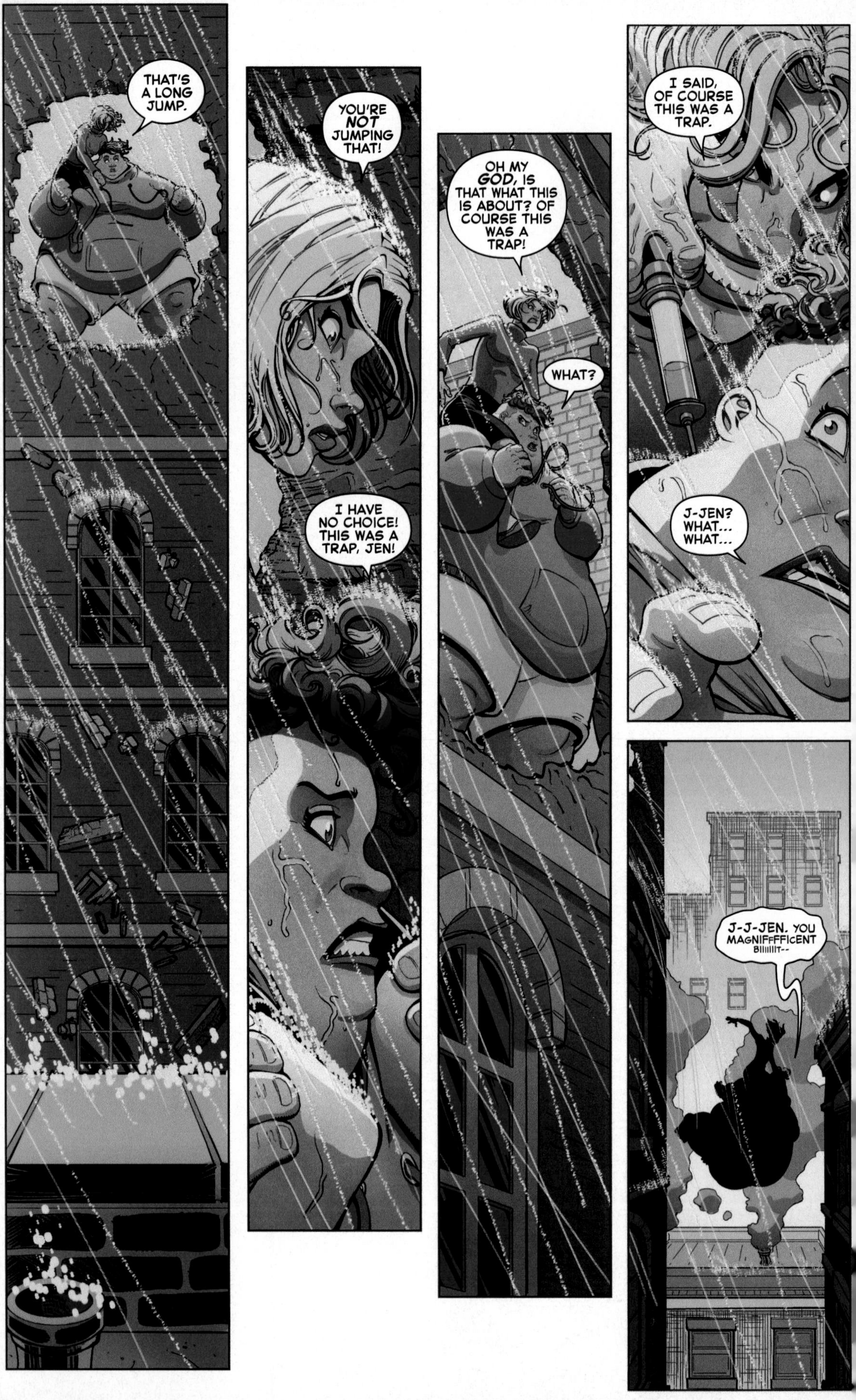
THAT'S A LONG JUMP.
YOU'RE NOT JUMPING THAT!
I HAVE NO CHOICE! THIS WAS A TRAP, JEN!
OH MY GOD, IS THAT WHAT THIS IS ABOUT? OF COURSE THIS WAS A TRAP!
WHAT?
I SAID, OF COURSE THIS WAS A TRAP.
J-JEN? WHAT... WHAT...
J-J-JEN. YOU MAGNIFFFFICENT BIIIIIIT--

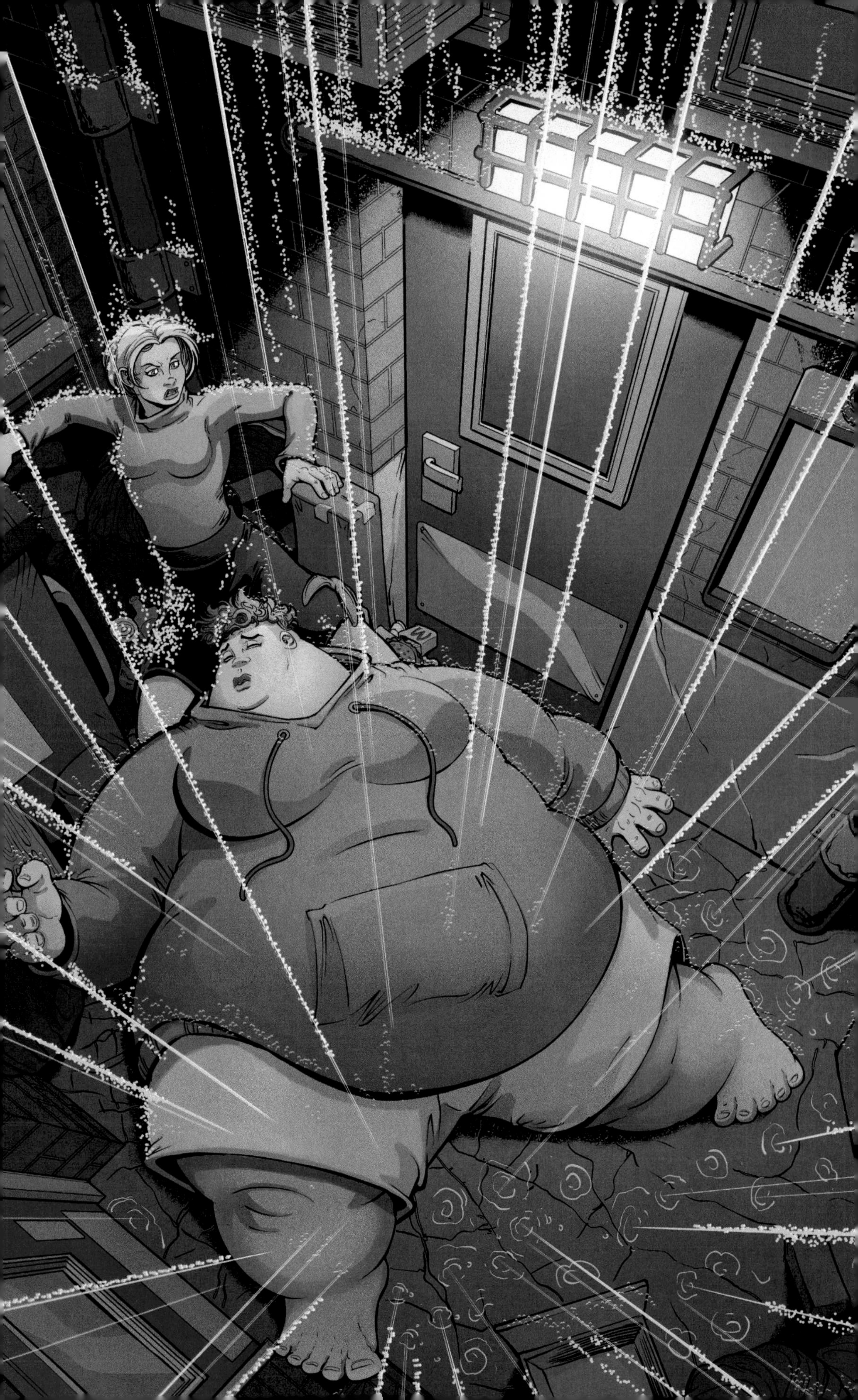

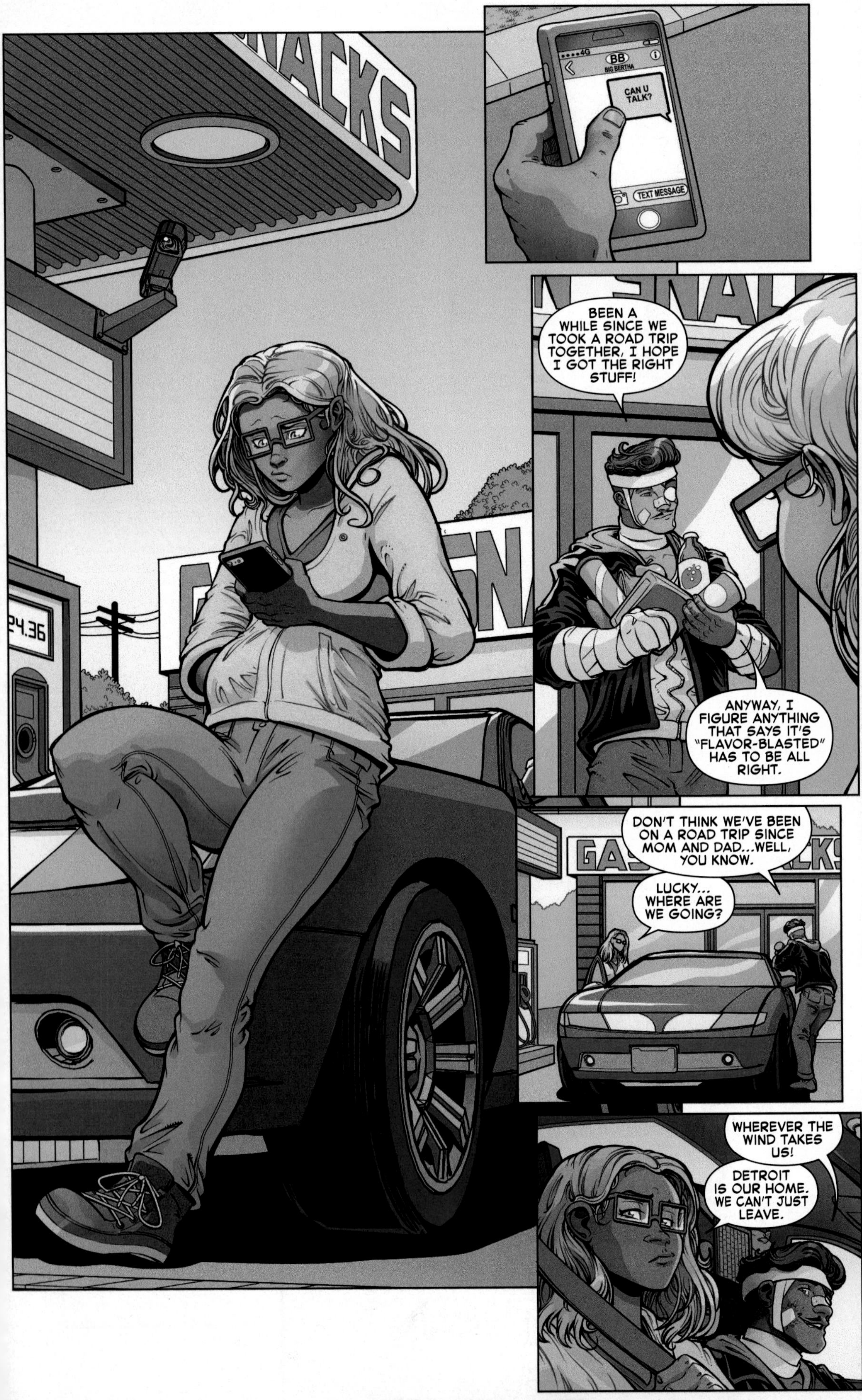

BB
BIG BERTHA
CAN U TALK?
TEXT MESSAGE
BEEN A WHILE SINCE WE TOOK A ROAD TRIP TOGETHER, I HOPE I GOT THE RIGHT STUFF!
ANYWAY, I FIGURE ANYTHING THAT SAYS IT'S "FLAVOR-BLASTED" HAS TO BE ALL RIGHT.
DON'T THINK WE'VE BEEN ON A ROAD TRIP SINCE MOM AND DAD...WELL, YOU KNOW.
LUCKY... WHERE ARE WE GOING?
WHEREVER THE WIND TAKES US!
DETROIT IS OUR HOME. WE CAN'T JUST LEAVE.

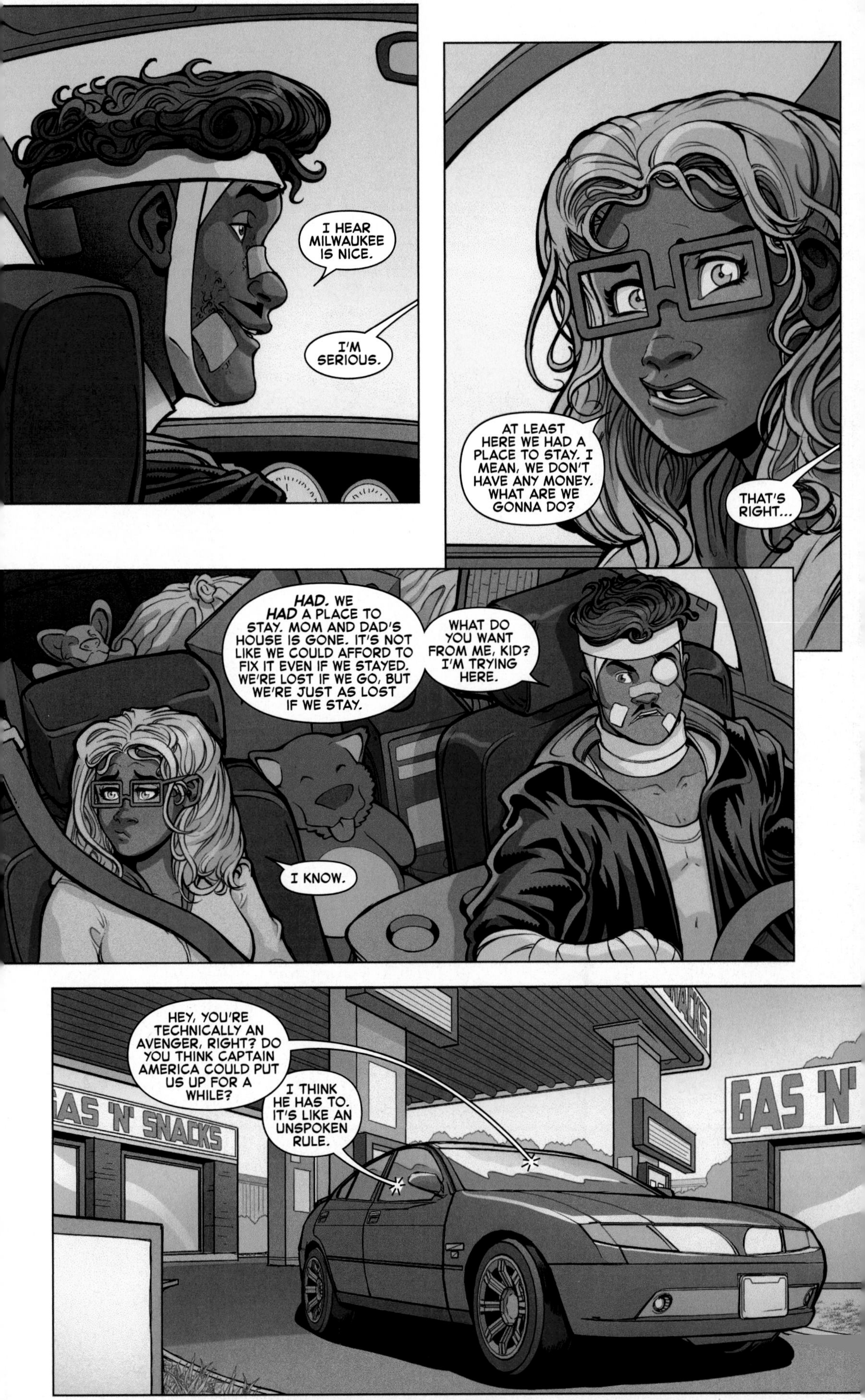
I HEAR MILWAUKEE IS NICE.
I'M SERIOUS.
AT LEAST HERE WE HAD A PLACE TO STAY. I MEAN, WE DON'T HAVE ANY MONEY. WHAT ARE WE GONNA DO?
THAT'S RIGHT...
*HAD.* WE *HAD* A PLACE TO STAY. MOM AND DAD'S HOUSE IS GONE. IT'S NOT LIKE WE COULD AFFORD TO FIX IT EVEN IF WE STAYED. WE'RE LOST IF WE GO, BUT WE'RE JUST AS LOST IF WE STAY.
WHAT DO YOU WANT FROM ME, KID? I'M TRYING HERE.
I KNOW.
HEY, YOU'RE TECHNICALLY AN AVENGER, RIGHT? DO YOU THINK CAPTAIN AMERICA COULD PUT US UP FOR A WHILE?
I THINK HE HAS TO. IT'S LIKE AN UNSPOKEN RULE.
GAS 'N' SNACKS
SNACKS
GAS 'N'

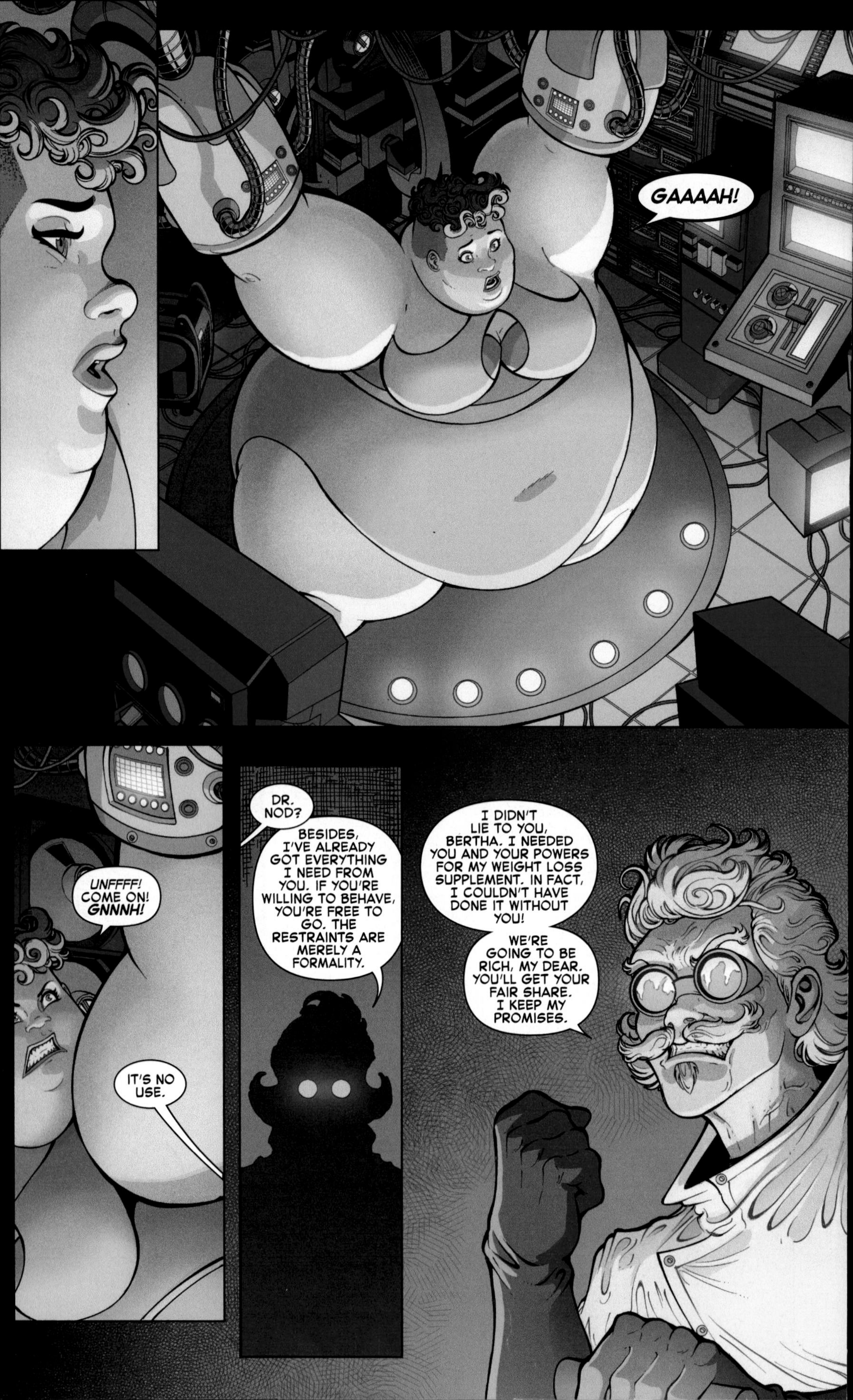
GAAAAH!
UNFFFF! COME ON! GNNNH!
IT'S NO USE.
DR. NOD?
BESIDES, I'VE ALREADY GOT EVERYTHING I NEED FROM YOU. IF YOU'RE WILLING TO BEHAVE, YOU'RE FREE TO GO. THE RESTRAINTS ARE MERELY A FORMALITY.
I DIDN'T LIE TO YOU, BERTHA. I NEEDED YOU AND YOUR POWERS FOR MY WEIGHT LOSS SUPPLEMENT. IN FACT, I COULDN'T HAVE DONE IT WITHOUT YOU!
WE'RE GOING TO BE RICH, MY DEAR. YOU'LL GET YOUR FAIR SHARE. I KEEP MY PROMISES.

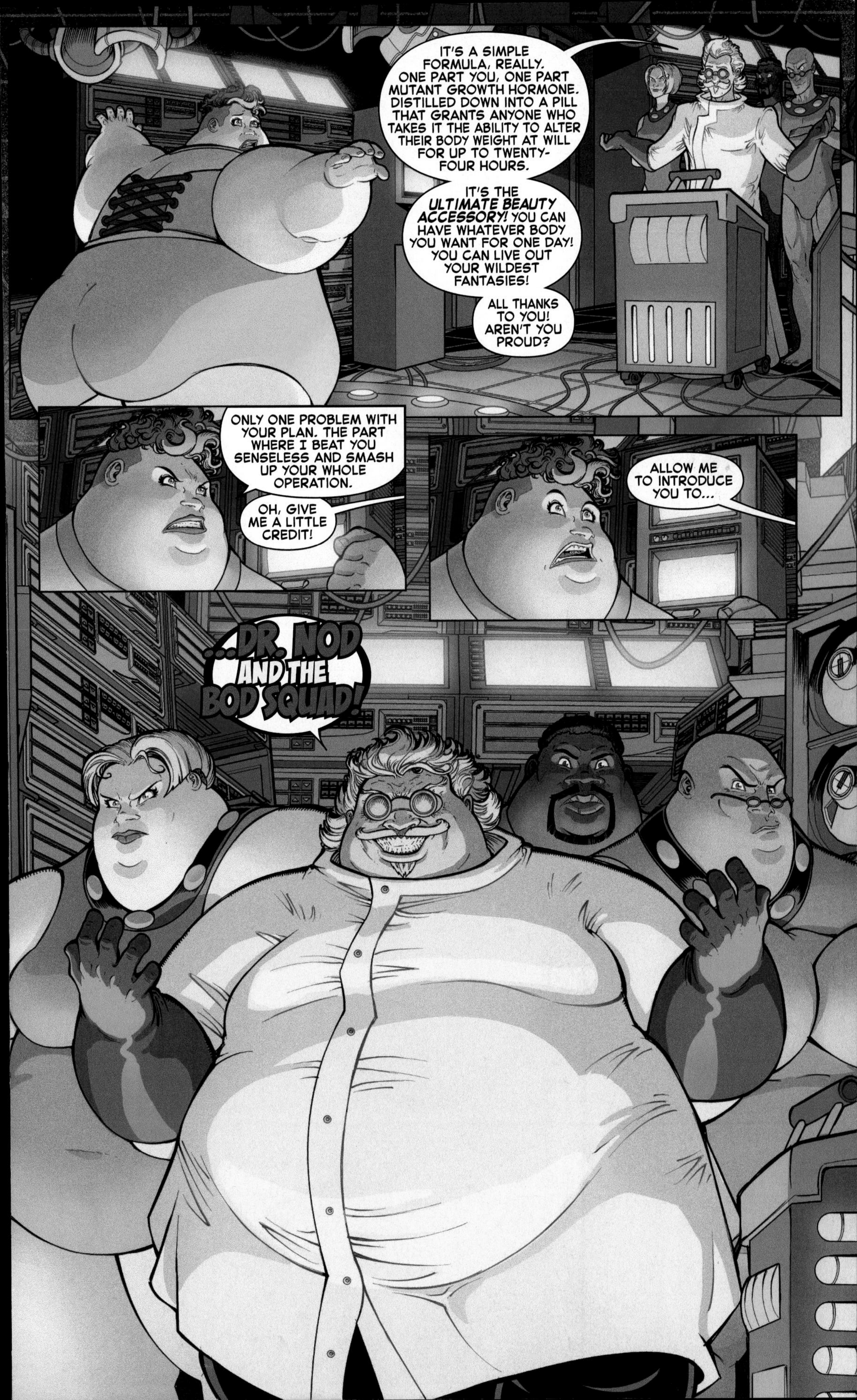
IT'S A SIMPLE FORMULA, REALLY. ONE PART YOU, ONE PART MUTANT GROWTH HORMONE. DISTILLED DOWN INTO A PILL THAT GRANTS ANYONE WHO TAKES IT THE ABILITY TO ALTER THEIR BODY WEIGHT AT WILL FOR UP TO TWENTY-FOUR HOURS.
IT'S THE ULTIMATE BEAUTY ACCESSORY! YOU CAN HAVE WHATEVER BODY YOU WANT FOR ONE DAY! YOU CAN LIVE OUT YOUR WILDEST FANTASIES!
ALL THANKS TO YOU! AREN'T YOU PROUD?
ONLY ONE PROBLEM WITH YOUR PLAN. THE PART WHERE I BEAT YOU SENSELESS AND SMASH UP YOUR WHOLE OPERATION.
OH, GIVE ME A LITTLE CREDIT!
ALLOW ME TO INTRODUCE YOU TO...
...DR. NOD AND THE BOD SQUAD!

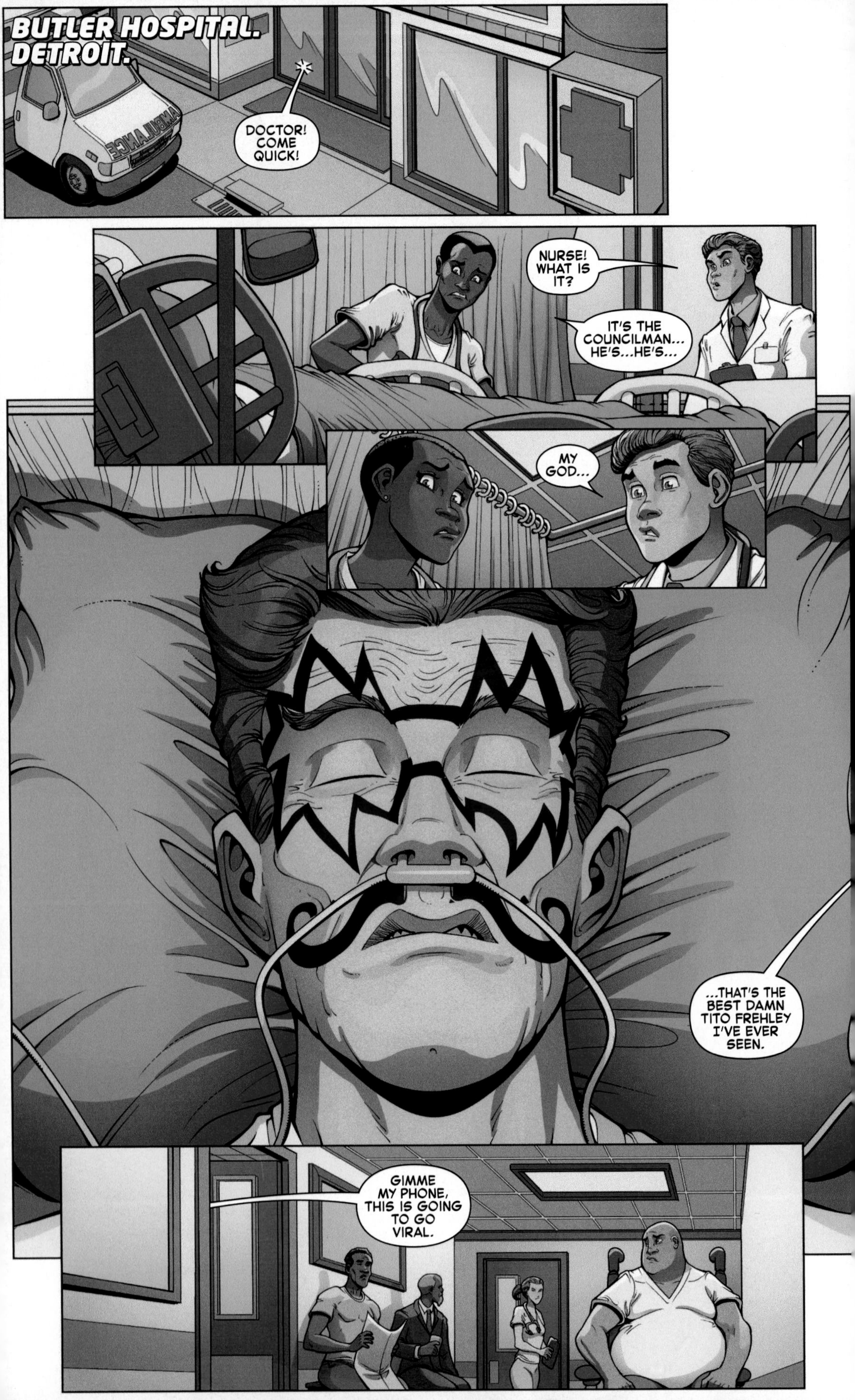
BUTLER HOSPITAL. DETROIT.
DOCTOR! COME QUICK!
NURSE! WHAT IS IT?
IT'S THE COUNCILMAN... HE'S...HE'S...
MY GOD...
...THAT'S THE BEST DAMN TITO FREHLEY I'VE EVER SEEN.
GIMME MY PHONE, THIS IS GOING TO GO VIRAL.

# The Great Lakes Avengers

Send letters to
MHEROES@MARVEL.COM
marked "Okay to Print"!

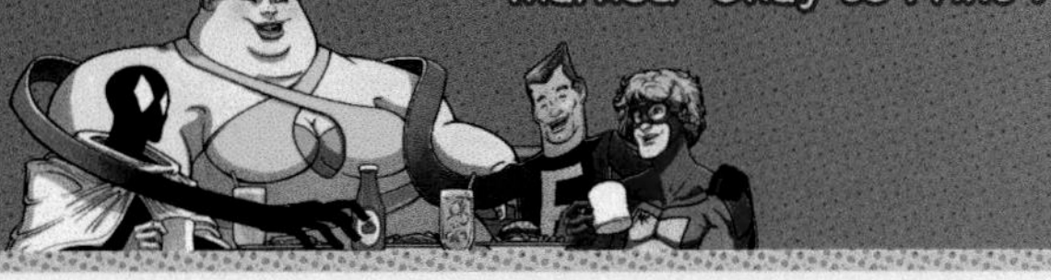

Okay, okay, we said we'd take anyone, but it turns out our writer and Great Lakes Avengers hiring director Zac Gorman is...a bit of a picky-pants? So we're still looking for new members! Let's see who we've got this week!

---

Dear Mr. Gorman,

Hello! I'm writing to express my interest in a continually open position as a member of the Great Lakes Avengers. I believe my very okay powers and access to a reliable, fuel-efficient vehicle make me an excellent recruit!

First, I'd like to highlight my power. I did not get my power from some freak accident in a laboratory, nor was I zapped by cosmic rays. Rather, I was born with the amazing ability to never get headaches! This fact usually agitates my human friends, but would be a great asset to the GLA, especially if they tangle with a villain with mental powers. It would also come in handy when answering phones or speaking at press conferences.

Secondly, I believe another land vehicle would be a great asset to the GLA. My Pontiac Vibe (which I'd rename "Advil") would be another tool to help the GLA fight crime. Currently, I'm one state below HQ, but close to the highway, so getting to Detroit wouldn't be a problem. Or I could run a regional office that sends cases to the GLA? The possibilities are endless!

Thank you for your consideration for this highly prestigious, cannon-fodder position in the Great Lakes Avengers!

Sincerely,
Nate Logan

**I suppose it's possible to have a superpower that prevents headaches, Nate, but I'd like to take a moment to consider another possibility. What if you've ALWAYS had a headache? Perhaps you've had a headache so long that having a headache has become your default state!**

**Speaking of states, "one state below" can mean one of two things when referring to Michigan: Indiana or Ohio. I'm not going to say which one, but residency in one of those states immediately disqualifies you for membership in the Great Lakes Avengers. Sorry, but it's not up to me. It's in the bylaws.**

Good day, Zac. I would like to toss my idiomatic hat into the ring (not my real one--I've lost too many good hats that way) in an attempt to bolster the ranks of the GLA. Among my numerous, but un-astounding, super-powers are the following:

1. Needless sesquipedalianism. This power to overuse long words demonstrates itself.

2. Information absorption. As a trivia junkie, it has come in handy in the past but in recent years it seems to work best with comic books and animation.

3. Pattern recognition, especially regarding odd typographical errors. For example, on the letters page of GLA #4, there were three instances where the letter pattern "fi" was mysteriously blanked out. What made this more odd is that they were not the only occurrences of that letter pattern. That's when I noticed that the 3rd, 7th and 11th occurrences of this pattern were the missing ones. After doing some research, I found a 7-11 just off the M-3 in Cadillac Square, which must be where the team gets their coffee.

If admitted to the team, I could be called The Insufferable Prat if it won't get me confused with Reed Richards.

Regards,
Ray Davis

**I appreciate you're letter, Ray, but it's important too remember that random typos are just that..completely random. Cloes the spy books. Maybe take a vacation. They're are better things to do with your time than comnig up with nonsense theories!**

Hello, I am here to tell you about my powers and name to, of course, join the Great Lakes Avengers. I am known as Dr. Boi. My name has absolutely nothing to do with my powers. At all. My power is to make any conversation awkward. Yes, it is VERY powerful. The GLA could use an asset like me. My powers do not stop there; in fact, they get better. I have my own spider-sense. I get a very bad migraine and a mini anxiety attack when there is a conversation that needs "awkwardation." But not only that, I can remember things from years back that don't AT ALL matter. Like, for instance, "I put my pencil in a cabinet!" But I can't remember names. That is the amazing extent of my amazing powers. Amazing, right?

With all goofs, jokes and memes aside, I really like your comics. I'm from Michigan and I was so happy you made it take place in Detroit, and I'm glad you brought back Mr. Immortal. He is my favorite. Thank you, and have a great day.

Malachi Blades
Lyon Township, MI

**Dear Malachi "Dr. Boi" Blades,**

**Dr. Boi is a fine super hero name, but have you considered "Malachi Blades"? Or maybe that's the whole problem! With a name like Malachi Blades, it's fair to assume that everyone you meet suspects you of being an elite assassin. It's no surprise that people feel awkward when they think you might backflip through a window onto a speeding motorcycle at any moment! As far as your spotty memory goes, I assume that's probably a byproduct of the brainwashing that happened when you went through assassin school. It's probably normal.**

**Thank you for your letter, Malachi!**

Dear Great Lakes Avengers,

My name is Sormo, a name I masterfully shortened from "sore mouth"--which is an unfortunate side effect of my superpower. My power itself is that my teeth grow and shrink randomly and at their own will. Although this power only causes me pain, I've been thinking recently that if I were to bite someone, it may be a useful power in a fight. Please give me a chance to join your team--I have below-average fitness and am very comfortable wearing spandex! Side note: Could you recommend a good dentist in Detroit?

Charlie Cooke,
Brisbane, Australia

**Dear Charlie "Sormo" Cooke,**

**I've got bad news and worse news. The bad news is that I'm afraid our roster doesn't have a slot right now for someone whose teeth grow and shrink randomly. The worse news is that I now have a new, horrific nightmare that will assuredly wake me up from sleep in the middle of the night, a cold flop sweat on my forehead, as I clutch desperately at my teeth to make sure they're still there and of a normal size.**

**Zac**

---

**Do you have a painfully mundane talent that qualifies you to be a member of the Great Lakes Avengers? If so, ~~dang, use it to do some good...why are you here, even?~~ send us your application! We will even take people who can just make beds real nice. That's an important life skill!**

---

## NEXT:

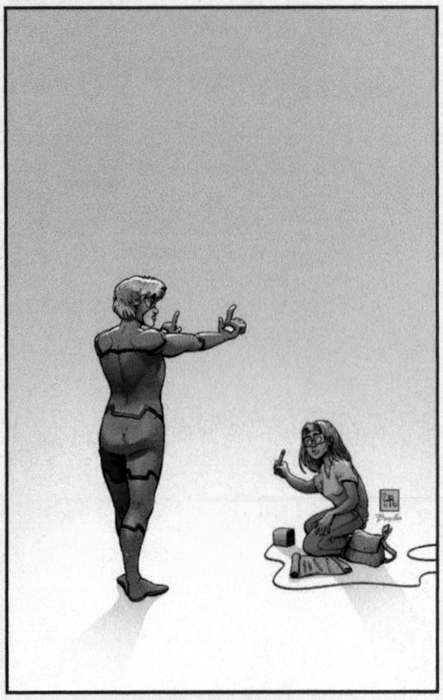

## REVENGE OF THE BOD

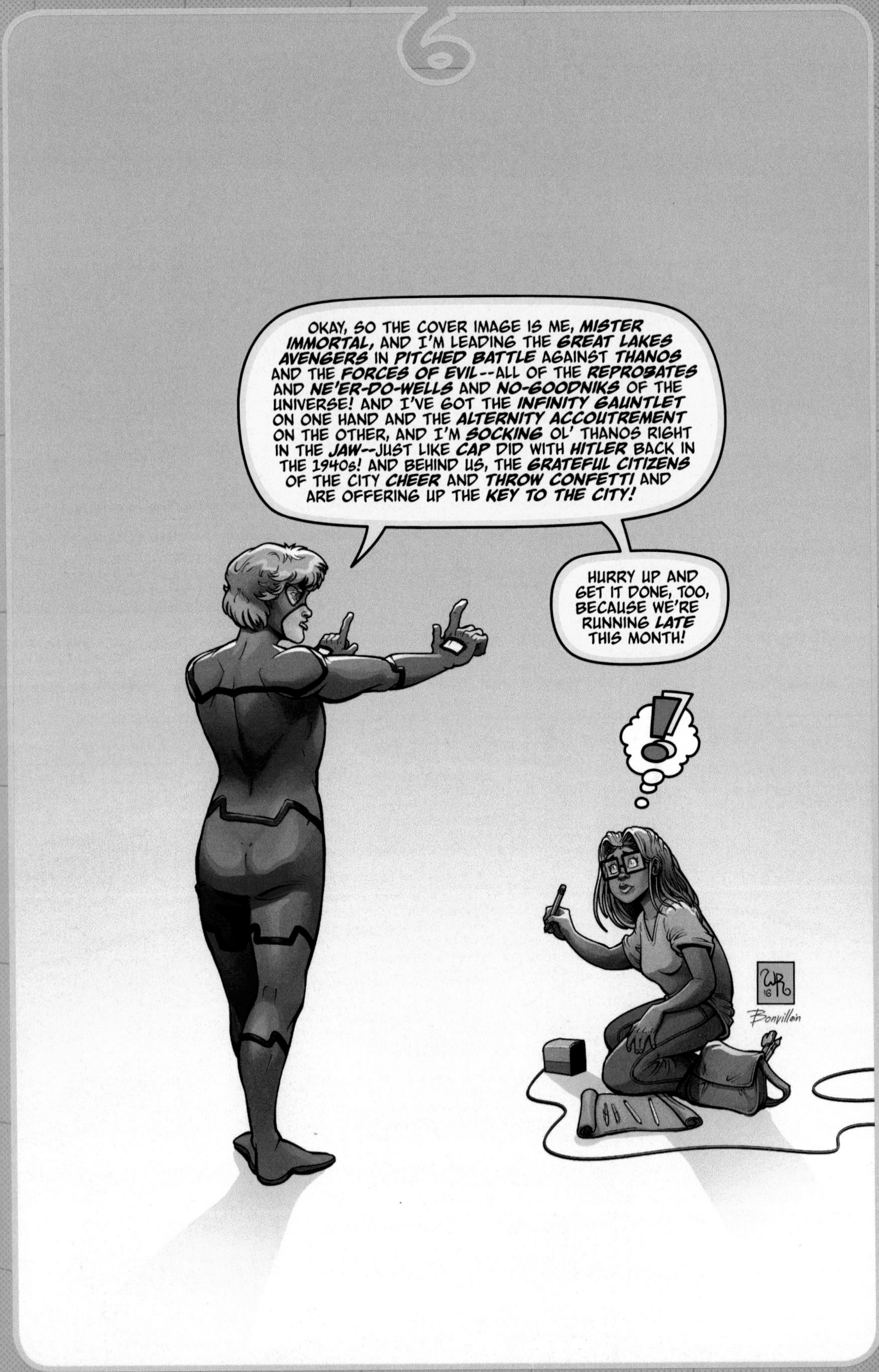

OKAY, SO THE COVER IMAGE IS ME, MISTER IMMORTAL, AND I'M LEADING THE GREAT LAKES AVENGERS IN PITCHED BATTLE AGAINST THANOS AND THE FORCES OF EVIL--ALL OF THE REPROBATES AND NE'ER-DO-WELLS AND NO-GOODNIKS OF THE UNIVERSE! AND I'VE GOT THE INFINITY GAUNTLET ON ONE HAND AND THE ALTERNITY ACCOUTREMENT ON THE OTHER, AND I'M SOCKING OL' THANOS RIGHT IN THE JAW--JUST LIKE CAP DID WITH HITLER BACK IN THE 1940s! AND BEHIND US, THE GRATEFUL CITIZENS OF THE CITY CHEER AND THROW CONFETTI AND ARE OFFERING UP THE KEY TO THE CITY!
HURRY UP AND GET IT DONE, TOO, BECAUSE WE'RE RUNNING LATE THIS MONTH!
!?
Bonvillain

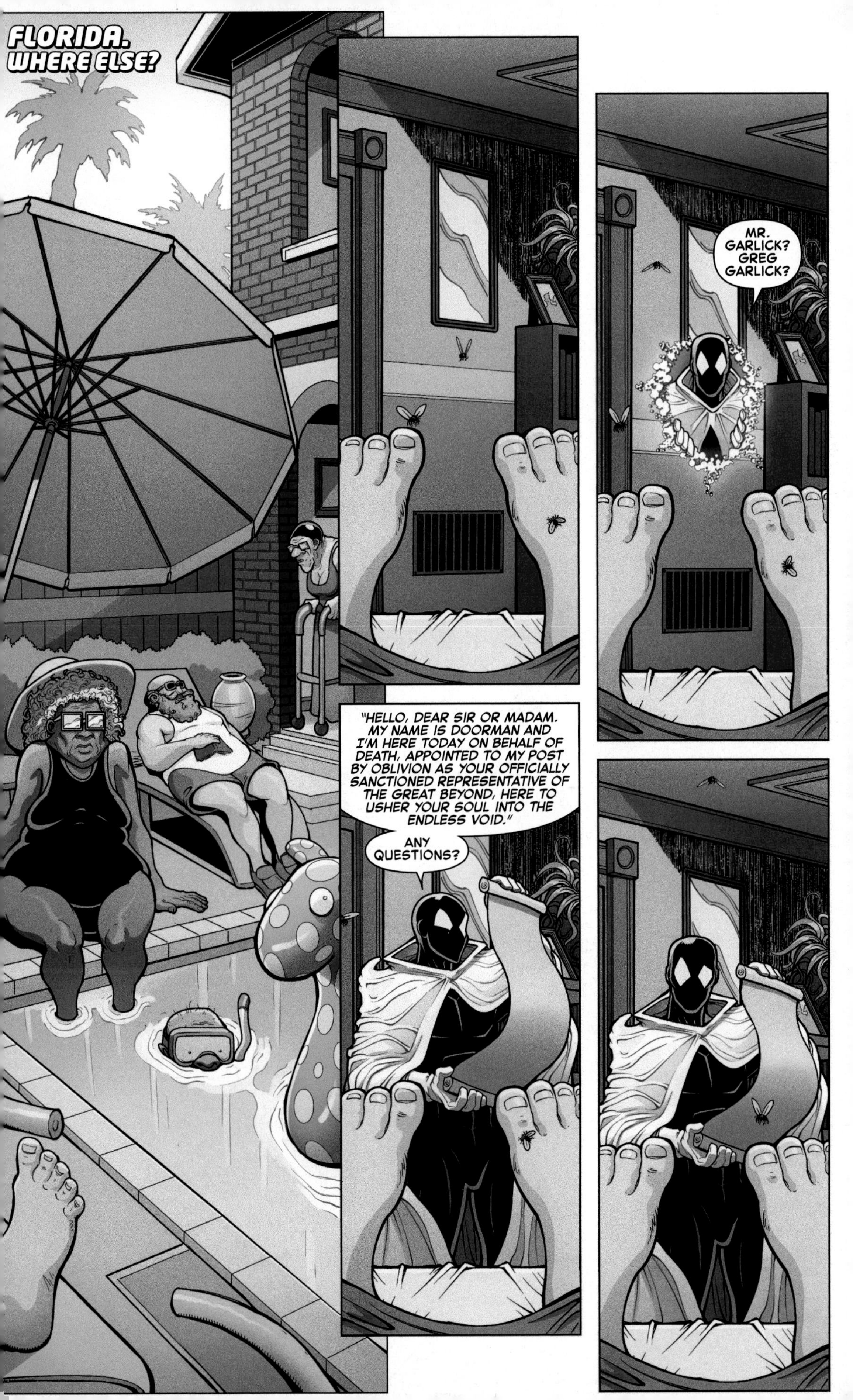
FLORIDA. WHERE ELSE?
MR. GARLICK? GREG GARLICK?
"HELLO, DEAR SIR OR MADAM. MY NAME IS DOORMAN AND I'M HERE TODAY ON BEHALF OF DEATH, APPOINTED TO MY POST BY OBLIVION AS YOUR OFFICIALLY SANCTIONED REPRESENTATIVE OF THE GREAT BEYOND, HERE TO USHER YOUR SOUL INTO THE ENDLESS VOID."
ANY QUESTIONS?

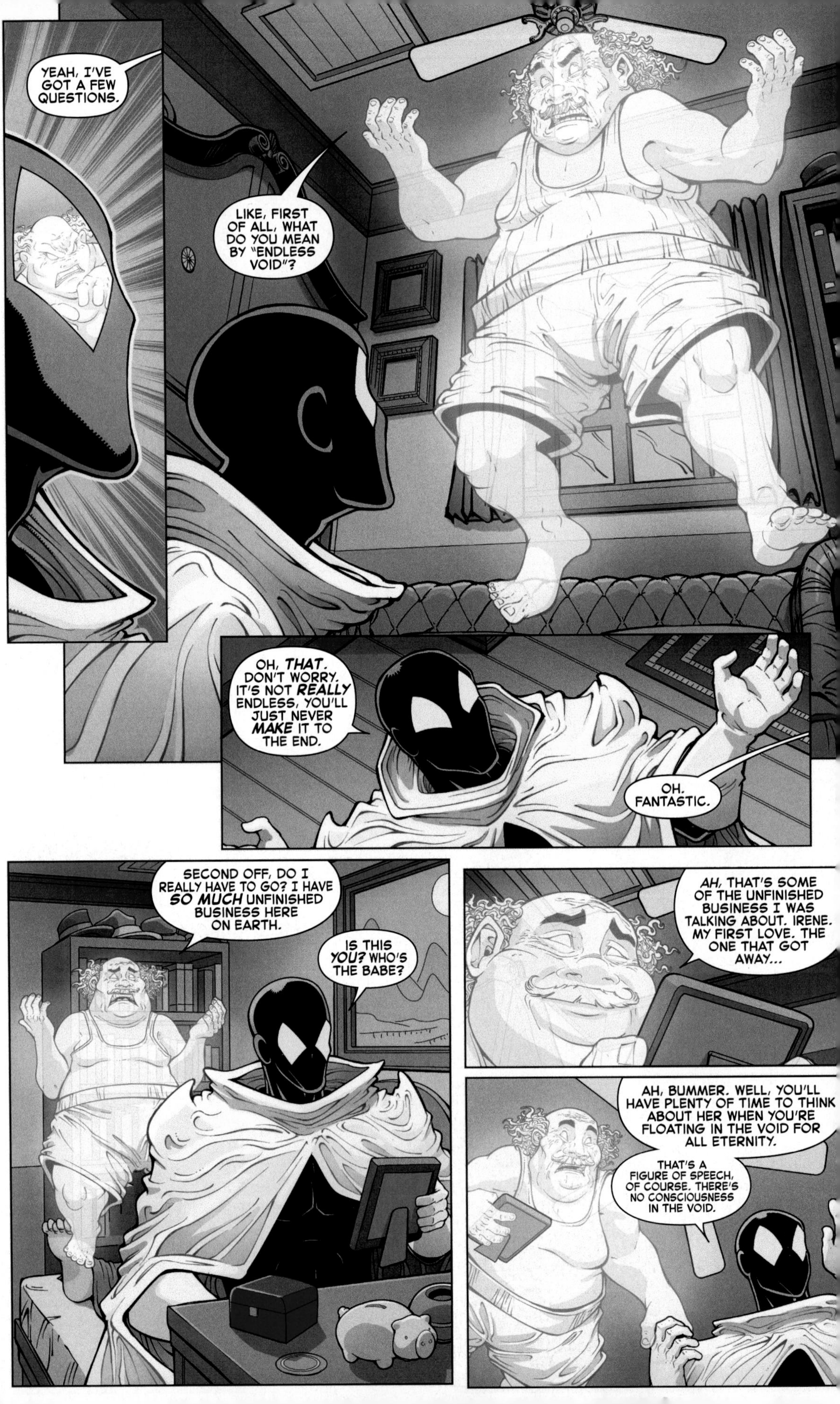
YEAH, I'VE GOT A FEW QUESTIONS.
LIKE, FIRST OF ALL, WHAT DO YOU MEAN BY "ENDLESS VOID"?
OH, *THAT*. DON'T WORRY. IT'S NOT *REALLY* ENDLESS, YOU'LL JUST NEVER *MAKE* IT TO THE END.
OH. FANTASTIC.
SECOND OFF, DO I REALLY HAVE TO GO? I HAVE *SO MUCH* UNFINISHED BUSINESS HERE ON EARTH.
IS THIS *YOU?* WHO'S THE BABE?
*AH,* THAT'S SOME OF THE UNFINISHED BUSINESS I WAS TALKING ABOUT. IRENE. MY FIRST LOVE. THE ONE THAT GOT AWAY...
AH, BUMMER. WELL, YOU'LL HAVE PLENTY OF TIME TO THINK ABOUT HER WHEN YOU'RE FLOATING IN THE VOID FOR ALL ETERNITY.
THAT'S A FIGURE OF SPEECH, OF COURSE. THERE'S NO CONSCIOUSNESS IN THE VOID.

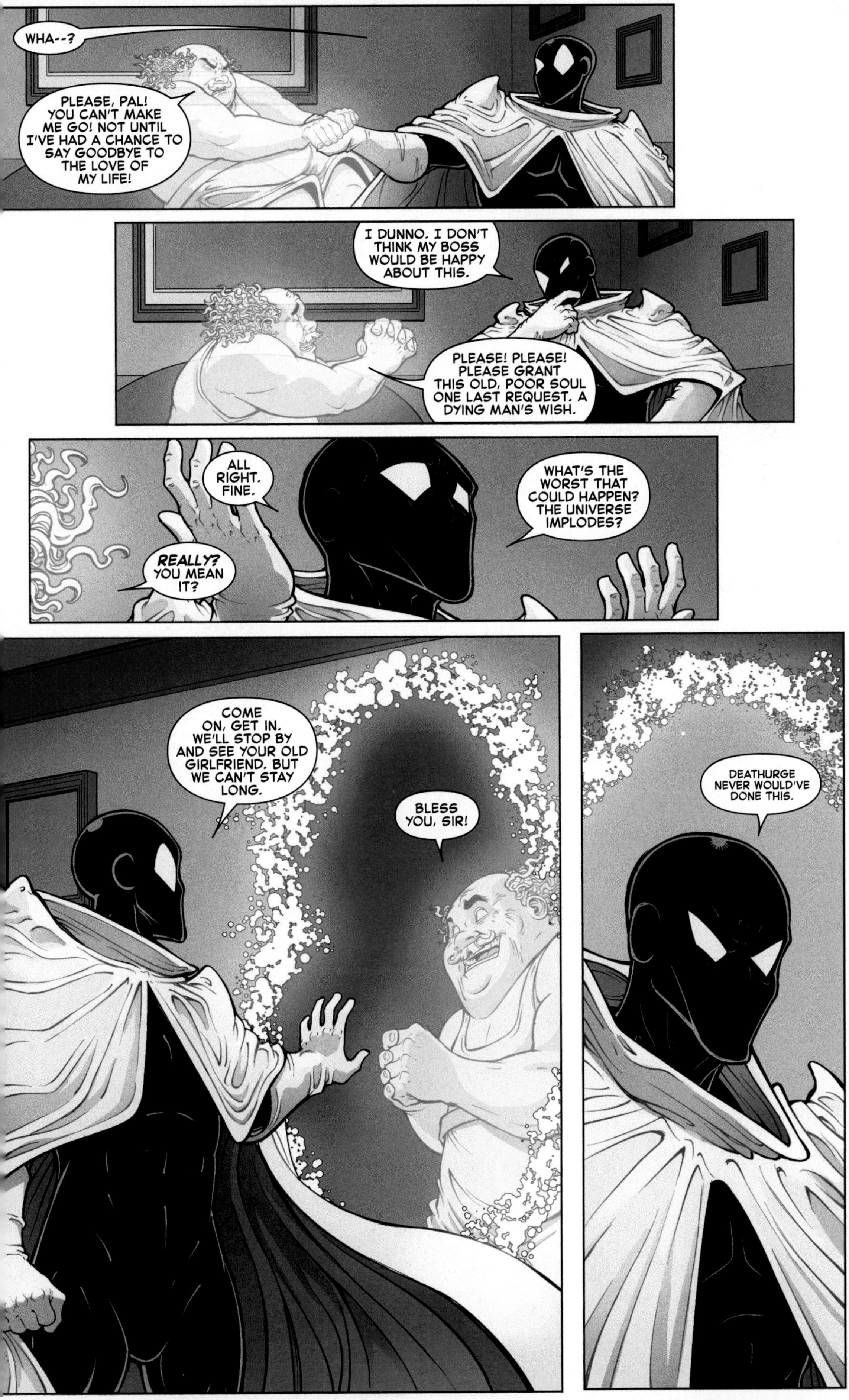
WHA--?
PLEASE, PAL! YOU CAN'T MAKE ME GO! NOT UNTIL I'VE HAD A CHANCE TO SAY GOODBYE TO THE LOVE OF MY LIFE!
I DUNNO. I DON'T THINK MY BOSS WOULD BE HAPPY ABOUT THIS.
PLEASE! PLEASE! PLEASE GRANT THIS OLD, POOR SOUL ONE LAST REQUEST. A DYING MAN'S WISH.
ALL RIGHT. FINE.
REALLY? YOU MEAN IT?
WHAT'S THE WORST THAT COULD HAPPEN? THE UNIVERSE IMPLODES?
COME ON, GET IN. WE'LL STOP BY AND SEE YOUR OLD GIRLFRIEND. BUT WE CAN'T STAY LONG.
BLESS YOU, SIR!
DEATHURGE NEVER WOULD'VE DONE THIS.

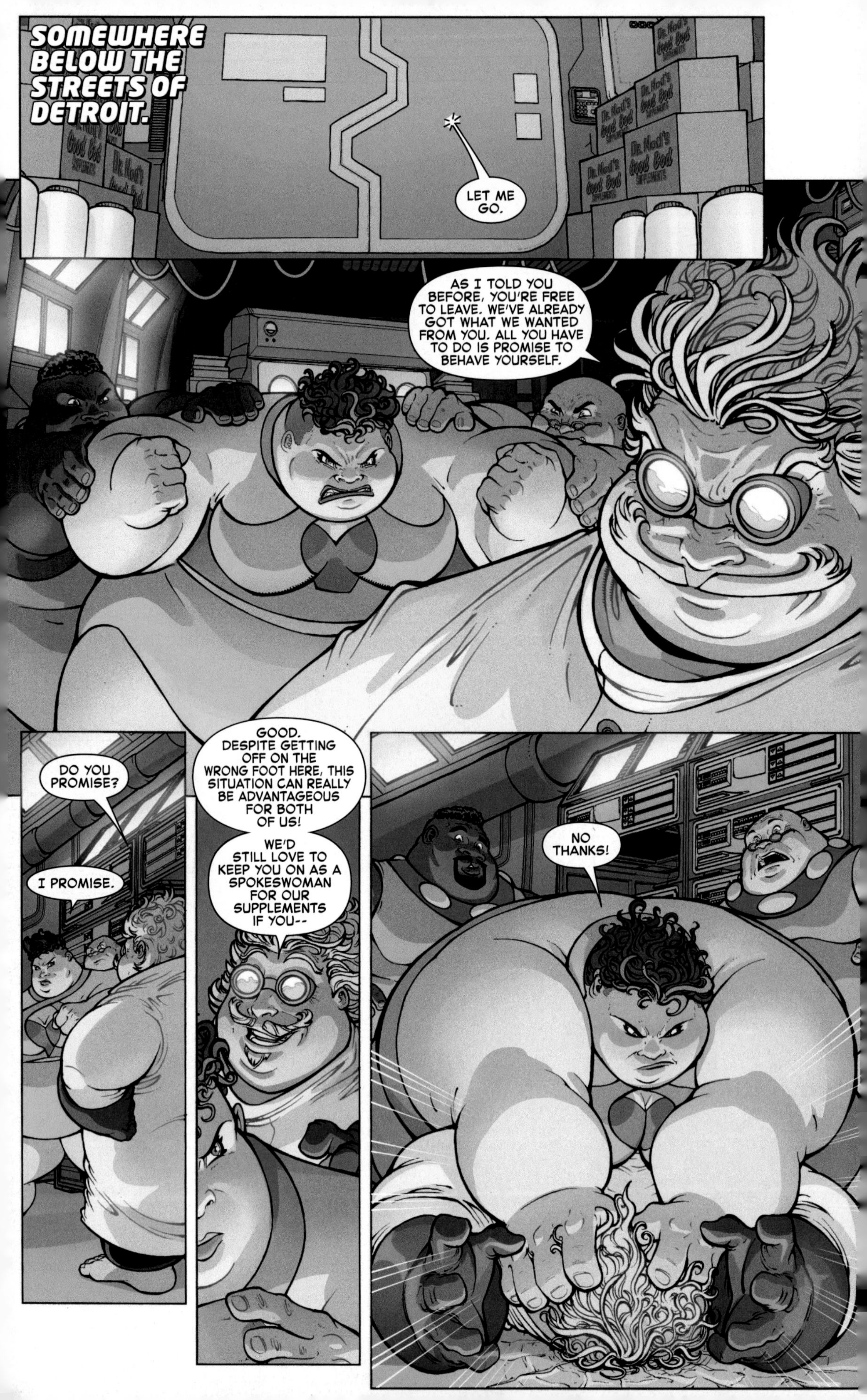
SOMEWHERE BELOW THE STREETS OF DETROIT.
Dr. Nod's Good Bod SUPPLEMENTS
LET ME GO.
AS I TOLD YOU BEFORE, YOU'RE FREE TO LEAVE. WE'VE ALREADY GOT WHAT WE WANTED FROM YOU. ALL YOU HAVE TO DO IS PROMISE TO BEHAVE YOURSELF.
DO YOU PROMISE?
I PROMISE.
GOOD. DESPITE GETTING OFF ON THE WRONG FOOT HERE, THIS SITUATION CAN REALLY BE ADVANTAGEOUS FOR BOTH OF US!
WE'D STILL LOVE TO KEEP YOU ON AS A SPOKESWOMAN FOR OUR SUPPLEMENTS IF YOU--
NO THANKS!

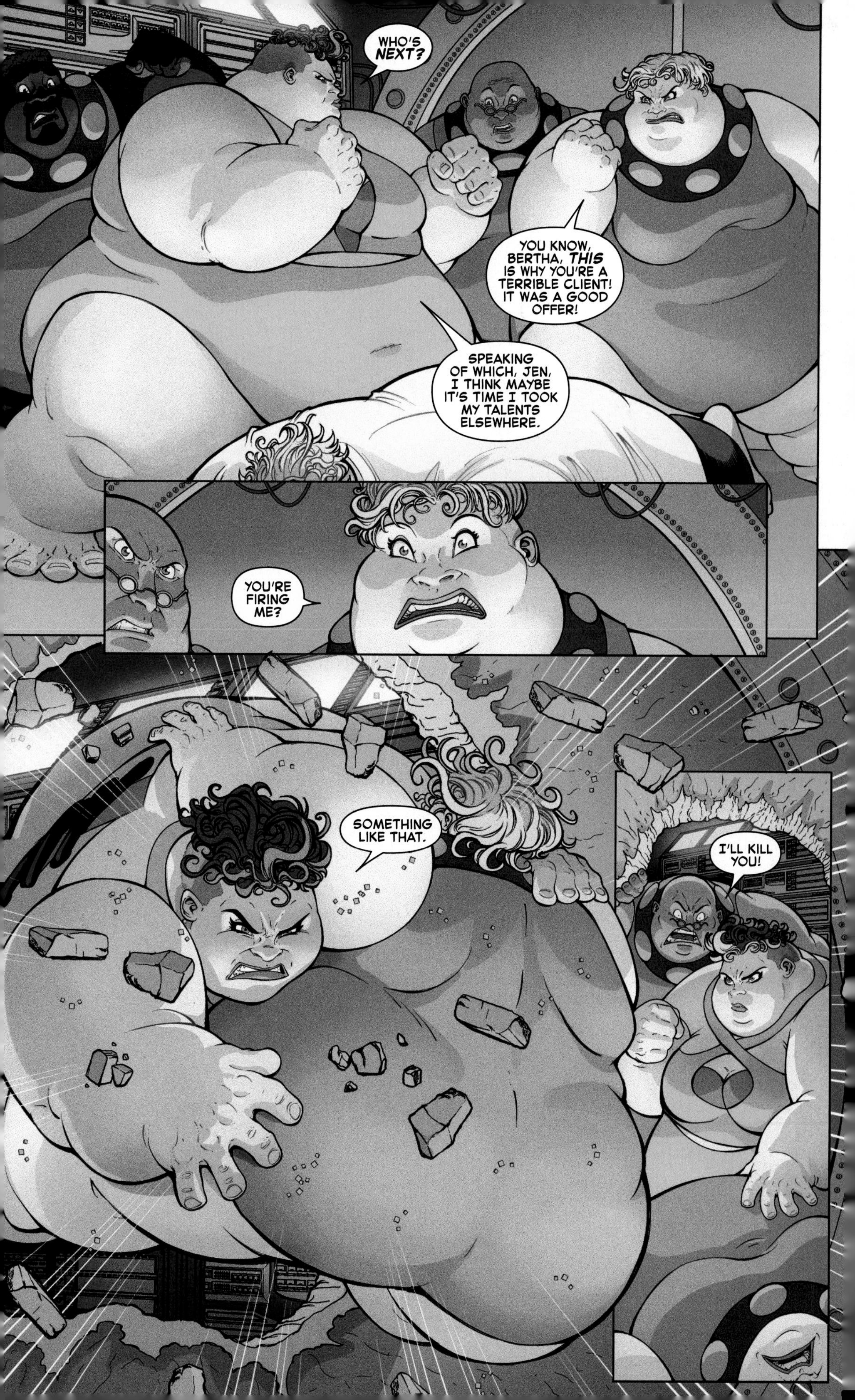
WHO'S NEXT?
YOU KNOW, BERTHA, THIS IS WHY YOU'RE A TERRIBLE CLIENT! IT WAS A GOOD OFFER!
SPEAKING OF WHICH, JEN, I THINK MAYBE IT'S TIME I TOOK MY TALENTS ELSEWHERE.
YOU'RE FIRING ME?
SOMETHING LIKE THAT.
I'LL KILL YOU!

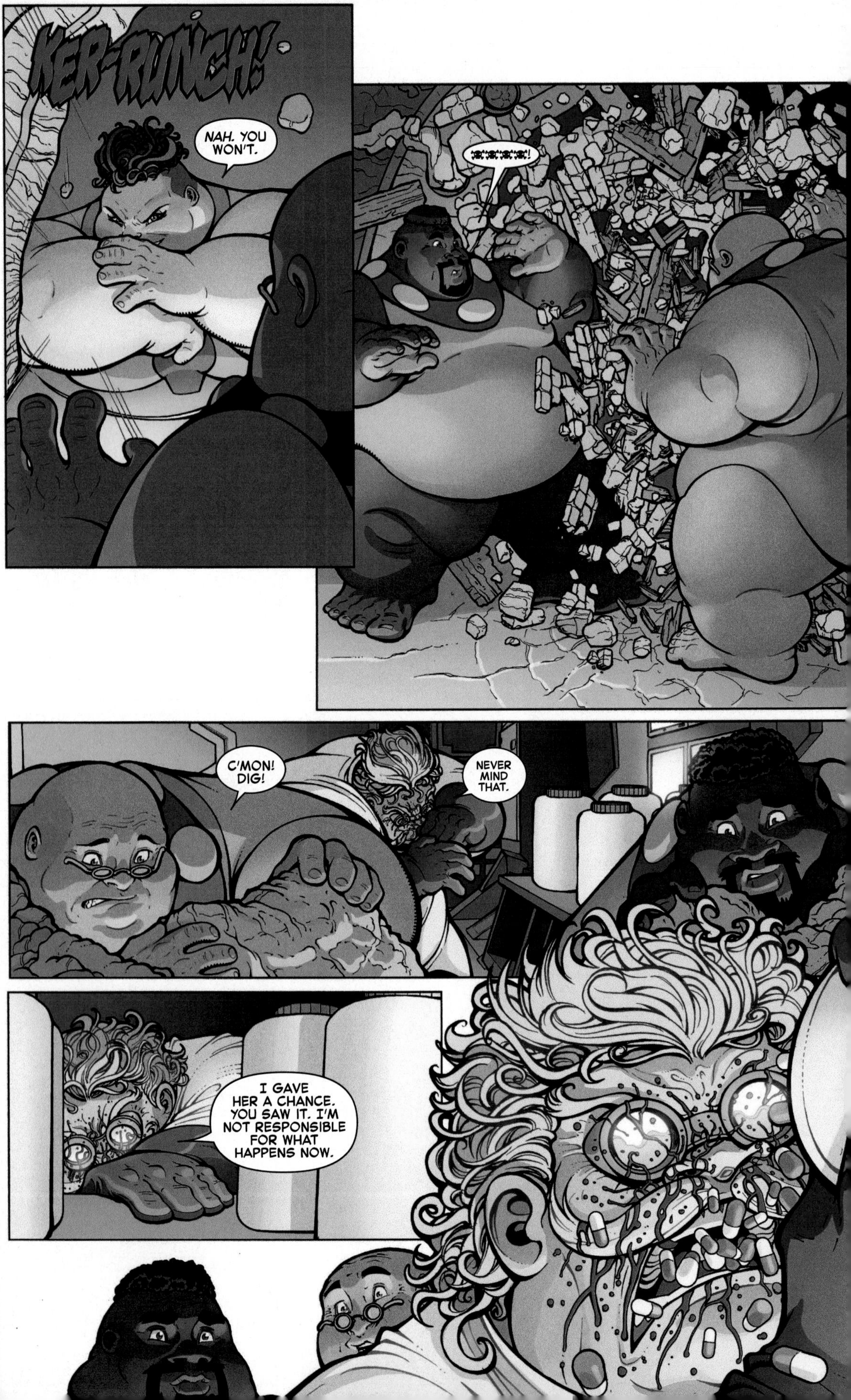
KER-RUNCH!
NAH. YOU WON'T.
C'MON! DIG!
NEVER MIND THAT.
I GAVE HER A CHANCE. YOU SAW IT. I'M NOT RESPONSIBLE FOR WHAT HAPPENS NOW.

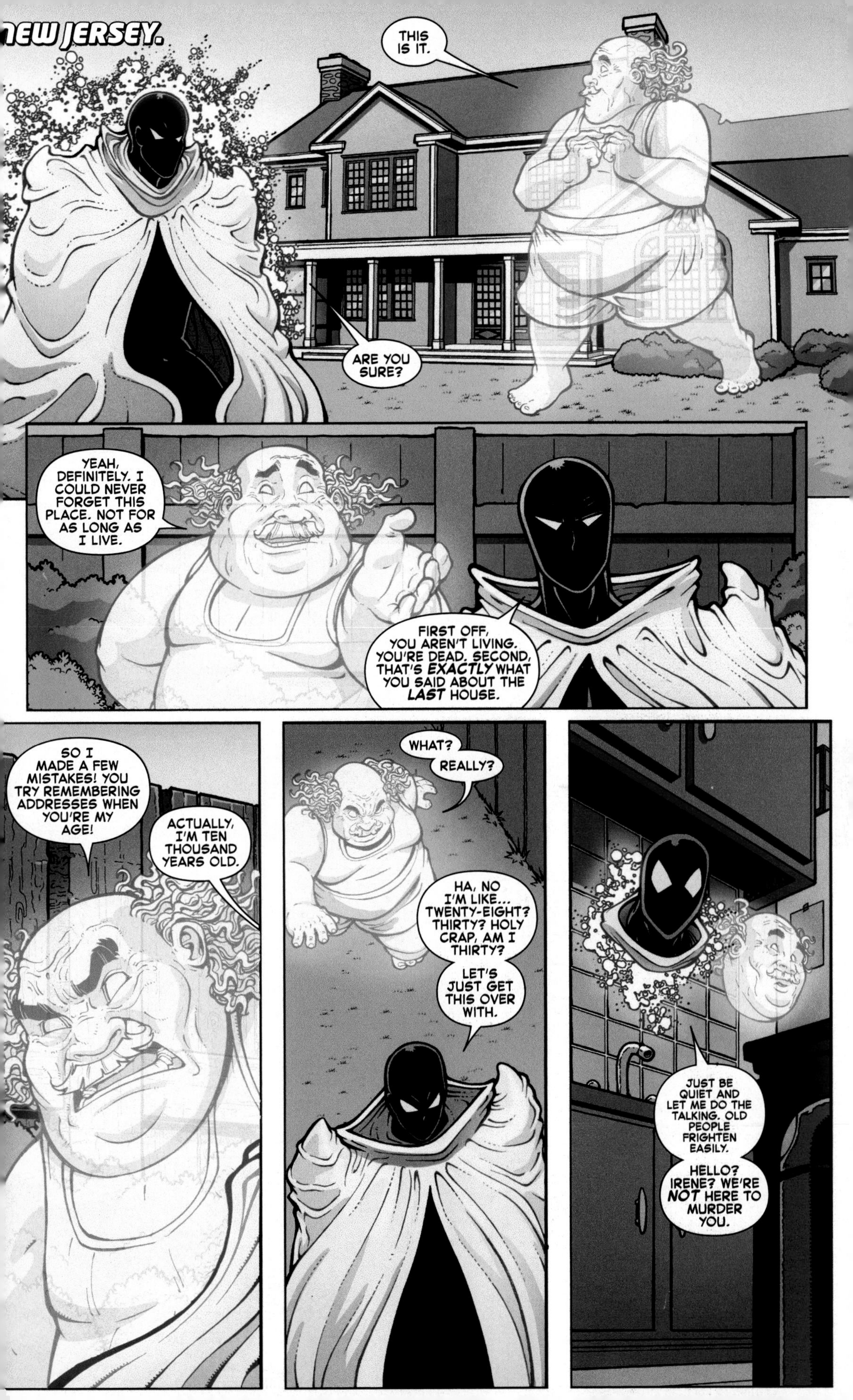
NEW JERSEY.
THIS IS IT.
ARE YOU SURE?
YEAH, DEFINITELY. I COULD NEVER FORGET THIS PLACE. NOT FOR AS LONG AS I LIVE.
FIRST OFF, YOU AREN'T LIVING. YOU'RE DEAD. SECOND, THAT'S EXACTLY WHAT YOU SAID ABOUT THE LAST HOUSE.
SO I MADE A FEW MISTAKES! YOU TRY REMEMBERING ADDRESSES WHEN YOU'RE MY AGE!
ACTUALLY, I'M TEN THOUSAND YEARS OLD.
WHAT?
REALLY?
HA, NO I'M LIKE... TWENTY-EIGHT? THIRTY? HOLY CRAP, AM I THIRTY?
LET'S JUST GET THIS OVER WITH.
JUST BE QUIET AND LET ME DO THE TALKING. OLD PEOPLE FRIGHTEN EASILY.
HELLO? IRENE? WE'RE NOT HERE TO MURDER YOU.

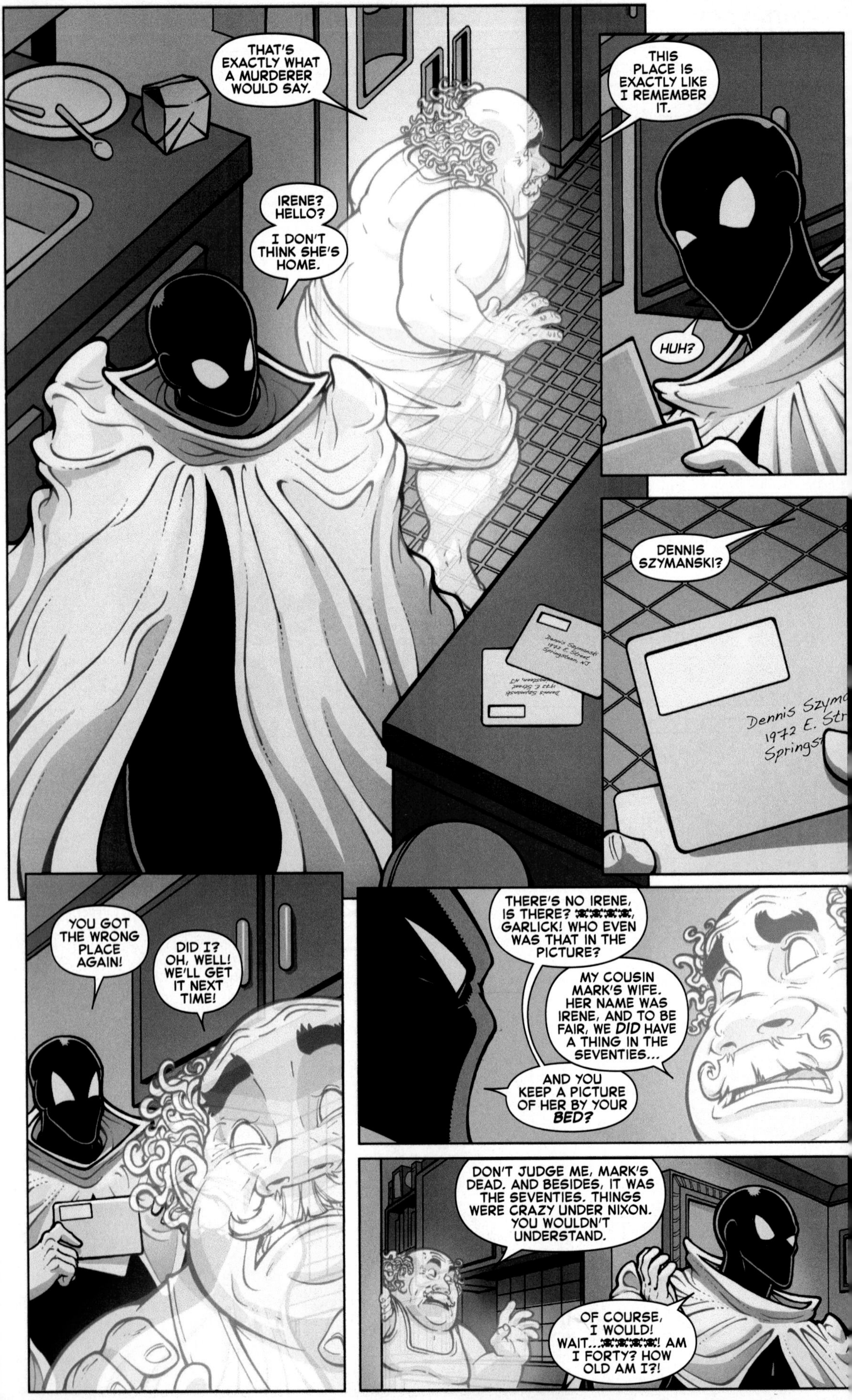

THAT'S EXACTLY WHAT A MURDERER WOULD SAY.
IRENE? HELLO?
I DON'T THINK SHE'S HOME.
THIS PLACE IS EXACTLY LIKE I REMEMBER IT.
HUH?
DENNIS SZYMANSKI?
Dennis Szym
1972 E. Str
Springs
YOU GOT THE WRONG PLACE AGAIN!
DID I? OH, WELL! WE'LL GET IT NEXT TIME!
THERE'S NO IRENE, IS THERE? , GARLICK! WHO EVEN WAS THAT IN THE PICTURE?
MY COUSIN MARK'S WIFE. HER NAME WAS IRENE, AND TO BE FAIR, WE *DID* HAVE A THING IN THE SEVENTIES...
AND YOU KEEP A PICTURE OF HER BY YOUR ***BED?***
DON'T JUDGE ME, MARK'S DEAD. AND BESIDES, IT WAS THE SEVENTIES. THINGS WERE CRAZY UNDER NIXON. YOU WOULDN'T UNDERSTAND.
OF COURSE, I WOULD! WAIT... ! AM I FORTY? HOW OLD AM I?!

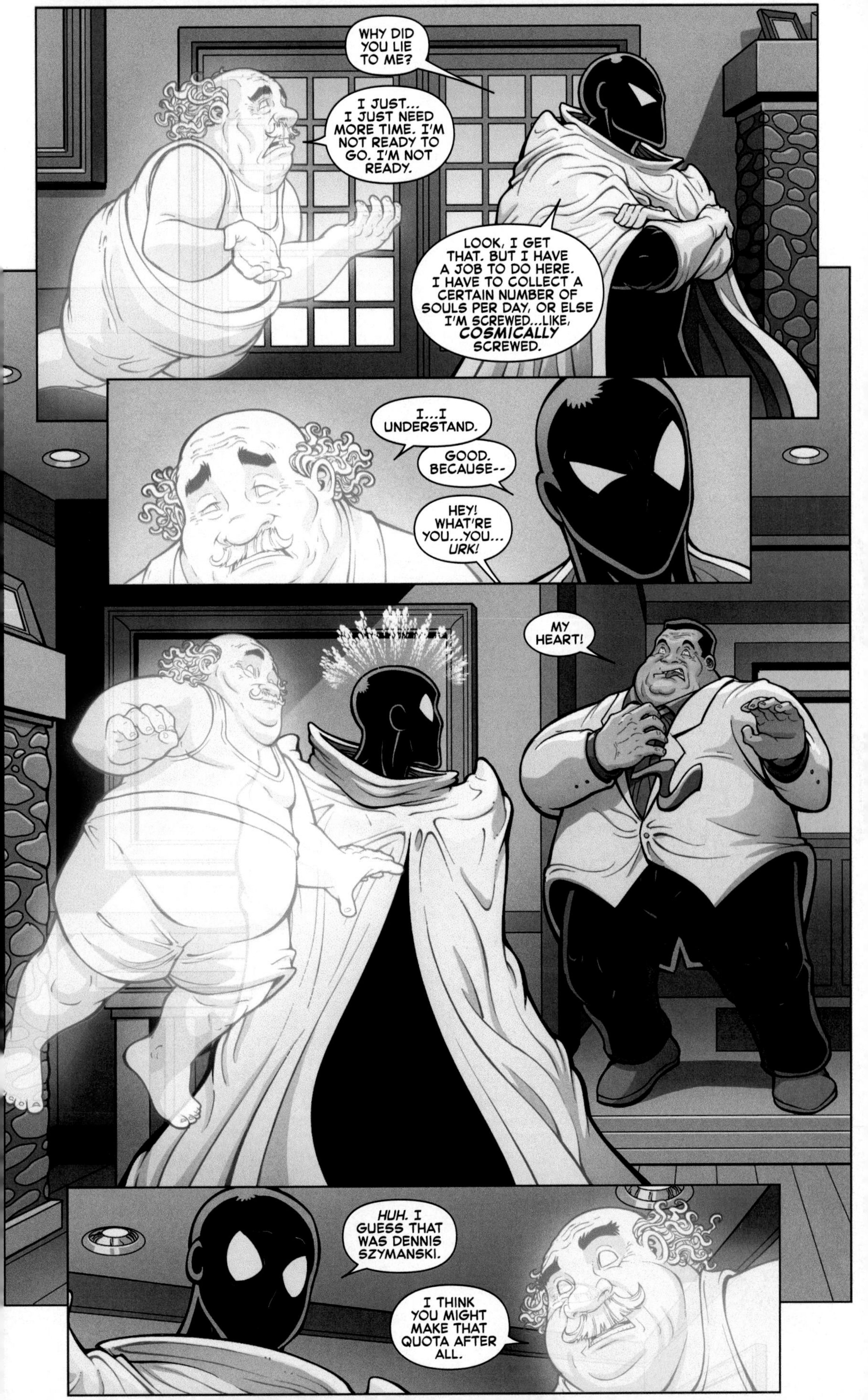

WHY DID YOU LIE TO ME?
I JUST... I JUST NEED MORE TIME. I'M NOT READY TO GO. I'M NOT READY.
LOOK, I GET THAT. BUT I HAVE A JOB TO DO HERE. I HAVE TO COLLECT A CERTAIN NUMBER OF SOULS PER DAY, OR ELSE I'M SCREWED...LIKE, *COSMICALLY* SCREWED.
I...I UNDERSTAND.
GOOD. BECAUSE--
HEY! WHAT'RE YOU...YOU... *URK!*
MY HEART!
*HUH.* I GUESS THAT WAS DENNIS SZYMANSKI.
I THINK YOU MIGHT MAKE THAT QUOTA AFTER ALL.

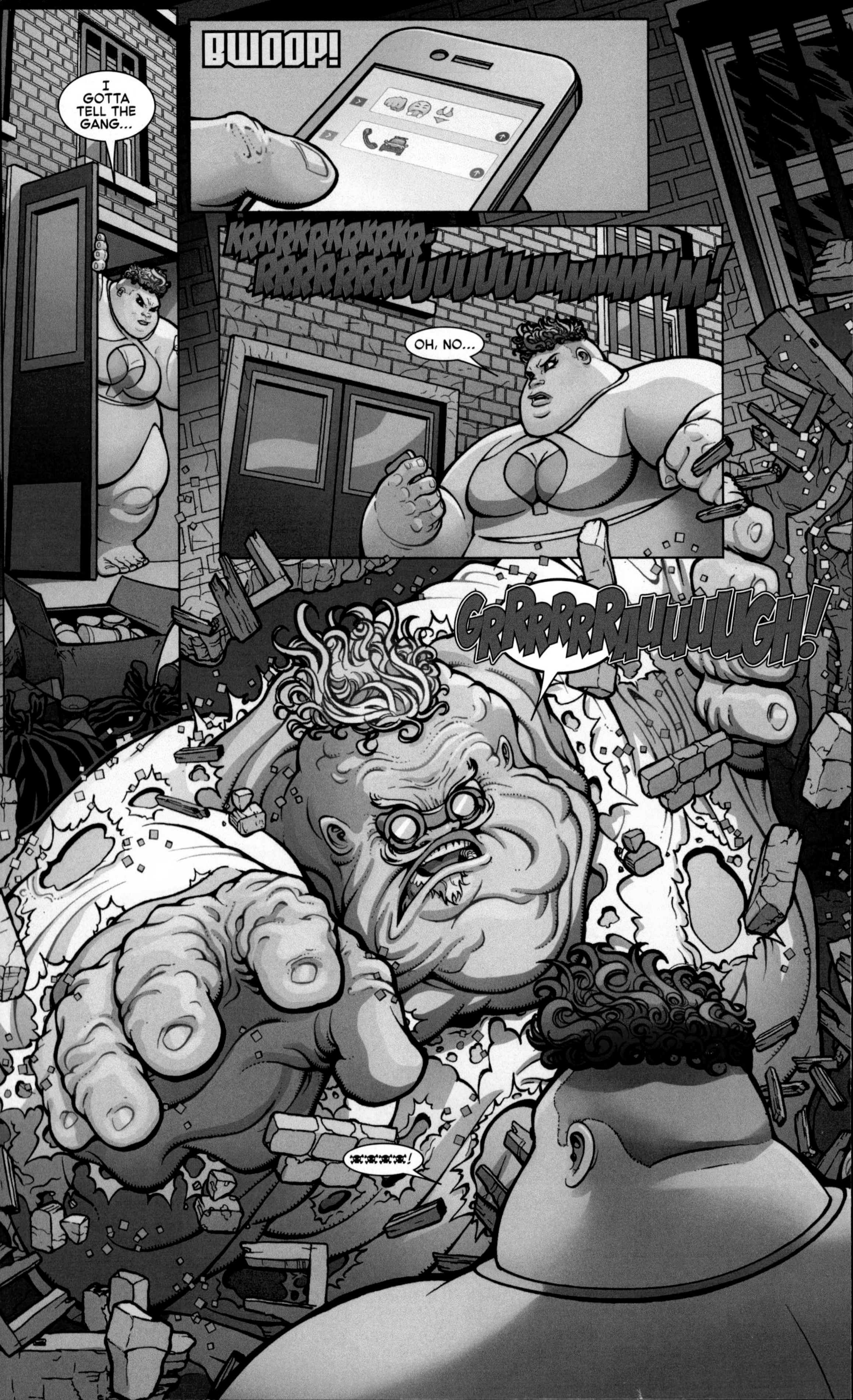

I GOTTA TELL THE GANG...
BWOOP!
KRKRKRKRKRKRKR-RRRRRRRRUUUUUUUMMMMMM!
OH, NO...
GRRRRRRAUUUUGH!

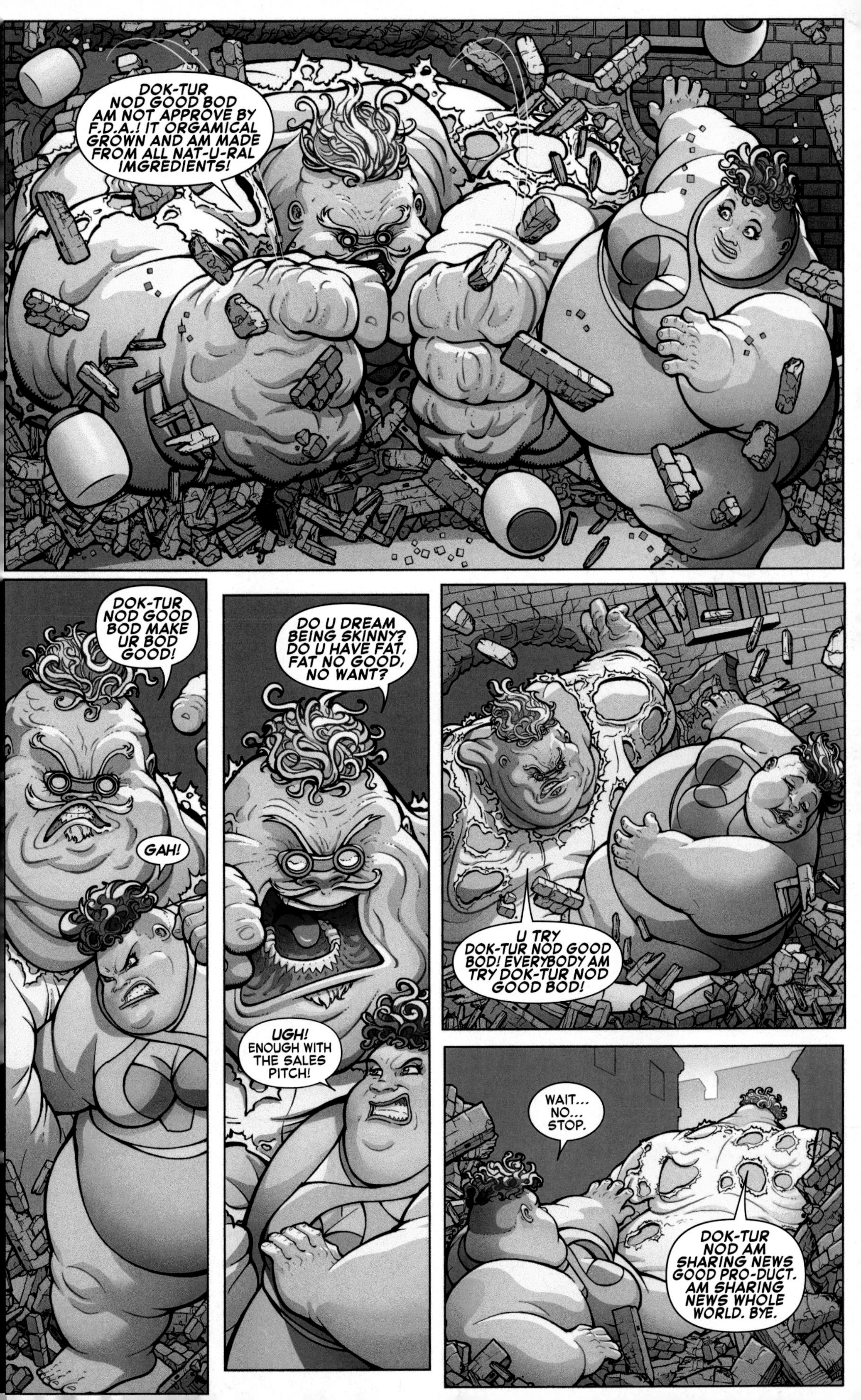
DOK-TUR NOD GOOD BOD AM NOT APPROVE BY F.D.A.! IT ORGAMICAL GROWN AND AM MADE FROM ALL NAT-U-RAL IMGREDIENTS!
DOK-TUR NOD GOOD BOD MAKE UR BOD GOOD!
GAH!
DO U DREAM BEING SKINNY? DO U HAVE FAT, FAT NO GOOD, NO WANT?
UGH! ENOUGH WITH THE SALES PITCH!
U TRY DOK-TUR NOD GOOD BOD! EVERYBODY AM TRY DOK-TUR NOD GOOD BOD!
WAIT... NO... STOP.
DOK-TUR NOD AM SHARING NEWS GOOD PRO-DUCT. AM SHARING NEWS WHOLE WORLD. BYE.

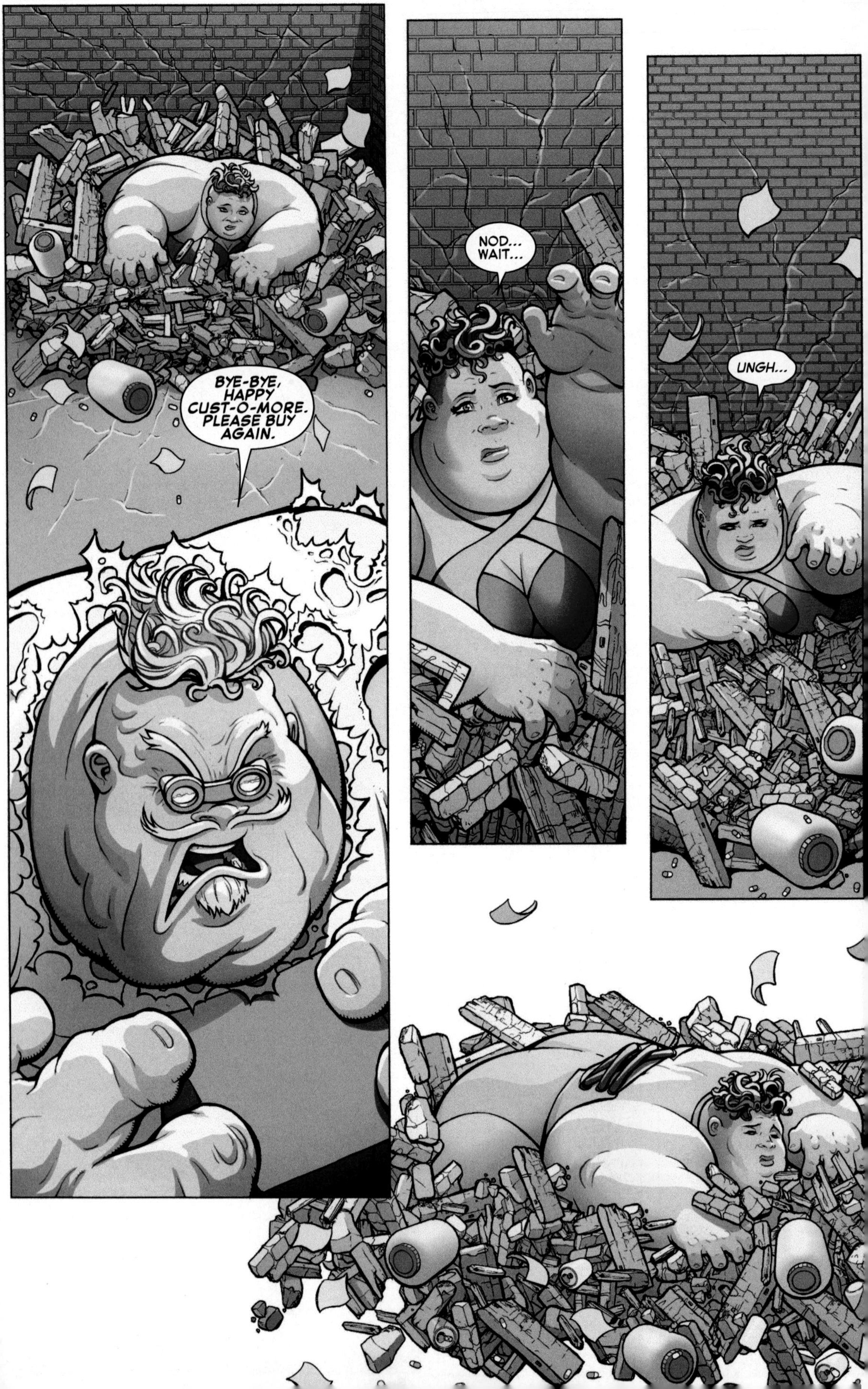
BYE-BYE, HAPPY CUST-O-MORE. PLEASE BUY AGAIN.
NOD... WAIT...
UNGH...

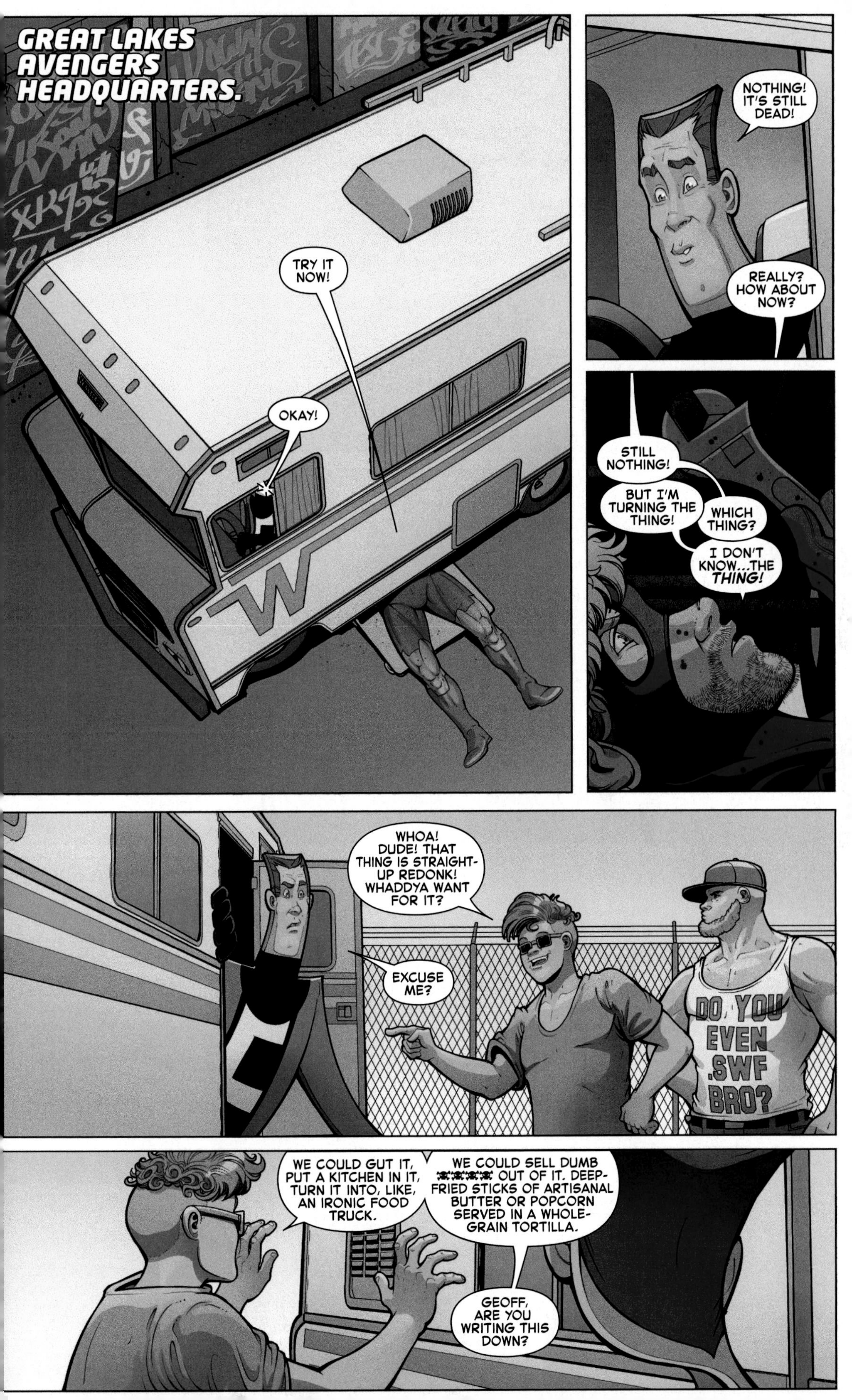
GREAT LAKES AVENGERS HEADQUARTERS.
TRY IT NOW!
OKAY!
NOTHING! IT'S STILL DEAD!
REALLY? HOW ABOUT NOW?
STILL NOTHING!
BUT I'M TURNING THE THING!
WHICH THING?
I DON'T KNOW...THE *THING!*
WHOA! DUDE! THAT THING IS STRAIGHT-UP REDONK! WHADDYA WANT FOR IT?
EXCUSE ME?
DO YOU EVEN .SWF BRO?
WE COULD GUT IT, PUT A KITCHEN IN IT, TURN IT INTO, LIKE, AN IRONIC FOOD TRUCK.
WE COULD SELL DUMB ☠☠☠☠ OUT OF IT. DEEP-FRIED STICKS OF ARTISANAL BUTTER OR POPCORN SERVED IN A WHOLE-GRAIN TORTILLA.
GEOFF, ARE YOU WRITING THIS DOWN?

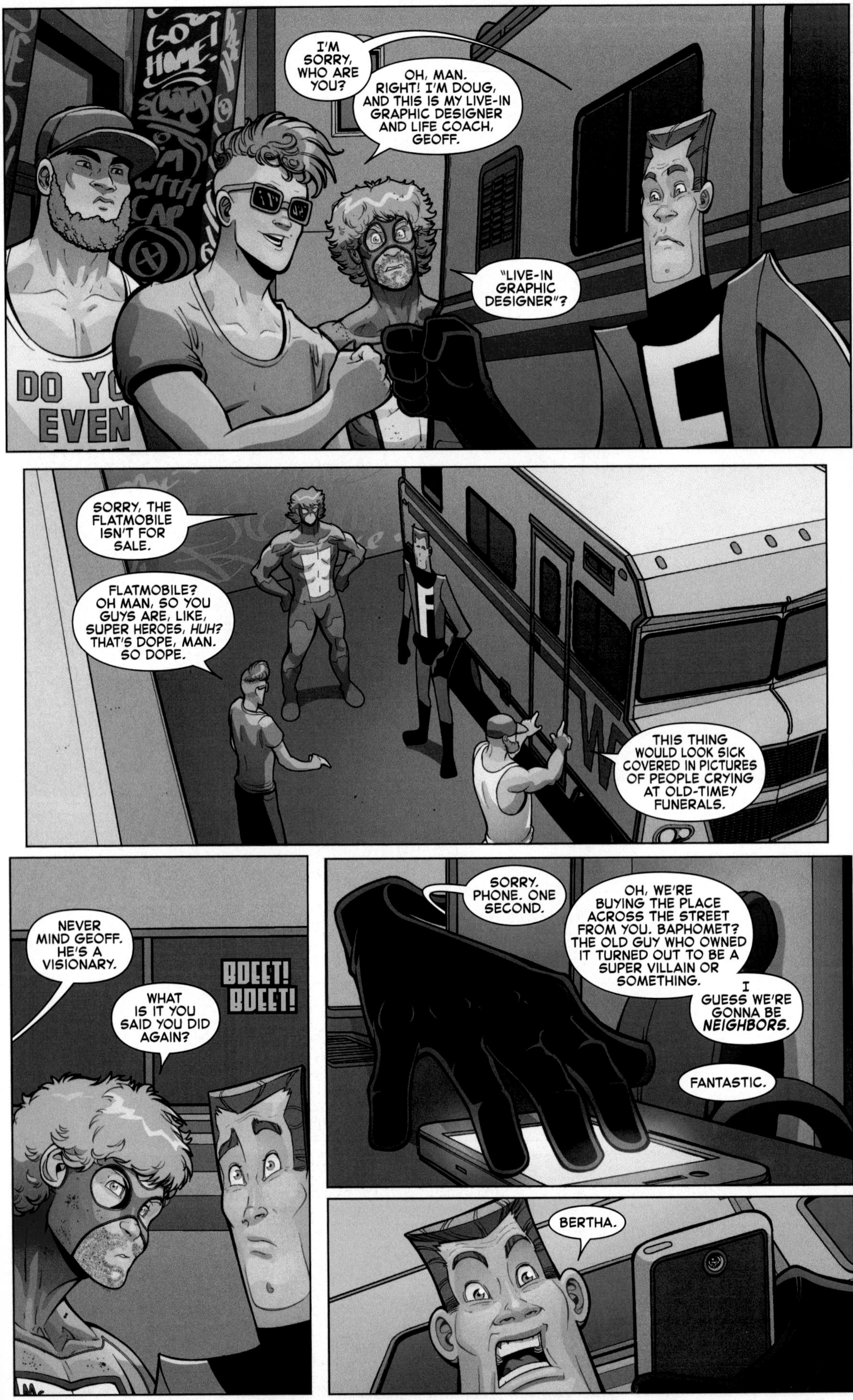

I'M SORRY, WHO ARE YOU?
OH, MAN. RIGHT! I'M DOUG, AND THIS IS MY LIVE-IN GRAPHIC DESIGNER AND LIFE COACH, GEOFF.
"LIVE-IN GRAPHIC DESIGNER"?
SORRY, THE FLATMOBILE ISN'T FOR SALE.
FLATMOBILE? OH MAN, SO YOU GUYS ARE, LIKE, SUPER HEROES, *HUH*? THAT'S DOPE, MAN. SO DOPE.
THIS THING WOULD LOOK SICK COVERED IN PICTURES OF PEOPLE CRYING AT OLD-TIMEY FUNERALS.
NEVER MIND GEOFF. HE'S A VISIONARY.
BDEET! BDEET!
WHAT IS IT YOU SAID YOU DID AGAIN?
SORRY. PHONE. ONE SECOND.
OH, WE'RE BUYING THE PLACE ACROSS THE STREET FROM YOU. BAPHOMET? THE OLD GUY WHO OWNED IT TURNED OUT TO BE A SUPER VILLAIN OR SOMETHING.
I GUESS WE'RE GONNA BE ***NEIGHBORS.***
FANTASTIC.
BERTHA.

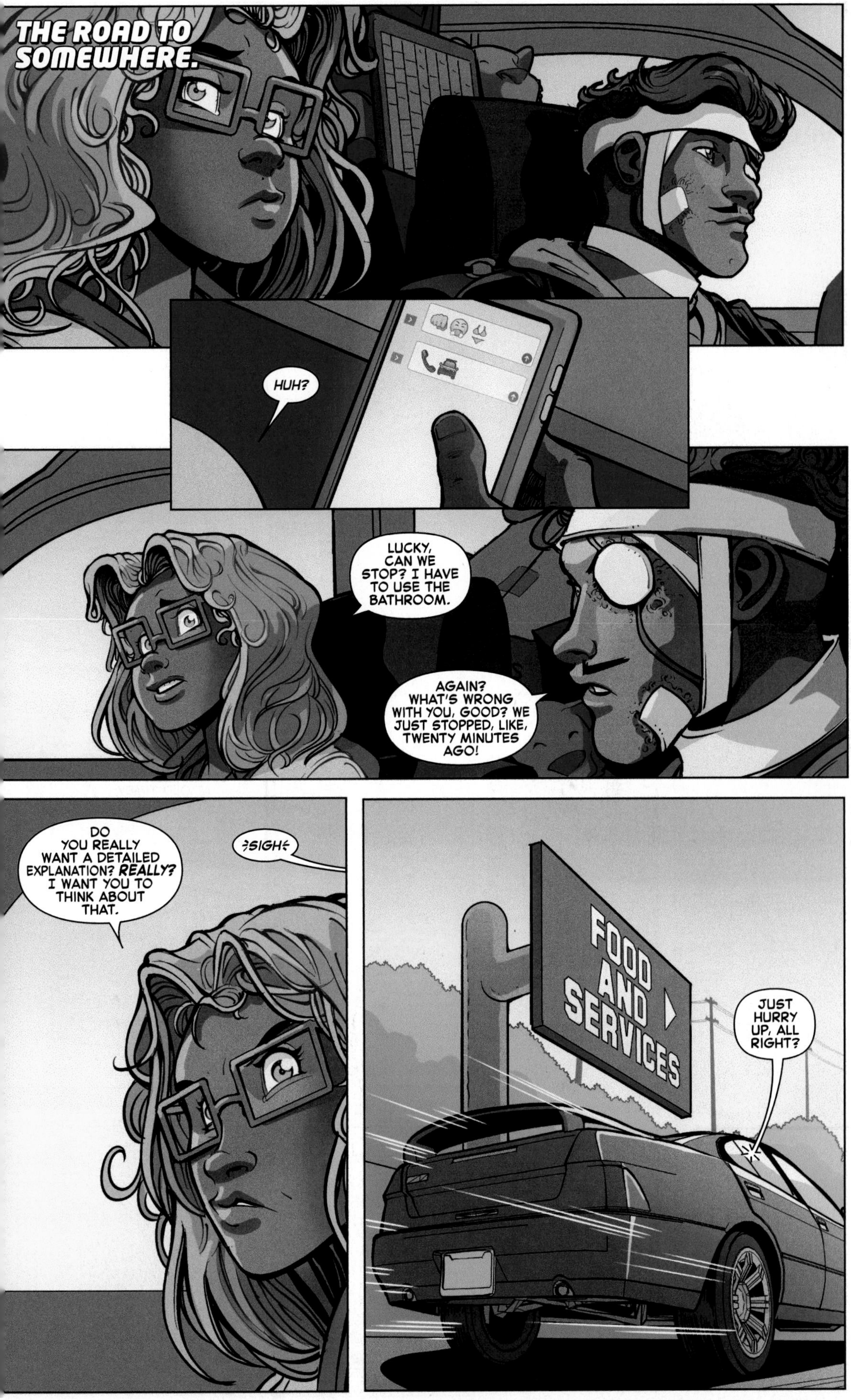
THE ROAD TO SOMEWHERE.
HUH?
LUCKY, CAN WE STOP? I HAVE TO USE THE BATHROOM.
AGAIN? WHAT'S WRONG WITH YOU, GOOD? WE JUST STOPPED, LIKE, TWENTY MINUTES AGO!
DO YOU REALLY WANT A DETAILED EXPLANATION? REALLY? I WANT YOU TO THINK ABOUT THAT.
SIGH
FOOD AND SERVICES
JUST HURRY UP, ALL RIGHT?

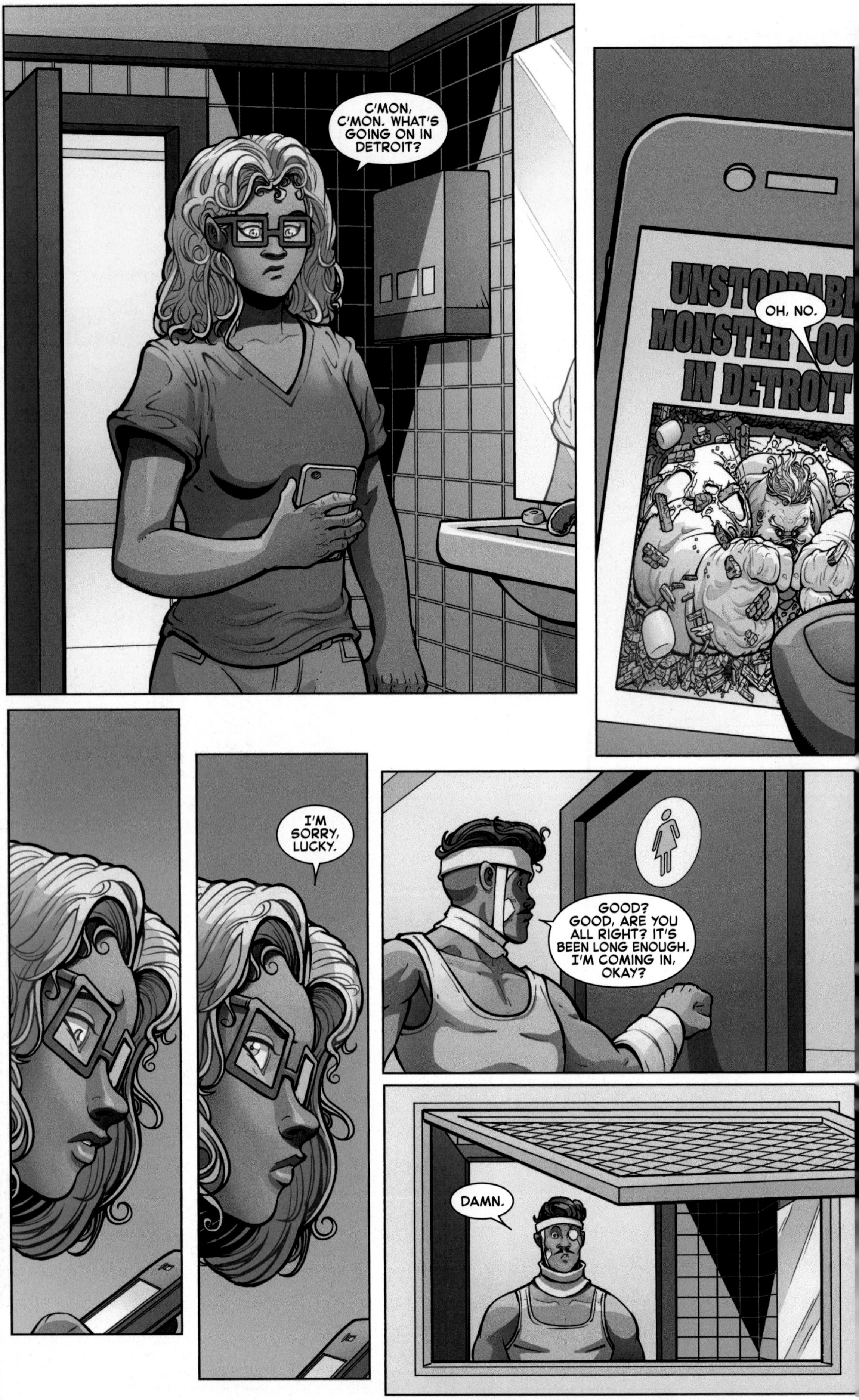
C'MON, C'MON. WHAT'S GOING ON IN DETROIT?
UNSTOPPABL
MONSTER LOO
IN DETROIT
OH, NO.
I'M SORRY, LUCKY.
GOOD? GOOD, ARE YOU ALL RIGHT? IT'S BEEN LONG ENOUGH. I'M COMING IN, OKAY?
DAMN.

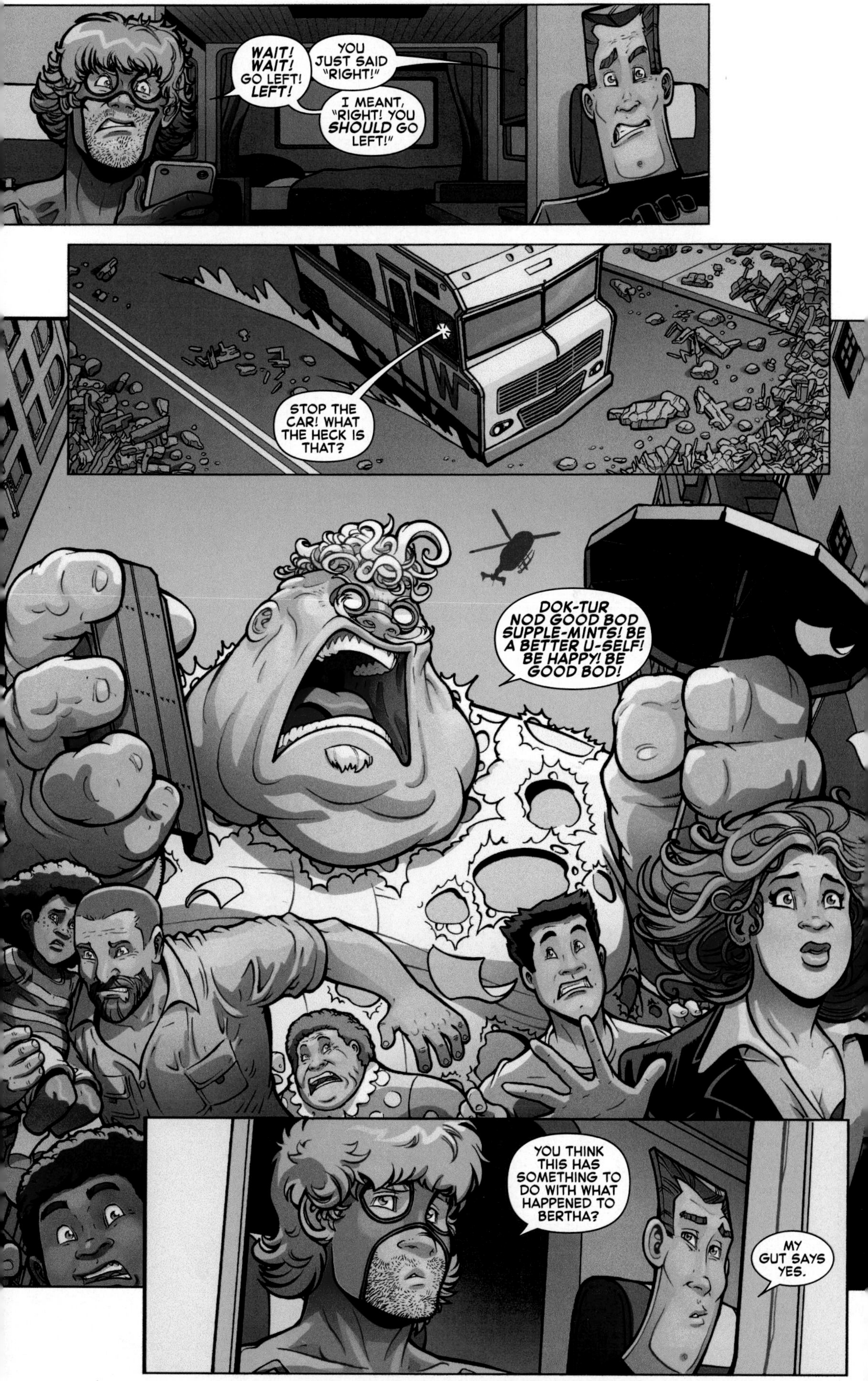
WAIT! WAIT! GO LEFT! LEFT!
YOU JUST SAID "RIGHT!"
I MEANT, "RIGHT! YOU SHOULD GO LEFT!"
STOP THE CAR! WHAT THE HECK IS THAT?
DOK-TUR NOD GOOD BOD SUPPLE-MINTS! BE A BETTER U-SELF! BE HAPPY! BE GOOD BOD!
YOU THINK THIS HAS SOMETHING TO DO WITH WHAT HAPPENED TO BERTHA?
MY GUT SAYS YES.

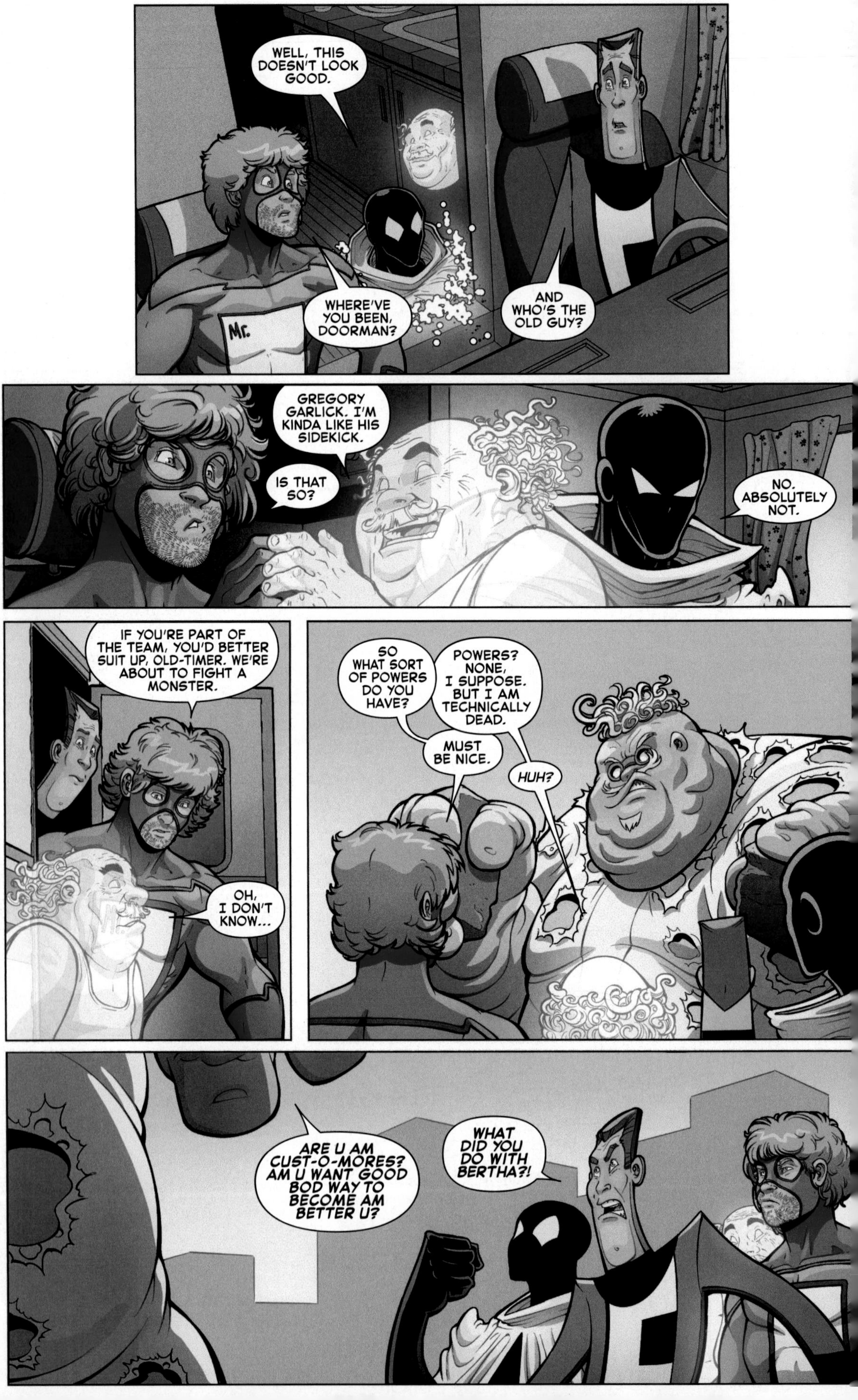
WELL, THIS DOESN'T LOOK GOOD.
WHERE'VE YOU BEEN, DOORMAN?
AND WHO'S THE OLD GUY?
Mr.
GREGORY GARLICK. I'M KINDA LIKE HIS SIDEKICK.
IS THAT SO?
NO. ABSOLUTELY NOT.
IF YOU'RE PART OF THE TEAM, YOU'D BETTER SUIT UP, OLD-TIMER. WE'RE ABOUT TO FIGHT A MONSTER.
OH, I DON'T KNOW...
SO WHAT SORT OF POWERS DO YOU HAVE?
POWERS? NONE, I SUPPOSE. BUT I AM TECHNICALLY DEAD.
MUST BE NICE.
HUH?
ARE U AM CUST-O-MORES? AM U WANT GOOD BOD WAY TO BECOME AM BETTER U?
WHAT DID YOU DO WITH BERTHA?!

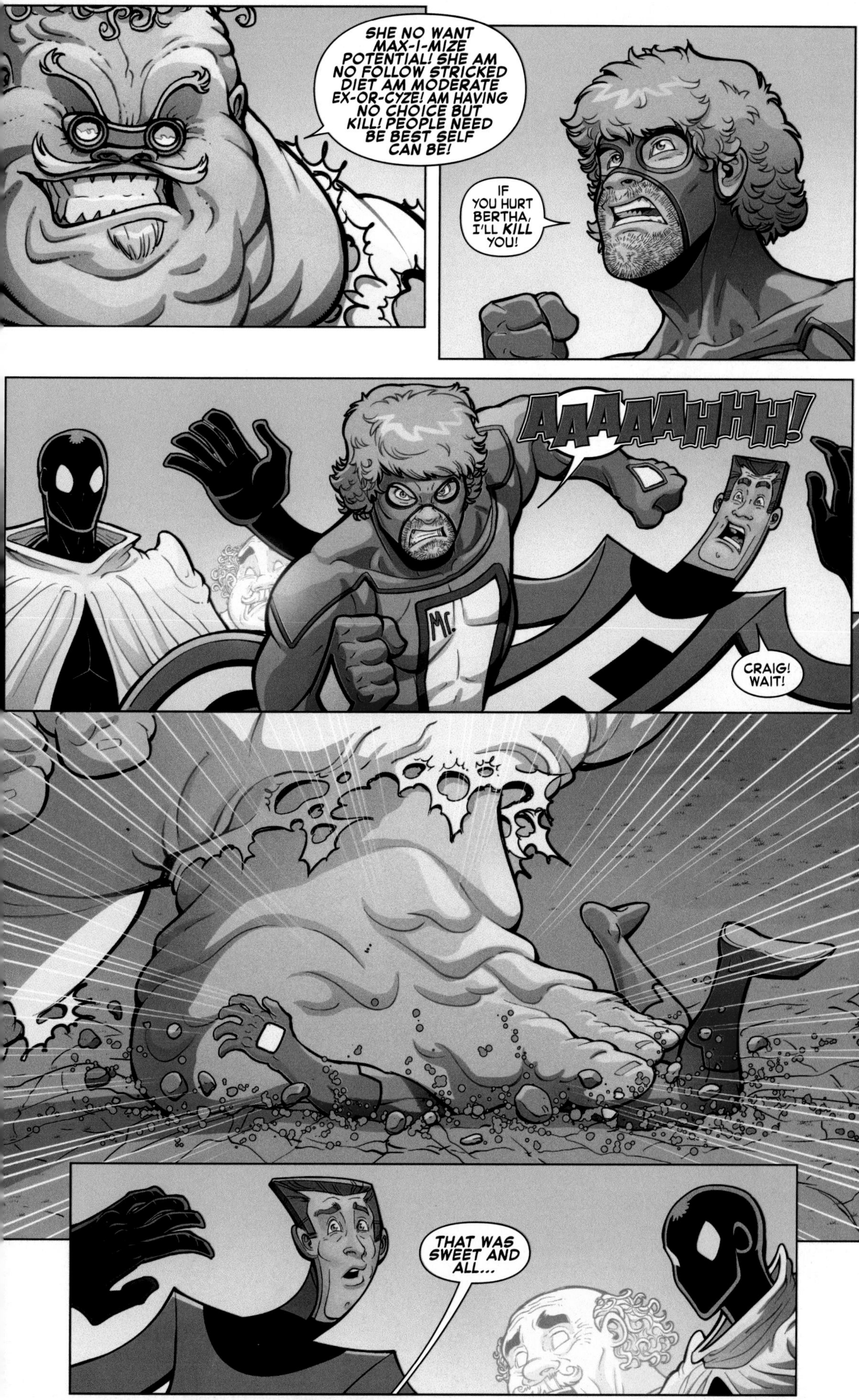
SHE NO WANT MAX-I-MIZE POTENTIAL! SHE AM NO FOLLOW STRICKED DIET AM MODERATE EX-OR-CYZE! AM HAVING NO CHOICE BUT KILL! PEOPLE NEED BE BEST SELF CAN BE!
IF YOU HURT BERTHA, I'LL *KILL* YOU!
AAAAAHHH!
CRAIG! WAIT!
THAT WAS SWEET AND ALL...

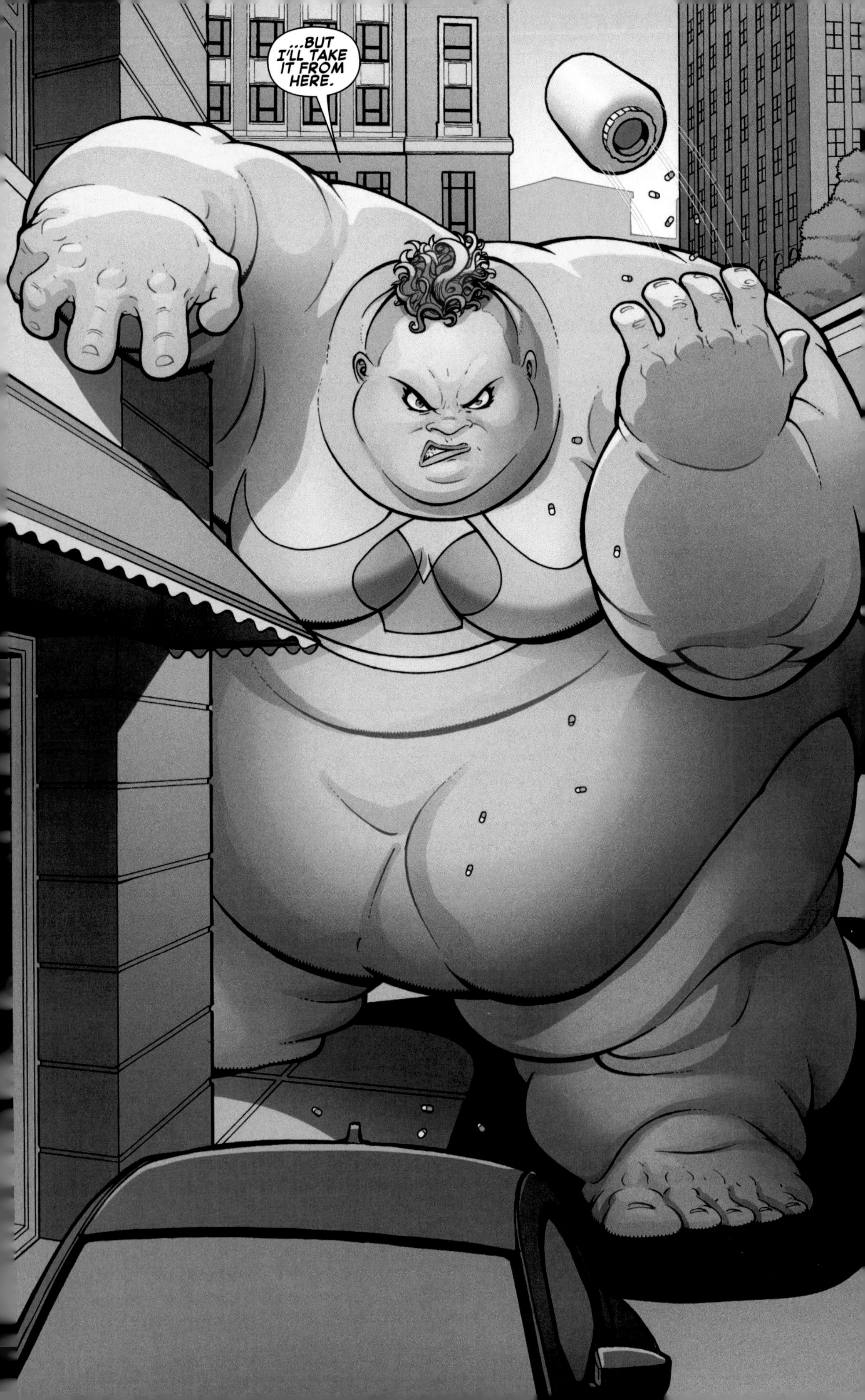
...BUT I'LL TAKE IT FROM HERE.

# The Great Lakes Avengers

Send letters to
MHEROES@MARVEL.COM
marked "Okay to Print"!

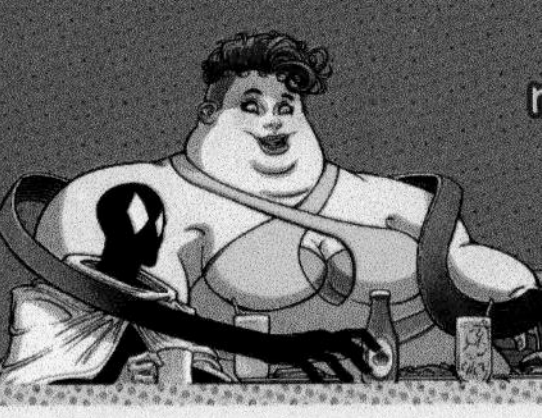

We're nearing the end of our talent search, Merry Marvelites, but Zac Gorman still has a few astonishingly average applicants to weed out before we can assemble our team into a legit minor-crimefighting unit. Take it away, Zac!

---

Unlike all of those other "heroes" who think they may be too good for the Great Lakes Avengers, I fully understand the importance of belonging to a team such as yours. In order to help make the universe a safer place, I would like to volunteer to be an honorary member of the GLA.

I realize I'm only the 17th most powerful being to come from our planet, give or take, but I'm sure that I can get much better. Dr. Strange (a nickname that I gave to the guy who lives in the alley behind our apartment, not the Sorcerer Supreme) told me that my skills would be best utilized under your tutelage.

When I was younger, I lost both of my eyelids in a freak bicycle accident. As I sat staring at the folds of skin that once were attached to my head, I closed my eyes to hold back the tears. What?! My eyelids had grown back!

Years later, a lawnmower engine that I was working on exploded. The shrapnel took off my right eyelid. Within seconds, I was blinking again. In a fit of shock, I began tearing my eyelids off. After creating a pile of around two dozen or so, I came to a realization. I have regenerative powers!

After an unfortunate mishap that left me without toes on my right foot, I found out that it's limited to my eyelids. That may not sound like much, but it has been extremely useful since I began my career in fighting crime.

If I need to sneak into a building after it's closed, I can smash eyelids into the door hole under the strike plate so that it doesn't lock properly. Vicious guard dogs that need distracting? Their owners obviously don't know how tasty an endless supply of eyelids can be to an animal that thinks with its teeth.

The most amazing aspect of my powers though is instant first aid. If the eyelids are applied to wounds after immediately coming off of my body, they will adhere to injuries with all of the benefits of the owner's real skin. A living bandage on the team would be sure to have its advantages.

Thank you very much for any consideration to be a part of your fine organization.

Darrick Patrick (The Eyelid)
Dayton, Ohio

P.S. I always keep honey, cinnamon, and mint in my utility belt. Bad breath or a nervous nature? With a quick pull of my eyelid, you'll never be without chewing gum...of sorts.

**Dear Darrick "The Eyelid" Patrick,**

**You were so close. You practically had the job. It was yours. Right up until that last sentence. Maybe we can look at this as a learning experience. Next time you're in an interview, maybe don't mention people chewing on your eyelids. That's all. I know it might come up organically in conversation sometimes--somebody asks for a piece of gum, let's say--but I really urge you to think twice about it. It's fairly disgusting.**

Dear Great Lakes Avengers,

I have the ability to break almost any kind of wood, usually before noon. I call myself Morning W-- ...on second thought, how about the GLA's cook? Food probably goes right through Doorman :), Flatman doesn't seem to need much, Big Bertha... okay, how about PR? I've been a fan of GLA since the Hawkeye/Mockingbird days; maybe I can advertise for the GLA? Not really a super-power, but hey, you said you'll take anybody--right? At least until I hone my skills enough to fight.

George Tabet

**I see what you did there, George. I see what you did.**

Dear Great Lakes Avengers,

I heard there's an opening and I guess I want in! If you must really know, my name is Brett Leaf, and I reside in Milwaukee, Wisconsin. My powers are the ability to never be put on hold while on the phone (I know...CRAZY, right?!?!?) Secondly, I can turn myself into any kind of leaf that I want. Just don't expect much from me during winter. I swear I'm good, I've only had a cold one with Red Skull one time, I even made him pay!

Brett Leaf
Milwaukee,WI

**Finally, somebody with real powers! Just think of all the different leaf possibilities! Maple, elm, oak, and...dare I even say it.. palm! The only thing troubling me is your willingness to associate with one of the world's most despicable villains, although I suppose we can make an exception for somebody capable of turning into a banana leaf.**

Dear Great Lake Avengers,

I am so excited to be writing you! I know this is going to sound strange, but my name is Dinah Lyric Soar. I am the daughter of your former teammate, Dinah Soar, who you thought died, she was actually shifted to a neighboring dimension, Earth-617. However, something went wrong and she ended up in the past. There she met a very nice musician/private investigator named Larry Lyric and they fell in love. They eventually married and I was born. I grew up with a pretty regularly life, all things considered. Mom taught me to fly and her native tongue. Everything was pretty great until about a year ago, my sonic powers began to change slightly. Instead of a sonic scream, it seemed to do a number of different things. My dad discovered the different abilities had to do with different pitches. I could cook a mean grilled cheese sandwich with a B-flat for instance. I also learned how to summon pigeons, which was super useful to mess up statues. One day, a few weeks ago, I hit a note I'd never hit before and was whisked away to your world. So here I am, just waiting to join you guys and be a member like my mother.

I sure do miss Mom and Dad, but I'm ready for new adventures! I do so hope you will let me join!

Thank you again,

Dinah L. Soar
Detroit, formerly of Earth-617, now Earth-616

**Dear Dinah L. Soar,**

**Wow! What a load off everyone's minds! I told Mr. Immortal and he was overjoyed--although the part about her marrying somebody else did seem to give him pause. Of course, the membership is yours! In fact, there's a rarely used clause in our team charter which gives preference to the children of members, so the membership process should be a breeze. We might even waive your enrollment fee, or at least reduce it by 10%. Either way, welcome aboard!**

---

**We're very excited to show you our final lineup for the All-New, All-Different, All-Pretty-Boring Great Lakes Avengers Support Squad--also known as A.N.A.D.A.P.B.G.L.A.S.S. (We're working on the name, but the fact that it spells out a word near the end there is promising, right?) Come back next issue to see if you and your extraordinarily mundane powers made the cut!**

---

## NEXT:

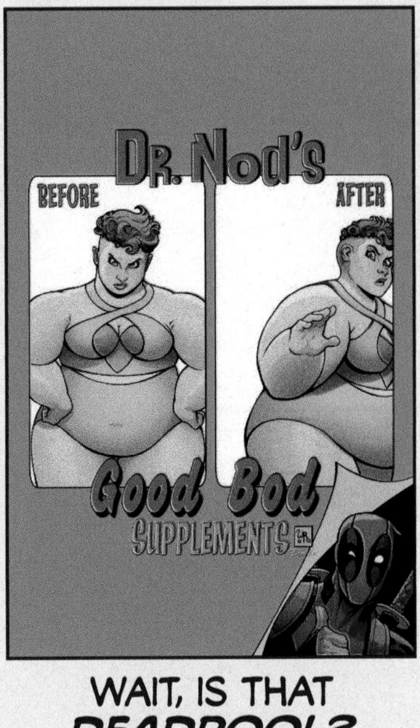

DR. NOD'S
BEFORE
AFTER
Good Bod
SUPPLEMENTS


## WAIT, IS THAT *DEADPOOL?*

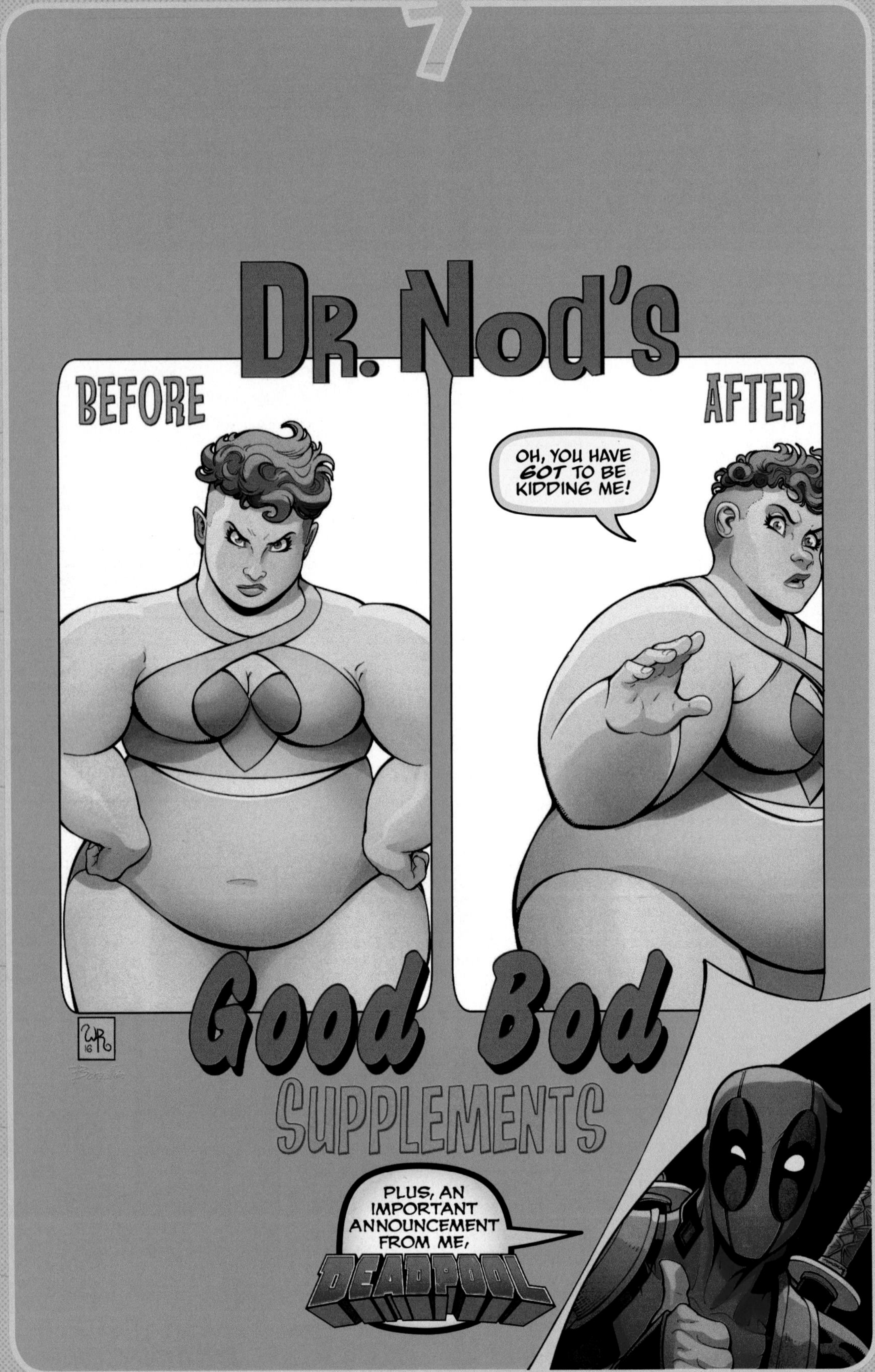

DR. NOD'S
BEFORE
AFTER
OH, YOU HAVE GOT TO BE KIDDING ME!
Good Bod
SUPPLEMENTS
PLUS, AN IMPORTANT ANNOUNCEMENT FROM ME,
DEADPOOL

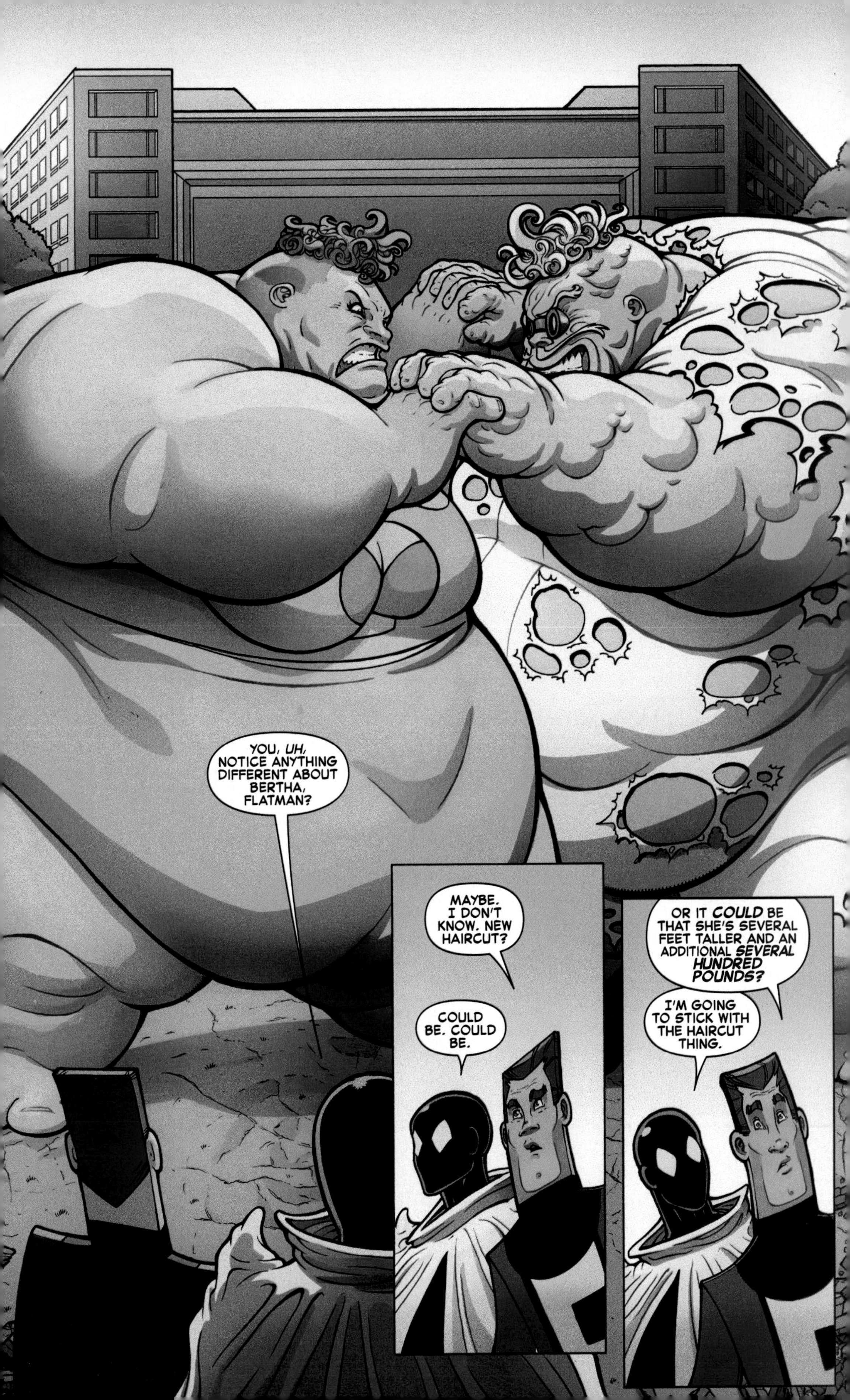
YOU, UH, NOTICE ANYTHING DIFFERENT ABOUT BERTHA, FLATMAN?
MAYBE. I DON'T KNOW. NEW HAIRCUT?
COULD BE. COULD BE.
OR IT COULD BE THAT SHE'S SEVERAL FEET TALLER AND AN ADDITIONAL SEVERAL HUNDRED POUNDS?
I'M GOING TO STICK WITH THE HAIRCUT THING.

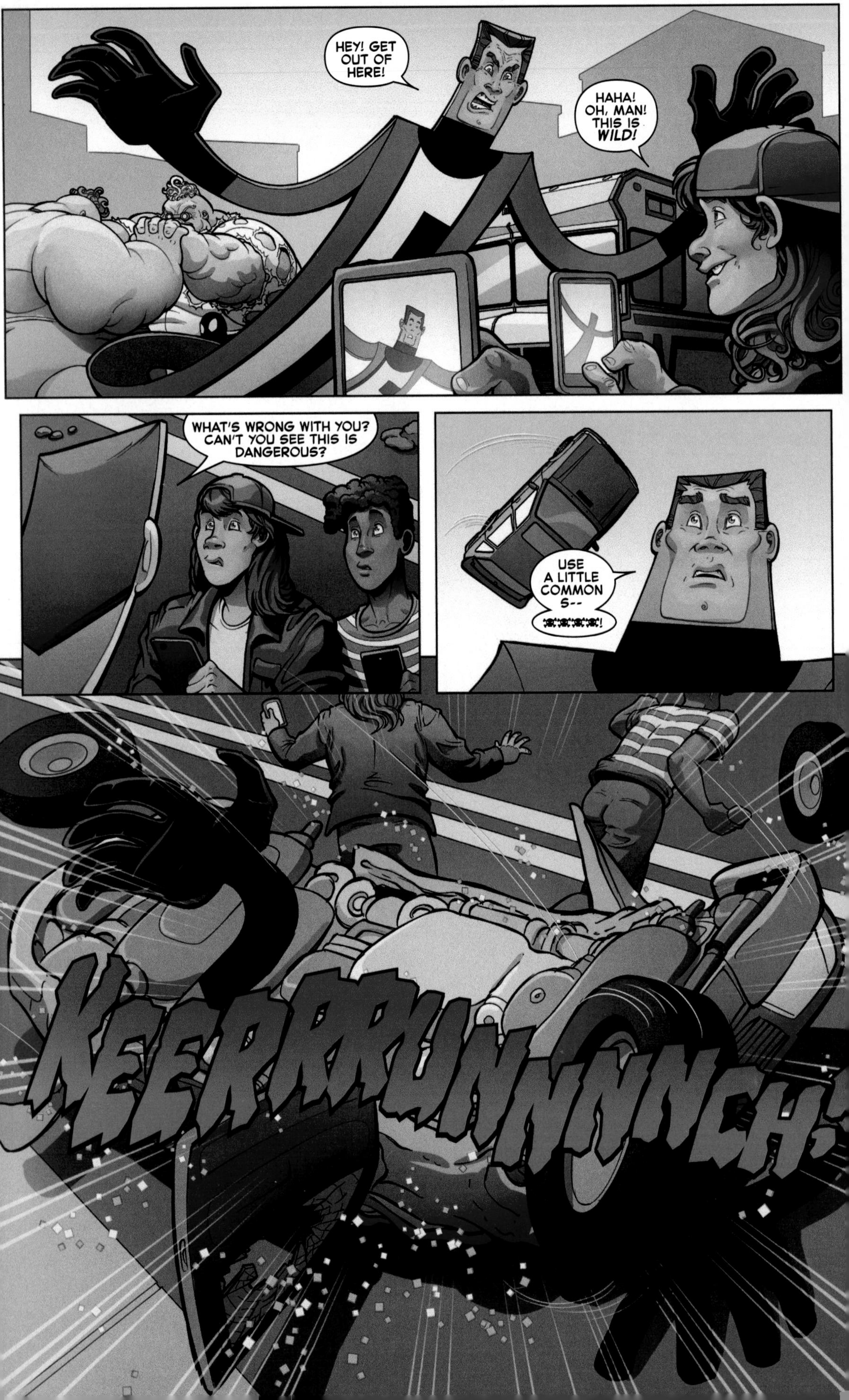
HEY! GET OUT OF HERE!
HAHA! OH, MAN! THIS IS *WILD!*
WHAT'S WRONG WITH YOU? CAN'T YOU SEE THIS IS DANGEROUS?
USE A LITTLE COMMON S--
KEERRRRUNNNNNCH!

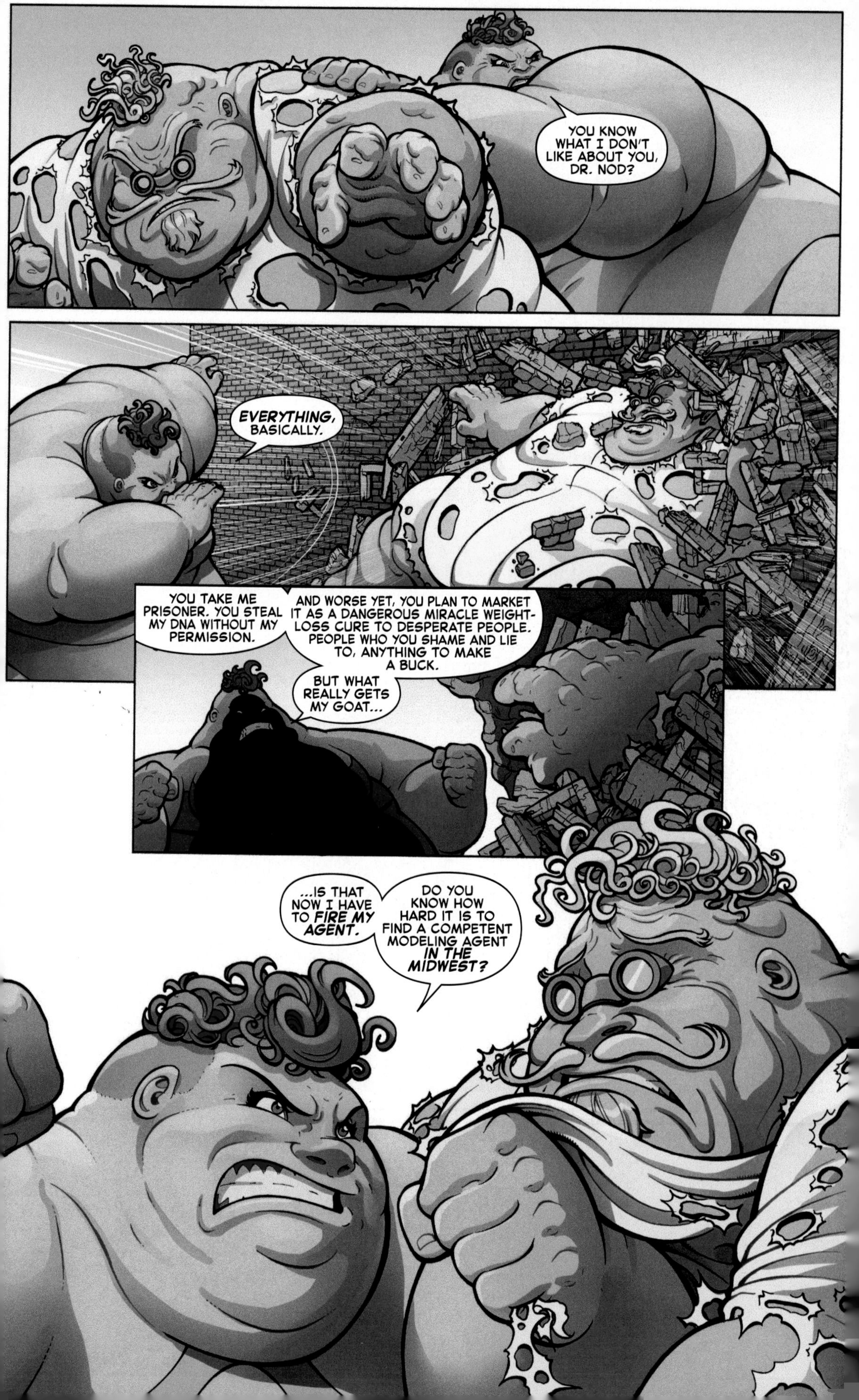

YOU KNOW WHAT I DON'T LIKE ABOUT YOU, DR. NOD?
*EVERYTHING,* BASICALLY.
YOU TAKE ME PRISONER. YOU STEAL MY DNA WITHOUT MY PERMISSION.
AND WORSE YET, YOU PLAN TO MARKET IT AS A DANGEROUS MIRACLE WEIGHT-LOSS CURE TO DESPERATE PEOPLE. PEOPLE WHO YOU SHAME AND LIE TO, ANYTHING TO MAKE A BUCK.
BUT WHAT REALLY GETS MY GOAT...
...IS THAT NOW I HAVE TO *FIRE MY AGENT.*
DO YOU KNOW HOW HARD IT IS TO FIND A COMPETENT MODELING AGENT *IN THE MIDWEST?*

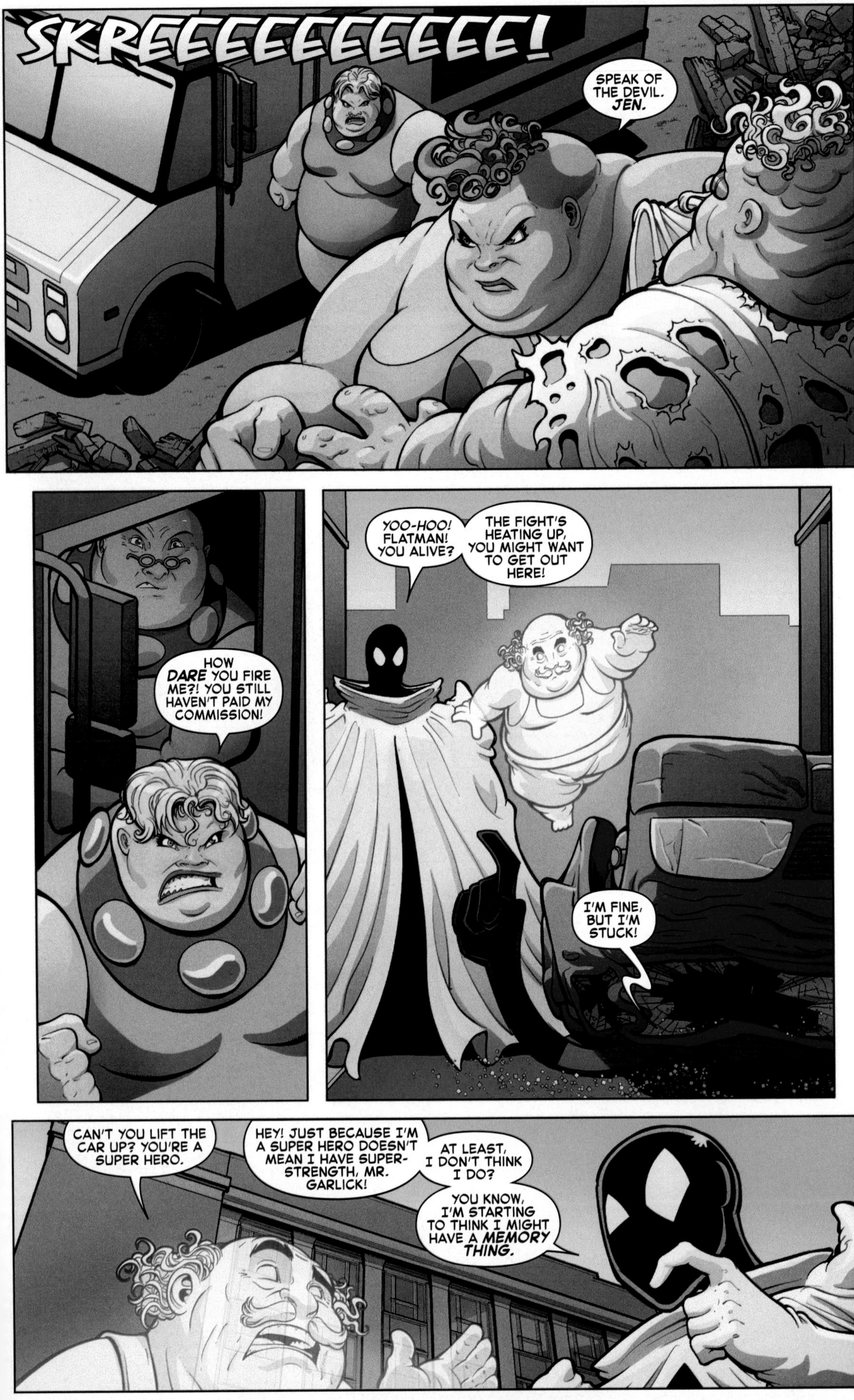
SKREEEEEEEEEE!
SPEAK OF THE DEVIL. JEN.
HOW DARE YOU FIRE ME?! YOU STILL HAVEN'T PAID MY COMMISSION!
YOO-HOO! FLATMAN! YOU ALIVE?
THE FIGHT'S HEATING UP, YOU MIGHT WANT TO GET OUT HERE!
I'M FINE, BUT I'M STUCK!
CAN'T YOU LIFT THE CAR UP? YOU'RE A SUPER HERO.
HEY! JUST BECAUSE I'M A SUPER HERO DOESN'T MEAN I HAVE SUPER-STRENGTH, MR. GARLICK!
AT LEAST, I DON'T THINK I DO?
YOU KNOW, I'M STARTING TO THINK I MIGHT HAVE A MEMORY THING.

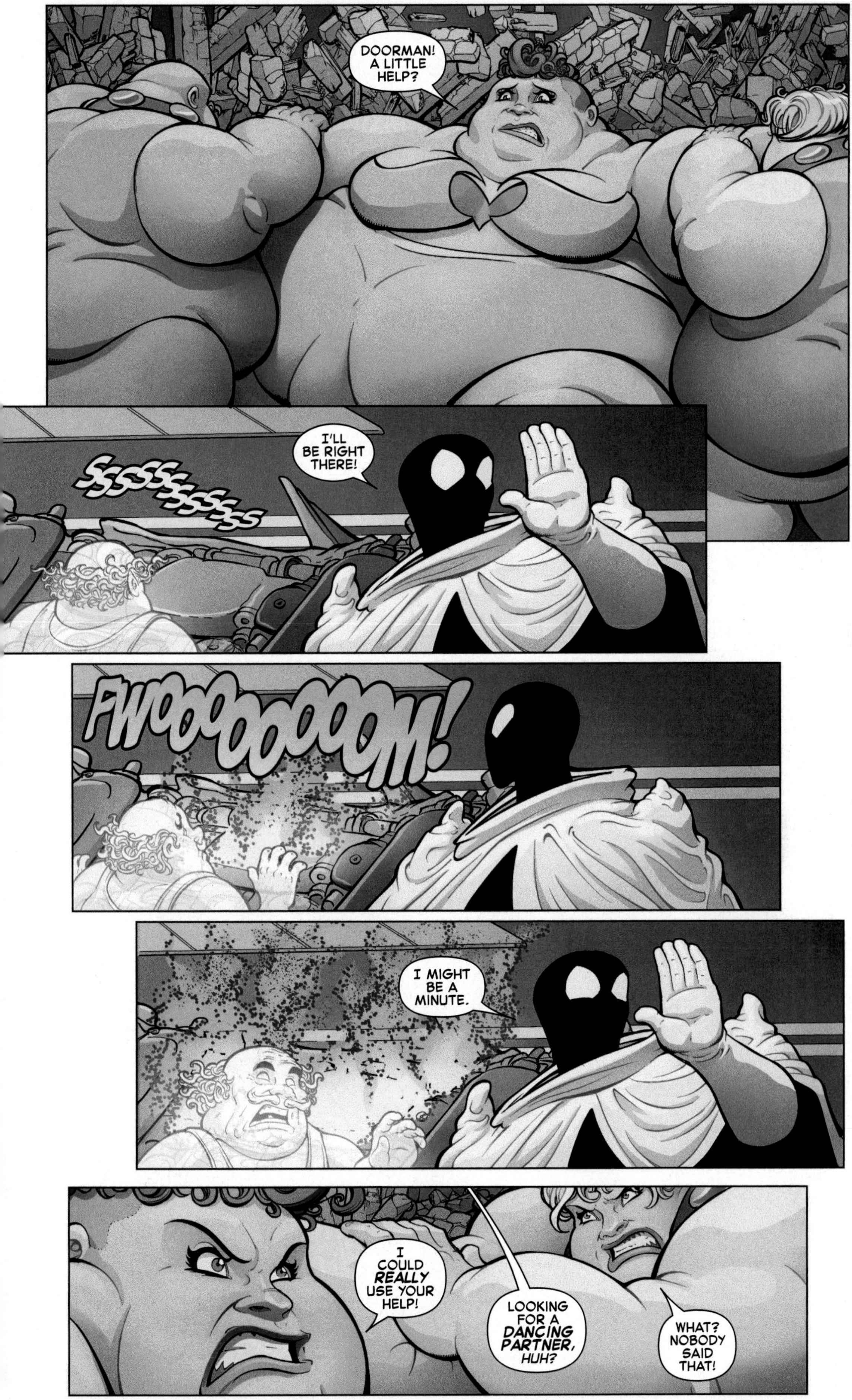
DOORMAN! A LITTLE HELP?
I'LL BE RIGHT THERE!
SSSSSSSSSSS
FWOOOOOOOOM!
I MIGHT BE A MINUTE.
I COULD *REALLY* USE YOUR HELP!
LOOKING FOR A *DANCING PARTNER,* HUH?
WHAT? NOBODY SAID THAT!

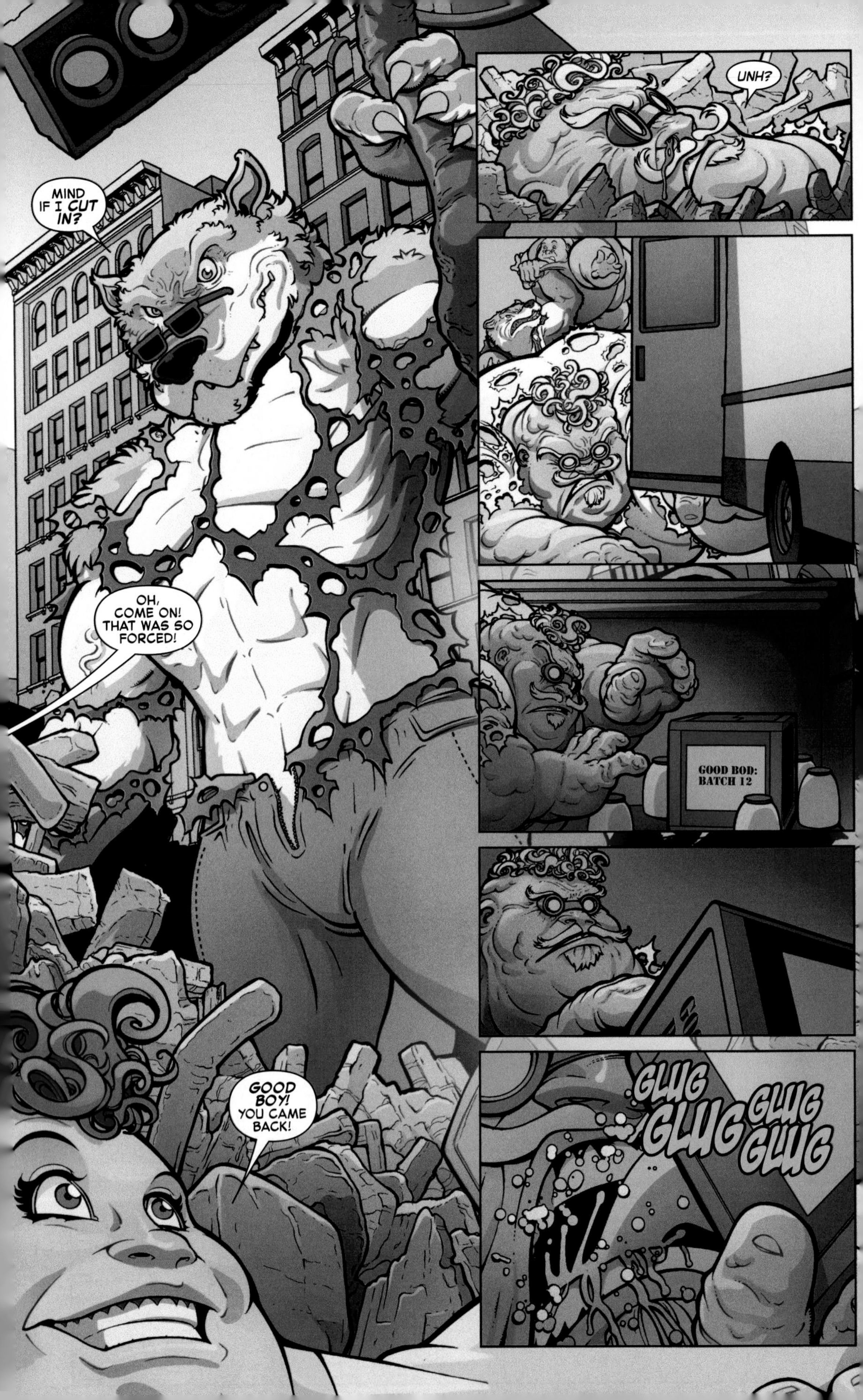
MIND IF I CUT IN?
OH, COME ON! THAT WAS SO FORCED!
GOOD BOY! YOU CAME BACK!
UNH?
GOOD BOD: BATCH 12
GLUG GLUG GLUG GLUG

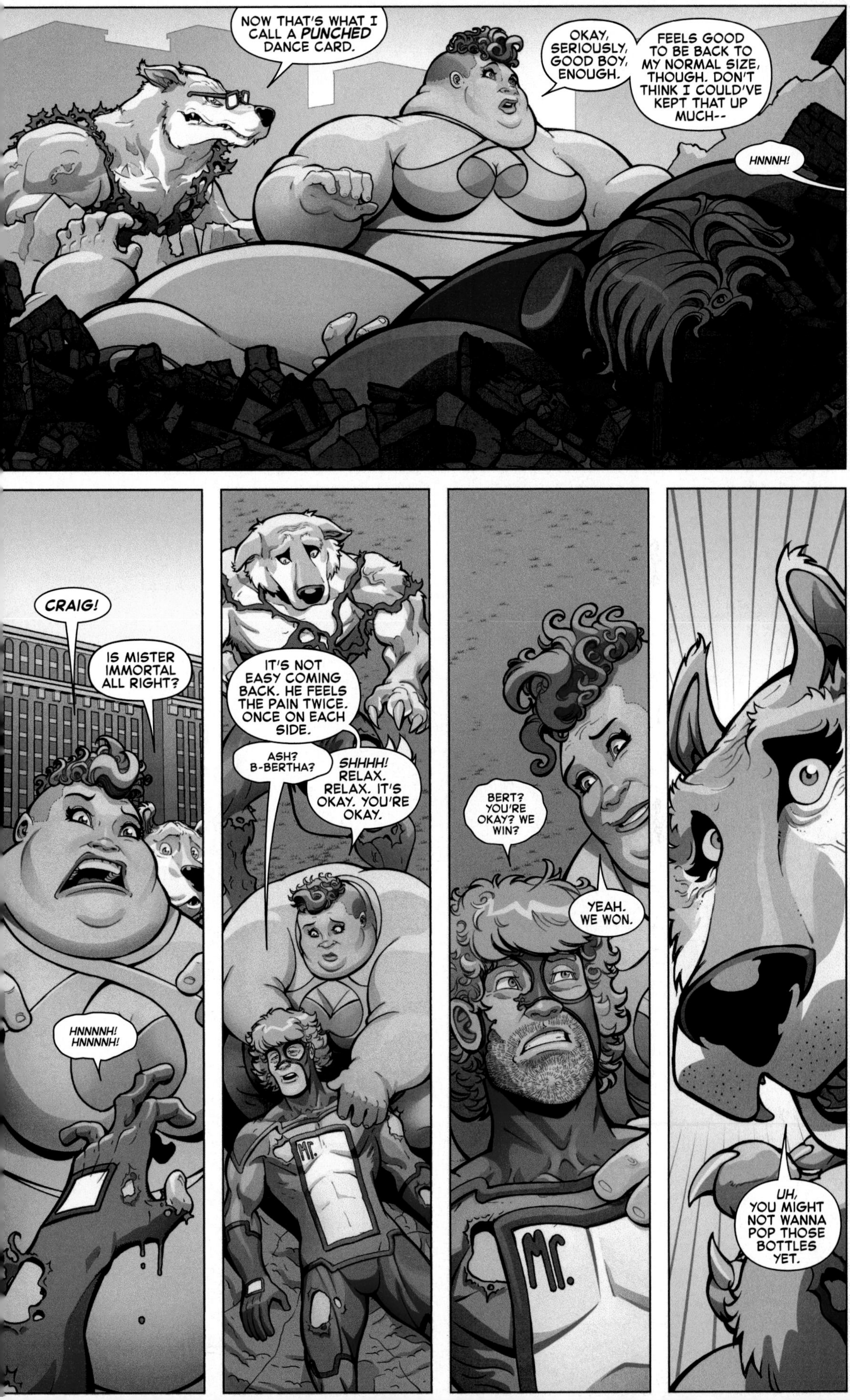
NOW THAT'S WHAT I CALL A *PUNCHED* DANCE CARD.
OKAY, SERIOUSLY, GOOD BOY, ENOUGH.
FEELS GOOD TO BE BACK TO MY NORMAL SIZE, THOUGH. DON'T THINK I COULD'VE KEPT THAT UP MUCH--
*HNNNH!*
*CRAIG!*
IS MISTER IMMORTAL ALL RIGHT?
*HNNNNH! HNNNNH!*
IT'S NOT EASY COMING BACK. HE FEELS THE PAIN TWICE. ONCE ON EACH SIDE.
ASH? B-BERTHA?
*SHHHH!* RELAX. RELAX. IT'S OKAY. YOU'RE OKAY.
BERT? YOU'RE OKAY? WE WIN?
YEAH. WE WON.
*UH,* YOU MIGHT NOT WANNA POP THOSE BOTTLES YET.

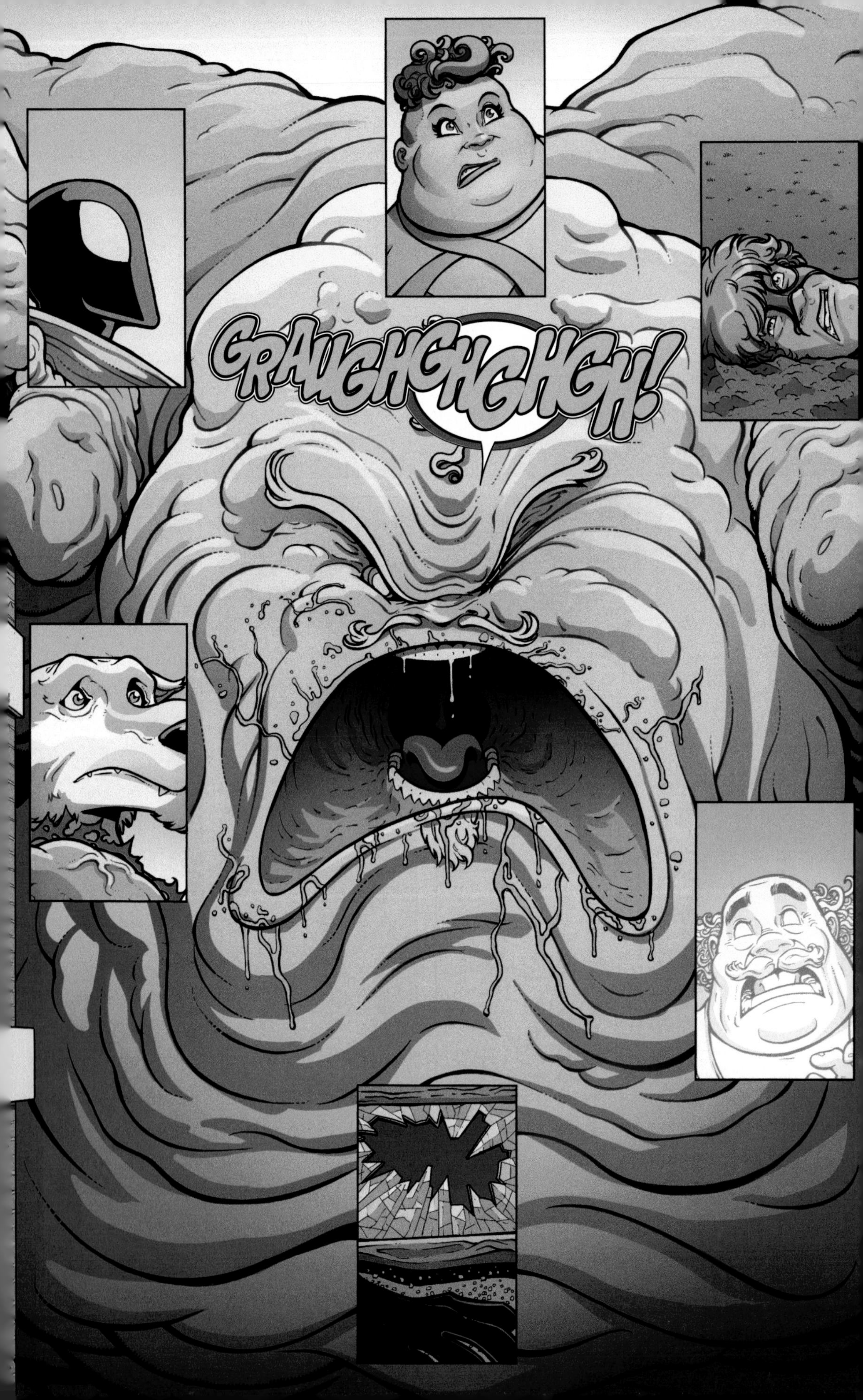
GRAUGHGHGHGH!

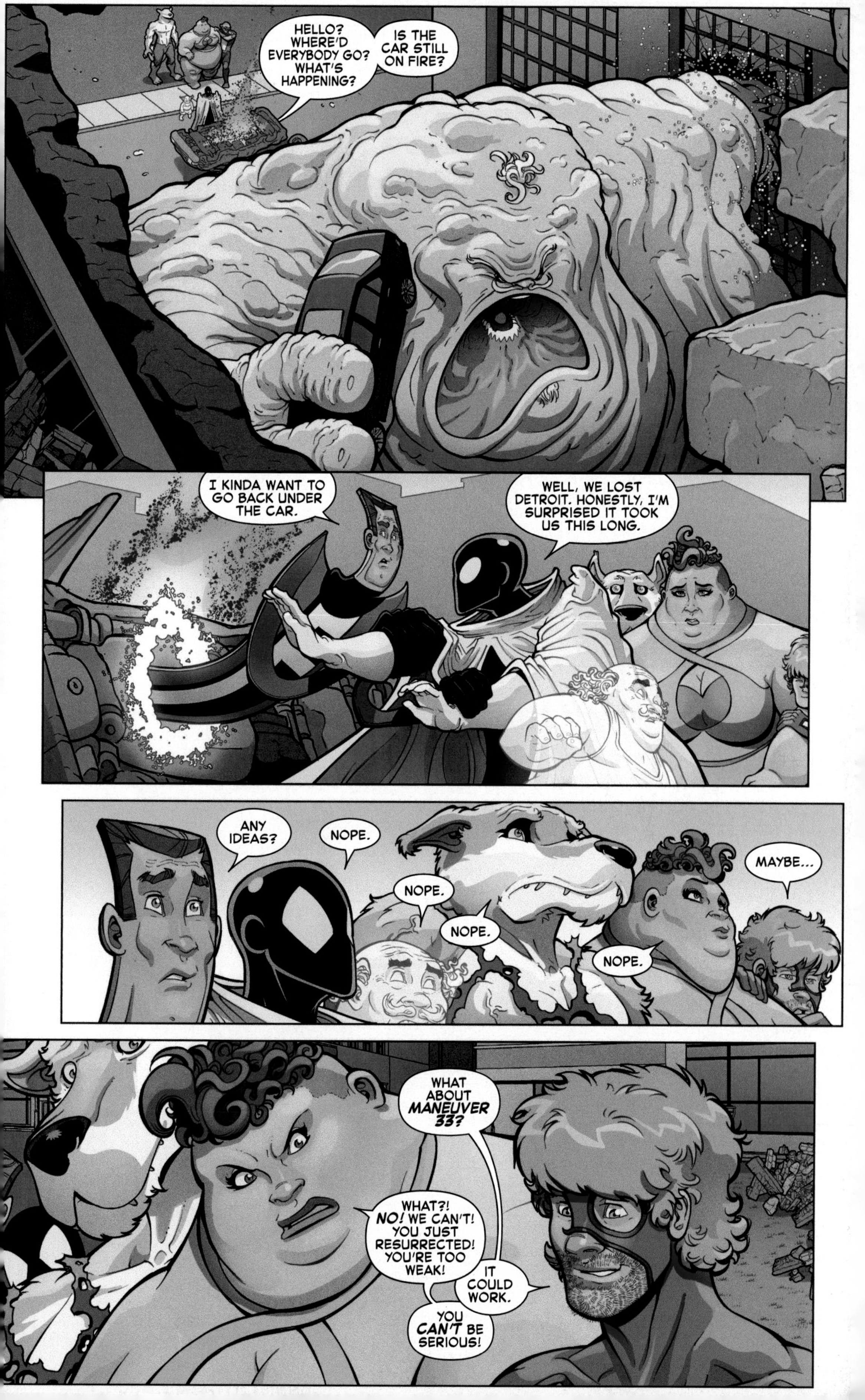
HELLO? WHERE'D EVERYBODY GO? WHAT'S HAPPENING?
IS THE CAR STILL ON FIRE?
I KINDA WANT TO GO BACK UNDER THE CAR.
WELL, WE LOST DETROIT. HONESTLY, I'M SURPRISED IT TOOK US THIS LONG.
ANY IDEAS?
NOPE.
NOPE.
NOPE.
NOPE.
MAYBE...
WHAT ABOUT *MANEUVER 33?*
WHAT?! *NO!* WE CAN'T! YOU JUST RESURRECTED! YOU'RE TOO WEAK!
IT COULD WORK.
YOU *CAN'T* BE SERIOUS!

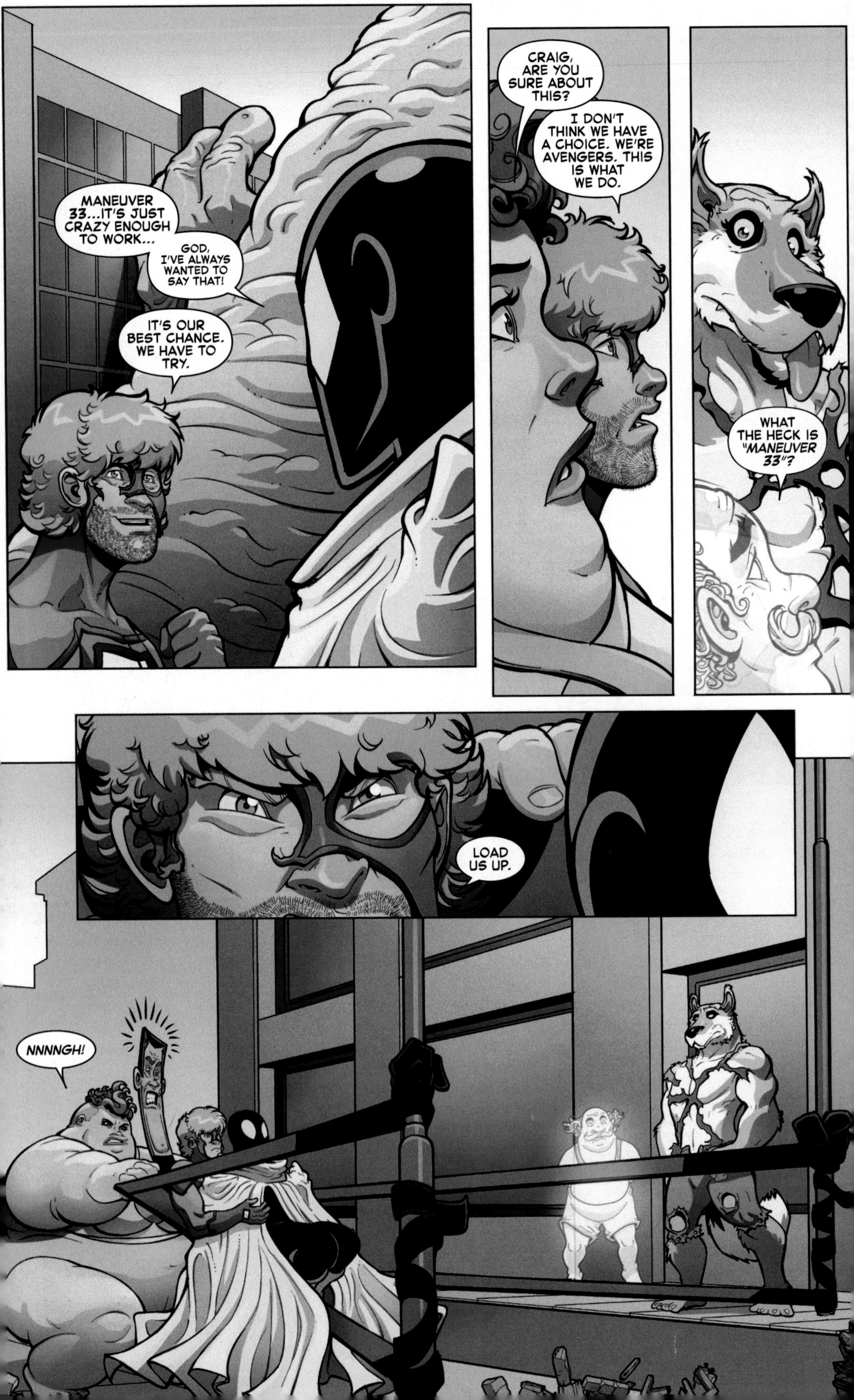
MANEUVER 33...IT'S JUST CRAZY ENOUGH TO WORK...
GOD, I'VE ALWAYS WANTED TO SAY THAT!
IT'S OUR BEST CHANCE. WE HAVE TO TRY.
CRAIG, ARE YOU SURE ABOUT THIS?
I DON'T THINK WE HAVE A CHOICE. WE'RE AVENGERS. THIS IS WHAT WE DO.
WHAT THE HECK IS "MANEUVER 33"?
LOAD US UP.
NNNNGH!

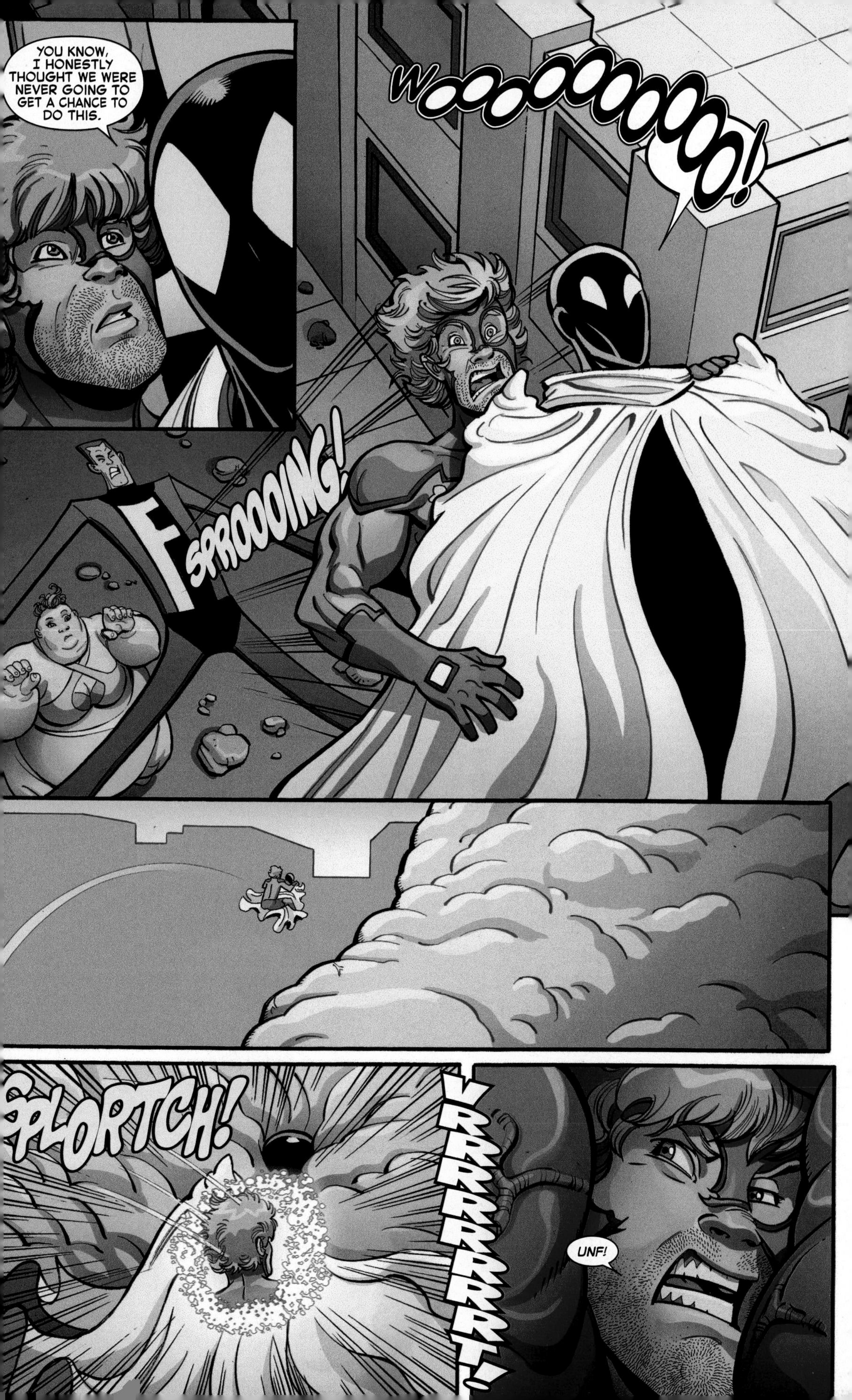
YOU KNOW, I HONESTLY THOUGHT WE WERE NEVER GOING TO GET A CHANCE TO DO THIS.
WOOOOOOOOOOOO!
SPROOOING!
SPLORTCH!
VRRRRRRRT!
UNF!

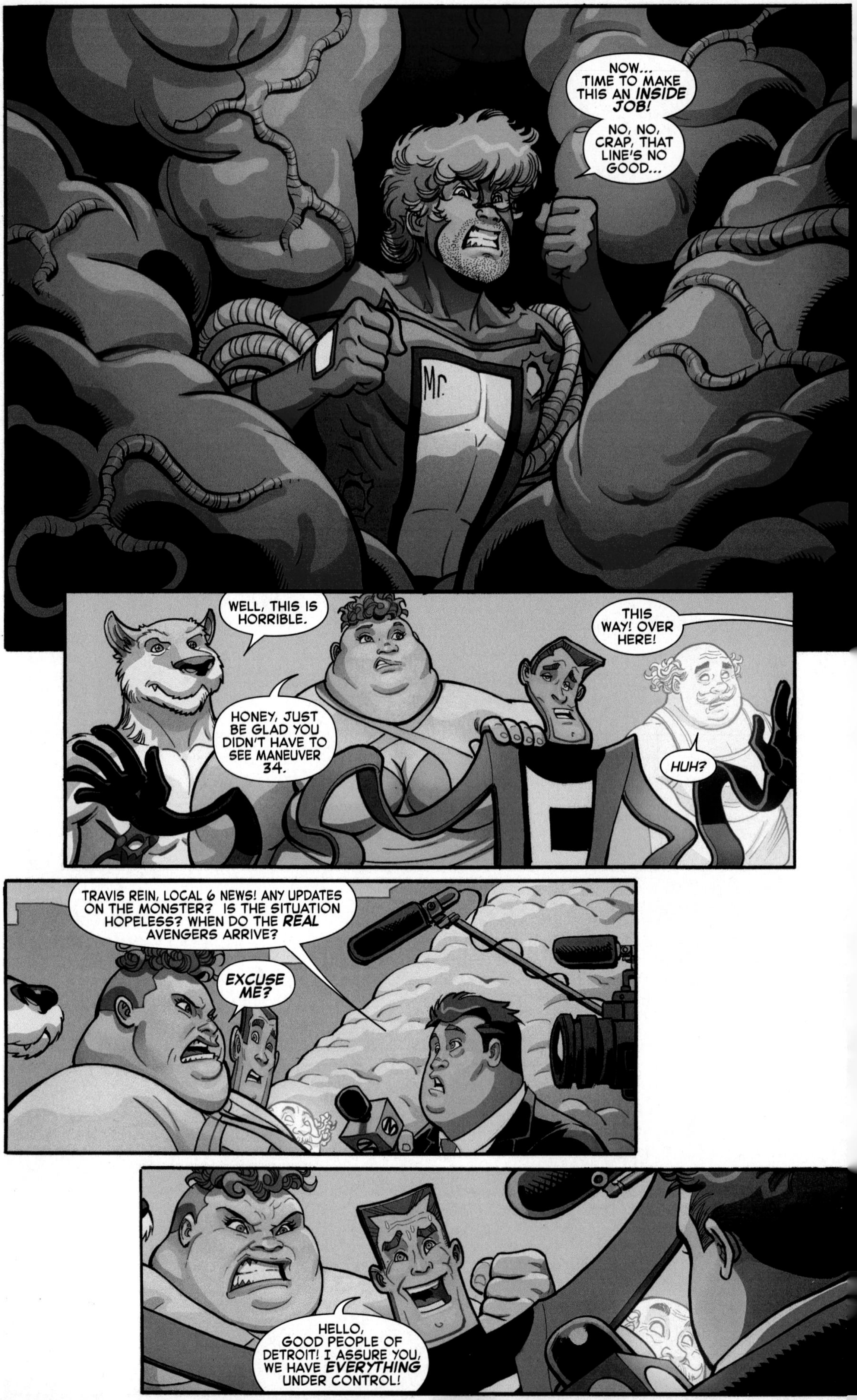
NOW... TIME TO MAKE THIS AN INSIDE JOB!
NO, NO, CRAP, THAT LINE'S NO GOOD...
Mr.
WELL, THIS IS HORRIBLE.
HONEY, JUST BE GLAD YOU DIDN'T HAVE TO SEE MANEUVER 34.
THIS WAY! OVER HERE!
HUH?
TRAVIS REIN, LOCAL 6 NEWS! ANY UPDATES ON THE MONSTER? IS THE SITUATION HOPELESS? WHEN DO THE REAL AVENGERS ARRIVE?
EXCUSE ME?
HELLO, GOOD PEOPLE OF DETROIT! I ASSURE YOU, WE HAVE EVERYTHING UNDER CONTROL!

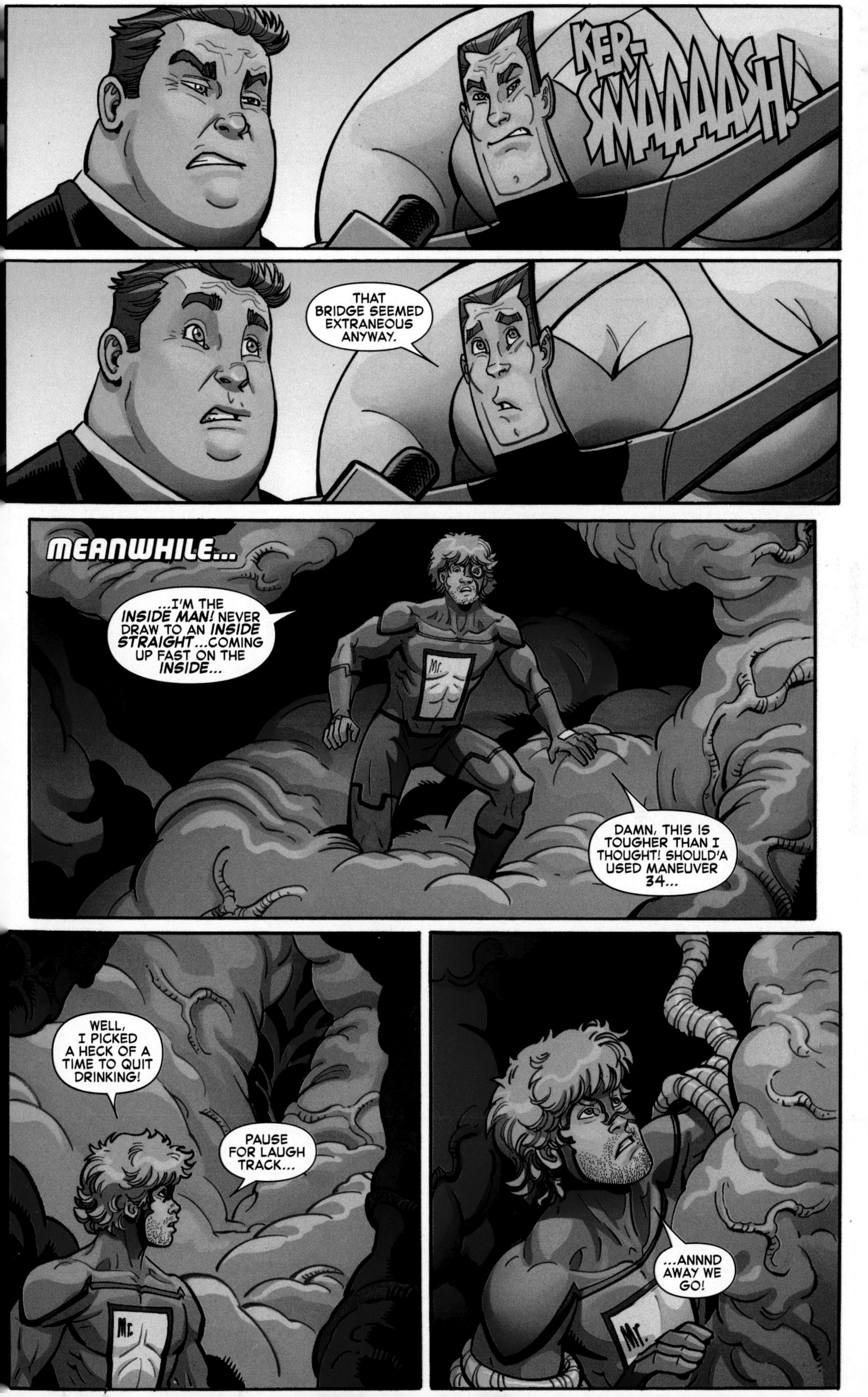
KER-SMAAAASH!
THAT BRIDGE SEEMED EXTRANEOUS ANYWAY.
MEANWHILE...
...I'M THE *INSIDE MAN!* NEVER DRAW TO AN *INSIDE STRAIGHT*...COMING UP FAST ON THE *INSIDE*...
DAMN, THIS IS TOUGHER THAN I THOUGHT! SHOULD'A USED MANEUVER 34...
WELL, I PICKED A HECK OF A TIME TO QUIT DRINKING!
PAUSE FOR LAUGH TRACK...
...ANNND AWAY WE GO!

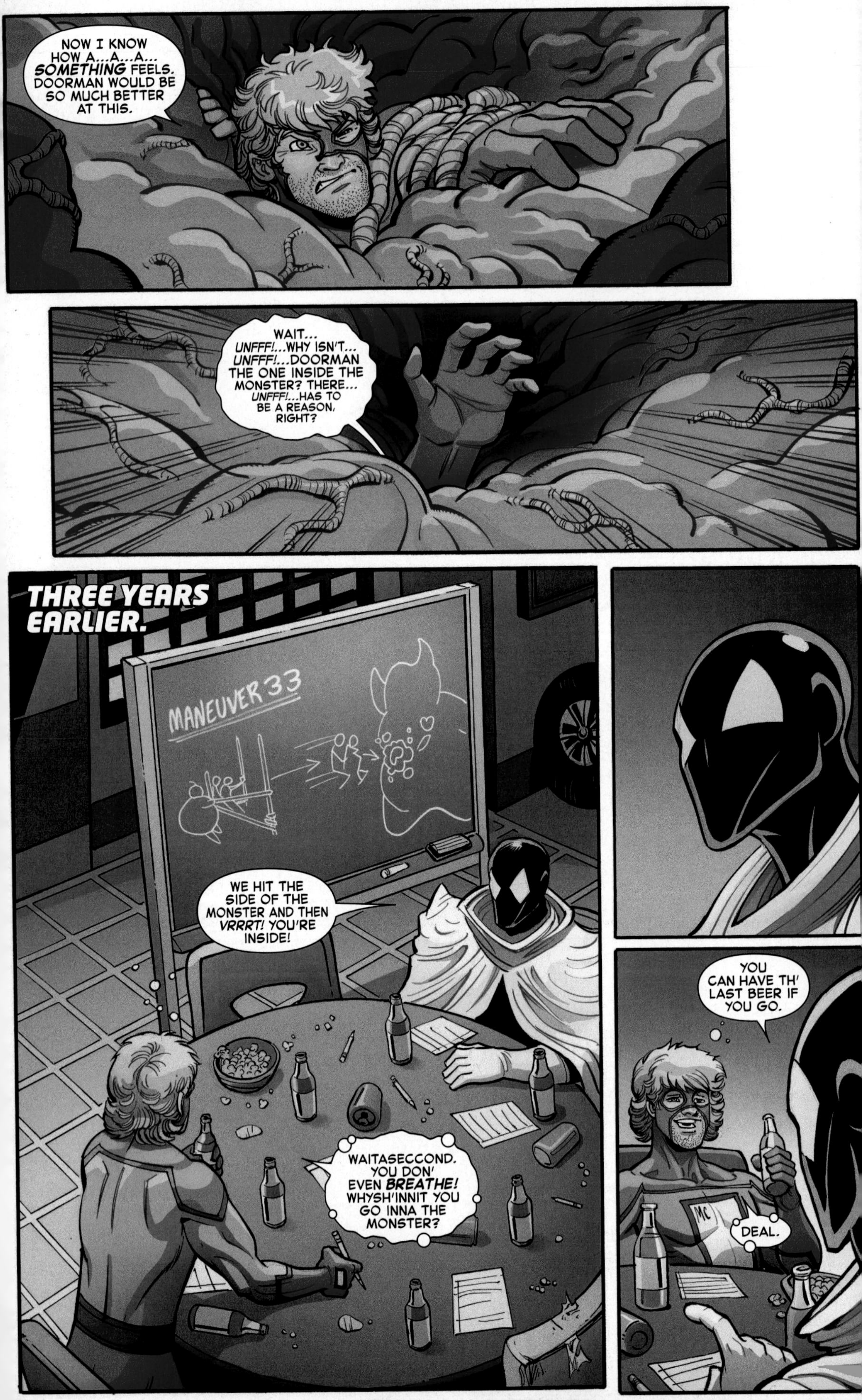
NOW I KNOW HOW A...A...A... SOMETHING FEELS. DOORMAN WOULD BE SO MUCH BETTER AT THIS.
WAIT... UNFFF!...WHY ISN'T... UNFFF!...DOORMAN THE ONE INSIDE THE MONSTER? THERE... UNFFF!...HAS TO BE A REASON, RIGHT?
THREE YEARS EARLIER.
MANEUVER 33
WE HIT THE SIDE OF THE MONSTER AND THEN VRRRT! YOU'RE INSIDE!
WAITASECCOND. YOU DON' EVEN BREATHE! WHYSH'INNIT YOU GO INNA THE MONSTER?
YOU CAN HAVE TH' LAST BEER IF YOU GO.
DEAL.

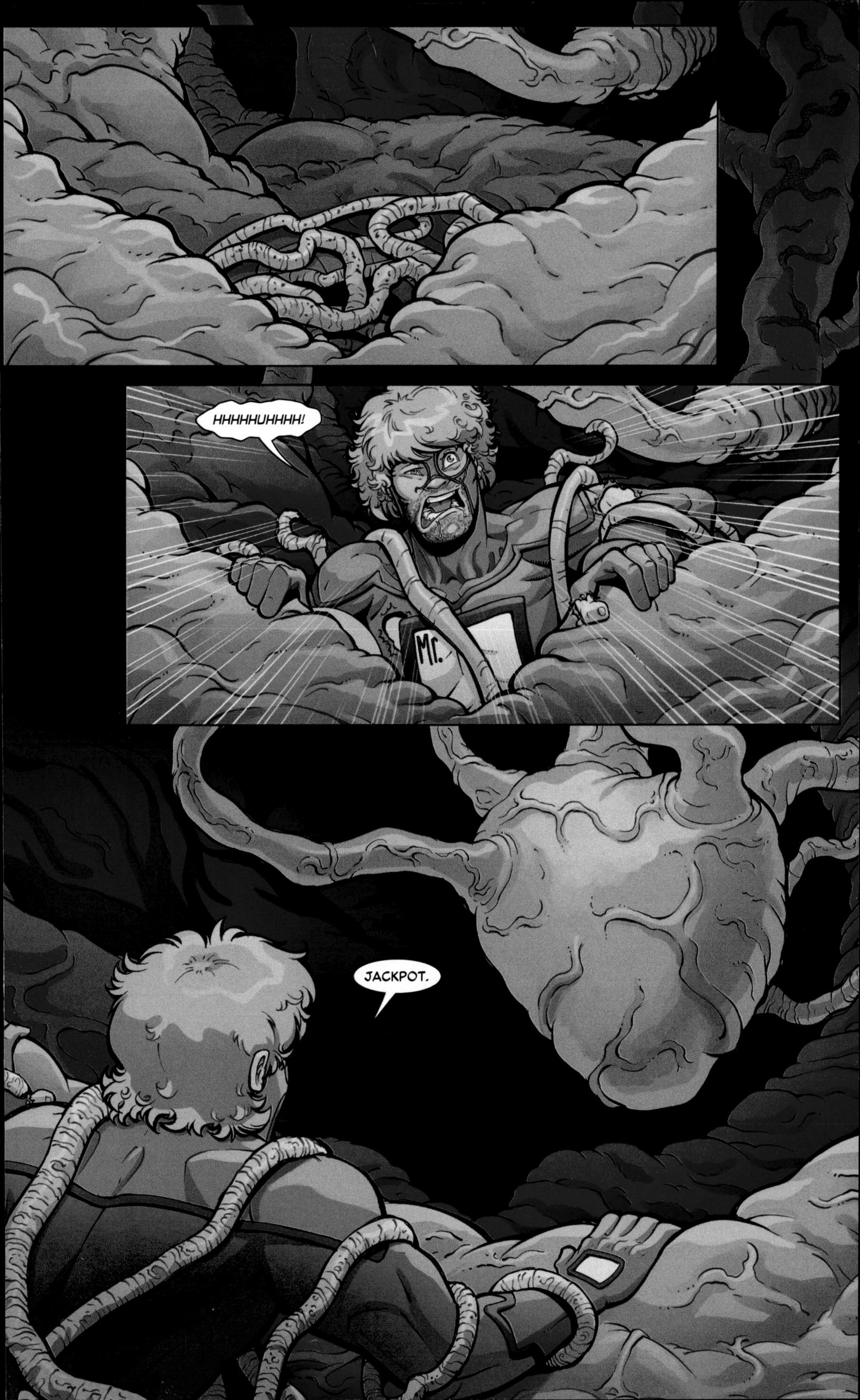
HHHHHUHHHH!
Mr.
JACKPOT.

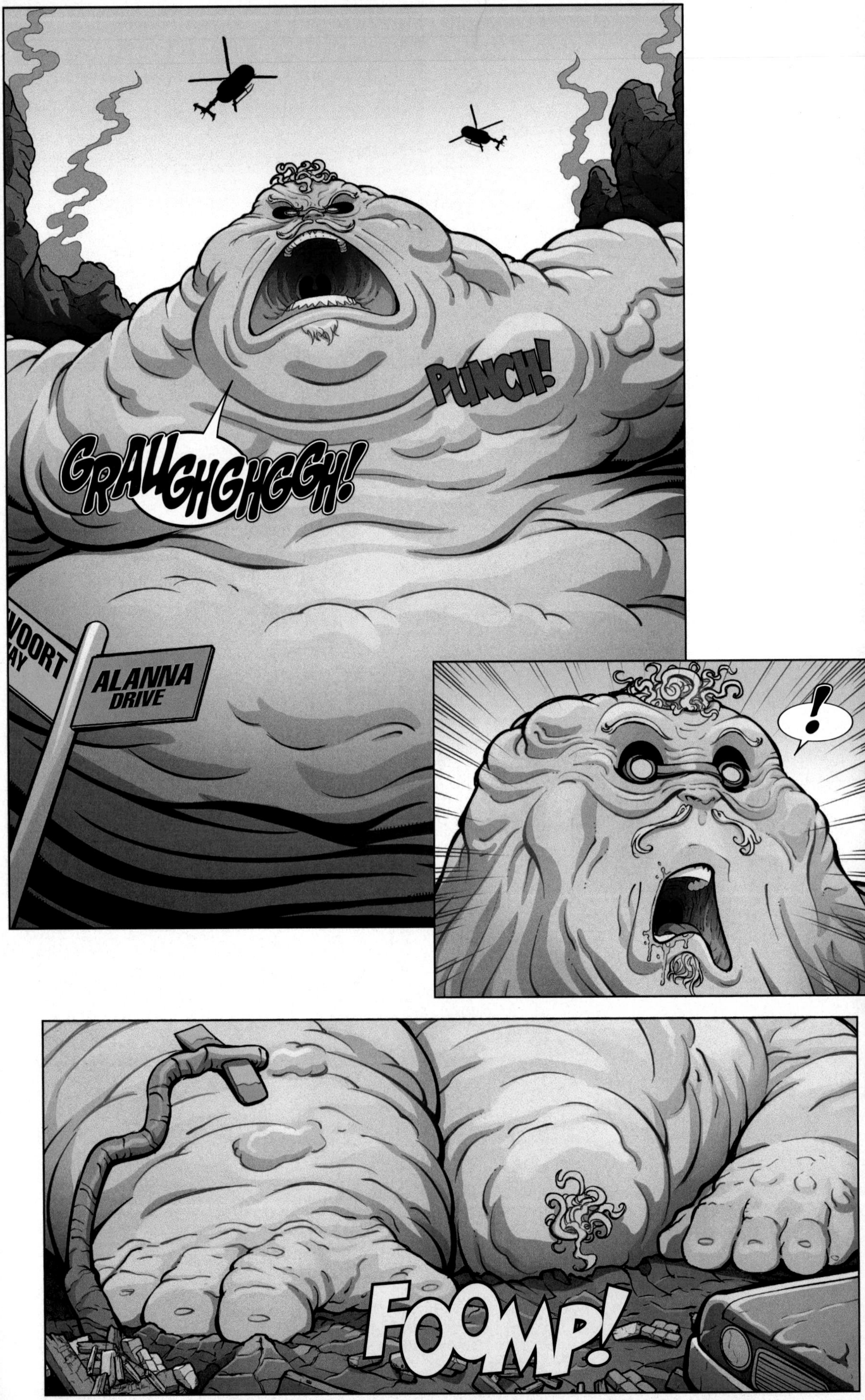
PUNCH!
GRAUGHGHGGH!
ALANNA DRIVE
!
FOOMP!

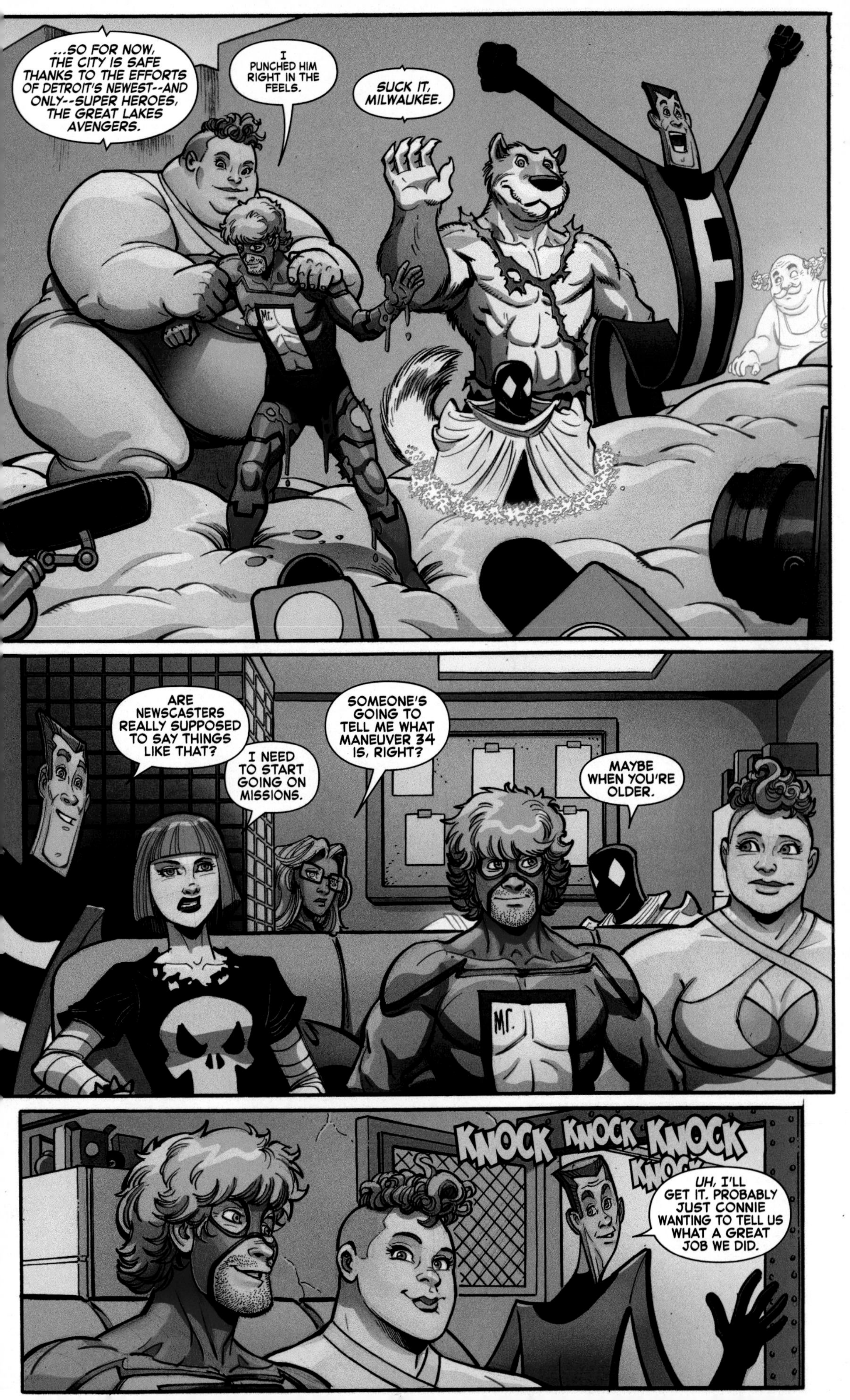
...SO FOR NOW, THE CITY IS SAFE THANKS TO THE EFFORTS OF DETROIT'S NEWEST--AND ONLY--SUPER HEROES, THE GREAT LAKES AVENGERS.
I PUNCHED HIM RIGHT IN THE FEELS.
SUCK IT, MILWAUKEE.
ARE NEWSCASTERS REALLY SUPPOSED TO SAY THINGS LIKE THAT?
I NEED TO START GOING ON MISSIONS.
SOMEONE'S GOING TO TELL ME WHAT MANEUVER 34 IS, RIGHT?
MAYBE WHEN YOU'RE OLDER.
KNOCK KNOCK KNOCK KNOCK
UH, I'LL GET IT. PROBABLY JUST CONNIE WANTING TO TELL US WHAT A GREAT JOB WE DID.

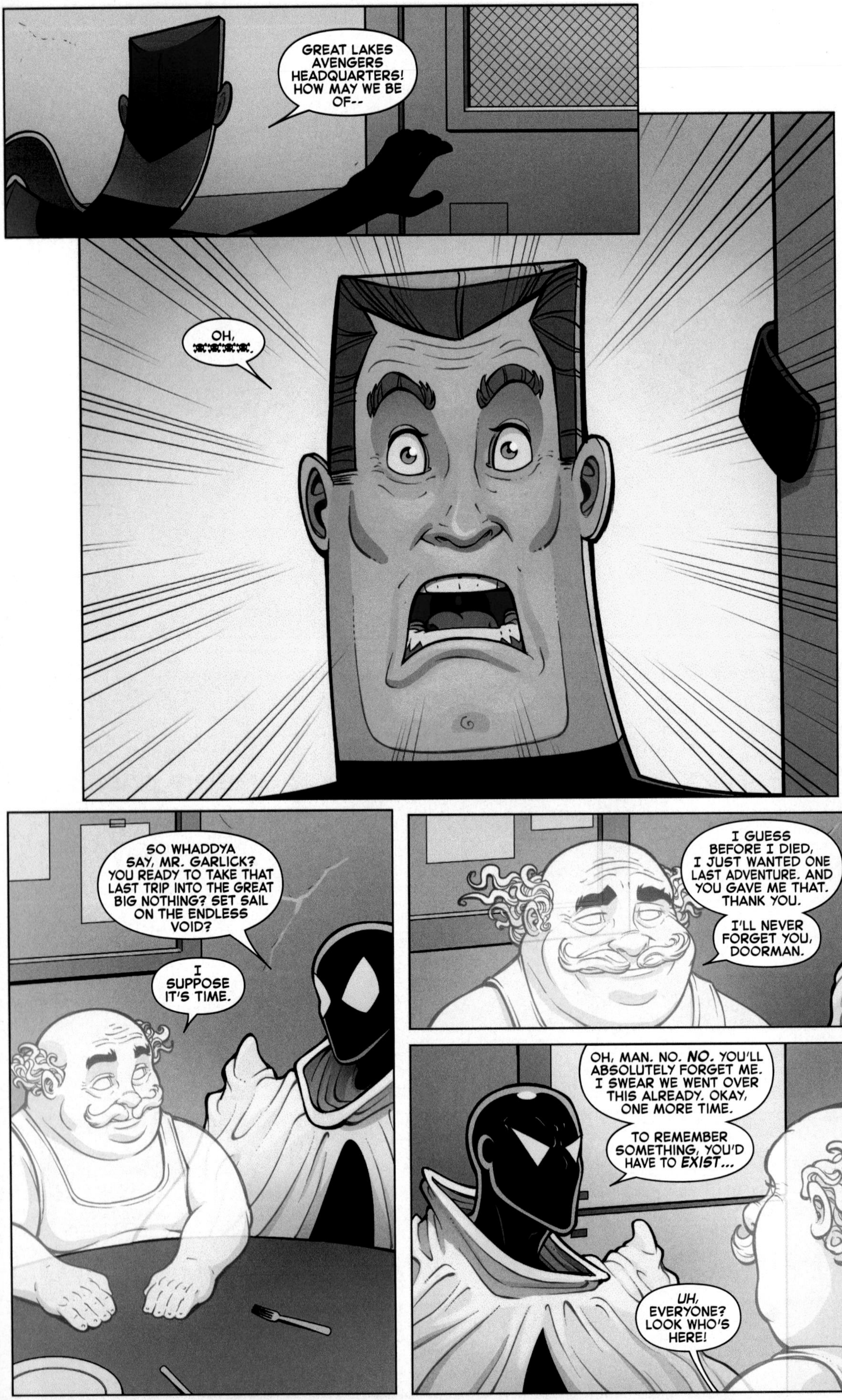
GREAT LAKES AVENGERS HEADQUARTERS! HOW MAY WE BE OF--
OH,
SO WHADDYA SAY, MR. GARLICK? YOU READY TO TAKE THAT LAST TRIP INTO THE GREAT BIG NOTHING? SET SAIL ON THE ENDLESS VOID?
I SUPPOSE IT'S TIME.
I GUESS BEFORE I DIED, I JUST WANTED ONE LAST ADVENTURE. AND YOU GAVE ME THAT. THANK YOU.
I'LL NEVER FORGET YOU, DOORMAN.
OH, MAN. NO. NO. YOU'LL ABSOLUTELY FORGET ME. I SWEAR WE WENT OVER THIS ALREADY. OKAY, ONE MORE TIME.
TO REMEMBER SOMETHING, YOU'D HAVE TO EXIST...
UH, EVERYONE? LOOK WHO'S HERE!

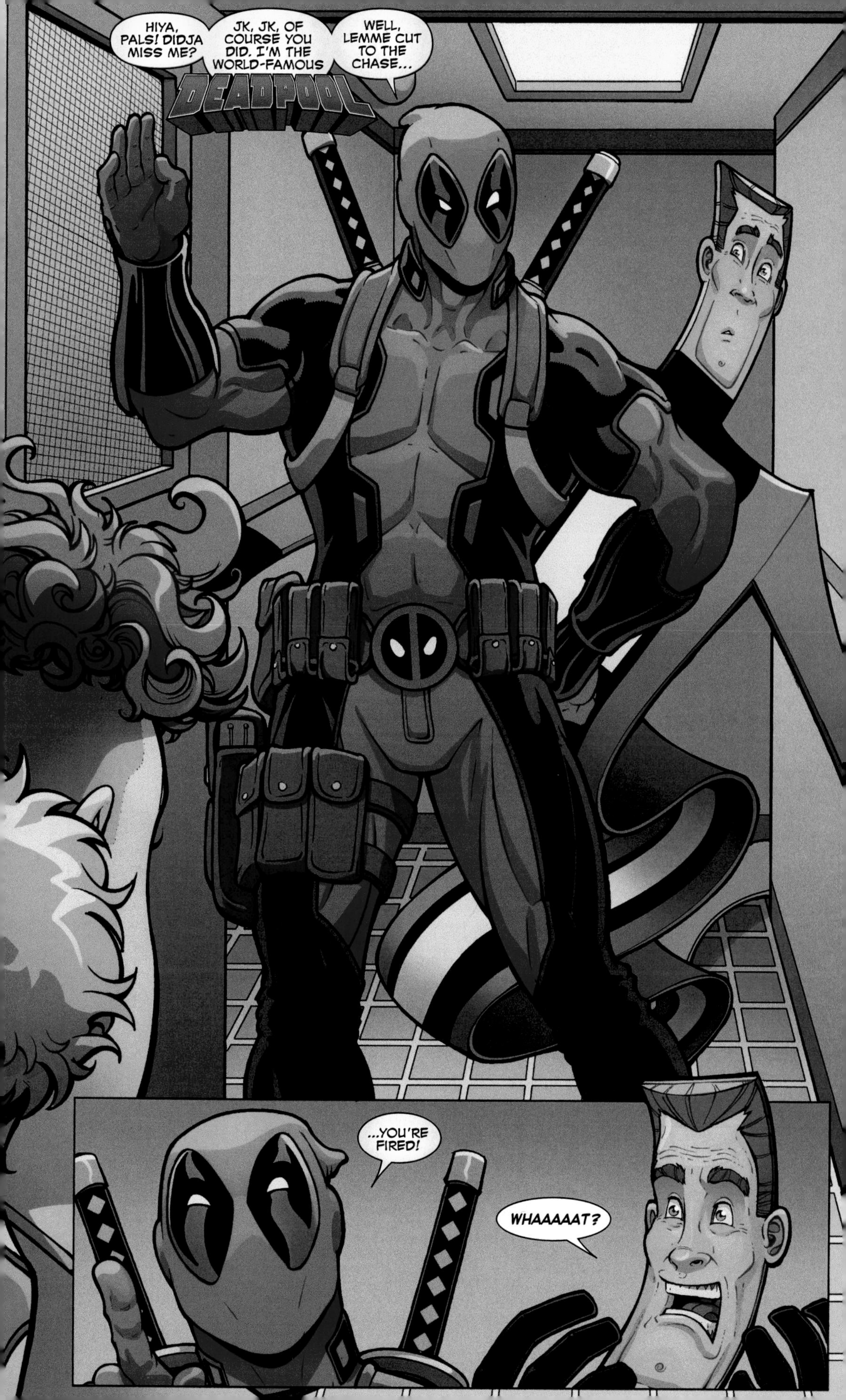
HIYA, PALS! DIDJA MISS ME?
JK, JK, OF COURSE YOU DID. I'M THE WORLD-FAMOUS
DEADPOOL
WELL, LEMME CUT TO THE CHASE...
...YOU'RE FIRED!
WHAAAAAT?

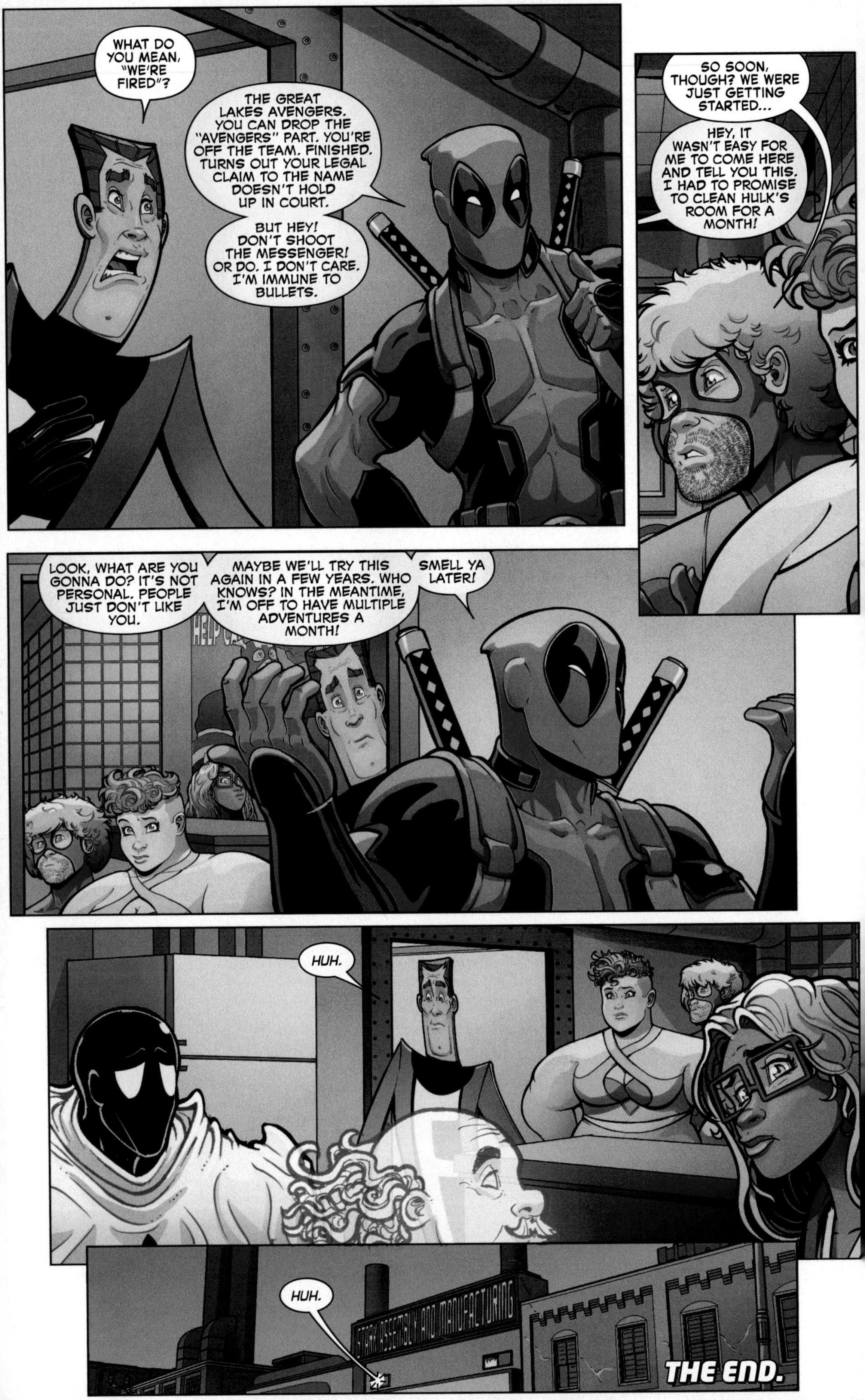
WHAT DO YOU MEAN, "WE'RE FIRED"?
THE GREAT LAKES AVENGERS. YOU CAN DROP THE "AVENGERS" PART. YOU'RE OFF THE TEAM. FINISHED. TURNS OUT YOUR LEGAL CLAIM TO THE NAME DOESN'T HOLD UP IN COURT.
BUT HEY! DON'T SHOOT THE MESSENGER! OR DO. I DON'T CARE. I'M IMMUNE TO BULLETS.
SO SOON, THOUGH? WE WERE JUST GETTING STARTED...
HEY, IT WASN'T EASY FOR ME TO COME HERE AND TELL YOU THIS. I HAD TO PROMISE TO CLEAN HULK'S ROOM FOR A MONTH!
LOOK, WHAT ARE YOU GONNA DO? IT'S NOT PERSONAL. PEOPLE JUST DON'T LIKE YOU.
MAYBE WE'LL TRY THIS AGAIN IN A FEW YEARS. WHO KNOWS? IN THE MEANTIME, I'M OFF TO HAVE MULTIPLE ADVENTURES A MONTH!
SMELL YA LATER!
HUH.
HUH.
STARK ASSEMBLY AND MANUFACTURING
THE END.

It's time at last, eager applicants! For six issues we've listened to you extoll the dubious virtues of your "skills" and "abilities," and we can finally release the full roster of All-New, All-Different, All-Pretty-Boring Great Lakes Avengers Support Squad™, as chosen by our hiring manager/writer, Zac Gorman. Did you make the cut? Find out below!

# The Great Lakes Avengers

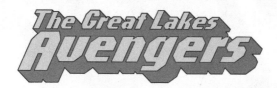

## ACCEPTED

Congratulations! With your uniquely mundane talents and ability to charm Zac Gorman, you've earned your acceptance into the ranks of the All-New, All-Different, All-Pretty-Boring Great Lakes Avengers Support Squad™! There's no pay and you'll probably die pretty fast, but you'll die knowing that you contributed to the glorious legacy of a team that Hawkeye called cool one time. So that's something, right?

The Cheesemonger
Brian Knight
John Bonnett
Brett Leaf
The Mega Horbz
Baron Von Papergreat
Malachi "Dr. Boi" Blades
Dinah L. Soar

## WAITLISTED

Sounds like Zac didn't hate you, but he didn't LOVE you, you know? Or maybe you were just overqualified! Let's face it, you're probably too good for us. Most people are. But when one of the chumps on the "accepted" list kicks it, we'll call you! For realsies!

Aeromajor
Damien White
Mark Duck
George Tabet
King Pumpkin
Dan Tandarich
The Insufferable Prat

## REJECTED

Sorry, buddy--we know we said we'd take anybody, but if you're on this list, you did SOMETHING to break our bylaws/gross out Zac Gorman/bum us the heck out. But it's not the end of the world--there's always the All-New, All-Different, All-Pretty-Boring West Coast Avengers Support Squad™, but they only meet in 1984, so I hope you also have time travel powers.

Awesome Shucks Man
Tim Menuis
Nate Logan
The Perfect Parker
Sormo
The Eyelid

Members of the A.N.A.D.A.P.B.G.L.A.S.S.™ should report to GLA headquarters as soon as--wait, what? We're not Avengers anymore? The book is canceled? Well, dang, that was a lot of wasted manpower. We better wrap this up before Zac tries to shake us down for his hiring manager salary.

The important thing is that you all learned a valuable lesson about friendship. We're not sure what lesson, but you learned it, all right! You learned the heck out of it.

*Arrivederci!*

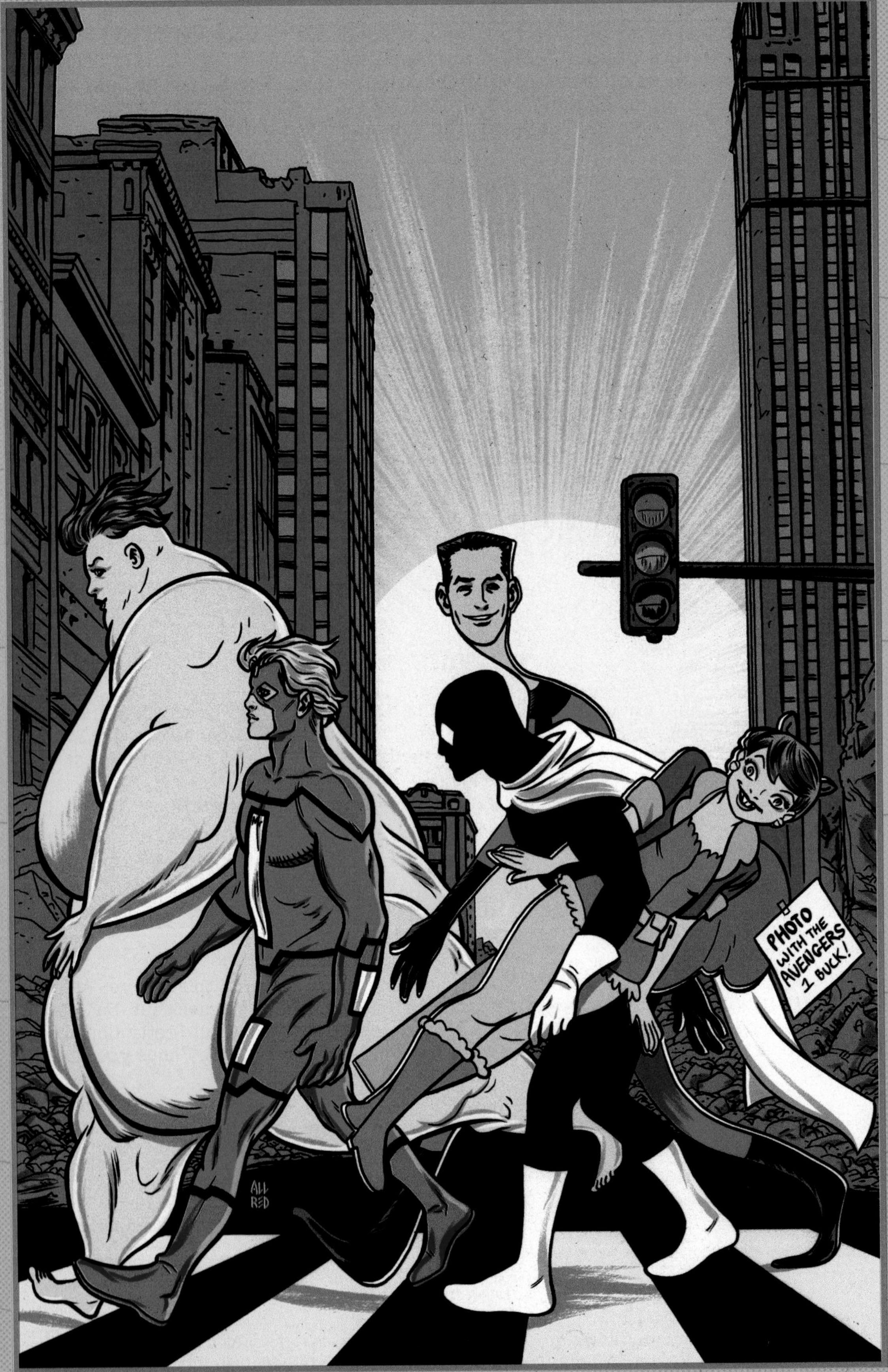
ALL RED
PHOTO WITH THE AVENGERS 1 BUCK!

MICHAEL ALLRED & LAURA ALLRED

1 VARIANT COVER

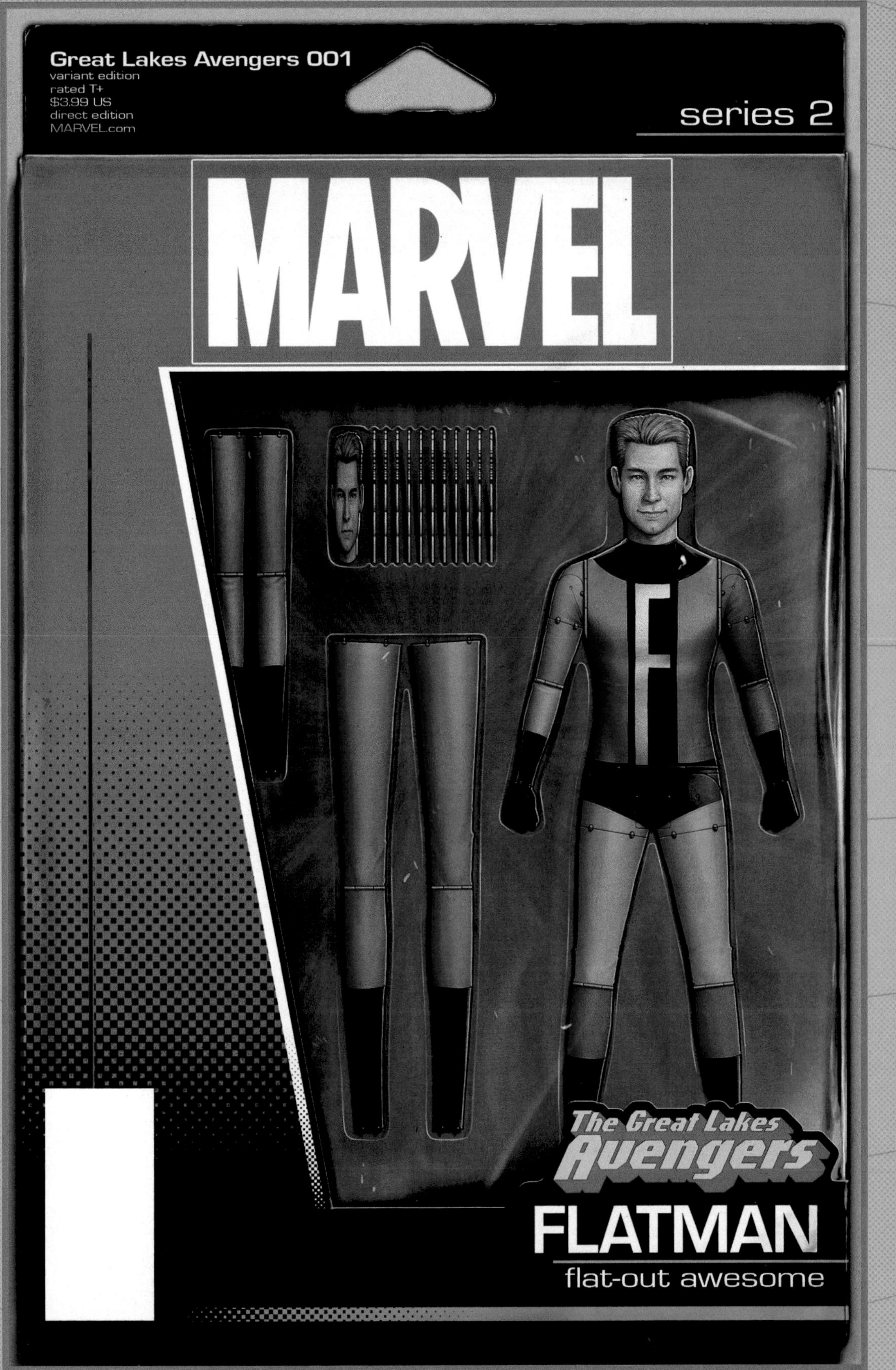

# Great Lakes Avengers 001

variant edition
rated T+
$3.99 US
direct edition
MARVEL.com

series 2

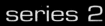

The Great Lakes
Avengers
## FLATMAN
flat-out awesome

# JOHN TYLER CHRISTOPHER
1 ACTION FIGURE VARIANT COVER

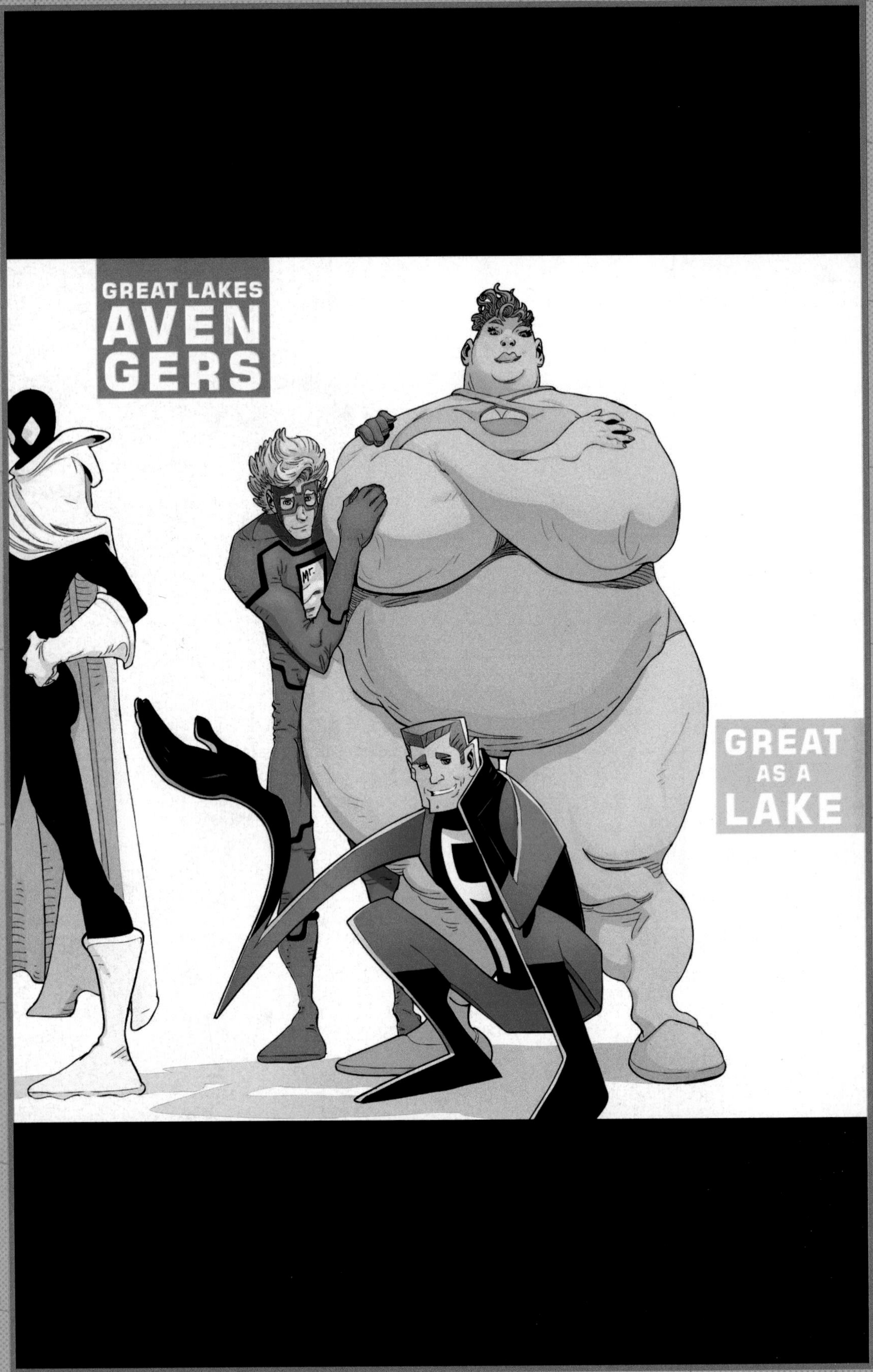
GREAT LAKES
AVEN
GERS
GREAT
AS A
LAKE

DAMION SCOTT & NATHAN FAIRBAIRN

1 HIP-HOP VARIANT COVER

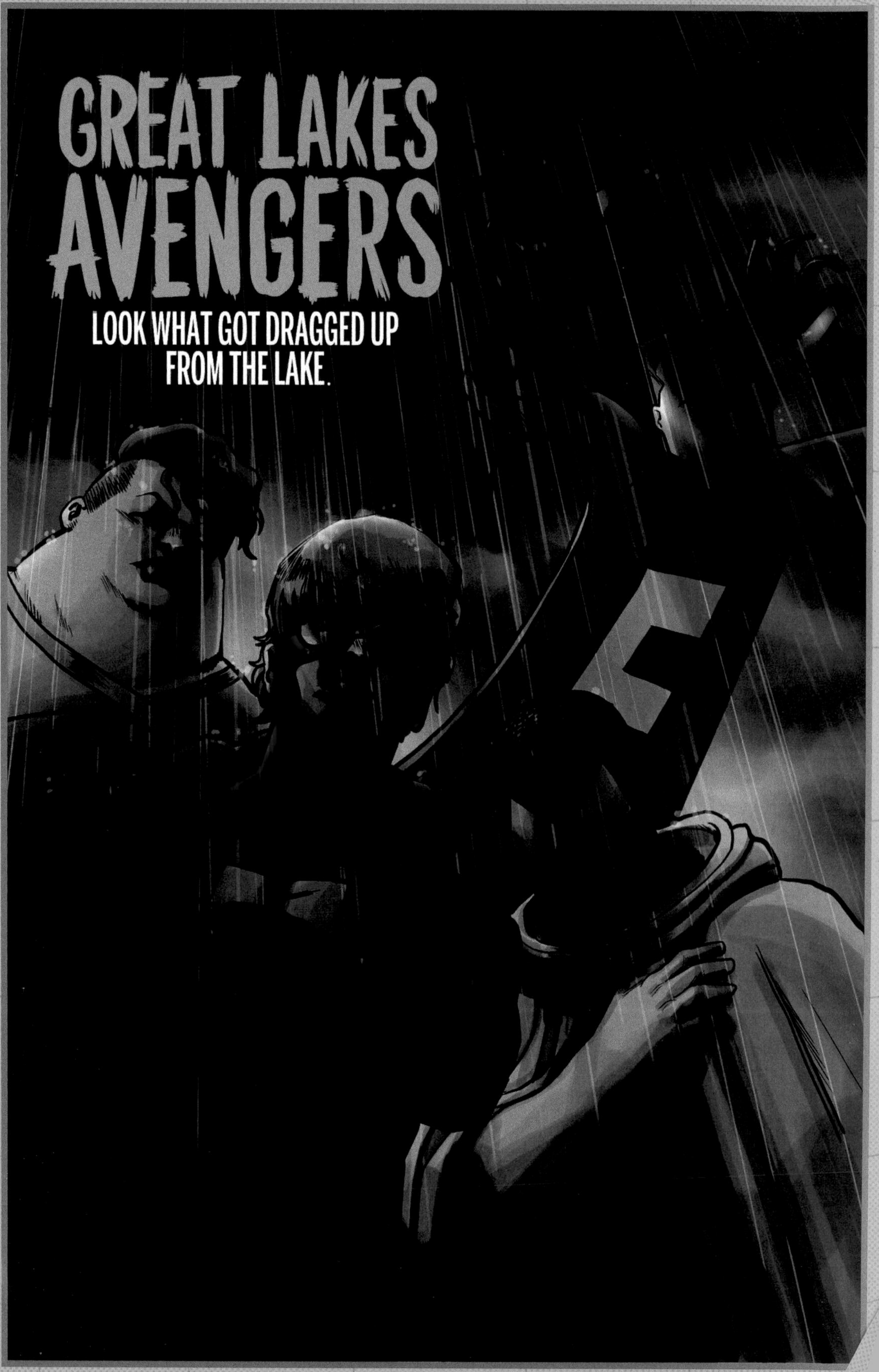
GREAT LAKES AVENGERS
LOOK WHAT GOT DRAGGED UP FROM THE LAKE.

CHIP ZDARSKY
2 VARIANT COVER

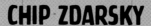

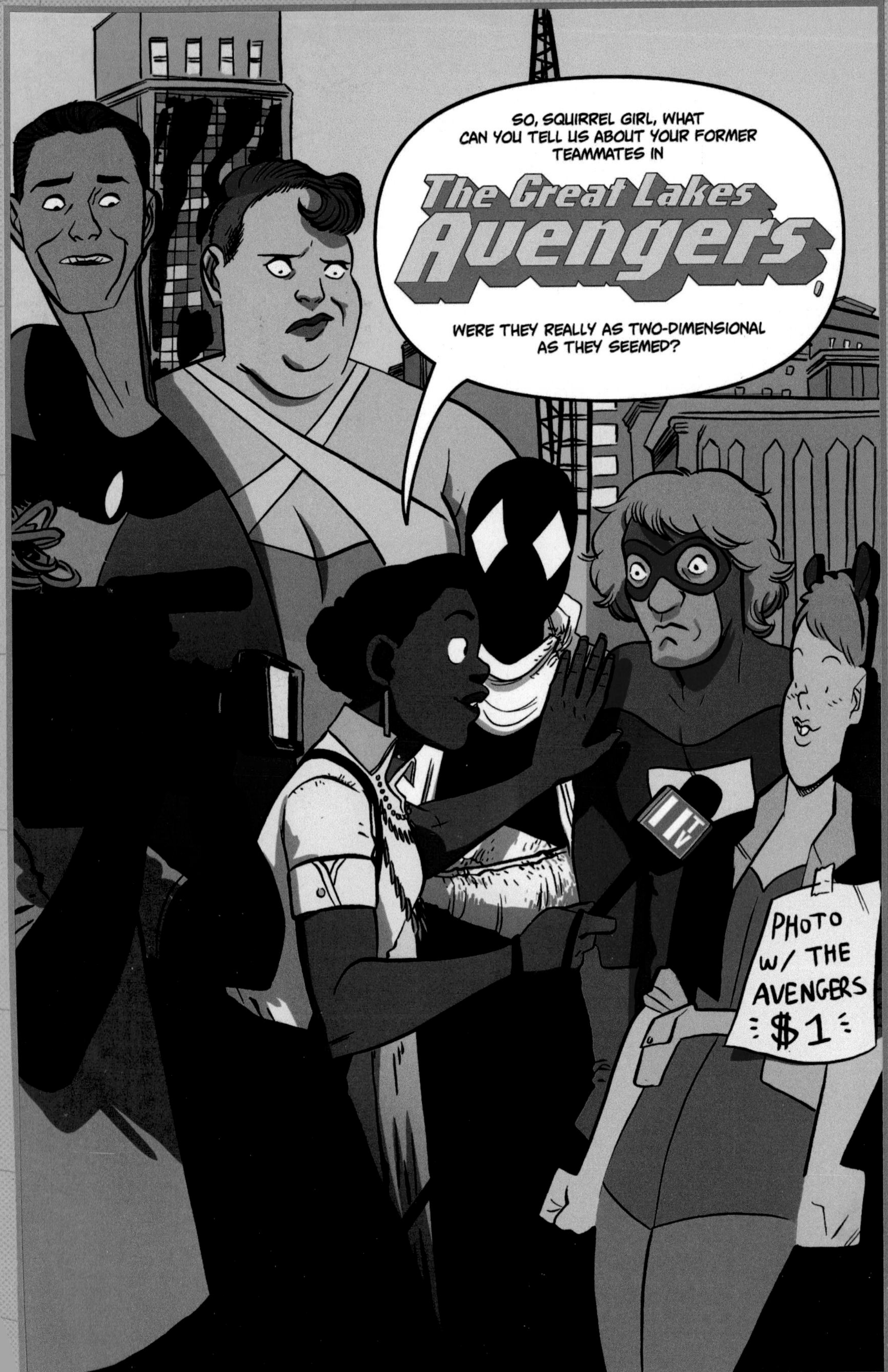
SO, SQUIRREL GIRL, WHAT CAN YOU TELL US ABOUT YOUR FORMER TEAMMATES IN
The Great Lakes Avengers,
WERE THEY REALLY AS TWO-DIMENSIONAL AS THEY SEEMED?
PHOTO W/ THE AVENGERS $1

ERICA HENDERSON

3 VARIANT COVER